Plays and

1969 - 1983

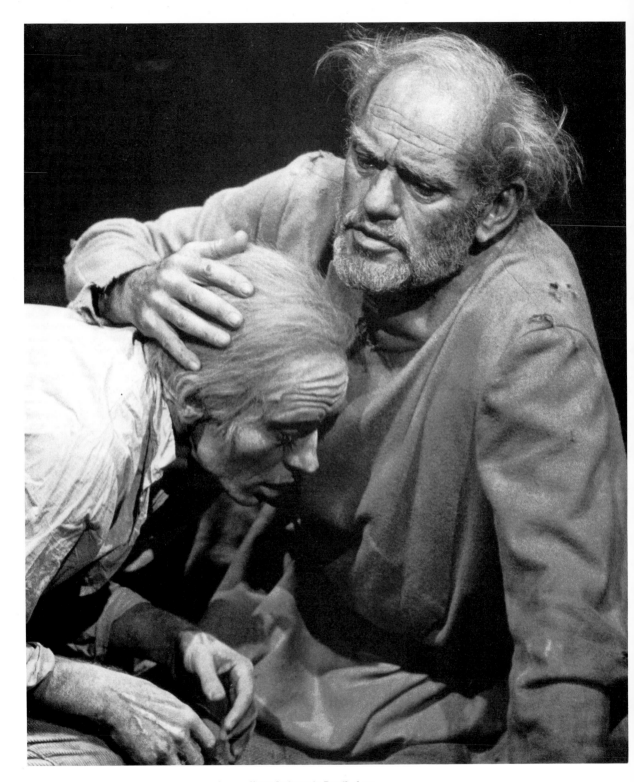

Harry Andrews in Bond's *Lear*

The Best of

Plays and Players

1969 - 1983

Edited by
PETER ROBERTS

with photographs
from the archives of
DONALD COOPER

Methuen Drama

A Methuen Dramabook

First published in Great Britain in 1989 by Methuen Drama
Michelin House, 81 Fulham Road, London SW3 6RB
and in the United States of America
by HEB Inc 70 court Street, Portsmouth, New Hampshire 03801
Copyright © 1989 Peter Roberts

Photographs copyright © 1989 Donald Cooper
(Except where otherwise stated)

A CIP catalogue record for this book
is available from the British Library

   ISBN 0-413-53720-7
   ISBN 0-413-53720-X Pbk

Printed in Great Britain
by Butler & Tanner Ltd,
Frome, Somerset

Contents

Preface

Plays and Players, which made its first appearance in October 1953, was the brainchild of its publisher, Philip Dossë. He had started his own company – Hansom Books – to publish a series of seven monthly magazines on the arts; the first was *Dance and Dancers* which came into being in January 1950. Before that Philip Dossë had been working on a greyhound newspaper and it was always said of him that he began his arts empire with the ballet magazine because he had fallen in love with a dancer whose identity however remained a mystery.

Like Lilian Baylis, founder of the Old Vic Company, Philip Dossë was a cheeseparing eccentric with nothing to invest in his enterprise except a great deal of manic energy. That made him a difficult man to work for and an unlikely patron of the arts. Yet his magazines did undoubtedly make a valuable contribution to postwar British cultural life in the 30 years that he published them. The roll-call of his titles reads, in alphabetical order, *Art and Artists*, *Books and Bookmen*, *Dance and Dancers*, *Films and Filming*, *Music and Musicians*, *Plays and Players* and *Records and Recording*. Yet, in the 12 or so years that I worked for him in various short-lease basement premises in the Victoria area of London, I do not ever remember his saying that he had been to a theatre, cinema or concert or that he had read a book or listened to a recording.

What was there in it for him? Since he was unwilling to delegate – he would often even operate the company switchboard himself – he had neither the time nor the energy to enjoy the arts to which his magazines were devoted. He certainly did not do it for money. He could never afford to go on holiday, wore second-hand clothes, drove a very modest car, mostly used to distribute magazines, and lived in a council flat with his mother who was co-director of his publishing company without ever making an appearance in the office.

Outside his own subterranean business premises he was rather a shy man and did not therefore take advantage of the entrée to the arts cocktail circuit to which his position as an arts publisher entitled him. Undoubtedly his magazines gave his bachelor life a sense of busy purpose as well as some insight into the politics and the working of cultural life in the Britain of the period, if not to direct enjoyment of it. His journals also gave him some power. Although the salaries he paid his editors were as atrocious as their working conditions, getting out his magazines each month was an exciting and challenging occupation as well as one that could be a stepping-stone to better things. This meant he could indulge in playing one editor off against another, and in this hothouse atmosphere of intrigue and occasional backstabbing his staff all learned to dread the handwritten notes scribbled on scrap-paper demanding their presence in his office.

Apart from being journalistic jacks-of-all-trades – critic, gossip writer, sub-editor, proof reader, messenger and layout artist – Philip Dossë's editors had to deploy considerable skills in ensuring that their contributors were eventually paid their nominal fees. In this, timing was a matter of the utmost importance and it was helpful to take careful account of grapevine indications of the mood of the moment. The writers most unlikely to get paid were those from overseas who were least able to press their claims on the phone. Sometimes these hardworking commentators from far off would choose to holiday in London thinking to float their break on the accumulated Hansom Book fees only to receive on their apearance the smallest payment-on-account to get rid of them. After a few years as assistant editor and editor of *Plays and Players*, I learned to open London bank accounts for some of them and invent unexpected appearances so that their fees could never amount to such proportions that settlement would be a permanent impossibility.

After thirty years of penny-pinching endeavour the harsh economics of totally unsubsidized magazine publishing caught up with Philip Dossë in the summer of 1980 in the form of a personal overdraft so extended he could stretch it no further to pay either his editors and their contributors or his printers. He carried out a carefully planned suicide in the flat where his mother had recently predeceased him. The magazines he had built up over so many years of hard grind did not reappear until the autumn of 1982 when they were acquired by Brevet, a subsidiary of the Croydon (UK) Printing Company who printed them.

Before concentrating on *Plays and Players*, meanwhile thanking the various contributors for permission to reproduce their articles here, it would be appropriate to list the editors of the magazine in the thirty years covered by this anthology: Ronald Barker, October 1953 to October 1955; Frank Granville

Barker, November 1955 to April 1962; Peter Roberts, May 1962 to June 1972; Peter Buckley, July 1972 to January 1973; Peter Ansorge, February 1973 to January 1975; Michael Coveney, February 1975 to June 1978; Simon Jones, July 1978 to February 1979; Robin Bean, March 1979 to June 1980; Peter Roberts, October 1981 to October 1983.

When Ronald Barker produced the first issue in October 1953 – which incidentally sold for one shilling and sixpence (or 7½p) – the coronation of Elizabeth II had recently brought over the first major wave of sightseeing tourists whose increasing presence was to prove such an important factor in the prosperity of post-war British theatre. But at that time there was no Chichester Festival Theatre to welcome them and the Royal Shakespeare Company was still seven years off. The National Theatre Company did not come into being until ten years later and the National Theatre building on the South Bank was not opened until *Plays and Players* was already well over twenty years old. Instead there were starry summer seasons given by an ad hoc Shakespeare Memorial Theatre Company in Stratford, while in London the Old Vic under Michael Benthall was struggling with its five-year plan to present all 37 Shakespeare plays in the First Folio on an inadequate budget. In the conservative world of West End theatre dominated by H. M. Tennent's 'Binky' Beaumont, a recently demobilised Peter Saunders was trying to break into the management game and, finding the established impresarios keeping the best theatres to themselves, had opened *The Mousetrap* the year before at the tiny Ambassadors.

In 1953 the often cosy and parochial world of intimate revue, in which a rising star called Dora Bryan was making her mark, had not yet been shattered by the arrival (in 1960) of the satirically irreverent and politically-conscious *Beyond the Fringe*. In 1953 Sandy Wilson's *The Boy Friend* began the British theatre's slow process of recovery from the acute inferiority complex brought on by the ultra-professional and all-prevailing American musical. This complex was to be further eased in the 1960s and 1970s, first by Lionel Bart (*Fings Aint Wot They Used T'Be*, *Oliver!*, *Lock Up Your Daughters*) and later by Andrew Lloyd Webber and Tim Rice (whether operating jointly or separately).

'Director's Theatre' – the in-phrase of the 1960s reflecting the achievements of giants like Joan Littlewood with her Theatre Workshop at Stratford East and Peter Brook with the newly-formed Royal Shakespeare Company – was to make itself felt towards the end of the magazine's first decade. It was, however, in the field of new writing that the biggest changes took place following the magazine's début. At the start of the 1950s writers like Noël Coward, Emlyn Williams and J. B. Priestley, all of whose best work had been done in the 1930s, were still names very much to be reckoned with, though their postwar work proved on the whole to be disappointing. T. S. Eliot with *The Cocktail Party* and *The Confidential Clerk* and Christopher Fry with *The Lady's Not For Burning* and *Venus Observed* had given rise to much excited speculation about a renaissance of poetic drama in the second Elizabethan era. But this new movement came to little as the new reign actually began. Rather, two years after the magazine started its long life, it was the founding of the English Stage Company at the Royal Court in 1956 under George Devine and its deliberate championship of new dramatic writing that led to something far more enduring. In Sloane Square a first generation of writers as diverse as John Osborne, John Arden and Arnold Wesker were to compete for interest with others being launched elsewhere like Harold Pinter, Brendan Behan and Shelagh Delaney. And they were to be followed in the 1960s and the 1970s by wave after wave of new arrivals including Edward Bond, Peter Nichols, David Hare, Howard Brenton, Tom Stoppard, Michael Frayn, Simon Gray, Peter Shaffer, Caryl Churchill and many others.

In the 1950s when *Plays and Players* first came into being the giants of the theatre had not been the writers but the actor knights and dames – Olivier, Guinness, Richardson, Gielgud and Redgrave; Ashcroft, Evans, Robson and Thorndike. Looking back over the three decades spanned by these two volumes it is fascinating to see how those leading players reacted – or did not react – to the new writing and how new generations of players came along to interpret the new dramatists. Olivier, before moving on to be founder director of the Chichester Festival Theatre and then the National Theatre Company at the Old Vic, enthusiastically embraced the New Wave by starring in Osborne's *The Entertainer* in 1957, whilst Gielgud retreated into Shakespeare anthology programmes and delayed coming to terms with the new writing until much later when he appeared – along with Richardson – in Storey's *Home* in 1970 and Pinter's *No Man's Land* in 1975. Ashcroft, as a leading player with the Royal Shakespeare Company, which under Peter Hall started doing new plays as well as classics, was also on the Council of Management of the English Stage Company and therefore put herself in the vanguard of new developments, in contrast to Robson who went into a premature retirement on the south coast. Fortunately the new waves of writers were matched by new waves of players, beneficiaries of the recently introduced local authority grants that placed a different sort of young hopeful at the drama academies, who destroyed the finishing school atmosphere at many of them: actors such as Tom Courtenay, Albert Finney and Joan Plowright. Some of the new players, like Vanessa Redgrave, Judi Dench and Ian McKellen, did much of their finest work in the classics, whilst others like Alan Bates tended to adhere to the long run system in the West End (albeit in plays by Pinter and Gray) rather than taking advantage of the improved working conditions offered by the repertoire system in the new ensembles.

Over the years all this activity has been reflected in *Plays and Players* in different ways by different editors. But I think it is fair to say that throughout the magazine has occupied the middle ground: it has never been a mainly pictorial record of the year in the (largely West End) theatre like *Theatre World*, which was incorporated with it in 1962, nor was it primarily a champion of the avant-garde like *Encore*, which it also took over in the 1960s. It certainly gave due prominence to the new writers and was fortunate to have on its panel of reviewers critics like Martin Esslin and John Russell Taylor who had both written invaluable guides to the new movements. But in so doing it reported widely also on the classics, the musicals and the staple fare of the West End. Nor did it neglect the regions as new theatres were built (and companies founded or extended) such as those in Nottingham, Exeter, Sheffield, Colchester and Birmingham. And the magazine played a useful role in providing a shop window for young critics – Michael Billington, Michael Coveney, Robert Cushman, Frank Marcus and Benedict Nightingale all reviewed regularly for *Plays and Players* before going on to be the critics of, respectively, the *Guardian*, *Financial Times*, *Observer*, *Sunday Telegraph* and *New Statesman*. Nor was theatre overseas neglected. *Plays and Players* has been fortunate to have some distinguished contributors in this section such as Robert Brustein in North America. In putting together this anthology, however, I have rarely drawn on these reports as I believe readers will chiefly want to recall what a British theatre magazine had to say about the British theatre. Otherwise I have tried to provide a fair reflection of the magazine's balance of interviews and reviews and regional contributions.

When I first took over the editorship in 1962 it had been the practice at the end of the year to write a light-hearted 'Credits and Discredits' summarising the year and to invite a single authority to write a critical résumé. I thought that it might be more interesting to invite the London theatre critics as a whole to vote for the performances and productions which had most impressed them during the previous twelve months and in the process to contribute thumbnail sketches indicating what had led them to make the choices that they did. Thus, after 1962, the 'Credits and Discredits' disappear from this anthology and are replaced by a summary of the London critics' poll each year. It would have been nice to be able to reproduce the whole of the critics' end-of-the-year comments but that idea had to be set aside in view of the space available.

Since the 'Credits and Discredits' and the summary of the critics' poll provide a brief annual summary of the theatrical highlights, I have not written another myself but have assembled a series of notes on each year which I hope will jog some memories of what was happening in the world as a whole and so enable the mix of reviews and interviews to be read in a global context rather than in a theatrical vacuum.

It has been an enjoyable experience tracing the original contributors, some of whom have dispersed far and wide. I would like to thank them for their co-operation and the publishers for their patience as these two volumes were slowly put together. I hope that they may be enjoyed partly as a tribute to the magazine's founder publisher, Philip Dossë, whose fearful energies provided a constant dynamo over so many years as his editors came and went.

Peter Roberts

List of Illustrations

Except where stated otherwise, all photos are by Donald Cooper.

11

1969

It was the year that De Gaulle resigned in France to be succeeded by Pompidou while Willy Brandt was elected West Germany's new Chancellor. Franco named Prince Juan Carlos as his successor in Spain and Golda Meir became Israel's new Prime Minister. The USA won the space race by landing astronauts on the moon.

The liner Queen Elizabeth II made her maiden voyage and Concorde her maiden flight. In Britain the Open University was founded and the seven-sided 50-pence piece made its appearance as the halfpenny vanished. London's Victoria Line underground was opened.

It was a lively year for new writing in the theatre with Peter Nichols' The National Health, *Charles Wood's* H *and David Storey's* The Contractor *heading the list of premières.*

1969

Winston Carve-up

Philip French reviews Hochhuth's Soldiers *at the New*

Like Peter Weiss's *Marat/Sade*, Günther Grass's *The Plebeians Rehearse the Uprising* and Heinar Kipphardt's *In the Matter of J. Robert Oppenheimer, Soldiers* has a strong, almost self-sustaining situation taken more or less directly from life and then shaped by the author for his own dramatic purposes. One feels indeed that the German theatre has been re-created by such exercises in ironic perception; where French dramatists were forced by German occupation to call up ancient myths in the cause of current reality (as Sartre, Camus and Anouilh were) and Eastern European playwrights have little choice but to utilise allegorical forms and Aesopian language, so the liberated young Germans have been compelled to face and employ immutable reality.

As staged by Clifford Williams, *Soldiers* is rather a bald play lasting around three hours. The first act is set on HMS Duke of York en route for Scapa Flow early in 1943 where Lord Cherwell explains to Churchill the aims of area bombing of German civilian populations and Churchill has an uneasy confrontation with General Sikorski, the leader of the Polish government-in-exile, whose intransigence threatens the tenuous Anglo-Russian alliance. The second act takes place later that year in Churchill's bedroom, where the PM evinces his ability to switch abruptly not only from front to front but from the cosmically significant to the personally trivial; the act ends with a portentously ambiguous discussion between Churchill and Cherwell concerning the possibility that Sikorski might suffer a fatal aeroplane accident on his return from a Middle-Eastern tour. The last act is laid in the garden at Chequers; dramatically and thematically this is the pay-off with a confrontation between Churchill and the most outspoken opponent of area bombing, Bishop Bell of Chichester, and the announcement that Sikorski has died in a plane crash – an occurrence that leads a Polish officer to suggest assassination and others to greet the event with stunned silence.

Clifford Williams is one of this country's best directors and he has produced these three scenes with characteristic clarity, economy and insight. John Colicos's impersonation of Churchill is perfect beyond description; compared with his performance the similar efforts by Richard Burton and Patrick Wymark, not to mention the American Dudley Field Malone in the 1943 movie *Mission to Moscow*, pale into insignificance. Ralph Koltai's simple sets are first class and are dominated by the brooding presence of a huge radar saucer which functions realistically in Act I and, as respectively, a ceiling and an arbour in Acts II and III. Throughout, the device serves as a constant symbolic reminder of the play's meaning – the nature of technological warfare and the depersonalising distance it puts between attacker and victim.

On stage the play has three major merits: firstly, it discusses important issues intelligently; secondly, it sets up various resonances that continue long after one has absorbed these issues (e.g. the relationship between the two old soldiers, Sikorski and Churchill, and the way they've adapted to modern warfare, set against the fact that Britain entered the war to aid Poland and was soon siding against Polish interests with the Russian invaders); thirdly, there is simple entertainment on the lines of Emlyn Williams's evenings with Dylan Thomas and Charles Dickens, Hal Halbrook's Mark Twain show, Max Adrian's GBS and so on. (In

Hochhuth's *Soldiers*, the play that rocked the National finally reached the stage at the New (now Albery) Theatre, London with John Colicos as Churchill. 1969.

raising this latter aspect I don't set out to trivialise the play or be flippant; this is what grips an audience, is an astonishing achievement by a playwright who speaks indifferent English, and is important to some of my later observations.) The weaknesses of the play lie in the utterly wooden fictional characters who talk in the clichés of old war movies and in the author's primitive sense of dramatic structure and development (which is rather different from a healthy disregard for the rules or the creation of new forms).

What we see at the New Theatre, however, has been carved from a text that would take some seven hours to perform and has been published in Robert David MacDonald's admirable translation (André Deutsch). Williams has used a considerably shortened version of the three central acts and dropped the prologue and epilogue entirely. No doubt he had little choice, but the original

17

text creates quite a different impression from the stage performance. The prologue, for instance, proposes a short-term polemical purpose, i.e. to persuade audiences that the Geneva Conventions protecting non-combatant civilians should be extended to include aerial attack. (This purpose, of course, is apparent rather than real and has led some critics to suppose that Hochhuth is campaigning for more rigorous and humane rules of war, whereas this is part of his ironic design, for the title *Soldiers* is itself ambiguous. On the other hand, there is no question of his suggesting that Churchill's aim to exterminate Nazism was not wholly admirable and justified.) The framework of the play is the ruins of Coventry cathedral in 1964 where, on the centenary of the first Red Cross meeting in Geneva to draw up conventions of war, an international gathering has come together to consider the implementation of new conventions. Furthermore, we are introduced to a play-within-a-play (the one we see at the New Theatre) and its fictional author, a dying bomber command veteran. This fictional author's son is now an RAF officer with NATO serving under an ex-Luftwaffe German-for-all seasons, who is the only unequivocally corrupt character in the whole play. Thus at the beginning and end, the issues raised are openly debated and the Churchill play itself (called 'The Little London Theatre of the World') is presented as the projection of a single man's own convictions and anxieties. Unfortunately there are passages in *Soldiers* that are so dense with historical argument and analogy that no director could make them theatrically viable (they make the early historical arguments in *Henry V* appear simple and lucid); at the same time the stage directions form an important part of the piece and contain some of Hochhuth's most penetrating writing. In short, Hochhuth has written an unperformable play – his second one, for *The Representative* comes into the same category. It isn't a play of fact, or a documentary; rather it recalls William Styron's description of his book *The Confessions of Nat Turner*, 'less an historical novel in conventional terms than a meditation upon history'. This is not to say that I consider Hochhuth an artist of comparable distinction to Styron, but he is a man who has thought long and felt deeply about his material and is worthy of our greatest respect and attention. With Black Power advocates, Styron ran into bitter criticism and bore insults not unlike those directed at Hochhuth from another direction.

Within the context of the complete play the allegation of Churchill's connivance in the death of Sikorski is sustained by the passion of the fictional playwright. Thematically it takes on the greatest importance in relation to the questions: what is the difference between murdering a single man you know and slaughtering hundreds of thousands of nameless civilians? In the national interest can either or both acts be justified and on what terms? (Let us not forget that the most profitable film shown in the Western world during the past couple of years has been Robert Aldrich's *The Dirty Dozen*, a grotesque war movie concerning, twelve condemned men who are spared the gallows to execute a secret mission – the deliberate incineration of unarmed German officers and their civilian companions – in flagrant breach of the Geneva Convention. Or that the most popular hero of our time is James Bond, whose double-O prefix signifies that he is licensed to kill, and does so in strict obedience to orders; in his creator's words, Bond is 'a blunt instrument in the hands of his superiors'. Bond and *The Dirty Dozen* are, as they say, only entertainment, and nobody seems to mind too much.) Yet I feel very uneasy about this when moving from the text and the stage version to the area of public debate. There can be no rules laid down as to what distortions are permissible in the cause of art or propaganda. If (as John Wain and others believe) it is acceptable to elevate the mentally disturbed thief Claud Eatherly to symbolic status as 'the Hiroshima Pilot' (which he wasn't) or to write any kind of imaginative historical fiction, then why cannot Churchill be dealt with as he is here? No one who has seen or read the play could doubt that Churchill emerges from *Soldiers* as a massive, tragic hero (or is at least intended to); and in his lifetime he was a public personality, consciously self-projected into the world of myth, a calculating theatrical performer, an emblematic, iconic figure. Still, I feel that Hochhuth could have made his polemic points without such overt allegations, for these have had the dual effect of reducing·moments of his play on the stage to crude melodrama (the end of Act II especially) and corrupting *ab initio* the profitability of the public debate that was bound to ensue. The fact that Hochhuth actually believes in the plot against Sikorski can be ignored in discussing the play though not in examining the public debate.

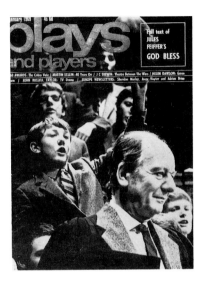

The discussion that followed *The Representative* (excellently recorded by Eric Bentley's anthology *The Storm Over the Deputy*) focused upon the play's central subject, the responsibility towards the Jews of Pope Pius XII. The furious debate that *Soldiers* has provoked is concerned with one aspect of the play – was Sikorski assassinated? And, if so, did Churchill know anything about it? The debate hasn't, in the predictably heated atmosphere, related this to the play's principal concern; on the contrary, the majority of those involved have ignored or obfuscated the crucial issues. For one who has spent so much time studying history and the realm of *realpolitik*, Hochhuth reveals himself as astonishingly naïve. I say this because I do not feel that *Soldiers* could have been as potentially powerful if Hochhuth had set the same events in Outer Carpathia or Ancient Sparta. The value of his work lies in the urgency that comes from his use of real and recent historical situations. But in adopting this method, in setting out to exploit material that already possessed a tremendous explosive charge for the public, he took upon himself aesthetic and social responsibilities that he hasn't fully acknowledged or discharged. In suggesting this, I must reiterate that I am not impugning either his integrity or that of his staunchest supporters; nor am I attempting to erect any artistic or dramaturgical principle; what I am doing, though, and seriously, is questioning his judgment.

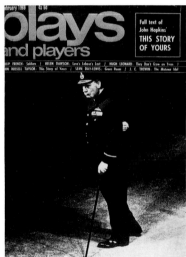

The Director in Rep

Max Stafford-Clark on the
Edinburgh Traverse*

*Max Stafford-Clark was
Artistic Director of the
Edinburgh Traverse 1968–1974.

Probably the most important single fact about the Traverse is that it seats only 60 people. For this has dictated both its problems and its artistic policy from the very outset. The history of the early years of the Traverse has already been swept away in the cross-fire of rivals scrambling to claim the position of founder. But this much is certain: in 1963 a group of Edinburgh citizens decided that they would like something to supplement the wholesome repertory fare already provided by the Gateway, and the Traverse emerged as a small club theatre in a dilapidated tenement building some 150 yards below Edinburgh Castle.

The premises had previously been used as a brothel, and successive managements have often thought of returning to that policy in times of financial stress. In its first two years the Traverse offered a diet of Arrabal, Sartre, Ionesco, Genet, Mrozek and de Ghelderode tempered with the occasional Noël Coward and Bernard Shaw and a superb *Ubu Roi* which has since become something of a myth – all good avant-garde stuff in a city accustomed to an annual three-week cultural orgy followed by 49 weeks' starvation. But it was not until the production of John Antrobus's *You'll Come to Love Your Sperm Test* at the end of 1964 that the Traverse started the new writers' policy on which its reputation has largely been made. In the four years since then the Traverse has produced some 40 premières by British writers and another 35 British premières of American or European plays – a record unequalled by any other theatre in this country.

The present policy continues this reckless pursuit of new writers while at the same time, since May, we have added a permanent company of six resident actors who have appeared in four out of the eleven productions since that time. By definition they are a young company as only people without family obligations can afford to stay for long under the Traverse's pitiful salaries. When the company are not performing or rehearsing for a specific production the time is spent in Workshop sessions where we have undertaken a number of projects, including the fermentation of a closer actor-audience relationship. The result of this was seen in a play called *Comings and Goings* by Megan Terry which the company performed over the summer. The play progresses through a series of transformation scenes which trace the relationship of a young couple from smooth take-off to forced landing. But although only two characters ever appear on stage at one time the play is designed for a flexible company as any actor can substitute for any other at any period in the action. In the original New York production the means of changing the actor was in the hands of a sort of umpire who spun a wheel with each actor's name on it at fixed points in the course of the play. In the Traverse production the audience were given two relay batons (one for actors and one for actresses) which they could raise at any point in the course of the play. In later performances a second sophistication was added and the audience were also able to change the scripted text to an improvisation on the same theme and back again. Nobody would claim that this was an enormous breakthrough in audience participation but by entrusting the audience with this simple responsibility a very close and easy atmosphere was established. It also made the audience more directly responsible for a 'good' or 'bad' performance, but most important of all it made each particular performance very special to the audience there that night – each show being vastly different from any other.

I think this is the ultimate weapon in the theatre's armoury for the war it must wage against rival media if it is to survive. For theatre still behaves as though its only rivals in the field of entertainment were the toothdrawer and the occasional bear-fight. The arrival of cinema and television, not to mention soccer and pop music, mean that theatre must redefine its position in order to survive. It must cease to attempt jobs which cinema and television can do better. I see this process of redefinition as being one of the Traverse's main jobs, equipped as we are to take risks that are difficult for larger regional theatres and perhaps even for the London underground theatres where the pressure to win an audience often seems destructive.

If the shape of the building is a decisive factor in the Traverse's policy so too is Edinburgh itself. On the one hand there is generous tradition of Scottish Liberalism, patronage of the arts, Edinburgh's regard for herself as a European cultural capital, Athens of the North and so on. While on the other hand there are the firmly entrenched legions of John Knox aided by artillery blasts from the Scottish *Daily Express* ('the liquidation of the Traverse Theatre would be a useful first step towards Edinburgh's cultural advancement', 30 April 1968). The odd demented Councillor and the Scottish *Daily Express* have both become occupational local hazards for anyone mounting anything more adventurous than *Mary Poppins*. *The Scotsman*, too, although usually firmly committed to the middle of the road, has occasionally been known to weigh in with the heavy morals – most recently about Rosalyn Drexler's rock musical *The Line of Least Existence*. ('The Traverse has forfeited any right to call itself a theatre for the next month . . .', etc.) But even though one is fighting moral battles that have been won elsewhere 50 years ago, at least what we do concerns people one way or another. The permissive society is, of course, simply splendid but too often becomes mere indifference. In Edinburgh if you care at all about a theatre like the Traverse you have to demonstrate your fidelity by practical support otherwise the next time you turn down The Royal Mile the Corporation will have turned us into a launderette.

Every theatre that has depended in any way on new British writers has found it a bit chilly in the draught that has inevitably followed the breakthrough of British theatre in the fifties. There seem to be no cosmic issues left to our writers, only personal neuroses, while in America the issues that are tearing the country apart have also been responsible for the creative energy of the Off-Off-Broadway scene. This re-focus of energy has, from London to New York, been reflected in the Traverse's policy. Over the last two years the Traverse has been the first British theatre to stage Paul Foster, Lanford Wilson, John Guare, Rosalyn Drexler and Megan Terry. But as well as this the Traverse recognises its obligations to find British writers. In the pipeline are commissioned works from Stanley Eveling, Adrienne Kennedy, C. P. Taylor, John Rudlin and Sean Hignett. Rosalyn Drexler threatens to write a play about Mary Queen of Scots and, most ambitious of all, is a project entitled *Dracula* on which eight different writers (six of them from Edinburgh) are currently

working. This will be the first play to have emerged from our workshop and is a joint investigation between the team of writers and the resident company on man's preoccupation with evil – 'the beast in man'. Scenes are improvised, written, fed to the actors, regurgitated and rewritten. Whether it will be horrific I can't foretell but it has certainly been most exciting to work with in rehearsal. This, then, is the Traverse's role to continue to give new writers an opportunity to see their own words in action and to develop a resident company who will be able to sing these words with a contemporary theatrical voice.

Bond Unbound

Martin Esslin reviews Saved *and* Narrow Road to the Deep North *at the Royal Court*

Nothing could have shown up the idiocy of British stage censorship in its declining phase than the reaction of the public – and even the critics! – to the revival of *Saved* at the Royal Court. After the grotesque antics in which the moral health of the nation was supposedly to the preserved by the imposition of a fine and the banning of the play, less than four years later it is staged, received with quiet respect and recognised to be a moral tract for the times, no less. Can anyone be proved to have been depraved or corrupted by it? Has it led to sadistic orgies? Or riots in the streets of Chelsea? Where, then, are all the arguments which maintained stage censorship in being for decades? 'Oh well, old boy, if you allowed that sort of thing, who knows what might happen?' Well, now we know the answer. *Nothing*, except that some people emerge from the theatre with a deeper insight, a greater compassion for the sufferings of some of their fellow human beings.

What a brilliant play *Saved* is, and how well it has stood the test of time! Bond has succeeded in making the inarticulate, in their very inability to express themselves, become transparent before our eyes: their very speechlessness is made to yield communication, we can look right inside their narrow, confined, limited and pathetic emotional world. This is the final step and the ultimate consummation of the linguistic revolution on the British stage: what a distance we have come from the over-explicit clichés of the flat well-mannered banter, the dehumanised upper-class voices of an epoch which now appears positively antediluvian – although its ghost-like remnants still haunt the auditoria around Shaftesbury Avenue. *Saved* is a deeply moral play: the scene of the stoning of the baby, which led to the first outcry about it, is one of the key points in its moral structure. Pam conceived the baby irresponsibly, without love; because she did not want it, she does not care for it; because she does not care for it, the baby cries incessantly and gets on her nerves; because it gets on her nerves she drugs it with aspirin; and so, when, caring more for the man with whom she is infatuated than for her child, she leaves it alone in its pram, the baby does not respond to the at first casual and quite well-meant attentions of the gang; because it does not respond, they try to arouse it by other means, and that is how they gradually work up to greater and greater brutality, simply to make the mysteriously reactionless, drugged child show a sign of life. There could not be a more graphic illustration of the way in which lack of responsibility and lack of understanding, lack of

Edward Bond's *Narrow Road to the Deep North* at the Royal Court Theatre, London
with Kenneth Cranham and Gillian Martell. 1969.

intellectual and moral *intelligence*, lies at the root of the brutality of our age. The SS man who kills a Jew just lacks the insight and imagination to picture his victim's feelings, the bomber pilot who drops bombs on civilians does not *see* his victims, and therefore does not trouble to think about them. The baby in the pram is neglected because his mother cannot picture him as a human being like herself; the boys of the gang kill him because, having been made into an object without consciousness, they *treat* him like a mere object.

In his note in the published version of the play, Bond himself calls it an optimistic piece, because of Len's loyalty to the girl who rejects him. It is true: Len is a touching character in his stubborn devotion to the girl. And yet I am not at all convinced that this is the main message of *Saved*. Why indeed is the play called *Saved*? As far as I can see the only direct reference to the title is in the scene when Pam is trying to win the murderer – and perhaps the father? – of the child, Fred, back after his release from prison. Len, who foresees that she will be rebuffed, has come with her to the café where the reunion is to take place. When Fred *does* reject her with contempt, Pam wants to believe that he is doing this because of the presence of Len – a rival. She cries out: '*Somebody's got a save me from 'im.*' The irony of the title, therefore, seems to me to lie in the fact that Pam at the end has lost Fred and continues to live in the same house, the same household as Len, and that, although all speech has ceased in that house, she will inevitably go on living with him, in every sense of the word. So that, eventually, she has *not* been saved. A closer study of the text reveals many equally subtle and complex insights and ironies: the way in which, for example, after the marvellous and horrifying scene where Len has to repair a ladder in the stocking of Pam's mother and is surprised in that compromising position by her husband, finally the two men find each other and establish a line of communication – the relationship between Len and his real rival, Fred; the brilliantly observed marital warfare between Pam's parents, and so forth.

William Gaskill's production is as excellent as it was in the first run in November, 1965. Kenneth Cranham is probably more credible as Len than John Castle, because he is a little less glamorous; Adrienne Posta is equally convincing. Queenie Watts, as Pam's mother, Mary, manages to be both an old hag and to exude genuine sexual attraction when dressing up in her nylons. And the rest of the cast are equally good, with John Barrett truly outstanding as Pam's father. My only quarrel with the new production is with the use of an – in itself breathtaking and brilliant – montage of images of affluence and horror between the scenes. It appears to suggest that an attempt is being made to link the plight of the characters in the play with the growth of television advertising and sexual titillation by pop entertainment in our age. This seems to me to introduce a pretty false note: Edward Bond himself, in his note, speaks of the devaluation of morals through their insidious association with intellectually disreputable religious dogma as the root of the play's problem; this is a far deeper, more convincing analysis. Indeed, the story could have happened in the East End of London thirty years ago as well as today; where was the telly then – or the affluence? If the theatre *is*, as I fervently

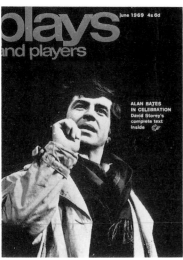

believe, a marvellous tool for genuine social analysis, then we must be very careful not to fall for superficially effective clichés of this kind.

At first glance there could be no greater contrast than that between *Saved* and Bond's latest play, *Narrow Road to the Deep North*. Here the dialect of the speechless, there the clarity of stylised poetic speech; here deepest London, there the farthest, most exotic orient. Yet, a closer look reveals the common ground. Here, as there, the problem of the disastrous influence of a morality based on an intellectually bankrupt religion, here as there the *horror* of violence which expresses itself in *images* of violence. Written, very rapidly, to serve as a comment on a conference about city planning held in Coventry last June, *Narrow Road* is a meditation on how to create a 'good city'. Laid in Japan at the time when the first Westerners had landed there, the play shows the creation of a city by Shogo, an upstart who becomes a bloody tyrant, and its capture by the forces of missionary English colonialism. We see the story mainly from the point of view of the old poet and priest Basho: on his way to the deep north, where he is seeking enlightenment in meditation, Basho finds an exposed baby, abandoned by his parents in a time of famine. Should he have saved it? He lets it die. When he returns thirty years later a city has been built on the spot, by Shogo, who may be that very baby who grew up resentful and evil because he had no love as a child (like Pam's baby in *Saved*). Shogo is overthrown, with Basho's help, by the Commodore and his Bible-toting missionary sister – or concubine – Georgina. And when, in the ups and downs of battle, that Victorian harridan sob-sister is pressed to reveal the identity of the young legitimate heir to the throne, who is hidden among her pupils, she lets a whole form of children die, rather than betray that one child – and goes mad. And Kiro, who was refused as a pupil by Basho and has become a friend of the tyrant Shogo, finally, confronted with all these moral dilemmas, commits hara-kiri, just at the moment when a man, who is drowning, calls for his help. The man saves himself by his own exertions; Kiro dies. The message is clear: not in speculation about moral principles lies salvation, but in one man's active help for another: if Basho had given that abandoned baby his love and care, if he had taken Kiro as his pupil – could not so much bloodshed and evil have been averted? But Basho, the poet, preferred his meditation far up there in the deep north; it is up there that he met the Commodore and Georgina and told them about the more populous south; what would have happened if he had not selfishly devoted himself to poetry and meditation (which only led to the conclusion, after many years, that there was nothing to learn in the deep north); what would have happened if the artist had not indulged in his selfish search for 'enlightenment' and self-expression?

This is a beautiful parable play, very Brechtian in its mixture of orientalism (used as an 'alienation effect' to show familiar problems in an unexpected light) and moral didacticism. It is Brechtian also in the spareness and economy of its writing. The performance, in a beautiful set of simple polished wood, by Hayden Griffin, is fully adequate, although it did not arouse me to great enthusiasm. Peter Needham (Basho), Jack Shepherd (Shogo) and Gillian

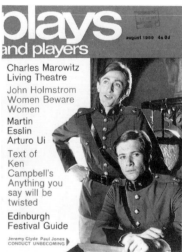

Martell (Georgina) are outstanding; the rest of the cast don't seem to me to catch the full flavour of the style. But, in spite of this, the quality and the message of the play comes through, loud and clear.

1969

Keep It Mum

John Holmstrom reviews In Celebration *at the Royal Court*

Family reunions have long provided dramatists with a resonant arena where clashes of temperament, Oedipal simmerings or sibling rivalries can erupt with a satisfying wham. Oddly enough, David Storey's Yorkshire stablemate, David Mercer, began his career as a playwright (and his celebrated trilogy of socialist breakdown) with a play in which two emigré sons return from the South with their middle-class wives to bury their mother and comfort their engine-driver father; ructions and heart-searchings ensue. Here the worries were mainly social and political – children growing away from their parents through education and ambition, rejecting many of the values that suckled them yet unable to find anything really admirable to put in their place – whereas Storey's new play *In Celebration* turns out to be less a matter of ideologies than of strictly familial love-hate. Three sons travel up to a Northern mining town – without wives, though two of them are married – to celebrate their parents' fortieth wedding anniversary. The eldest, Andy (Alan Bates), is a dangerous, destructive jester who has thrown up his legal practice to be a half-hearted abstract Gauguin; the middle one, bachelor Colin (James Bolam), is a rather smug socialist careerist, a labour relations manager to a large industrial firm; the youngest, Steven (Brian Cox), is a teacher who has just abandoned a study of society that he's been working on for seven years, and it's soon clear that he's in a mood of suicidal depression, intensified by reunion with his family. He was always the quiet, studious one – Silent Steven – but now he's more like the Angel of Death. 'What's wrong?' they keep asking him, but he can't or won't explain.

Colin is the model son who brings flowers, correct and considerate but oddly unlovable. Andy is his opposite, a tousled charmer who under the affectionate banter nurses contempt for his tough little Dad (Bill Owen – magnificent) and vindictive hatred for his cosy, sweet-natured Mum (Constance Chapman). Dad, it emerges, got her with child four decades ago and they had to marry, though for Mum it was a social come-down. Having failed to kill herself and the child, she contented herself with enslaving Dad and emasculating her surviving sons (the first died at seven of pneumonia) by raising them in the social scale. They all feel a loss of identity, but only Andy feels vicious – regarding his mother as a sainted vampire and his father as a pathetic animal, burrowing on his back in a thirteen-inch seam and plodding home to idolise his wife. The reunion centres on a grand beano at the Hotel Excelsior. Andy has already given tongue before it, raising the forbidden topic of Jamie, the dead son, and hinting to his brothers that he wants to smash the sanctified image of Mum. Afterwards, when they have returned home in a glow of togetherness, he breaks out wantonly in the presence of Dad, mocking and scourging him with the damned-up contempt of years. What animates this monster of revenge? Because, as a little boy, when his mother was expecting again and wanted to lessen the domestic burden, he had been farmed out to a friendly neighbour and for five weeks was refused entry to the house. Deep down, he has never forgotten or forgiven it. But he doesn't fully confront Mum with his hatred. The play ends with a sort of battered truce; the sons depart, and Dad, who has never quite understood what it was all about, wipes the whole thing from his mind and settles back into domestic bliss.

David Storey's *In Celebration* at the Royal Court Theatre, London with Alan Bates, James Bolam, Brian Cox and Bill Owen. 1969.

The first thing to be said about *In Celebration* – because most reviewers have made it sound worthy and dull – is that it is highly intelligent, highly theatrical and often wickedly funny. Storey has the knack of charging naturalistic settings with terrible possibilities of revelation, lighting a long, invisible fuse whose length to the powder-keg one can only guess. He's not in the least avant-garde, and who cares? He makes one sit on the edge of one's seat and listen, more than almost any dramatist of his generation. He gets beautifully the unease of complicated, uprooted children, faced with the hideous furnishings and embarrassing respect of their parents; he sets them skating gingerly on the thin ice of homely chaff and platitude, and some inspired arabesques result. Vicious Andy is not an entirely fresh creation – he has links with Osborne, and with the mocking hero of Alun Owen's *Progress to the Park* – but Alan Bates plays him superbly, and many of his sallies are memorable. 'He couldn't knock a fly off a rice pudding,' he says of managerial Colin. 'He'd negotiate with it first.' The other main comic treat is quite extraneous, a dapper, elderly Scots boozer

27

from down the road (observed with rosy accuracy by Fulton Mackay) for whom happiness is a warm H-bomb shelter.

The reason why the play isn't as wild and electrifying as *The Restoration of Arnold Middleton* is that the three sons are tiresomely schematic characters – the Revenger, the Crippled, the Crucified – who never convince one that they could have sprung from any womb, let alone the same one. Steven's agonised silence begins by being enigmatic, ends by merely irritating; Andy's spoutings gush too fluently from a dangerous vein of elegant, snooty rhetoric which Storey, like Mercer, sometimes gets stuck in. And the 'explanation' for Andy's daemon is as pat and implausible as the imaginary child in *Virginia Woolf*. Mum, on all the evidence in the play, could never have been such a monster as to bolt the door to her weeping little son; it's a concocted piece of *Angst* that doesn't fill the bill. (I believe this is why Storey dodges the *scène à faire*, the confrontation with the mother towards which everything had been building: it would have collapsed under the weakness of motivation.) One has seen plenty of examples in real family life of 'disfigurement . . . by totally innocent hands', but the results are seldom as daemonic as Andy or as mysteriously doomed as Steven. I'd say Colin's loneliness is about right. But faults apart, have I made it sound worthy and dull? I hope not. Much of it sparkles. And Lindsay Anderson, who since *If . . .* can do no wrong for me, has done no wrong here. The performance is spot-on.

NOVEMBER
1969

The Silver Tassie

Reviewed by Hugh Leonard at the Aldwych

Only O'Casey could have written *The Silver Tassie*, and probably only Yeats could have rejected it. It is a bad, a terrible play. Perversely, but not incompatibly, it is also a masterpiece; and the clue to its rejection and the bitter aftermath lies in the collision of two personalities as different as Adam and God. Yeats, the patrician, believed that he and Lady Gregory had invented O'Casey. They had staged his three great slum plays, and from the stage of the Abbey Yeats had defied the mob, hailing O'Casey as the worthy incumbent of that 'cradle of genius'. He was, in a sense, their performing dog, although they had at least the grace to acknowledge the excellence of the performance. The dog, to labour the metaphor, was an unpredictable brute. O'Casey had enough chips on his shoulder to fuel a bishop's bonfire. Myopic, self-educated and reared in squalor (this by his own account; there is conflicting testimony), he was an injustice-collector. Admittedly, there was plenty to collect: his plays had evoked howls of Jansenistic outrage; and by criticising the performances of the Abbey Players in lesser works than his own, he found himself barred from the theatre's green room. Another man might have shrugged off the hostility and not cared that even the lavish praise of his partisans was tinged with a condescension evoked by the tag of 'slum playwright'; but O'Casey was translucently thin-skinned. He went to London, was lionised, wrote *The Silver Tassie* and submitted it to Yeats.

The reaction can be imagined. For Yeats, the ideal theatre was a drawing room, the ideal audience an assembly of verse-minded dilettantes. With *Tassie,* O'Casey had barged, hob-nail boots and all, into the sanctum of poesy; Yeats was being challenged on his own ground, the apprentice was attempting to take over the factory. It is certain that Yeats sincerely believed the play to mark a falling-off in O'Casey's work, but there is nothing so galling as to throw breadcrumbs to a man, whose response is to shower you with pieces of cake. Yeats rejected *Tassie,* and, where O'Casey was concerned, to reject the work was to reject the man. In his rage he threw the entire sad mess into the correspondence columns of the Irish press, vowing never again to submit a play to the Abbey. The promise was kept, but I have seen a letter in which he admitted to keeping every new play away from other managements until the Abbey had the opportunity of asking for it. 'But the Abbey', he wrote, 'proud lady that she is, passes me by with her head in the air.' In the event, Yeats was more myopic than O'Casey. Ireland lost a playwright; O'Casey, raddled with rage and bitterness, lost a theatre.

Looked at coldly, *Tassie* is thin and diffuse enough to vindicate Yeats's rejection. Its hero, Harry Heegan, goes off to war; he returns crippled; his girl-friend leaves him for the man who saved Harry's life in the trenches; finally, embittered and deserted by all except a blinded comrade, he crushes the 'tassie', the symbol of his former manhood. As one might expect from O'Casey, this frail anecdote is compressed into a quarter of the text; the rest is farce. But the performing dog seems to have wearied of going through the same old tricks once more; his clowns, Sylvester and Simon, are faint echoes of the Captain and Joxer; Mrs Foran (pronounced at the Aldwych to rhyme with 'sporran') is a shadow of Mrs Grigson in *Gunman.* The comedy set pieces seem to have been prefabricated and slipped in arbitrarily; they might be vaudevilles, entitled respectively: *Sylvester and Mrs Foran Under the Bed, Sylvester Takes a Bath* and *Simon and the Telephone.* It is symptomatic of O'Casey's loss of interest in the realism of *Juno* and *Plough* that here he brazenly heaps Sylvester and Simon into the same hospital ward as Harry, as fellow-patients, and with their neighbour, Susie Monican, as the nurse in charge. More serious is the almost total absence of family ties. Sylvester is Harry's father, but there is hardly one word uttered to indicate the relationship. The same holds good of Mrs Heegan: these creatures exist in a dramatic Limbo.

One of the Sunday reviewers waxed glowingly in praise of O'Casey's great compassion. It is the lack of this very quality which, for me, flaws the play most fatally. The creator of Juno Boyle and Bessie Burgess has here given us a gallery of predatory women verging on caricature. Susie is a religious maniac of no discernible denomination, whom a nurse's uniform transmutes into a vapid, callous ninny. Mrs Heegan's only maternal passion is an obsessive love for her separation allowance. Mrs Foran cannot wait to get her husband off to the trenches so that she can be 'single again'. Jessie – Harry's fiancée – is a nasty, if believable piece of work: as endearing as barbed wire. One can see from the beginning that Harry is in for a rough time. By surrounding him with vultures, O'Casey attempts to underline the tragedy; instead, he suborns truth: not every – perhaps not any – war victim comes home to face a welcoming committee of monsters. Towards the end of the play, Harry is prevailed upon to sing a negro spiritual, but as the balloons are released in the adjoining ballroom, his listeners – including his parents – desert him uncaringly. We are meant to feel sorry for Harry, but our reaction is to resent being got at so shamelessly: his defecting audience would, at worst, have interrupted his song and wheeled him with them into the ballroom. O'Casey here betrays his class to suit his purpose.

O'Casey's *The Silver Tassie*, revived at the Aldwych Theatre, London for the Royal Shakespeare Company by David Jones. 1969.

As for Harry himself, Irving Wardle has suggested that he echoes O'Casey's own rage at the rejection of *Tassie*. This is putting the cart before the horse with a vengeance, but I know what Mr Wardle means. The betrayed fury which Harry spews out in the last act is unmistakably O'Casey's. But here, having called it a bad play, I must try to explain why it is perhaps a great one. Harry, like his creator, is not one to suffer in silence. He pursues the faithless Jessie and her new lover like a fury, lashing them with his tongue, spinning his wheelchair in a crazed parody of a waltz, cursing his shattered legs. The spectacle is unedifying: Harry's upper lip is anything but stiff; to be brutal about it, he is a cry-baby. It is O'Casey's magnificent language and the eloquence of what is no more than a scream of futile rage against war which make the play almost unbearably moving. The war scene in the second act is superb, as is John Bury's setting. An enormous cannon dominates what is left of a church in Flanders; flanked by a crucified Christ and a crucified Tommy, the soldiers chant in an obscene lampoon of the Mass: war, too, O'Casey is saying, is both an obscenity and a sacrifice. The language here is as monotonous as the mock-Gregorian chant; it is the concept and the staging which, in this scene alone, disarm criticism, and it is the brilliance of this second act which suggests that Yeats rejected *Tassie*, not for its faults, but for its virtues.

David Jones has directed the play lovingly, but at times with an excess of reverence. The first act, in particular, needs more ebullience: it is realistic, but not naturalistic, and Sylvester and Simon need not be as hangdog as O'Casey and Mr Jones makes them. Elsewhere, there is much to praise. The hospital scene, which is reputedly unworkable, succeeds very well; and Mr Jones has extracted some notable performances – above all from Patience Collier, whose Mrs Heegan could not possibly be bettered. The accents were, inevitably, all over the place, Miss Collier and Clifford Rose excepted. Frances Cuka, who was altogether splendid in a becoming red wig, treated us to an accent so richly her own that she should have it patented at once. David Waller and Clifford Rose were fine as the croneys; one would have welcomed a more beerily extroverted performance from both gentlemen to make up for the lassitude of the writing, but from Mr Waller in particular there came a characterisation of such kindly dignity as to do the part more justice than it deserved. Helen Mirren brought Susie to life – an impressive feat; while Sara Kestelman as Jessie Taite was excellent and right; but one wished again that the performances as a whole were less polite. This was unmistakably a 'British' production, and the Irish – in speech and behaviour, at any rate – are less subtle than Mr Jones perhaps realises. As Harry, Richard Moore started uneasily; the early boisterous speeches seemed alien to him. Later, he was extremely moving.

An American reviewer of one of O'Casey's volumes of autobiography describes it as '. . . misshapen, seamed with horrid flaws, sinfully human and wilfully pigheaded . . . wild and sometimes beautiful'. The description fits *The Silver Tassie*. It is wrong, muddled and clumsy, and even though O'Casey invests it with genius it ought not to work. The nearly unforgivable thing is that it does.

1969 Awards

voted for by the London Theatre Critics

Best new play: *The National Health* by Peter Nichols (Old Vic)

Best new musical: *Anne of Green Gables* by Donald Harron and Norman Campbell

Best performance (Actor): Leonard Rossiter in *Arturo Ui*

Best performance (Actress): Peggy Ashcroft in *A Delicate Balance/Landscape* (RSC)

Most promising actor: Alan Howard in RSC repertoire

Most promising actress: Polly James in *Anne of Green Gables*

Best director: Trevor Nunn for *The Revenger's Tragedy* and *The Winter's Tale*

Best designer: John Bury for *Silence* (Aldwych)

The mosaic of snap judgements on 1969 which follow are compiled from 16 contributors who voted in eight categories – some voting more than one way in one category, others preferring not to vote in certain areas where no offering seemed to merit a bouquet.

One critic voted twice in the New Play category so that Peter Nichols' *The National Health* emerged as the Best Play of 1969 with eight votes from a total of 17. The late Joe Orton's *What the Butler Saw* collected two votes as did Albee's *A Delicate Balance*, Miller's *The Price* and Barry England's *Conduct Unbecoming*. Pinter's *Landscape* received one vote.

There were two abstentions in the Best New Musical slot so that *Anne of Green Gables* receives the accolade of 1969's Best Musical with a total of seven votes against the five cast for *Promises, Promises* and the two for *Dames at Sea*.

One critic again voted two ways for the Best Performance by an Actor, so that Leonard Rossiter polled nine votes with four going to Ian McKellen as Richard II and one vote going to Tom Courtenay, Michael Lonsdale, Ian Richardson and John Clements.

In the Best Performance by an Actress category there was one abstention and the voting ranged over eleven artists with Peggy Ashcroft receiving this category's nomination with a total of three votes, one for her performance in *Landscape* and two for *A Delicate Balance*, both parts being seen at the Aldwych. Eileen Atkins received two votes for her performance in *The Sleepers Den* at the Royal Court Theatre Upstairs and Margaret Leighton two for her Cleopatra at the Chichester Festival.

In the Most Promising New Actor category one critic again voted two ways so that Alan Howard receives this nomination for his work with the Royal Shakespeare Company with a total of 4 votes out of a possible 17 which in fact ranged over 11 artists. Paul Jones and Jeremy Clyde both received two votes for their performances in *Conduct Unbecoming* as did Brian Cox for his performance in *In Celebration*.

Left: Best new play: Peter Nichols's *The National Health* with Paul Curran and Robert Walker. 1969

Above: Best performance: Leonard Rossiter in Brecht's *Arturo Ui*. 1969

In the Most Promising New Actress category there was one abstention and one critic voting two ways in that Polly James in the title-rôle of *Anne of Green Gables* is thus named with a total of three votes from a possible 16. Twelve artists were mentioned and amongst these Susan Carpenter for her performance in *Dear Janet Rosenberg, Dear Mr Kooning* and Helen Mirren for her Cressida both received two votes.

Voting in the Best Production and Best Set categories was tighter (seven and eight names being put forward respectively). With a total of five votes (three for *The Revenger's Tragedy* and two for *The Winter's Tale*) Trevor Nunn emerges as the director for 1969. And John Bury, also with a total of five votes, for his set for Pinter's *Silence* at the Aldwych is the designer. Michael Blakemore received three votes for his productions of *Arturo Ui* and *The National Health* and John Barton two for his *Troilus and Cressida*. Piero Gherardi received four votes for his set of *The White Devil* and Ralph Koltai two for his designs for *Back to Methuselah*. Both are National Theatre productions.

1970

Britain's General Election returned the Conservatives under Heath with renewed efforts to gain UK entry to the Common Market quickly following. In Egypt Sadat succeeded Nasser. An attempted assassination of Pope Paul VI was made at Manila airport. South Africa was expelled from the International Olympics Committee over apartheid. Oil was discovered in the North Sea. The Jumbo Jet – the Boeing 747 – made its appearance.

In the British Theatre it was a bright and varied year with Albee's Tiny Alice, *Bolt's* Vivat! Vivat Regina!, *Hampton's* The Philanthropist, *and Storey's* Home *grabbing the headlines – some way after the talking points of Tynan's* Oh! Calcutta! *at the Roundhouse and Peter Brook's now legendary* A Midsummer Night's Dream *at Stratford.*

Hedda Gabler at the Cambridge

reviewed by Martin Esslin

One of the most difficult aspects of drama criticism is the work of the director: where does the actors' contribution end, where does the director's contribution start? Was an actor's brilliant performance due to his own creative imagination or was it suggested by the director? If only one could see the same director's work on the same play with a totally different set of actors! Then one could really separate the actors' and the director's share of the total success or failure of the production. To those who have had a chance of seeing Ingmar Bergman's production of *Hedda Gabler* at the Royal Dramatic Theatre in Stockholm (and briefly at the World Theatre Season at the Aldwych), a visit to the same production with the actors of the British National Theatre at the Cambridge Theatre therefore offers a unique opportunity for studying Bergman's personal contribution by comparing the two performances.

First of all: there is the overall conception. A non-naturalistic setting – the scene is all blood red, a few pieces of furniture, only the essentials: a piano, a settee, a chair or two, a bookcase. A small movable screen indicates that the set can represent not one but two – communicating – rooms in Tesman's house. And this underlies the basic conception of Bergman's approach: it enables him to counterpoint Ibsen's scenes by showing characters who are not on stage in Ibsen's text alone in the next room. This allows the director to use one of the theatre's greatest assets as against the cinema: the simultaneity of two sequences of events happening side by side. For example: the play opens – in Ibsen's text – with the dialogue between Aunt Julia and the maid: happy gossip about the returned honeymoon couple. But Bergman opens the play in the other room, with Hedda looking at herself in the mirror and expressing her utter disgust and nausea at knowing herself pregnant. And while the aunt and the maid indulge in their sentimental chit-chat we see Hedda in the other room staring in front of herself in despair and utter boredom.

The possibility of this split stage is used with the utmost intelligence and subtlety throughout, culminating in Hedda's suicide in full view of the audience, while the other characters sit in the next room in smug ignorance of what is about to happen. Secondly there is the handling and adaptation of the text: Bergman has cut and modernised the play and freed it from such period romanticism as the famous phrase about vineleaves in Loevborg's hair. As a result the play, while still essentially concerned with the problem of the frustrations of women in a Victorian bourgeois society becomes wholly accessible to a mid-twentieth century audience.

Moreover, Bergman has speeded the action up, playing the text in a continuous sequence – with one interval, but without elaborate pauses to indicate the lapse of time. This gives the action a filmic quality which is completely acceptable in an age as inured to television as ours.

The result is astonishing: theme and motivation of this allegedly enigmatic masterpiece emerge with blinding clarity. And we realise the depth of Ibsen's insight into the moral and human dilemma of gifted women in his time. The conventional view of Hedda as a wicked vixen disappears: this Hedda is a victim of society, of convention, of her upper class status. Ibsen shows us a gifted woman denied a creative outlet – because society does not allow a lady to work; and a passionate woman kept from the man she loves because society threatens the direct sanctions to those who break its sex taboos. Loevborg, a gifted man but an alcoholic, is not in a position to marry. Hedda loved him but when he wanted her to become his mistress, she threatened to shoot him; as a general's daughter she was afraid of scandal. Having got tired of dancing at provincial balls she finally *has* to marry and marries the dull but devoted scholar Tesman. When she returns from her honeymoon she learns to her horror that another woman, Thea Elvsted, *has* had the courage to run away from her husband and her home to live with Loevborg. And that her defiance of convention has enabled Loevborg to write a great book.

Hedda cannot endure seeing another woman achieve what she lacked the courage to do. Hence her hatred of Thea, her destruction of the manuscript which was the fruit of Loevborg's relationship with Thea, her destruction of Loevborg and finally her suicide. Hedda Gabler's destructiveness is frustrated creativity, her hatred frustrated love. That is why, in spite of her incredibly wicked actions she moves us as a true tragic heroine.

Maggie Smith's Hedda in many ways resembles her Swedish counterpart Gertrud Fridh in looks and gesture. But she is more regal, more majestic, cooler. And she has, in all her tragic frustration, the sense of humour and the timing of a born *comédienne*. This is a truly memorable performance. The three men in Hedda's life are less stately, less serious, and younger than the Swedish actors who played these parts. Jeremy Brett's Tesman is a wholly credible character. Not the usual bungling fool, but a very presentable, handsome young man who just happens to be somewhat too dull, too scholarly and socially inferior to his wife.

Robert Stephens as Loevborg is much less of the impressive scholar than Georg Arlin presented in the Swedish production. But he is very credibly a man of immense charm whose passionate nature has led him into dissipation – precisely because women of intelligence and breeding were unattainable, he has been driven into the brothels. John Moffatt (Brack) worthily completes the trio: he is a far younger man than conventionally cast. And quite rightly so, for in Norway one entered the career of a judge on leaving university. There is therefore no need for him to be an old codger. A younger Brack is far more convincing as a cynical seducer of married women. John Moffatt suggests the right mixture of dignity, cunning and coarseness.

This, then, is a rewarding evening: impeccable acting under a great director.

Oh! Calcutta! at the Roundhouse

reviewed by Helen Dawson

Probably the most disconcerting thing for the ordinary, sensible playgoer about *Oh! Calcutta!* at the Roundhouse, was the emergence of the rich man's Mrs Mary Whitehouse in the shape of the Dowager Lady Birdwood. One can only hope that her almost instant defeat will humble her into silence: the theatre needs its watchdogs, but of the artistic not the demi-moral variety. Moreover, the Dowager Lady Birdwood cannot even claim 'surprised shock' (as Mrs Whitehouse is prone to over the cocoa): no show in recent years has been so widely publicised, and there is surely no citizen in the land who could pretend he hadn't been warned.

However, Lady Birdwood has, at least temporarily, been squashed. The general critical reaction, on the other hand, could be termed world-weary which, seen in historical perspective, seems to me to be unfair. Whether one likes the revue, or whether one doesn't; whether one finds it funny, or whether one doesn't, it is, surely, a breakthrough. And, however hooded those eyes on the aisle, it is myopic to pretend that it isn't. Many of the critics explained at length how much the show set out to appeal to the desperately swinging middle-agers which, given the fact that almost all of them fall into this age-group is, somehow psychologically suspect. I don't see why sex in general, and this show in particular, is any more exclusively middle-aged than food, drink, reading or love.

The audience is, of course, middle-class, middle-aged and middle-brow. So are most audiences in the commercial theatre – and commercial *Oh! Calcutta!* certainly is, with high prices and low comfort. But whoever the people who are writing about it, whoever the people who are paying to see it, the revue *is* a breakthrough. Whatever one's previous experiences in avant-garde basements and attics, however daring *Hair* seemed at the time, *Oh! Calcutta!*, in a sense, crashes the barrier once and for all. It may not always be very subtle in its approach or artistic in its means, but it is a bold and triumphant attack on the taboos which have hedged in the Western theatre for centuries, not only by celebrating the human body, but by laughing at the activity which that body, in a 'cultured' society, has come to regard as its most unspeakable pastime. And, for all its faults, what pleased me most about *Oh! Calcutta!* was that its tone, given the circumstances of the occasion, was right. There was no sense of sneering or sniggering, it was all – despite the junior commonroom gags – good-natured and amiable, willing you to be on its side, encouraging you to have as much fun as the cast.

In the numbers when the emphasis was on the naked body, it was much more than this. The highest praise must go to Richard Pilbrow who was in charge of the infinitely subtle, consistently inventive and often extremely beautiful lighting. The nudes, whatever their individual merits, mingled together shade by shade, like moving sculpture. Far from depraving or corrupting, I should have thought it would have been extremely educative for any child to have witnessed grown-ups behaving as naturally and attractively as this. The other great credit is earned by Margo Sappington, who not only arranged the choreography, but also performed an exceptional dance with George Welbes, 'One on One', in which tutus and tights became as obscene as rather bad chocolate box designs when compared with Rembrandt. Another outstanding visual pleasure is provided by Brenda Arnau, a spectacular golden negress who recited John Cotgrave's 'To His Black Mistress', in a pearl cap and necklet.

As to the show's much publicised 'erotic' aspect, I would have thought that, especially in the non-verbal sketches, this was minimal. Certainly it was for a woman, for whether from stage fright or the temperature, the male members of the cast were resolutely unaroused – even when it was clearly in the interests of art that they should be. Sometimes this was covered up – as in the almost silent-film speeded up direction of a sketch revolving round the Masters and Johnson experiments in the laboratory in America – but usually nature had to be imitated. I wonder, however, whether the tone of the revue would change if this wasn't the case: as it is, the eroticism is still cerebral rather than specifically physical.

Another technical point: most of the musical numbers were spoilt by over-amplification of the Open Window in an upper gallery. Given the acoustics of the Roundhouse, words of songs were at all times inaudible, something, surely, that the director, Clifford Williams, who otherwise did an extremely intelligent job, could conquer. As to the sketches themselves: they are, as everyone has said, not funny enough. The funniest go on too long and others, frankly, need rewriting. It seems churlish in a show of such natural invention to complain that consistent wit is lacking, but even if it's regrettable, it's true. Of course, as most of the sketches are concerned with fantasy, it's unlikely that everyone in the audience will find every one equally sympathetic or amusing. In particular, I became bored with the 'period' sado-masochistic offerings, but even the best – like 'Will Answer All Sincere Replies', 'Until She Screams', 'Suite for Five Letters', 'Four in Hand' and 'Rock Garden', in which an old rancher prattles on about a particular shade of white paint, while his son cross-talks about a very small vagina – seem to be too pleased with their own rambling brand of cheekiness. I, personally, enjoy schoolboy humour but only in small doses.

The cast, in general, wasn't quite strong enough, but they also deserve medals for bravery, for it's probably not as easy as most people would think to be 'first' in an experiment of this kind. Many of them at least looked pretty seductive, and Bill Macy, with his little paunch and middle-aged mien, was an endearing contrast. And if none of them had quite the panache to make a virtue of the mediocrity of the punch lines, they certainly had genuine smiles and a pleasing tendency to send themselves up.

It would be nice to think that now the show has settled down, there could be some rewriting in the weaker scenes. But even if everyone concerned feels that they can relax and no more work is necessary, it would still be good to see *Oh! Calcutta!* transfer to the West End, become more generally available, and for other actors, writers and managements to feel confidence in developing the theatrical territory which it has revealed. Contrary to the Birdwood faction, it seemed to me to be a small, but healthy area of artistic exploration.

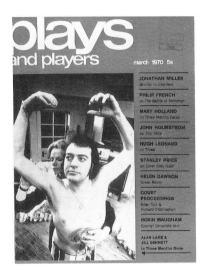

Director in Interview

Peter Brook talking to Peter Ansorge about his Stratford production of A Midsummer Night's Dream

The quartet of sleeping lovers lolled perilously upon swings suspended from the flies: Bottom lay motionless below seeming dead to the world. On another side of the stage, Oberon was waiting to catch a spinning plate on a pole tossed down by Puck from a high balcony. He missed, shrugged (Take 342!) and tried again. In the front stalls of the Stratford auditorium Peter Brook was watching the fraught rehearsal of *A Midsummer Night's Dream* calmly and without any visible signs of anxiety or doubt.

Brook surveys his actors like a subdued Moses bearing a hidden decalogue in his hands. He is directing the *Dream* unaided by the obvious pretty, pretty fairy enchantments. Props and movements have been shaped from a circus ring rather than a haunted wood. He doesn't worry when things go wrong – the actors must make their own magic. Mistakes are part of the performance, risks to be taken in the mastery of stage illusion.

During the second week of rehearsals, when the text had yet to be opened, the actors had improvised a happening around the theme of the *Dream*. 'It had extraordinary force and interest,' states Brook. 'But like all happenings it can never be repeated – it was there once and gone.'

The Tempest Roundhouse experiment notwithstanding, far from neglecting the text of a play, Brook's involvement in a work which interests him is total. For this Shakespeare comedy, his actors must never be allowed to forget that they are playing in the context of continual stage happenings, a world 'swift as a shadow, short as any dream'.

'After a long series of dark, violent, black plays I had a very strong wish to go as deeply as possible into a work of pure celebration. *A Midsummer Night's Dream* is, amongst other things, a celebration of the arts of the theatre. On one level the actors have to display a physical virtuosity – an expression of joy. Hence our production at Stratford involves acrobatics, circus skills, trapeze acts. Equally, certain parts of the play cannot be played without using a Stanislavskian sense of natural character development. There's the play we all know – and also a hidden play, a hidden *Dream*. That's the one the actors set out to discover for themselves.

'The *Dream* is a play about magic, spirits, fairies. Today we don't believe in any one of those things and yet, perhaps, we do. The fairy imagery which the Victorian and even post-Victorian tradition has given us in relation to the *Dream* has to be rejected – it has died on us. But one can't take an anti-magical, a down-to-earth view of the *Dream*. When I directed *Titus Andronicus* at this theatre sixteen years ago I was convinced that the play wasn't just a series of gory events but was a *hidden* play – the drama behind *Titus* was a ritualistic expression of a primitive cycle of bloodshed which, if touched, would reveal a source of immense, atomic power. In the same way, the interest in working on the *Dream* is to take a play which is apparently composed of very artificial, unreal elements and to discover that it is a true, a real play. But the language of the *Dream* must be expressed through a very different stage imagery from the one that served its purpose in the past.

'We have dropped all pretence of making magic by bluff, through stage tricks. The first step must be moving from darkness

to daylight. We have to start in the open – in fact we begin in a
white set and white light (the only darkness in the entire production occurs during the public encounters between Theseus and
Hippolyta). We present all the elements with which we are going
to work in the open. This is related to one of the key lines in the
play when the question arises about whether the man who is going
to play the lion should be a real lion or only pretend to be real.
Out of this academic and very Brechtian discussion comes the
formulation that the actor should say to the audience, 'I am a man
as other men are'. That is the necessary beginning for a play about
the spirit world – the actors must present themselves as men who
are like all other men. It's from the hidden inner life of the
performer that the magic, the unfolding possibilities of the play
must emerge. The core of the *Dream* is the Pyramus and Thisbe
play which doesn't come at the end of a highly organised work
just for comic relief. The actor's art is truly celebrated in this
episode – it becomes a mysterious interplay of invisible elements,
the joy, the magic of the *Dream*. The play can become an
exploration, through a complex series of themes, of what only the
theatre can do as an art form.'

Brook has several of his actors doubling, even trebling their
roles in the play. Most notably Alan Howard and Sara Kestelman
play both Theseus-Hippolyta and the fairy king and queen
Oberon-Titania. Was this for thematic or economic reasons?

'There were two motives. Firstly I wanted to do the play with a
small group. There is a quite different quality of involvement with
such a group than with a large cast where the actors come on, do
a little bit and then disappear for the rest of the evening. When I
directed the RSC experimental group in a version of Genet's *The
Screens* we used a small group in which one actor played two,
even three, roles. In this way you can take an actor much further
– if he reappears in a different part during a performance. Close
to this was the fact that in the *Dream* there are no set characters –

the more you study the comedy it becomes a comment on what makes a dream; each scene is like a dream of a dream, the interrelation between theme and character is more mysterious than at first sight. Theseus and Hippolyta are trying to discover what constitutes the true union of a couple, what can bring about the conjunction whereby their marriage can become true and complete. Then a play unfolds like a dream before their wedding in which an almost identical couple appear – Oberon and Titania. Yet this other couple are in an opposition so great that, as Titania announces in language of great strength, it brings about a complete schism in the natural order. She claims that her dispute with Oberon is the cause of the whole world going awry. Thus on the one hand we have a man and woman in total dispute and, on the other, a man and woman coming together through a concord found out of a discord. The couples are so closely related that we felt that Oberon and Titania could easily be sitting inside the minds of Theseus and Hippolyta. Whether from this you say that they *are* actually the same characters becomes unimportant.'

Peter Brook's innovative 'Dream' for the Royal Shakespeare Company at Stratford-upon-Avon. 1970.

I then asked Brook if he shared Jan Kott's view of the *Dream* – that far from being a 'celebration' the play contained a darker, more sinister exploration of love than is normally suggested. 'Most definitely. Kott wrote very interestingly about the play – though he fell into the trap of turning one aspect of the play into the whole. The *Dream* is not a piece for the kids – it's a very powerful sexual play.

'There is something more amazing than in the whole of Strindberg at the centre of the *Dream*. It's the idea, which has been so easily passed over for centuries, of a man taking the wife whom he loves totally and having her fucked by the crudest sex machine he can find. We had a long discussion about this at one point in rehearsals – we listed all the alternative animal-mates with which Titania might have been presented by Oberon. One realises that every other animal could have left Titania with a certain sexual nostalgia – it's a sort of romantic dream for a woman to be screwed by a lion or even a bear. The ass, famous in legends for the size of its prick, is the only animal that couldn't carry the least sense of romantic attachment. Oberon's deliberate cool intention is to degrade Titania as a woman. Titania tries to invest her love under all the forms of spiritual romance at her disposal – Oberon destroys her illusions totally. From Strindberg to D. H. Lawrence one doesn't find a stronger situation than that. It's not only an opposition between this ethereal woman and a gross sensuality that's coupled between Titania and Bottom – but the much darker and curious fact that it's the woman's husband who brings this about – and in the name of love! Yet there's no cynicism in Oberon's action – he isn't a sadist. The play is about something very mysterious, and only to be understood by the complexity of human love.'

If it is part of Peter Brook's intention to lead his actors through 'most of the schools of theatre that we know' during their performance of the *Dream*, it is also part of a preparation for a larger experimental programme which Brook is finally to begin in Paris this October. He has been trying to find a subsidy for his room in the French Ministry of Works, his 'empty space', for the past two years. As there are to be no public performances money has been difficult to find – but, of all places, a subsidy has finally come from Persia.

I asked Brook why so many directors were currently questioning the value of the work they were doing, uncertain about the state and future of our theatres themselves. Typically, he answered with confidence and faith. Unique among our directors, Brook has been questioning the meaning of the conventional theatre for years. Equally strangely he has been searching for and inventing new forms on his own, as though bent on rescuing the art of the theatre for a future, unknown generation:

'All questions of this sort exist or disappear in relation to the level of intensity that is reached. A low level Shakespeare production sets up boringly archaic barriers for an audience – all that is true life is only dimly perceived. All that is lukewarm, passive, conventional in an audience is brought into play. At that level one has to question the meaning of a performance – to ask what social function it performs.

'Above that, there's another level where in place of a lack of an intention, an intention *appears*. With that intention, which may be political or social, comes a force, a clarity of purpose and a meaning. It might involve doing a play about a dock strike in the right place at the right time.

'Then you approach the next level, which includes very few writers (of which Shakespeare is the strongest and unique example), when you suddenly discover an essential area where meanings between actors and an audience can be shared again, on a very different level to, say, a treatment, of a dock strike – but a

may 1970 5s

plays and players

MAGGIE SMITH and SHEILA REID in The Beaux' Stratagem / Old Vic

WILLIAM GASKILL   Director in interview
DAVID MERCER   John Russell Taylor writes
PRAGUE REVIVES   Peter Roberts in Czechoslovakia
HELEN DAWSON   at Measure for Measure
STANLEY PRICE   at The Beaux' Stratagem
JACK PULMAN   Happy Apple playtext

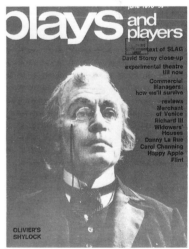

june 1970

plays and players

text of SLAG
David Storey close-up
experimental theatre
till now
Commercial
Managers:
how we'll survive
reviews
Merchant
of Venice
Richard III
Widowers'
Houses
Danny La Rue
Carol Channing
Happy Apple
Flint

OLIVIER'S SHYLOCK

meaning which is quite tangible. This form of intensity makes all questions of the play's relation to the past unimportant. It's happening *now* – whether the characters appear to be archaic or contemporary in their costumes and behaviour. All theatre begins when it is alive – all other theatre is dead. The theatre event that increases our power to perceive is something rare but, to my mind, to be cultivated at all costs.'

The Philanthropist at the Royal Court

reviewed by John Holmstrom

Christopher Hampton's new play, whose title promises inversions of Molière, opens with a Molièresque impromptu culminating in a young playwright, exasperated by the faint praise of friends on his latest work, blowing his brains out all over the back wall of the set. ('Rather too cerebral,' complains one of the friends later when the mess has been cleaned up.) The ghastly act, no less than the sick jokes that follow it, convulse the house with innocent mirth; it must be the most surprising and hilarious suicide of our age. But the violence, vulnerability and wild laughter are all of a piece, and are what make Hampton the most entertaining, as well as the most intelligent, of our young playwrights. Clearly he lives and writes on his nerves – twanging with resentments and puns – and one can't help feeling, behind the bilateral satire of the scene with the artist and his critical friends, some of the bottled-up frustrations of a Resident Dramatist. But he offers much more than autobiography.

His talent, having been somewhat muted by respect for history in his Rimbaud play *Total Eclipse*, now returns to the contemporary torments of *When Did You Last See My Mother?* The protagonist in both is a nervous man who feels out of place and at a disadvantage with competitors; but whereas Ian, in the earlier play, masked his nerves behind adolescent fooling and flyting, and though homosexually obsessed he still brought off the spirited seduction of a mature woman in his bed-sitter, Philip in *The Philanthropist* is an academic, keeping his nerves at bay behind a bland façade of civilisation and scholarship. His subject – as far removed as possible from the confrontations of real life – is philology, the passion for words. It is a sublimation, of course. Not very effective with humans, and women in particular, he can call words to his bidding, strip them to their bare origins, split, copulate or anagrammatise them, and have them ballet- or belly-dance before him, waving veils of accretion and association. In the harem of words, at least, he is unchallenged Sultan.

He has a girl-friend at the university, a fiancée even, as pretty as Jane Asher, though he doesn't realise how fed up she is getting with his feebleness and lack of assertion. A womanly woman in spite of herself, she longs to be controlled, and the last straw falls on their tottering relationship when, after a dinner-party in Philip's rooms, she is unwillingly removed by the unspeakable novelist Braham who beds her in his hotel while Philip is bedded, no less unwillingly, by the tireless nymphomaniac Araminta, who has stayed behind to help with the washing up.

No one, despite the surface gloss, could be less in control than Philip; and in the painful explication that follows the one-night fall, he admits that his desire to please at all costs – which of course succeeds in pleasing nobody – springs simply from fear of people, from inadequacy and avoidance of anything potentially embarrassing. A shaming story about a cripple in an oriental car park symbolises for him his own moral cowardice. He could even respect himself more if he behaved with the frank, vulgar cynicism of Braham, who on being told that the price of a prawn cocktail would feed a starving child for a week goes straight out and orders a prawn cocktail.

Christopher Hampton's *The Philanthropist* at the Royal Court Theatre and Mayfair, London with Jane Asher and Alec McCowen. 1970.

A play takes its tone from its hero, and where the hero is weak and hopeless one might expect a limp play, but *The Philanthropist* is far from that, though much of it is static and discursive: even – as disarmingly forecast in the prefatory scene – 'a conversation piece'. (We also have the *coups de théâtre*, but no pastoral interludes.) It is witty, and larky, and touching, and beautifully apposite in its illustration of Philip's psychic blockages. 'I'm a man without conviction – I think,' he confesses; and later, on being told that he spends too much time apologising, answers like a shot 'Yes, I know; I'm sorry'. Challenged to produce an anagram of *La Comédie Française*, he can do no better than 'A Defence o' Racialism'; but at the end, in agony of soul, from the proposal 'Imagine the Theatre as Real' his despairing mental computer returns 'I hate thee, sterile anagram'.

Luckily, too, the playwright can count on sufficient reserves of feebleness in his audience to ensure considerable identification with Philip. Though he is often presented as a farcical figure – by

Mr Hampton and by Alec McCowen who plays him irresistibly behind an elaborate semaphore of tiny wincing smiles – there is also a core of reasonableness to his inadequacy. It baffles him, for instance, to be accused of literal-mindedness. 'You never understand what I'm trying to say,' wails his furious ex-girlfriend. 'But I think I understand what you *do* say,' he counters modestly. Point taken.

Apart from the pleasures afforded by Mr McCowen, Charles Gray and Dinsdale Landen luxuriate in the roles of visiting monster and slothful colleague, and Jane Asher, after floundering in the more literary set pieces, improves as the story moves into pathos. I have to admit finally that I don't believe in Philip on realistic terms: there are many women that such a man would give deep, wombish satisfaction to, and he only works as a wild exaggeration of the playwright's neuroses. In which case, long may they thrive. Hampton's neuroses: No anthems so super? Not quite. See no human sports? Oh, but they do. At last I have it: and it almost rhymes.

> Hampton's neuroses
> Sport humane noses.

DECEMBER
1970

Nothing Like A Dame

Peggy Ashcroft talks to Margaret Tierney

'I feel that the theatre has developed quite astonishingly during my lifetime – I think in fact it's grown up to a very large extent.' Dame Peggy Ashcroft is the youngest of our theatrical Dames, but she can recall forty-four years during which the theatre has gone through possibly more violent upheavals than at any time in its history. Strangely, her prevailing sense is one of endless links in a chain.

'I think if I look back over the forty-four years I've been on the stage I see an enormous amount of change, but I also see a tremendous continuity. And perhaps this is what's always existed in the theatre. I think there's a state of perpetual revolution, existing side by side with roots that have been there since the Greeks. We tend to believe that what seems new in the theatre has never been done before, but this isn't really true. For instance, take the companies that like to work through improvisation. You have only to look back to the Commedia dell'arte, whose performers surely based their work on improvisation.

'I think the *function* of the theatre changes with the times. The Greek idea was that tragedy was there to purge you with pity and terror. I don't know whether we ask tragedies to do that for us now. I think we ask them to disturb us. So if you ask me what the function of the theatre is *at this moment* I would say "to disturb", to question, because we're living through a very disturbing period, and it is for the theatre to probe, as, for instance, did Edward Bond in *Saved*, which is a play asking a question of society.'

One of Dame Peggy's earliest successful roles was the daughter, Naomi, in Ashley Dukes's adaptation of *Jew Süss*, at a time when plays were more concerned with telling a story than presenting a message. My suggestion that this was a somewhat naïve goal seemed, in itself, to strike her as amusingly naïve. 'Certainly some of the plays I performed in then wouldn't be put on now, but then they wouldn't be written now. People write out of their age and circumstances, and I think the reason the theatre has changed so rapidly is because the world is altering so fast.

'*Jew Süss* started as a popular romantic novel before it was adapted into a play. At the time it was topical in its attitudes towards the Jews, which hadn't reached anything like the intensity of ten years later, under the Nazis. Neither the book nor the play would be written quite that way now, but plays are important in their own time, and should be seen in their own time. It's not necessarily a criticism of a play's value that it isn't valid for another age.

'Of course a *great* play is for always, and not just of its own time. But I don't think the theatre has to consist only of great plays. Take a play like *The Second Mrs Tanqueray*, which now is really a museum piece. You can't take that play seriously any more. But for its own time it was just as relevant as a play by Ibsen, which might deal with a similar theme, but still stands up today. How many of the plays we're doing today will stand up for future generations? It's anybody's guess.'

It's impossible to discuss the development of the theatre with Dame Peggy without coming to the subject of permanent ensemble companies. The establishment of such companies has been a lifelong ideal, and her own present association with the Royal Shakespeare Company, of which she is a director, can be traced back to an enthusiastic schoolgirl whose ideas about stage life were mainly formed by Henry Irving.

'I wanted to act since I was very young, about thirteen. And I had a completely romantic idea about the theatre, just from reading books about it. I hadn't been to see many plays, but I'd read about Irving's company at the Lyceum. But that was finished by the time I started, and there were no companies. It was the age of the drawing-room comedy, the West End show.' It was also an age when classical productions, without the protection of subsidies, had to stand or fall on their box-office appeal. The playwright's original truth became inevitably subordinate to the question 'Will this get them into the theatre?' At twenty-two Peggy Ashcroft's first professional contact with Shakespeare was playing Desdemona to Paul Robeson's Othello, in a cast that included Sybil Thorndike and Ralph Richardson. The cuts in the text infuriated the purists, but the spectacular, noisy and almost unmovable scenery delighted the public.

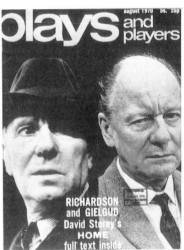

'There were several small art theatres round London, and Nigel Playfair was doing his productions at the Lyric, Hammersmith, the young actors' Mecca. Then there were the repertories, which was where one thought the really important theatre was. Also, I think any young actor of that period was interested in theatre abroad. One read Stanislavsky and knew about the Moscow Art Theatre, and the National Theatres in other countries, and wondered why we hadn't got one. There was the Old Vic, but that couldn't engage actors as a permanent company, only season by season.'

Her own first Old Vic season was in 1932 when, although only twenty-four, she entered the company as a leading lady to play ten major roles. They included Portia, Rosalind, Imogen, Juliet,

45

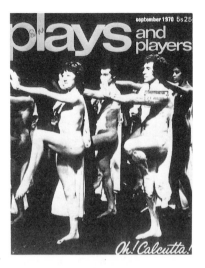

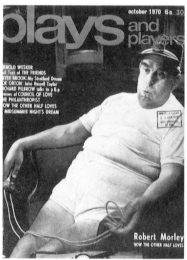

Miranda and Lady Teazle, all of which she was to play again at later stages in her career. 'It was a killing venture, quite beyond my scope at the time, and I knew it. And of course I suffered because I felt inadequate. And I remember the director Komisarjevsky (to whom I was later married) saying to me, "You must try to think that these are only studies for what you eventually may have the chance of playing. So use them, and don't worry if you can't make them what you feel they ought to be. One day you'll get nearer." And I did get another chance, at a time when I could bring more to them.'

In some cases the second chance came more than twenty years later. Portia, Rosalind, Imogen, Viola, are all roles that Dame Peggy tackled in her forties, prompting the critics to stand their priorities on end and produce a stream of ungallant remarks about her age, before proceeding to the real point of interest, her performance. 'Did they really?' The victim of these irrelevant obsessions is unbothered by them, and if anything amused. 'But didn't you know that all critics – and journalists' (with a wry look in my direction) 'are interested first of all in people's ages? Which is very superficial. Of course you have to screw up your courage if someone wants you to play Rosalind when you're fifty. But they probably have a good reason for asking you. In this country we're particularly ridden by the idea of age, but actors' ages should be separate from them. If they can convey what they want to convey, that's all that matters. When Peter Hall asked me to play Katherine the Shrew – at 52 – with Peter O'Toole – I hesitated, then accepted – and never regretted it.

'I think with the great parts, certainly Shakespeare parts, one is very lucky if one has the chance to play them more than once, because there is always something new to be discovered. And if the original production was long ago, that actually helps, because it's easier to put it out of your mind, and give the role a fresh approach.

'I don't think there are any parts at the moment I want to repeat, or any that I haven't played that I want to try – though I probably would be ready to do both. There aren't a great many Shakespeare plays left for me to do. The Nurse in *Romeo and Juliet* is a wonderful part, of course, and maybe some day I'll be asked to play that. Volumnia in *Coriolanus* doesn't interest me terribly, although I suppose that's an impertinent thing to say about what is considered one of the great Shakespearean roles. I think good modern roles have the greatest attraction for me now, and I hope they will turn up in plays I don't yet know about.'

The standard belief about the lack of good female parts outside the classics is something she doesn't wholly subscribe to. 'If you look back, even Shakespeare didn't write as many good women's parts as he wrote for men. But Ibsen – and I think this is very interesting – wrote a lot of his greatest parts for women. Even in *Rosmersholm*, Rebecca is really more interesting than Rosmer.

'Many of today's writers are young men who perhaps tend to write out of their own experience, and out of introspection, and consequently put more into their men's roles than their women's. But Edward Albee and Harold Pinter have written wonderful parts for women (for which I have been grateful). And one of my own favourites is Marguerite Duras' "mother" in *Days in the*

Trees. But thank goodness the emphasis today is not on writing wonderful parts for people, but on *plays*. And I think this is one of the reasons the companies and ensembles are so important.'

For someone who has worked with so many of the great names of the stage, to attempt to pick out individual influences must be an almost impossible task. Dame Peggy thought the directors played a vital role here. 'In my youth I would say the two greatest influences were Michel Saint-Denis, whom I worked with in *Three Sisters, The White Guard* and later *Electra*, and Komisarjevsky, who did a lot of the first productions of Chekhov in this country. He also did productions at Stratford (though I was never in them) which were thought at the time to be outrageous innovations, but are now talked about as classics.

'This is a good example of what I mean by continuity. Komisarjevsky influenced a lot of people who worked with him, such as John Gielgud. Gielgud was really the first person in my lifetime who tried to start a more or less permanent company. He couldn't sign people on for years, but he did keep a group of actors together whom he wanted to work with as an ensemble. I played in his season at the Queen's Theatre in 1937/38, and before that at the New Theatre. Among that group were George Devine, Glen Byam Shaw and Michel Saint-Denis, and these three started the Young Vic. That venture came to an end, unfortunately, and they went their different ways. But eventually George Devine started the Royal Court, which I think has caused the biggest change in the English theatre in my time. There was a basic alteration in the type of play that could be done in London. Authors who would never have been considered by commercial managements have had a platform since then.

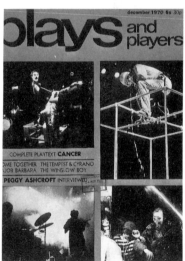

'Glen Byam Shaw went to Stratford, chose Peter Hall to work for him, and it was eventually through Glen that Peter Hall became the next director of Stratford. He in his turn invited Michel Saint-Denis to produce *The Cherry Orchard* and then become one of the directors of the company. So you get a sort of circle that goes on and on, each generation being influenced by the one before, but re-creating in its own way, and for its own time, and then influencing the next generation.

'There's a new generation at work in the present Stratford Company, and for me one of the pleasures of being there is the chance to work with young actors and directors; and seeing how much more democratic things are than when I was beginning! When I was young there was a gulf between the young and the old. The young had the most inordinate awe and respect for their elders, which was a pity because it separated them. In those days you just did what the director told you. Now there is more give and take, with everybody having something to contribute. And this, I think, is one of the marvellous things about the modern theatre.'

And what is wrong with it? 'Oh, as with most things – it's economics. In spite of all Equity has done – which is a lot – there is still too great a discrepancy between the top salaries and the bottom. But *that* should have an article all to itself.'

1970 Awards

voted for by the London Theatre Critics

Best new play: *The Philanthropist* by Christopher Hampton

Best new musical: *1776* by Sherman Edwards (music and lyrics) and Peter Stone (book)

Best performance by an actor: Laurence Olivier as Shylock

Best performance by an actress: Eileen Atkins as Elizabeth I in *Vivat! Vivat Regina!*

Most promising actor: John Wood in *Exiles*

Most promising actress: Anna Calder-Marshall as Sonia in *Uncle Vanya*

Best director: Peter Brook for *A Midsummer Night's Dream*

Best designer: Sally Jacobs for *A Midsummer Night's Dream*

At the end of twelve months' professional theatregoing, fifteen critics nominate the play, musical, performances, direction and design that most impressed them in the year that is over.

In the New Play category ten dramatists were mentioned. Christopher Hampton's *The Philanthropist*, which opened at the Royal Court and is now at the May Fair, received four votes. David Storey's *Home*, which also opened at the Royal Court and is now playing in New York after a transfer to the West End, received three votes. Storey's *The Contractor* also received one vote. The remaining seven dramatists all received one vote each. They were Edward Albee (*Tiny Alice*), Robert Bolt (*Vivat! Vivat Regina!*), Christopher Fry (*A Yard of Sun*), Günter Grass (*The Plebeians Rehearse the Uprising*), Peter Shaffer (*The Battle of Shrivings*), Anthony Shaffer (*Sleuth*) and Michael Weller (*Cancer*).

It was generally not considered a good year for New Musicals and, in this category, there were five

abstentions. But the Sherman Edwards and Peter Stone musical, *1776*, received six votes with one apiece going to *Carol Channing and her 10 Stout-Hearted Men, Lie Down, I Think I Love You, Mandrake*, and *Oh! Calcutta!*

Best new musical: *1776*, by Sherman Edwards (music and lyrics) and Peter Stone (book). 1970.

In the Performance by an Actor section, two critics voted two ways, and eight artists were nominated with Laurence Olivier's Shylock at the National Theatre collecting six of the 17 votes. Closest were John Gielgud with four votes (for *Shrivings* and *Home*) and Ralph Richardson with two (for *Home*). Also mentioned in this category were Robert Lang (*The Merchant of Venice*), Alec McCowen (*The Philanthropist*), Paul Scofield (*Uncle Vanya*), Donald Sinden (*London Assurance*) and John Wood (*Exiles*). As far as Performance by an Actress was concerned, it was a runaway success for Eileen Atkins in *Vivat! Vivat Regina!* who received eight of the 15 votes. Maggie Smith at the National received three votes, Elizabeth Spriggs at the RSC two, and one vote each went to Anna Calder-Marshall (*Uncle Vanya*) and Julia Foster (*Flint*).

Eleven artists were mentioned in the Most Promising Actor category with John Wood in *Exiles* at the Mermaid collecting three votes. Both John Kane (Puck in *A Midsummer Night's Dream*) and Nikolas Simmonds (*Palach*) received two votes. Eleven artists were also mentioned in the *Most Promising Actress* category in which one critic did not vote. Anna Calder-Marshall emerged as the year's most promising actress with

three votes for her performance as Sonia in *Uncle Vanya* at the Royal Court. All remaining artists received one vote each except for Rosemary McHale who got two (for *Slag* at Hampstead and Masha in the Cambridge Theatre Company's *The Seagull*).

A designer's award for the production of *A Midsummer Night's Dream*. **1970.**

Peter Brook's production of *A Midsummer Night's Dream*, which opened at Stratford-on-Avon in the summer and which opens in New York in the New Year, received seven votes. Harold Pinter's direction of *Exiles* was accorded five. Frith Banbury (*The Winslow Boy*), William Gaskill (*The Beaux' Stratagem*), Jonathan Miller (*The Merchant of Venice*) had a vote each.

Eight artists were mentioned in the design category with Sally Jacobs receiving the most with four for her work on *A Midsummer Night's Dream*. Julia Trevelyan Oman had three votes for her sets for *The Merchant of Venice*. Also mentioned, were Rene Allio with two for *The Beaux' Stratagem*, Farrah (twice for *Tiny Alice* and *The Plebeians*) and, once, Ian Breakwell (*Palach*), Jocelyn Herbert (*Home*), Reece Pemberton (*The Winslow Boy*) and Alan Tagg (*London Assurance*).

JANUARY, 1971

1971

The year that a coup brought Idi Amin to power in Uganda was the year François Duvalier of Haiti died – to be succeeded by his son Jean-Claude. Dom Mintoff was sworn in as Prime Minister of Malta. Chancellor Willy Brandt was awarded the Nobel Prize for his services in lessening East-West tension. Canadian Prime Minister Pierre Trudeau married Margaret Sinclair.

*In the UK Chancellor of the Exchequer Barber announced a spending programme to curb unemployment. In the world of the British theatre the momentum of new playwriting was sustained with new work from Pinter (*Old Times*), Peter Nichols (*Forget-Me-Not-Lane*) Edward Bond (*Lear*) and Simon Gray (*Butley*).*

JUNE
1971

Forget-Me-Not-Lane at Greenwich

reviewed by John Russell Taylor

Forget-Me-Not Lane, now transferred (from Greenwich) to the Apollo, looks very much like the play Peter Nichols has been in training to write for the last ten years. Not only does it bring together elements from at least five television plays – Nichols himself admits to using television plays as sketches for his theatre plays – but it neatly resumes most of his leading themes – the 'genetic trap' which eventually turns us into our parents, especially in the ways we most hated and despised them; the divisive effect of children on married life; the mechanics of parent-child and particularly father-son relationships – and offers, perhaps deliberately, a key to Nichols's work as a whole. Obviously one cannot take it as simply autobiographical, though Nichols admits that there are strongly autobiographical elements in it, and it has some curious similarities to another play of childhood reminiscences recently presented at the same theatre, John Mortimer's *A Voyage Round My Father*. But whether real or imaginary in detail, it does indicate very clearly how the various parts of Nichols' imaginative world fit together. It takes up again, as its starting-point (in time, if not in the theatre), the parent-child relationship in *The Gorge*, along with the abortive sexual encounter between an intelligent but painfully inexperienced boy and a much more earthy, knowing girl. This develops into the young-adult situation depicted in *The Continuity Man*, with the boy and his wife, who have now improved themselves with degrees, posh accents and all, coming back into the original family situation and being forced into a re-enactment of childhood patterns of behaviour.

This leads into a virtual rewrite of one of Nichols's best television plays, *When the Wind Blows*, in which a tea party brings together a young couple and the husband's parents, and develops into a life-and-death struggle over which couple will finally succeed in destroying the other's marriage. But what was there played largely as drama is here presented in the context of comedy, and the parents' marriage, though severely bent, does not break altogether. This time it is the son's marriage which breaks up, in very much the circumstances of *Daddy Kiss It Better*: husband's resentment of the demands children make on the wife's time and interest; wife's resentment at the way the husband forces her into the position of organiser, dominant partner, and then blames her for it. And at length the father dies, in just the way that the father died in *Hearts and Flowers*, and we see that with a few minor adjustments (the introduction of a brother to complicate the family and marital situation, in place of *Forget-Me-Not Lane*'s best friend) this is the same family exactly at a slightly later stage. (In fact, *Hearts and Flowers* was written in the midst of *Forget-Me-Not Lane*, as a footnote and a way of bringing the stage play into focus.) From all this you will gather that there is, to say the least, an enormous amount of material in *Forget-Me-Not Lane* – a family saga covering three generations, no less. And the most astonishing thing about it is the way Nichols has managed to organise his material in such a way that one has no feeling whatever of overcrowding, and certainly no feeling of bittiness. Technically the play is an extraordinary achievement; instead of seeming, as it well might, like a jigsaw puzzle, it has the richness and unpredictable intricacy of veined marble. It is a very theatrical play, with a central character-narrator who uses to the full the possibilities of stepping in and out of the action, now becoming himself deeply involved, now stepping back sadly or ironically to comment.

Peter Nichols's *Forget-Me-Not-Lane* premièred at Greenwich Theatre with Joan Hickson and Michael Bates. 1971.

The whole play, indeed, is built on a pattern of ironies, brilliantly manipulated. An effect will be meticulously built up, and then cheerfully undercut with some deflating comment or absurd juxtaposition. But the deflation is not merely destructive, a cancelling-out; instead it always brings us into something deeper, stranger, another layer in Nichols's complex, many-layered reality. This may be done by just one line, as when Frank, the hero-narrator, objects to being ticked off as 'sonny boy' by his father on the grounds that he is nearly forty and has three children of his own, and his wife at once tartly reminds him that at this stage he is nearly thirty and has only two children. Or it may be by a reflection that it is left to the audience to make, as when Frank, after recounting to us one of his most embarrassing experiences, when his puritanical father interrupted a blue comic's act at a local variety show, concludes that this put him off audience participation for life, and we automatically observe that this is a funny thing for Nichols to say (in so far, of course, as it is Nichols rather than his character who says it) when so much of his technique depends precisely upon the degree to which he gets his audiences to participate.

But more than by these overt devices, however ingeniously used, the play works its ironies on us by subtleties of structure. I

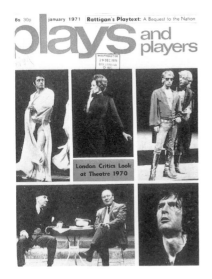

London Critics Look
at Theatre 1970

can think of few plays in the contemporary British theatre where the dramatic syntax is so functional. The form seems to be free, taking us backwards and forwards in time more or less at random. But if we stop and consider for a moment, each episode proves to be placed where it is, in relation to its surroundings, with the utmost nicety. The placing of the scene in the theatre, for example, right out of its chronological context, at the end of the play, gives it the effect of summing up, in microcosm, the whole involved relationship of father and son, and the characteristic they most obviously have in common, a strange and guilt-ridden sexuality. In the same way the exact order of Frank's reminiscences throws light on his character from half a dozen different directions, so that we find ourselves sympathising with him in an obvious, naïve way (seeing things through his eyes, we are put in his position), then gradually detaching ourselves as we see him less and less sympathetically – particularly from his wife's point of view – and come to apply to him and his family just what he has been saying about his parents and their relationship: that it is all a matter of interpretation, of where you stand at any given moment.

That may be how the play works, but it does not give much indication of what it is working for. As well as being a devastatingly acute dissection of the family situation (any family situation) it is, for a start, a riotously funny theatrical entertainment. Of course it is not 'just' funny; as we well know from *A Day in the Death of Joe Egg* and *The National Health*, Nichols is most serious when he is most funny, he has a unique gift of finding the laughter in pain without diminishing its painfulness. If you think about his plays, you don't know whether to laugh or to cry; but in the theatre, for the moment at least, you laugh. And in *Forget-Me-Not Lane* the laughter comes loud and long. The character of the father, beautifully played on but never over the edge of caricature by Michael Bates, is quintessentially the sort of parent who is fine in someone else's family but agonising in one's own, especially amid the manifold built-in embarrassments of adolescence. We laugh, as an outsider would, at his catch-phrases (beautifully graded, incidentally, to indicate the passage of time and shifts of relationship) and his little jokes, but at the same time we cringe along with his son at the sheer social horror of it all.

And above and beyond all that, the play is a hymn to the Forties, to the generation whose monument was the Festival Hall. Ah, the romance of the runaway barrage balloon, the big bands with the big beat, pin-ups of Betty Grable, slap-and-tickle in the shelters, the surrealistic splendour of casual bomb damage. Yet even here there is built-in irony. When Frank extols austerity (it sounds so much better than affluence) we see that he has been crippled by the times as much as by his individual family circumstances; adolescent in a masochist's paradise, he carries the psychological scars of guilt and repression into his own forties. If he ends by turning into his father (his lecture to his own now-teenage son of noise and motor-bikes is a masterly transposition of his father's thought-patterns into his own generation's liberal vocabulary) it is not only the genetic trap which has done this to him; it is the times he has lived through, and his understandable but misplaced nostalgia for them. But then it is a play one can go on and on about indefinitely. I must resist the temptation and offer at least token recognition to the immaculate playing of the whole cast – notably Anton Rodgers as Frank, Joan Hickson as his mother and Priscilla Morgan as his wife – the knife-edge timing of Michael Blakemore's direction, and the great functional ingenuity of Roger Butlin's many-doored semi-abstract set, which looks at the start as though it is going to be too cutesy and then is persuaded, like everything else in the play, to send itself up from time to time. But above all, the play's the thing – and this time it really is something to shout about.

'There are some things one remembers even though they may never have happened. There are things I remember which may never have happened, but as I recall them so they take place.' It is Anna speaking, the old friend refound in Harold Pinter's new play. It sounds like a key line – though, of course, for that very reason one should partly distrust it: if with this key Pinter unlocked his heart, then the less Pinter he. But all the same, it does provide a fair hint of the tone and method of this play, which stands in the same sort of relation to *Landscape* and *Silence* as did *The Homecoming* to the group of one-acts which preceded it. *Landscape* and *Silence* were about memory, the ambiguity of memory, the constant ability of man to redefine his past in terms of his present, to remember things as he would have them be rather than as they were, to relive and thereby re-create happenings in his mind which are if anything more real than present events in the world which surrounds him.

Old Times at the Aldwych

reviewed by John Russell Taylor

Harold Pinter's *Old Times* at the Aldwych Theatre, London with Dorothy Tutin and Colin Blakely. 1971.

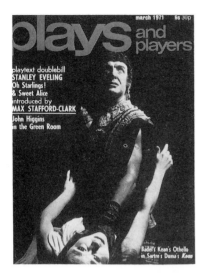

Old Times is also about this, but as befits a full-length play (even a very short full-length play) it is about more; it cannot afford to be, and it is not, merely meditative. It starts with deceptive directness and simplicity (or perhaps not so deceptive: the plays are direct and simple, the responses they evoke complex). Kate and her husband Deeley talk about an expected guest, Anna, of whom we learn that Kate once shared rooms with her, that she was not only Kate's best, but her only friend, and that on occasions she would steal Kate's underwear. To be precise, Deeley talks about her, eliciting brief, gnomic answers from Kate, whose role almost throughout the play is that of dreamy, uncommunicative object off whom the others bounce thoughts and feelings. It sounds like a conventional piece of exposition, preparing us for a classic Pinter situation in which an interloper arrives to disturb what we presume to be the settled peace of an existing domestic situation. Except that Anna is there already, a palpable presence in the background – as though she has always been there, always a psychological presence in the marriage, even before she walks forward as the lights come up to become a physical presence.

Once the three characters are in conversation together, the play quickly becomes an exchange, and then a battle, of memories. Anna chatters on about the past she shared with Kate as young secretaries in the culture-filled London of twenty years ago, and already we begin to wonder how accurate her memories are – do we really believe that these two people ever sat up half the night reading Yeats? Deeley hits back with a long recollection of his first meeting with Kate, whom he picked up at some deserted suburban fleapit where they were showing *Odd Man Out*, so that their relationship began, as it were, under the patronage of Robert Newton. Anna's immediate response to this is the mysterious statement about memory already quoted, and then a long story about the inexplicable appearance and disappearance of a man one night in their room, hers and Kate's. After which she drops in casually that *she* went with Kate that hot afternoon to see *Odd Man Out . . .*

And behind and beneath all this there seems to be something more: a battle over Kate, conflicting claims of ownership, conflicting definitions of her nature. Even something so apparently innocent as a medley of recollections from the good old songs they don't write any more becomes subtly a jockeying for position; it is fundamentally Anna's recollection, but Deeley keeps capping each quotation, taking it over and by implication making it his own. Even when Anna talks about Sicily, where she now lives, Deeley moves in with his own views, garnered from a filming trip: 'I've been there. There's nothing more to see, there's nothing more to investigate, nothing. There's nothing more in Sicily to investigate.' And in all this Kate remains more or less passive, withdrawn, the object. She even complains at one point that they both speak of her as though she were dead, so preoccupied are they with redefining their past, *her* past, to their own ends. And right at the end of the first act Anna seems to be winning the battle for Kate, by taking the conversation with a wrench back to the old times, speaking with Anna as though they are back in their flat together, telling her what to wear, suggesting one man or another to her attention. But Kate at the last makes her own move: she will run her bath herself. Anna and Deeley are left alone as the lights go down. But if the first act seems to be mainly a battle between Deeley and Anna for power over Kate, there are also implications of something else, a growing interest felt by Deeley in Anna. In the second act this comes to the fore, with Deeley insisting that he knew Anna too, in the old times, before even he knew Kate, and that in his experience she was not at all the genteel, cultivated figure she now represents herself as being. Gradually, as more and more memories are brought out and exchanged, cancelling each other out, or seeming to (for as Pinter pointed out long ago, 'The thing is not necessarily either true or false; it can be both true and false'), Anna and Kate blur, change places, until there is no knowing what happened to and with which.

At the end, when Kate at last speaks out, it seems to be in assertion of her existence, independent of Anna, her own choice of Deeley in place of Anna: Anna, in Kate's recollection, is seen as dead, smeared with dirt – but then she recollects trying to smear Deeley's face (if it was Deeley with her in the room) with dirt also. Only he refused, and suggested a wedding instead, and a change of environment. But by now the three are locked into some sort of erotic unity which cannot be broken quite so easily: in the silence after the last word spoken (by Kate) Deeley re-enacts the scene remembered (or imagined) by Anna in the first act, when she saw or thought she saw a man in their room, cradled by Kate, and at the end Anna is still there, as at the beginning – the three of them are there, separate but inescapably together.

Obviously this is a chamber play which depends very importantly on a precise balance of power among the three characters – and the three actors playing them. Vivien Merchant has the most immediately showy part as Anna, and plays it with the piquant, apparently prim sexiness and slightly sinister undertow which has become the hallmark of several Pinter women in her hands: one could not imagine the role any better played, or indeed any different. Dorothy Tutin in comparison has to make her effect largely by sheer presence, by saying little and radiating a lot – which she does extraordinarily well, so that we are constantly aware of Kate as, under it all, perhaps the moving, regulating force of the whole action. Colin Blakely as the mere man has less certain authority to portray – Deeley is the one who has to be changeable, emotional, unsure of himself – but does it with perfect economy and control. And Peter Hall's direction keeps the tension tight through pauses which are sometimes drawn out almost to the limit of tolerance. Every time one thinks Pinter must surely have gone as far as he can along his particular line he goes a step further, and produces something even more spell-binding and extraordinary. Heaven knows what he will do next, but we can be sure that it will prove both surprising and inevitable, the product of a major talent working at full maturity and power. There is none more exciting in the theatre today.

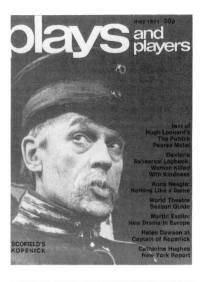

Dear Antoine at Chichester

reviewed by John Mortimer

A middle-aged playwright travels to Chichester. He has reached an important stage in his life at which, unknown to himself and some others, he may possibly be dead. He has, unquestionably, been dying since the age of seven. While there he encounters several old friends, women who may or may not have meant something to him in his past life, and critics. He takes a meal in the restaurant and finds that the waitresses are not really waitresses at all, but actresses who have failed in their dreams. (The cream is not cream either, but something which set out to be toothpaste and grew sentimental.) He enters a modern and functional building in the middle of which is set an ornate and funereal drawing room. There, with a certain hopeful innocence which has not been quite quenched by a life of impurity and disappointment, he hopes to learn something relevant to his plight.

The drawing room once belonged to a middle-aged playwright who is quite certainly dead, and in fact was not a middle-aged playwright at all but Sir John Clements in one of Sir Noël Coward's dressing gowns giving a remarkably English rendering of M'sieur Anouilh. He is surrounded by a number of women who may or may not have meant something to him, and a critic whom he clearly dislikes. There is Dame Edith Evans whom the audience applaud, not because she was and is an actress of genius, but because she is momentarily at a loss for a line. This reassures the audience and convinces them that it is all nothing but a play. Dame Edith's point is then reinforced by M'sieur Anouilh who shows us that all the characters on the stage are actors, rehearsing a play which the dead playwright on the stage has written and is now directing, about their reaction to his own death. The dying middle-aged playwright in the audience, who by this time is beginning to think about the long drive home, notices that the action takes place in a castle in Bavaria in 1913. He has not been to Bavaria and was just not alive in 1913. Uneasily he begins to wonder if he will meet, during the evening, anyone who will be able to tell him anything about himself.

In the interval the middle-aged playwright meets several critics and remembers that his function for the evening is not to make discoveries about his own life but to criticise. All around him stockbrokers, who may possibly be actors, are sitting on the grass drinking gin and tonic and pretending, not only to be alive, but enjoying it all hugely. The playwright remembers many evenings passed with M Anouilh when they were both younger, and the number of times he's heard the speech from *Colombe* in auditions. He goes back determined to try harder. He is rewarded, to some extent, by a brilliant scene in which the dead playwright invites the actors to say something heartfelt and interesting over his corpse. Monsieur Anouilh and the middle-aged playwright in the audience congratulate each other; actors don't exist until someone writes lines for them. Perhaps people don't either. As the play draws to a close the actors are leaving the Chateau. There are suitcases about, and a vague feeling of love misfired and a hammering as the castle is shut up. 'Oi, oi, Monsieur Anouilh,' says the playwright in the audience, 'You've pinched that from *The Cherry Orchard*.' 'Do you know a fine play by Chekhov,' says the playwright on the stage. 'It's called *The Cherry Orchard*.'

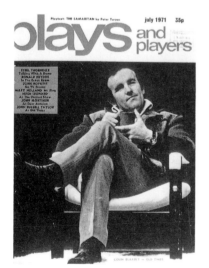

'Fooled you there,' says Monsieur Anouilh, 'I'm simply demonstrating that my playwright is well read and not above an occasional steal.' 'I don't know that play,' says the stage playwright's mistress. One question lingers on the air like the sound of a plucked guitar string. 'Was the whole thing set in 1913 so that someone could say they hadn't heard of *The Cherry Orchard*, or was it because Monsieur Anouilh likes the costumes?' The suspicion grows that Anouilh is not being a playwright but a critic: a critic who proves his points by scintillating theatrical images. Winter flashes into summer and here is Pirandello. Change the light and lo and behold, Chekhov. Bring on the avalanche for Ibsen, the ghosts of Strindberg. Each master plays his part, but we do not meet Monsieur Anouilh. He is, Mr Harold Hobson writes in the programme, reticent about himself. Sir John Clements makes it clear that the stage author has failed to communicate with those closest to him. The middle-aged playwright in the audience drives back to London feeling that he has learnt a lot about the theatre, and the technique of drama in the hands of a master technician, but precious little about M Anouilh and nothing at all about himself.

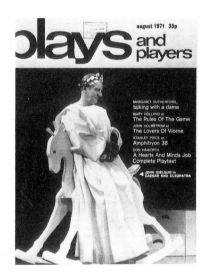

I don't know if there is actually any advantage to having read English at Cambridge – I've always thought there must be some, but have never quite been able to put my finger on what it is. Maybe I was just waiting for Simon Gray's new play, for which the experience provides at least the ideal jumping off ground. The central character is a don, teaching English somewhere in London University, and the whole action takes place in his office – or rather, the office he shares with an ex-pupil, now himself an academic and hopeful contender for preferment. In the course of the working day (though 'working' is hardly the *mot juste* where Butley is concerned) he has to contend with a succession of professional complications of various sorts: pupils to be supervised or put off, distraught colleagues to be managed, the professor to be kept if possible at the other end of the telephone. And all this, the professional and psychological placing of his hero, is done by Simon Gray, himself an English don in London University after having – but of course! – read English at Cambridge, with superb precision. I think one would guess anyway from the tone of conviction with which it is done, that the jockeying for position, the little professional jokes about theses and the subjects of academic study, are scarifyingly believable. But it's nice to know for sure – it gives the play an extra dimension.

The point, though, is what it gives an extra dimension to. And here the play stands admirably on its own inherent human interest. One immediate comparison springs to mind – *Look Back In Anger*, of all things. Butley, like Jimmy Porter, has a blistering command of invective, and is surrounded by people who seem, quite unaccountably, ready to sit still and let his torrents of rage and abuse break over them. There is even a wife who has taken herself off but might perhaps be willing to come back, and a younger male sidekick, sharer of Butley's home and (since this is

Butley at the Criterion

reviewed by John Russell Taylor

1971) unequivocally homosexual instead of, like Cliff, nebulously undefined in his sexual allegiances. But here the resemblances, though striking, end. Jimmy Porter, whatever Osborne's stage directions say, does come over as a kind of hero, an idealist who somehow wins the sneaking admiration of everyone round. Butley on the other hand has force but no real strength. The only thing that makes him bearable is that he is clearly doomed to defeat.

Simon Gray's *Butley* at the Criterion Theatre, London with Alan Bates and Richard O'Callaghan. 1971.

In fact, when you come down to it, every single other character in the play is stronger than he is. He can deliver pinpricks to their vanity without really deflating it, he can win any individual battle of words hands down but never looks within miles of winning the war. Basically this is because everyone else has something, worthy or unworthy, that he or she wants; Butley wants nothing. He is entirely negative, destructive. He is not interested in academic preferment for himself – he merely wants to stop other people getting it. He will never finish his own long-planned book on Eliot, and is therefore savagely contemptuous of his colleagues' studies of Byron or Herrick, which, whatever their value, will at least be finished and appear. He does not even want his wife; he is just determined that no one else shall have her – least of all the man he has already characterised as 'the most boring man in

London'. And though he goes out of his way to make it clear that there's nothing queer about him and that he has nothing but disdain for his pupil-flatmate's affair with a publisher, the way he carries on about the publisher and about any time the young man may spend with him suggests nothing more than the fury of a woman scorned.

Perhaps, indeed, it would not be going too far to see as the 'sub-text' of *Butley* (a term reassuringly branded with Butley's scorn) a reworking of Simon Gray's last play, *Spoiled*. Again, the central character is a teacher. Again the two most prominent people in his life are his wife and a young (or younger) male pupil. And again the wife is neglected in favour of – well, in *Butley* perhaps as well as *Spoiled*, in favour of an unacknowledged homosexual passion for the pupil. How else can one make complete sense of Butley's relations with Joey, to whom (as he intimates in the course of a barbed encounter with Joey's lover) he regards himself as more married than to his wife? Not that I see the play as a conundrum to which there is one simple, generally applicable solution. One might just as well say – though it would not nowadays be fashionable for anyone except Harold Hobson to say it – that Butley acts as he does because he is an evil man. Or because he has become disillusioned with the educational system, or has lost his passion for any sort of literature except the nursery rhymes he endlessly spouts. It doesn't really matter. The play as it stands, as given, provides at the very least a superb set-piece for the actor playing Butley, and Alan Bates seizes it with obvious relish. The dialogue crackles and tingles, and could easily be allowed to deteriorate into a monologue delivered vaguely in the direction of a succession of more or less captive listeners. But Harold Pinter's knife-edge direction never allows this to happen. The balances of the play are very delicately, exactly maintained, so that we understand, even when Butley seems most decisively to hold the centre of the stage, that the long silences of his adversaries are not admiring or merely passive. They can keep their own counsel because they have been here before, they know every move in the game, and draw strength from their knowledge of Butley's ultimate vulnerability. They don't say anything much because they know, and we come to know, that they don't need to.

The best of the supporting performances is the one we have to see most in this light; Richard O'Callaghan's as Joey. This is beautifully judged in terms of the thoughts going on within the often impassive exterior. We recognise that the character is sly and shifty, that he is, as Butley's wife has allegedly said, creepy. But at the same time we see why he has to be; that this is the only way of maintaining his precarious individuality under the incessant barrage of Butley's power-mania. More obvious, because he has a shorter, sharper role, is Michael Byrne's excellence as Joey's tough and perceptive lover, who at once recognises Butley's weakness and demolishes him completely. It is Simon Gray's singular triumph in the play that while hoping for and welcoming the demolition, we still feel some sympathy for Butley, some pathos in the man. And even, which is very much in the spirit of the play, some malicious pleasure at being able to pity him, since it is the reaction he would be least able to forgive.

Lear at the Royal Court

reviewed by John Holmstrom

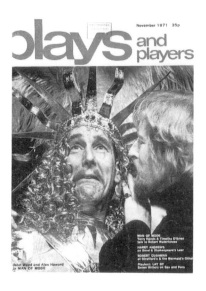

November 1971 35p

>lays and **players**

MAN OF MODE
Terry Hands & Timothy O'Brien
talk to Robert Waterhouse

HARRY ANDREWS
on Bond & Shakespeare's Lear

ROBERT CUSHMAN
at Stratford's & the Mermaid's Other

Playtext: LAY BY
Seven Writers on Sex and Porn

John Wood and Alan Howard
in MAN OF MODE

I take it we are all agreed, we shattered ones who have seen Bond's *Lear*, that it is an imposing and disturbing piece of work. The question that now lies before us is the quality of the disturbance and the nature of the imposition. To dispose first of the correspondences with the *Lear* of Shakespeare: Bond's old autocrat, more politically exercised, has his Goneril and Regan (here named Bodice and Fontanelle) but no Cordelia. The Cordelia who duly turns up is unrelated. Lear's wicked daughters flout him openly, and marry the rebel dukes of North and Cornwall against whose treason he is erecting a Hadriatic Wall. Civil war, therefore, is with us from the start, not a later development. Both dukes (North replacing Albany) are silly villains. There are a Gloucester and an Oswald of sorts, also a Fool – but more of him anon. There is no contest of filial devotion, and no apportioning of the kingdom; but many, many miles of blasted heath. The storm is mainly small-arms fire. Plenty of that too.

We first see Lear – an impressively craggy figure, of course, in the person of Harry Andrews who creates him at the Royal Court – personally executing a recalcitrant wall-worker to encourage the others. His daughters plead perfunctorily for clemency, not because they care about such things but purely to undermine Lear's authority. After they marry the rebel dukes (poor puppets scorned by their wives) the horrors begin in earnest, and Lear after rout in battle is a hunted man. His captured general is beaten up and hideously maimed – with the gloating co-operation of the sisters – and left to wander the countryside, deaf, crazed and tongueless.

Lear's troops have been brutal; the duke's are worse, and any however vaguely suspected of harbouring fugitives or associating with dissidents are summarily shot (men) or raped (women). Even their pigs are noisily butchered off-stage. One pair of victims are an admirable young farmer, known as the Gravedigger's Boy, and his timorous wife Cordelia, with whom Lear fatefully shelters for a time; but both survive the tragedy, considerably metamorphosed. Cordelia shows up again, rather improbably, as a ruthlessly practical partisan leader, who eventually defeats and slaughters the sisters and imposes a more moral but no less brutal regime. The Gravedigger's Boy, for his part, returns to Lear (temporarily imprisoned by the rebels) as an ashen ghost, a surrogate son of Fool, who suffers more in death than he ever had in life. Even as a ghost he is subject to mortality, watching his white body and graveclothes rot and shrivel; he is still alive enough at the end to be gored to death by swine. (Echoes here of the living deaths of *Early Morning*, though the meat is rather too gamy for anyone to venture a nibble).

Although the sisters are now overthrown and Cordelia's partisans are in command, Lear is still an outcast and a political embarrassment, a demoralising rustic *guru* (though too riddled with disgust and despair to be politically or indeed metaphysically effective). He still does harm, bringing death to the innocent while harbouring snivellers, and finally dies (shot, of course) while making a final futile symbolic attempt to demolish his futile symbolic wall.

Bond's play is a long scream of pain and horror, and nobody can seriously suspect that the author, in spite of some touches of pitch-black comedy, is enjoying himself. But I think it is open to serious criticism, both dramatically and philosophically. Theatrically it is monotonous largely because of its faithfulness to a vision which says that merciless people are horrible, but only the merciless survive. The endless succession of killings and maimings – so unremitting as to breed, finally, a self-protective frivolity in the onlooker (I find traces of it in my review) – which seem sentimental because they are so plainly set up only to be brutally snuffed out. Lear himself is more or less crazy from start to finish,

Edward Bond's *Lear* at the Royal Court Theatre, London with Harry Andrews as Lear and Mark McManus as the Gravedigger's Boy. 1971. (Photo: John Haynes)

and though his tone alters from blustering paternalism at the beginning to humane but total pessimism at the end, he is never balanced and always self-centred. (Even his fatherly concern for the Ghost is very perfunctory.) He is saying, presumably, in his naïve romantic desire at one moment to escape into the pastoral calm of a swineherd's life. But the play as a machine suffers badly from emotional sameness and negativity, without any solid central point of reference. All are either hunters or prey. One ends the evening more bludgeoned than moved.

As a treatise on man's inhumanity to man it fails too, I think, because it tells us nothing about society, only about war. The horrors of war are too well known, and none of us surely needs persuading of them in this day and age. The cruelties and dehumanisations of peacetime are subtler and more insidious, and Bond said more about degraded civilisation and its moral insanity in *Saved* than he has done here, in spite of the elevated tone. He has a marvellous way with simile, and Lear's view of his elder daughter ('Her voice is like chains on a prison wall . . . She walks like something struggling in a sack') is unforgettable, as is the description of a man's smashed hands 'like boiling crabs'. But such detail deserts Bond when he launches into what should be the central passages of the play: here he falls back on Fine Writing, a bald celtic rhetoric of wind, tears, leaves, pain and pity, which is desolatingly unhelpful. Like Shaw before him, he doesn't reckon much to the Bard – too accepting of society as it is, he thinks, and too verbal – but *King Lear* will continue to move us more and show us more about the nature of man.

Harry Andrews, grand and forceful as he is, goes down fighting against the gloom and monotony of his role. The most memorable performances come from the magnificent Carmel McSharry as Bodice – even her final panic has a brisk, formidable businesslike quality – from Rosemary McHale whose bobby-sox Fontanelle bounces with blood-lust, and from Mark McManus (three Mcs: how curious) who is deeply touching as the Boy/Ghost/Fool. 'Why are you crying?' Lear asks him at one stage. 'Because I'm dead,' sobs the ghost. 'I knew how to live. You never will.' When the play is as direct as that, it hits hard.

Bill Gaskill's direction serves it devotedly, with extreme skill and tact.

1971 Awards

voted for by the London Theatre Critics

Best new play: *Old Times* by Harold Pinter

Best new musical: *Catch my Soul* by Jack Good

Best performance by an actor: Ralph Richardson in *West of Suez*

Best performance by an actress: Peggy Ashcroft in *The Lovers of Viorne* and *Henry VIII*

Breakthrough actor: Anthony Hopkins, National Theatre

Breakthrough actress: Heather Canning, RSC

Director: Lindsay Anderson for *The Changing Room*

Designer: Farrah for *The Balcony*

Farrah's design for the Royal Shakespeare Company revival of Genet's *The Balcony*. 1971.

1972

The year Japanese Army Sergeant Yoko was found in the Guam jungle (still believing after 28 years in hiding that World War II continued) was the year Nixon was re-elected President and visited China to meet an ailing Mao Tse Tung. Allende declared a State of Emergency in Chile and Ceylon became the Republic of Sri Lanka. An airborne Hassan II of Morocco narrowly escaped assassination and Prime Minister Dom Mintoff ordered all British troops out of Malta.

Queen Elizabeth and Prince Philip made a state visit to France and Sir John Betjeman became Poet Laureate. Chancellor Barber announced tax cuts amounting to £1,200m, and Prime Minister Heath opted for direct rule of Northern Ireland with William Whitelaw as Northern Ireland Secretary.

In the British theatre bravura performances came from Laurence Olivier in the NT's revival of O'Neill's Long Day's Journey into Night, *Michael Hordern in Tom Stoppard's new play,* Jumpers, *Albert Finney in E. A. Whitehead's* Alpha Beta *whilst John Gielgud and John Mills feasted on Charles Wood's* Veterans *at the Royal Court.*

Long Day's Journey into Night at the New

reviewed by Hugh Leonard

That *Long Day's Journey Into Night* is a masterpiece is hardly in dispute. It seizes us with the tenacity of an old tart, it dares us not to be moved to tears of anger and compassion; and the miracle – every great play is a miracle – is all the more astonishing when one considers that not only is it awash with self-pity, but with factual untruths. Thirteen years ago, Kenneth Tynan wrote – and he is quoted in the programme for the National Theatre production: 'No more honest or unsparing autobiographical play exists in dramatic literature.' Honest? Well, I have no doubt that across thirty years O'Neill came to believe that his father had been a compulsive miser, his mother an incurable morphine addict, and his brother a latter-day Iago. The evidence says otherwise. Unsparing? In his dedication O'Neill declares that the play was written '. . . with deep pity and understanding and forgiveness for *all* the four haunted Tyrones'; and an American critic has called it 'a round-robin of recrimination'. But O'Neill is the only one who emerges from the 'long day' without, as the saying goes, a stain on his character: it is his father, mother and brother who are pilloried, not he.

The play is, necessarily, a distillation. On a summer's day in 1912, Edmund Tyrone (O'Neill) learns that he has tuberculosis and that his penny-pinching father intends to send him to the remedial equivalent of Dotheboys Hall. To compound his misery, his brother confesses his lifelong jealousy of Edmund: 'The first good chance I get [I'll] stab you in the back'; and his mother again succumbs to drug-addiction – and, it is implied, her case is hopeless. With respect to O'Neill's artistic purpose, even an 'internal' autobiography, such as Joyce's *A Portrait of the Artist*, owes at least a genuflection towards objective truth; he seems, however, to have been intent at all costs on perpetuating himself as a deeply-wronged tragic hero. James O'Neill was thrifty, but he was not a miser. He bought his wife expensive jewellery; later, he sent her to a series of expensive sanatoria; his sons were educated at private schools; and O'Neill himself said: 'My father, the Count of Monte Cristo always got me the classiest rowboats to be had, and we sported the first Packard car in our section of Connecticut.' The 'cheap old quack' who diagnoses Edmund's illness was in fact a reputable surgeon; and although O'Neill did go to the county sanatorium, he remained there only overnight and was then sent to a more progressive establishment on the advice of two eminent specialists engaged by his father. And, if Eugene's brother ever declared 'I hate your guts, kid', it is strange that there was no subsequent cooling of their friendship, Eugene being of a notoriously unforgiving nature. But the most revealing truth of all is one of omission. O'Neill ends the play on a starkly tragic note with his mother's drug-induced retreat into the kindlier past; he gives no indication that she was to be permanently cured of her addiction within two years.

It would be glib to assume that O'Neill sought to portray himself as the wronged and put-upon scion of a doomed family merely so that his later achievements might seem all the more creditable. Certainly, he was a life-long injustice seeker: he thirsted for betrayal, he created personal tragedy where often none existed. But perhaps a true explanation goes deeper. If I may over-simplify: there are two kinds of actor regarded as 'great': the actor

Constance Cummings and Laurence Olivier in Eugene O'Neil's *Long Day's Journey into Night.* 1972.

who *is*, and the actor who merely believes that he is, but with such obsessive ferocity that his belief communicates itself to us (Wolfit was perhaps a case in point). The same holds true of writers, and O'Neill was a terrible playwright who willed himself to be great. He had no eloquence, no wit, no real command of his medium; he was emotionally maudlin, too egocentric to understand others profoundly, and he remained a callow youth to the last. His plays are overlong, but cannot be cut, because their strength derives from repetition: when O'Neill makes a point, it is done so clumsily that it escapes us; when he makes it a fourth and fifth time, it bores us. But when he makes that same point for the twelfth time, we are his prisoners; he cares so passionately about what he is writing that we, too, must care. This is why O'Neill – in three plays at least – is a great tragic writer. He knew that he would never be a *natural* writer. Edmund's attempt to describe his

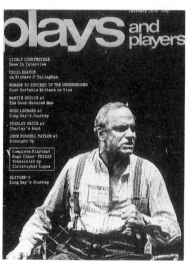

'epiphany' at sea is prose at its most embarrassingly purple, but at least he – and O'Neill – finishes the speech with: 'I just stammered. That's the best I'll ever do.' Lacking the orthodox paraphernalia of a playwright, it is at least feasible that O'Neill subconsciously assumed the symptoms in hopes of picking up the disease. Personal tragedy was an essential ingredient: either triteness or a sense of humour would have pierced and destroyed his obsession. *Long Day's Journey* is bad autobiography, but a magnificent play, all four hours of it. It is marred, not by its lack of factual candour, but by the guiltless passivity of Edmund.

Michael Blakemore's production can be faulted on details only. For all the quietness of the beginning, there is too much physical movement, as if an Equity ruling had decreed that every chair and sofa must be sat on at least once in the first hour. And the final act was perhaps under-lit – at least for an audience who by then was feeling the effects of eyestrain. Totally, however, the play was superbly executed, starting casually and rising imperceptibly towards the great set-pieces of the final act. And here, a confession. I had not previously seen a stage performance by Laurence Olivier; so *Long Day's Journey* was the fulfilment of an ambition extending back to the day when, at the age of 16, I was killed by an arrow during the Battle of Agincourt under Olivier's direction.

He began quietly, almost anonymously: a bull-like figure in a shabby suit, omitting O'Neill's hundreds of exclamation marks as he growled at his sons with the absent-mindedness born of a multitude of family squabbles. Within twenty minutes he had ceased to be Olivier, and was James Tyrone, creating a foundation from which – keeping pace with Mr Blakemore's production – he might unleash the thunderbolts of the last act. I was, I own, ready for the famous howls, but I did not expect to be so moved: not only by the pyrotechnics, but by the stubborn despair of his 'I'm not complaining, Mary'. At one point, Olivier quoted from *The Tempest*, and both we and he wondered whether it was James Tyrone or Olivier who was playing Shakespeare at that instant. The self-deprecatory gesture at the end worked brilliantly on both levels and evoked applause; but my own favourite moment came when, in a fit of exasperation, he aimed a kick at a chair and remembered in mid-kick that chairs cost money. There were also two spectacular descents from a table, and here again Tyrone's flamboyance excused Olivier's, but only just. It was his creation of a human being, flawed, magnificent and complete, which made the tricks unnecessary and the evening unforgettable.

The difference between creation and acting, although of a rare excellence, marked the gap between Olivier and his colleagues. As Mary Tyrone, Constance Cummings – although inflicted with a wig that looked like a wig – was moving, and admirably avoided the pitfall of being herself moved: the principle here being that when an actor feels sorry for himself it saves his audience the bother. Miss Cummings' final reversion to the convent schoolgirl was more than worthy of the play. As Edmund, Ronald Pickup had some of the most unspeakable lines ever visited upon an actor, and yet – as in the case of O'Neill – he compelled us to care. He has a sense of repose which is unusual in a young actor: the young O'Neill cannot have been so very different. Denis Quilley's emphasis of Jamie's clownishness perhaps softened the emergence of the inner rage – the clue here is that Jamie was to reappear as the hero of *A Moon for the Misbegotten* – and we never quite believe in his resentment of Edmund; and yet Mr Quilley's breeziness was perhaps a necessary counterweight. As the maid, Cathleen, Jo Maxwell-Muller was raucous and stage-Irish; worse, none of the affection she is required to show for Mary was apparent. A memorable evening and – in terms of length – a punishing one. I travelled 300 miles to see this production and would not begrudge an inch of the distance.

Company at Her Majesty's

reviewed by Robert Cushman

Phone rings, door chimes, in comes *Company*; and its triumphal entry would be a personal grief to me if it were not such a pleasure. I have felt that *Company* belonged to me for more than a year now, ever since buying an imported copy of the Broadway cast LP. (This also is now freely available in this country so, swallowing hard, I advise you to purchase it forthwith; it's the best show album ever made.) I could hardly believe my ears; here, at last, was the musical fulfilling its proper function, a modern comedy of manners set as every musical should be in New York, compact of numbers whose deftness, wit and intelligence sent the mind reeling as it searched in vain for precedents and parallels. A structure (I could glean so much from the sleeve-notes) apparently unencumbered by a conventional plot-line, or even a conventional time-scheme, but still unified and shapely. A hero whose saintly fortitude as the rest of the cast massacred his beautiful name (Robbie, Bobby, *Robbo*) marked him out as a hero of our time. All this and Elaine Stritch too.

You will have observed the danger. The songs by themselves made perfect, satisfying sense. Who needed a book? So it was that my first stage encounter with *Company* – in a lacklustre performance at the fag-end of its run in New York – was a disappointment. I could not match the show to my own preconceptions. But now here it is in London, tightened and restored to what must have been its pristine condition, and here am I – with reservations – loving it. The reservations first. For much of its length, George Furth's script gazes, with reasonable beadiness, at the antics of five sets of Manhattan marrieds – and evenings on this pattern are now among the recognised hazards of theatregoing. (There is an English example I am always citing but it is probably more apposite here to recall Robert Anderson's Broadway success and West End disaster *You Know I Can't Hear You When the Water's Running*.) And though the situations Mr Furth has devised for his pairings are serviceable if not particularly novel – one couple working off in karate practice the frustrations induced by dieting, another smoking pot for the first time – they are often unreasonably protracted. It gets – particularly in the first half – to seem a long time between songs. And when they do come along the economy of Stephen Sondheim's lyrics serves almost as a rebuke. 'The Little Things You Do Together' not only summarises the script's sardonic comments on marriage; it pre-empts them. 'It's things like using force together, shouting till you're hoarse together, getting a divorce together . . .'

plays and players
March 1972 35p

Marriage Lines:
interviews with
JILL BENNETT
DIANA RIGG
RACHEL ROBERTS

HAL PRINCE and
BORIS ARONSON
talk about Company

PETER CHEESEMAN
The Treatment of Terson

American Underground
in London

FRANK MARCUS
in The Green Room

ROBERT CUSHMAN
at Company

MARTIN ESSLIN
at All Over

JOHN RUSSELL TAYLOR
at Alpha Beta

Complete Playtext
Peter Terson's
FRED FREDDIE IS DEAD

ALBERT FINNEY
in Alpha Beta

plays and players
April 1972 35p

John Mills and John Gielgud in VETERANS Reviewed by
Ronald Bryden + MARY HOLLAND at The Great Exhibition
+ HUGH LEONARD at The Threepenny Opera + CECIL BEATON
on Isabel Jeans + Complete Playtext: SAM, SAM by
Trevor Griffiths

After that catalogue of the things that make marriage a joy, a sketch depicting a happy couple actually divorcing is anticlimactic. And what could follow the brilliant patter-song in which a bride-to-be breathlessly explains why she is Not Getting Married Today ('I telephoned my analyst about it And he said to see him Monday But by Monday I'll be floating in the Hudson with the other garbage.')? What does follow it is a scene in which she explains the whole thing again, more slowly. Not that the episode is a dead loss. It has some witty and touching lines; and it has Beth Howland. Miss Howland, a small brunette with frenetic button eyes, lost her way in the song on the second night (though not on the first – I thought I'd slip that in) but she was in total command of the dialogue. 'Ah' she cackled desperately at the suggestion that she was still attractive at thirty, 'an oldie but a goodie'. When it looked as if the wedding was off and thirty-five year old Robert proposed to her instead ('so they'll leave us alone') the atmosphere was electric.

Robert was there because Robert is always there – a permanent third person for his married friends to batten on ('Who takes the kids to the zoo/Who finished yesterday's stew') in return for which they do his living for him. The show charts his growing awareness of the flaws in this situation and when Mr Furth is intent on this, when he brings his husbands and wives into conflict with Robert rather than with each other, he does himself far more justice. And when he lines Robert up with a series of girl-friends he is winning all the way. Paradoxically this plotless musical is consummately plotted, with its central figure emerging in sharper relief with each scene. Trouble stirs again only at the end when one of Robert's married ladies finally makes a pass at him and her offer to take care of him jolts him into asking 'But who would I take care of?' This is meant to represent a Great Moral Step for Robert, whose love-life has hitherto consisted of a series of enviable one-night stands, and I didn't believe it. Could an intelligent man really have reached thirty-five without at any rate paying lip-service to the idea that love involves giving? (To act on it is quite another thing.) But, the fatal words once out, Robert is irretrievably committed – to, among other things, the performance of a soaring and strenuous ballad called 'Being Alive'. The Sunday papers have arrived as I write this, and I see that Mr Hobson (in *The Sunday Times*) finds this number an 'exceptionally high point' and Miss Dawson (in *The Observer*) calls it 'pretty soupy.' Both are right. The song is cunningly constructed, and it would take a tougher throat than mine to remain unlumped as the music swells and Robert comes down in favour of togetherness. Nor can his analysis of its constituents ('Someone to hurt you too deep Someone to know you too well') be called unrealistic, while the line which somebody interjects 'You've got so many reasons for not being with someone but you haven't got one good reason for being alone' is hardly to be quarrelled with. All the same we are being preached at and it would be nice if this of all musicals had resisted the temptation to prescribe as well as describe. It does the second so well.

Apart from all that, the show is faultless. Mr Sondheim's lyrics are literally incomparable, a series of exquisite glancing blows with every character singing in an individual voice; his music moves beneath, as smooth and unpredictable as quicksand. Words and music are mixed as in a perfect cocktail (a whisky sour, I think.) One number, *Barcelona*, makes unremarked history; it does the work of a whole scene, and musicalises an entire conversation. The two breeziest show-stoppers, however, utilise familiar conventions; three birds lament Robert's lack of co-operation in a forties close-harmony trio, 'You Could Drive a Person Crazy' and the entire posse of husbands and wives do duty as a chorus-line (individuals high-kicking being more fun than nonentities) in an all-inclusive barnstormer 'Side by Side by Side' whose lyrics should you get the chance to listen to them, are particularly devastating.

The sets (Boris Aronson) can be disposed of along with the choreography (Michael Bennett); both are streamlined and move like a dream. My favourite wife was Teri Ralston, who salvages the pot-smoking scene by her unbelieving joyousness as she sinks giggling under the influence and my favourite husband Kenneth Kimmins, a balding eager beaver who bounds knowingly on to offer Robert a spare girl ('Call me tomorrow, I want the details') and sweetly and wistfully intones the score's most ambiguous tribute to marriage, 'Sorry-Grateful'. And always there is Elaine Stritch, the good-humoured bad-time girl, tossing off her routines with a look-no-hands abandon and mowing down the opposition with every acid line. Larry Kert as Robert stands up to her very well; he looks guileless, can sing, dance and listen. Donna McKechnie can sing and dance (marvellously) too, even act a bit; and Annie McGreevey, as the gabbiest of Robert's girls success-fully gives the lie to her own dictum that 'Smart remarks do not a person make', though I don't know that she has to deliver quite so many of them in the audience's lap; this is a gaffe unworthy of a Harold Prince production, considering the quality of the acting in his and Sondheim's latest show *Follies*.

Now *Follies* is a show I really want to hang on to.

A backcloth of Victorian melodrama. An antique desert peopled by rogues, mountebanks, comic Cockneys and romantic egoman-iacs. Threading their midst, a figure of garrulous, spinsterish saintliness, putting chaos to rights with a gracious vagueness which somehow always issues as toughest common sense. An implicit lesson about the humility of greatness, making people behave better by treating them as you'd want them to treat you . . .

You can't tell me Charles Wood didn't write *Veterans* for John Gielgud with one eye over his shoulder on *Captain Brassbound's Conversion*. It's too long-armed a coincidence that the only two plays of their kind in the language – undisguised dramatic portraits of the actors for whom they were written – should be the adoring Moorish fantasia Shaw devised for Ellen Terry and the equally loving Turkish comedy Wood has run up for Ellen Terry's great-nephew. The family likeness even extends to both Terrys' reluc-tance to accept the tendered homage. Ellen Terry took six years to agree to play *Brassbound*, and then only for a season of six

Veterans at the Royal Court

reviewed by Ronald Bryden

matinées. It's to be hoped success will change Gielgud's mind as it changed hers, and extend the life of *Veterans* past four meagre weeks at the Court.

Charles Wood's *Veterans* at the Royal Court with John Mills, Ann Bell, John Gielgud and Gordon Jackson. 1972.

For, like Shaw, Wood has pinned down a theatrical legend for posterity. Voytek's set for the Turkish film location of *Veterans* is trebly appropriate. A vast strip of dusty gold canvas curving from flies to footlights, it isolates the two ageing actors of the title, perspiring in their canvas chairs, in a celluloid limbo – beyond the hot, narrow continuum of their work is darkness. Both it and their conversation suggest a giant swatch of film discarded on the cutting room floor, as indeed they are – Wood makes no attempt to hide that his play is additional footage retrieved from the experience of scripting Tony Richardson's *Charge of the Light Brigade*. But it's also, far more than any film yet made, a permanent record of the white magic of Gielgud. Future students of acting who wish to understand his peculiar grace will refer, not to *The Charge*, Agate's notices or Rosamund Gilder's line-by-line analysis of his *Hamlet*, but to this; just as anyone seeking the key to Ellen Terry's charm turns to *Brassbound*.

Like Shaw's, Wood's comedy has weaknesses as a play, the result of combining a love-letter for posterity with a lampoon for yesterday's gossip columns. *Veterans* bristles with good, sharp jokes about how the umpteen millions Richardson's *Charge* cost, and lost, evaporated in the Turkish sunshine. Kippers are flown from Beirut. Technicians stand idle in scores while their director giggles. Turkish cavalry disappears sporadically to hunt rebellious students. But these are showbiz in-humour, already yellowing at the corners like Shaw's satire in *Brassbound* on the sort of spectacular nonsense on which Irving wasted Ellen Terry's talent. If *Veterans* were no more than this, it would merely be journalism; bright, barbed but ephemeral. It makes the same error Shaw did, hoping to beguile Irving into playing Brassbound, to appear in its last act, tamed and ludicrously frock-coated, at Ellen Terry's chariot-wheel. 'He means them to laugh at me,' Irving commented accurately, and refused. Unable to cast the rest of *The Charge* company as themselves, Wood has had to produce muffled, generalised performances. Frank Grimes does best as an empty-headed young star with a yacht, ten-gallon hat and holding company. But John Mills softens the already blurred figure of Gielgud's old crony-enemy 'Dotty' D'Orsay, who almost gets thrown off the film for exposing himself to an ambassador's daughter. Much of the best opportunities are offered by the invented characters of a queenly Scottish unit cook and a sun-crimsoned Cockney electrician. They're seized by Gordon Jackson and Bob Hoskins.

What raises *Veterans* from gossip to history is Wood's transparent worship of Gielgud, shining through every line as ardently as Shaw's platonic passion for Ellen Terry. With the same loving ear which recreated the squaddie-dialect of *Dingo*, the Anglo-Indian cadences of *H*, he has captured the Gielgud voice in words. 'To my utter shame and constant sorrow, I never did do anything like my bit,' he mourns, comparing his theatrical war-record with 'the marvellous oil-stained things' Dotty did in naval epics. 'Haven't you ever told him to fuck off?' asks the director, about a tiresome supernumerary. 'He wouldn't, though,' explains Gielgud simply. 'Then one's been unpleasant to no purpose.' All the backstage legends of Gielgud's tactlessness are exploited for full risible value. ('They ought to get on together. They're both insufferable.') But they're fitted into the framework of a nature in which exquisite politeness is in constant tug-of-war with iron, unbending truth about artistic value. 'Haven't you ever had one before?' he asks Dotty, elated by his first Oscar nomination 'How very nice!' The attempted warmth can't conceal his astonishment that anyone should regard an Oscar as worth having.

The total impression is of a kind of saint of the theatre. Unable to lie about the value of his work and other people's, he's equally unable to imagine that his greatness entitles him to special treatment. 'Am I cheap?' he asks the director, genuinely unsurprised. 'I suppose I must be. There must be some reason why I'm so constantly employed.' The one thing he can't stand is amateurish inefficiency. 'I withdraw my labour!' he quavers, plucking off his toupee, when the director leaves him sweltering and uninstructed on a wooden horse-substitute. Having walked off the set, he's at a loss. All three of his homes have been lent ('If only people wouldn't take invitations so seriously') to friends. 'There doesn't seem anywhere I can go,' he explains humbly, 'without

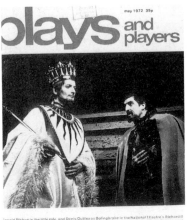

Ianald Pickup in the title role, and Denis Quilley as Bolingbroke in the National Theatre's Richard II. Alan Bennett in the Green Room • Kenneth More, Denis Quilley and David Warner on Theatre and politics • Emile Littler and Joe Layton on Money and the Musical • Cecil Beaton photographs Alan Webb • Michael Redgrave on taking over from Alec Guinness (Voyage Round My Father) • Max Stafford-Clark; Traverse Workshop Goes To War • Jeremy Sandford on TV Drama • Complete Playtext; David Hare's The Great Exhibition

Ronald Bryden on Gone With The Wind • Hugh Leonard at Maid of The Mountains • John Holmstrom at Big Wolf • Frank Cox at Coriolanus • Complete Playtext; WITHIN TWO SHADOWS by Wilson John Haire, production reviewed by Mary Holland • Cecil Beaton photographs Paul Scofield • Irving Wardle in Florence • Millicent Martin, John Neville, Angela Richards in The Beggar's Opera reviewed by Helen Dawson ▼

being a nuisance'. It must be the most endearing portrait of an actor ever drawn. Obviously it helps to have Gielgud impersonate himself, his timing of each joke on himself as perfect as the modesty with which he offers it. Ronald Eyre's reticent direction helps too, leaving the lines to work for themselves. But the real satisfaction of the piece is to see Wood's long devotion to the most undervalued of our great actors (he created the role of Havelock in *H* for him, but Gielgud refused it) flower at last in a play which gives life and depth and to that crystal professional virtue, explaining to the future why, since Ellen Terry, no actor has been more beloved by his peers.

DECEMBER

1972

Green Room

Clive Barnes condemns the agony and preposterousness of first nights, the worst of all possible worlds

A theatrical first night in New York, or for that matter in London, is an injustice, a fraud and an abomination; it should be rejected almost as firmly as slavery. The typical first night is a cross between a witches' sabbath, a dowdy fashion show and a minor horse race. It brings no credit on the theatre and the idea of it being glamorous is on a par with the idea of whores being good-hearted. Some of both are true, but most are straightforward commercial propositions, like Christmas or the wholesale marketing of lung cancer. What is wrong with a theatre first night? After all, here is a climax in a playwright's career, a golden chance for an actor, an occasion when the brightest people in town – critics and fellow artists – can come and see theatrical history made. Here is the culmination of what might be a lifetime's effort; a time when stars are born and less lucky souls shipwrecked.

Only Hollywood can really do justice to a 'glittering Broadway first night' because only Hollywood has the gall – and in fairness I suppose the ignorance – to lie about it. The dream is rather pretty. How many times have we seen it in those humble little Hollywood musicals about bright Broadway musicals. The gorgeous limousines driving to the door, the lovely people – ambassadors accompanied by horizontals so grand that they are allowed to walk upright in polite society, the cream of the town, and best of all, the critics, elegant, suave and knowing, all looking either like George Sanders or Basil Rathbone, wearing scarlet-lined opera capes and whistling sinisterly through their teeth – and the bright lights of the foyer. Never forget the bright lights of the foyer. Inside the cheerful auditorium the scene is animated. Bright eyes look around questioningly and gay banter lightly fills the air. Backstage all is excitement; call boys are running everywhere, agents are smoking cigars and backers are merely smoking. The producer, a well-preserved man in his late 90s, is giving warm words of encouragement to the eager little chorus girls, who every so often laughingly cross themselves and adjust their bra straps.

Now the show begins, and in a surge of sentiment everyone realises there is no business like show business. The audience rocks with laughter with only the archetypal critic frowning in his opera cape. At last he slyly smiles, then beams, then roars with uncontrollable laughter, shaking in his seat like an out-of-hand earthquake. The young boy-friend of the girl-who-is-about-to-become-a-star watches the critic shuddering with merriment,

*Clive Barnes, British-born critic of *The Washington Post* and formerly of *The New York Times*.

winks happily at the well-preserved producer who smiles with a simple radiance. The critic strolls out of the theatre, clasping the producer warmly as he leaves. The crowds open respectfully for him, he signs an autograph or two, then enters his chauffeured limousine and proceeds to his elegant office. Here, sipping champagne, he dictates his praises to a tape recorder. Meanwhile a mad party is in progress – the show is a hit, a gorgeous, fantabulous hit. The producer is clasping everyone and the girl who has just been made a star is telling the world that she cannot believe it. Now the critic enters, still wearing his opera cape, and in a respectful silence reads his notice to the crowd. The author – a forgotten figure up to now – comes up to him and kisses his hand. The press agent orders a new marquee and sends out the advertisements for the next day's paper. That's Broadway for you – the glittering, lovely Great White Way, street of a thousand dreams and a million heartbreaks. And that is a first night to remember.

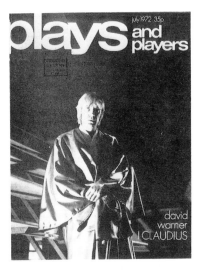

The reality is somewhat different. First nights start early – about seven o'clock, to give the critics some more or less reasonable chance to write a notice on time, and to let the audience make it more or less on time through the murderous cross town traffic. Few people have had time to eat – only to drink. The scene in the grubby foyer is frantic. People are elbowing their way through to the auditorium, most of them with the manners of pigs on slaughter day. The press agent stands by the ticket collector, watching for the press to enter and biting his nails and losing his hair. Usually one of the press is late (sometimes it's me as I combine no sense of direction with no sense of time) and the curtain has to be held a minute or two. The auditorium is depressing. Faded gilt, uncomfortable seats, and an audience that looks as though it has dressed (if it has dressed) rather too quickly. An expensive scent of alcohol and musty perfume fills the air, most of it gin and after-shave. The critics are a fine body of men, but few of us wear opera capes and only Henry Hewes looks remotely like George Sanders, although I personally might claim some distinction as looking like a rather uneven cross between Peter Lorre and Sydney Greenstreet.

The performance is, to a greater or lesser extent, a disaster. It almost certainly was better at the previews, it will soon get much better still, but this particular performance is rarely up to snuff. It may be perfectly adequate, but it certainly is not typical. This is due to the audience. The audience consists of the backers, the critics, such friends as the producer still has left, and glamorous professional first-nighters who do not know that plays often give other performances too.

This hand-picked and monstrous audience hardly laughs, never cries, but applauds and cheers rapturously at every opportunity – some conceivable, some less so, and some almost aborted. The critics appear to be on some kind of contract arrangement never to react visibly or audibly. The hard core backers – and everyone else with a stake in the show – are too busy observing the splendid performances being given by the non-reacting critics to notice the actors. The actors' turn, in fairness, will come at the party afterwards. The actors themselves are frozen with nerves, knowing, half the time, full damn well that the producer has a closing

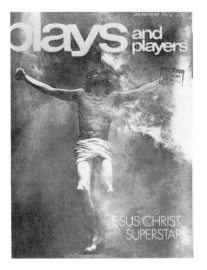

notice in his pocket and that he is only praying for the bad notices that will get him out quickly. As the curtain falls, or usually just a little before the curtain, the critics and such misguided fools as would be mistaken for critics, tumble out of their seats and rush madly for the exits as if they had been given prior notice of a three-alarm fire. In this rush men, women and producers can be knocked down if they are not careful. Once outside the critics brush themselves down and proceed quietly to their various cubbyholes all over town. There, in the space of an hour or so, they have to write a considered opinion of a work that might represent the endeavour of a lifetime. The newspaper critics have between 600 and 1,000 words, while television and radio critics have about 200. Meanwhile, as this fevered cerebration is proceeding, the cast are removing their make-up, receiving their friends and eventually going on to a first-night party. This is traditionally in Sardi's – but there are, I believe, other inferior places. (What I say is if you are going to die at least die in Sardi's and Vincent Sardi can have that quote as a gift.)

The television notices are received in Sardi's and news of them floats around. WQXR, the *New York Times's* radio station, usually carries an idea of the *Times's* view on its 11 o'clock news. This is actually based on the beginning of the *Times's* notice, which is not usually finished until 11 p.m. The *Times's* notice proper is available after 12.15 a.m. All the notices are assessed – particularly as to whether or not they are 'money notices'. A money notice is one conducive to a line forming at the box-office the following morning; no other notices are welcome. Most producers, I think, would prefer a pan to an 'if-and-but' notice – especially if the balance of an 'if-and-but' notice is favourable; for while not producing a storm to the box office, the producer feels he must keep going to see if the play catches on. Producers and backers alike prefer a sharp opinion. Unfortunately for them, hardly any plays are either so good or so bad as to justify such boldly opinionated reviews. Most plays are mediocre and notices must reflect that mediocrity. Now the verdict is more or less in. As someone recently said, they know whether to order beer or champagne – although critics' judgements are, in fairness, much less decisive than producers pretend – and the first night is over in either joy or tears, triumph or disappointment. Now, I ask you, is this any way to run a theatre?

There is no artistic need for a first night whatsoever, and I think we are probably about to see its decline and fall. The alternative to a first night is obvious, and it is an alternative that the more enterprising and younger producers are turning to in increasing numbers. The new idea is to call the last five or six previews 'press performances'. The critics choose which of these they would like to attend, but all their notices appear on the same day. This is the system that is used by Richard Barr and Harold Prince. I also know that both Alexander Cohen and David Merrick are at least interested in this new way of theatrical life.

The advantages for the actor and the critic are enormous. The actor, who is not told in advance who is out in front, does not have the tension of the first night circus. No performance is make or break and he is able to be himself. For the critic the system has two important aspects: first, he is sitting with a genuine audience, an audience he can really feel himself part of, which, in a communal art such as the theatre, does give the right ambience for his own sensibilities to flourish. It is a ghastly thing to sit in an unnaturally picked audience and to feel that you are almost as much on display as the actors themselves. Second, it gives that all-important day or two for reflection. Critics vary in their writing methods. For myself, I actually enjoy the rush back to the office and then putting down my immediate reactions as fairly as I can and as quickly as I can. I have trained myself for this kind of journalism, and with modesty I do it as well as most. But I would much appreciate the benefit of second thoughts. You look at a notice the morning after and, once in a while, you deeply regret the wounding crack of the night before. At least twice a season most critics, if they are honest, will admit that they feel they might have missed on a play, and occasionally it goes the other way. Often you are fair when you should have been generous, and occasionally generous where it would have sufficed to have been merely fair.

I am becoming more and more convinced that the first night and all it stands for is not only barbaric but, more hopefully, obsolescent. As a journalist I have little difficulty in meeting any deadline anyone asks me to meet, but as a writer I cannot accept the rightness of the present ferocious system. Why should I have to make up my mind definitively while I am walking to my office? Why not give all critics – if they want it – a time for contemplation, a period where the first fiery reaction can sink in; a period where we might even be able to shape some of our present rough-hewn prose into at least a semblance of grace? The playwright, the actor, the director, the producer, the backer, are ready to complain at the insensitivity of critics. But are they also prepared to assist the critic to do his best possible job? Kill the first night, kill it, kill it.

I and Albert

1972 Awards

voted for by the London Theatre Critics

Best play: *Jumpers* by Tom Stoppard

Best musical: *Company* by Stephen Sondheim (music and lyrics) and George Furth (book)

Best performance (Actor): Laurence Olivier in *Long Day's Journey into Night* (National)

Best performance (Actress): Constance Cummings in *Long Day's Journey into Night* (National)

Best performances in a supporting role (Actor): Denis Quilley for work at the National

Best performance in a supporting role (Actress): Yvonne Antrobus for *The Effect of Gamma Rays . . .*

Most promising actor: Peter Egan for *Journey's End*

Most promising actress: Veronica Quilligan for *A Pagan Place*

Best production (Director): Michael Blakemore for *The Front Page*

Best production (Designer): Victor Garcia for *Yerma*

With a dearth of new plays around, Tom Stoppard's *Jumpers* was a walkover winner getting the solo nod from 11 out of 16 critics. E. A. Whitehead's *Alpha Beta* was nominated by three critics, although two of them (Harold Hobson and Felix Barker) split their votes, and only Herbert Kretzmer gave it his 100 per cent. Alan Ayckbourn's *Time And Time Again*, Sam Shepard's *The Tooth of Crime*, and David Hare's *The Great Exhibition* each received one vote apiece, while Harold Hobson, full of theatrical *joie de vivre* nominated Edna O'Brien's *A Pagan Place*, Howard Brenton's *Hitler Dances*, William Douglas Home's *Lloyd George Knew My Father*, and Noël Coward's *Private Lives*. Well, considering the competition, why not.

    Company was the easy choice as Best Musical. An almost perfect package combining, under Hal

Left: Best play: Tom Stoppard's *Jumpers* at the Old Vic with Michael Hordern. 1972.

Above: Best production: Michael Blakemore's production of *The Front Page* for the National Theatre. 1972.

Prince's marvellous staging, the acid/witty score of Stephen Sondheim with George Furth's sharply drawn book about living death in the urban jungle and set in Boris Aronson's cage of glass and aluminium. Two strong plus factors were a no-holds-barred performances by Elaine Stritch, and Michael Bennett's electric choreography, especially as performed by Donna McKechnie.

The new smash hit *Applause* also received two votes as did both *Jesus Christ Superstar* and *Joseph and the Amazing Technicolour Dreamcoat* from the pens of the ubiquitous Tim Rice and Andrew Lloyd Webber. *Trelawny* was mentioned by two critics while outsiders were *Cowardy Custard* (from the right) and *George Jackson's Black And White Minstrel Show* (from the left).

Both top acting honours came from the National's production of O'Neill's *Long Day's Journey Into Night,* with Laurence Olivier and Constance Cummings' performances judged the best of the year. Olivier was nominated by 10 critics, while runner-up was Michael Hordern with three votes for his tour de force performance in *Jumpers*. Albert Finney was also mentioned by three critics, one of whom split his vote, but it was Olivier all the way.

Miss Cummings received six votes out of the 16, while two votes apiece were received by Jill Bennett for *Hedda Gabler* and Julia Foster for both *Notes On A Love Affair* and *The Day After The Fair.* Other actresses cited were Rachel Roberts (*Alpha Beta*), Lou Jeffrey (*Pip Simmons' Alice*), Joan Plowright (*The Doctor's Dilemma*), Janet Suzman (*Antony and Cleopatra*), June Ritchie (*His Monkey Wife*), Lauren Bacall (*Applause*), and Nuria Espert (*Yerma*).

In the supporting categories, 12 different nominations were received for Best Performance by an Actor, eight for an Actress. Denis Quilley emerged as the winner in the former for his outstanding work at the National, while Yvonne Antrobus's performance in *The Effect of Gamma Rays . . .* was the top choice. Quilley received three votes, just topping James Villiers (*Private Lives*) and Peter Barkworth (*Crown Matrimonial*); Miss Antrobus, four, winning over Angela Richards (*The Beggar's Opera*) and Julia Foster. Maureen Lipman also received a pair of votes for her performance as the street hooker in *The Front Page*.

Most Promising New Actor and Actress is always a difficult choice and this year it again provided a bit of confusion. Although hardly a 'newcomer to the scene', Peter Egan's status as a lead was consolidated by his brilliant performance in *Journey's End* and this induced the critics to vote him the most Promising. Neither of the runners-up could be considered 'new' either since both Julian Curry (*The Black And White Minstrel Show*) and David Schofield (*The Tooth of Crime*) are well seasoned actors, but then promising and new don't always mean the same.

One thing that can definitely be said for Veronica Quilligan is that she is indeed new, since her performance in *A Pagan Place* was her first professional appearance, and with it she not only stole the hearts of even the most hardened critic, but proved the clear winner out of a field of eight nominations as the Most Promising New Actress of 1972.

The National Theatre crowned its triumphant season by presenting not only the Best Production of 1972 – *The Front Page* – but also the runner-up – *Long Day's Journey Into Night* . . . Both were directed by Michael Blakemore, clearly the director of the year.

Victor Garcia's production of *Yerma*, presented at the World Theatre Season, was mentioned somewhere by nearly every critic, but the only category where it managed to top all others was in Design, Garcia's magical trampoline set, which he designed with Gabian Puigserver, was the core of this exciting production and one of the most extraordinary devices seen in the theatre in many years; a feat of design and production that stood out in a very grey year.

A design award for Victor Garcia's production of *Yerma* with Nuria Espert. 1972.

1973

The year that Watergate began its inexorable move to engulf President Nixon was also the year that Juan Peron and his wife Isabel were elected President and Vice President of Argentina. Israel's Prime Minister Golda Meir had an historic meeting in Rome with Pope Paul VI. Whilst remaining Head of State in Spain, Franco resigned as Prime Minister appointing to succeed him Admiral Carrero Blanco who was later assassinated. Kidnapped John Paul Getty III was found in Southern Italy after a ransom payment reputedly of 2.8 million dollars. Picasso died at 91.

Britain endured a fuel crisis, a State of Emergency and Prime Minister Heath's 3-day week. Princess Anne married Captain Mark Phillips. In the theatre talking points were provided by Christopher Hampton's Savages, *Alan Bennett's* Habeas Corpus, *Peter Shaffer's* Equus *and not least Richard O'Brien's musical,* The Rocky Horror Show.

The Island of the Ardens

*Pam Gems interviews John
Arden during rehearsals of* The
Island of the Mighty *by the RSC
at the Aldwych*

I was told that he was a shy man, and to try and see him separately from Margaretta . . . presumably she usually does the talking. As it happened he had come over from Ireland before his wife, who, as often before, has collaborated with him on the play we are going to talk about. So we agree to meet at the RSC rehearsal rooms. It's a rotten November night, the rush hour, and I have just had £20 pinched from my purse. We walk over to the pub together and Arden doesn't say a word.

John Arden is a spare, light man, young in the face, and is immediately remarkable for a wild head of coke-coloured hair. He moves like a countryman; people in London walk from their knees down, and he springs across the room to get me a shandy and himself a beer. We don't know what to talk about first because we don't know each other. Anyway he isn't shy. He is sharp, and prudently careful, and his voice is very strong and resonant, and he is much better looking than the whey-faced pictures he sees fit to have printed on the backs of his books. He does look dreamy, partly the glasses. Now and then, when he sharpens up, the direct gaze, because of the magnification of the glasses, becomes a glare. Having the habit of looking into the faces of people I talk to, I get this look from time to time, and together with the hair it makes him seem slightly mutated . . . something crested, night-flying.

But he couldn't be more matter of fact, or direct. The reason that we haven't seen more of his plays in the last two years is that John Arden went to India and was very ill for a long time. He got hepatitis and nearly died. As he has written, in the foreword to *The Bagman*, (the play itself was actually written before the journey) the influence of this visit was predictably profound. Since the liver is now clinically accepted to be the seat of the emotions, it seems to have been a relevant illness. I want to know about the politics there. Well, he says, to the Indians, *all* westerners are right wing. What did you see? What about the green revolution? (Shirley Williams told me there is a lot of trouble with contraception programmes since at this time in India people believe that the green revolution will solve all the problems of maintaining the increasing population). Yes, he says, we travelled. 'At one place we stopped by a dam, and we got the interpreter to ask some of the people who were sitting around if they were better off with the extended cultivation and increased yields. And everybody smiled, and the translators said . . . they say that the *landowners* are, indeed, better off. For them, it is the same.'

So what about *The Island of the Mighty* . . . is that a political play? He is so full of the first week of rehearsal that I lose him at once. He says 'Well, I'm in the middle of it, I've been rewriting, it was in three parts originally you see.' He pauses and mumbles something about getting on all right with David Jones the director so far, and not being up in actors, having been away, but thank goodness, the casting seems OK. He opens up, and is edgy about the large permanent company, not the size, which he needs, but the necessity for some degree of rigidity, and fixed forward planning.

'In Sheffield last week,' he says, 'we played *Ballygombeen* in the round so we had to make changes in one quick rehearsal. Then when we opened that evening, the Monday, there were only people on two sides, so the production had to be reshaped during the actual performance, which we did, and it worked.' He has seen a model of Timothy O'Brien's set of *Island of the Mighty* and heard bits of music, and David Jones has been flexible and agrees that as things come together changes will no doubt be necessary. But, says Arden, gloomily, when Margaretta arrives, a week on Friday, she's going to be fresh, 'there'll be a full run through by then and she'll see exactly where it's all wrong. And I bet we won't be able to change it, and there'll be the musicians' union, and the sets will have been painted.' Still, he says, 'it's all right so far. As far as I can see, and that's no distance at all. Nothing's there yet.' I ask him about King Arthur and he is very happy with Patrick Allen whom he has known, as most of us have, mainly for series work on television, and whom he has found responsive, alive to suggestion and genuinely inquisitive.

The Island of the Mighty, he says, was written first of all as a trilogy for the BBC, which promptly then went into one of its 'broke periods'. There had been an earlier play on Arthur, abandoned. Just after the project with the BBC was shelved he was approached by the unhatched egg of the National Theatre of Wales . . . had he got anything that would do for their inauguration? 'Well I have this trilogy about Arthur. "Marvellous," they said, "couldn't suit us better." "Well no," I said, "actually it's set on the border of Scotland,"' and he gives me one of his glares so I don't like to say that like everybody else I think of Arthur messing about around Somerset and the Bristol Channel. It didn't matter because the Welsh said could they have it anyway. So he reworked the trilogy, and together with Margaretta, rewrote the whole thing into a long pageant-play, with music and dancing . . . the very thing for a national occasion. And then the Ardens went to India and John was ill, and eventually it did occur to them to

John Arden's *The Island of the Mighty* at the Aldwych Theatre. 1973.

wonder what Wales was doing with the play. The answer was, nothing. The money had never surfaced, the design was laid low, nobody had thought to tell him. Meanwhile the play still ran round his head.

So Peggy Ramsay, his agent, sent it to the RSC. 'They said it was great. And kept it properly filed. For a year. Until Ronald Bryden joined the RSC as play-picker, found *The Island of the Mighty* and that was that.' It has had to be shortened to four hours, so that people can catch buses and trains, and Arden has been doing a lot of rewriting. He's still on about the need for changes, the need to keep the thing alive, and I say, 'but they've got the playwright, living, for once in a while, this must make it possible and easier'. He looks entirely unconvinced. He says, of course, it's possible, that this was done until very late on with Gaskill and Finney in *Armstrong's Last Goodnight*, 'I want this play on. It's a piece of work and it wants doing. But when you set a thing this size in motion . . . at the moment I can only trust that . . .'

It is time for another drink and I can't pay because my money's been pinched and he says I must be firm about this and sort it out. We talk about children and he has four boys and I say how old and he says the oldest is 14. Mine is 21 and I make a knowall face. Which he doesn't miss. There is about him a sagacious masculinity, much more of the country than the town. He could easily be a farmer with an eye for a gimpy leg, no fool in the auction ring. I think to myself that he's probably a lively lover though you'd likely have to set fire to the hearth rug to get his head out of a book. I can't really tell much about him. He's too sharp.

'You'd better come and have a word with Margaretta next week,' he says. And adds again that he isn't a rabble rouser, that he is a writer, and likes a quiet life. But that sometimes matters intrude which blend actuality into the plays. 'Take this new piece,' he says . . . 'well, it's about land hunger. At the time of Arthur people pushed west from Asia till some fell in the sea and came to England. And the play is about this, and about the ordinary people, who live daily lives through these massive upheavals, and how they are affected while playing no conscious part whatsoever in these violent changes in their lives and history. The visit to India has affected the play, just as living in Ireland has meant the writing of *The Ballygombeen Bequest*. But I am not a "committed" writer, in the present usage of that phrase.'

What are you writing now?

'I'm helping to write a play about James Connolly, and in spite of everything I've just said this *will* be a political play.' Partly, he adds, 'because Connolly's personal life was one of blameless family affection . . . therefore one has only the politics.'

He gets up to go and suddenly asks me if I have seen *Oh! Calcutta!* I get careful and say Andy Warhol's *Pork* was much better, but that I liked the first sketch in *Oh! Calcutta!* about American provincials wife-swapping and getting tangled up in the hardware. However, Ken Tynan should worry. Yes, he muses. 'He asked me for something you know.' He looks so grave and Yorkshire that I have to try not to laugh and he then says that he did indeed send Tynan a piece, he sent *Squire Jonathan*, and Tynan, thank God, sent it back and said it belonged on its own.

Ten days later I arrange to meet the redoubtable Margaretta d'Arcy in the same pub. I get told things. That she is Irish, Marxist, very committed, when she turns up the fur flies, she will knock my head off, Willie Gaskill wouldn't let her inside the Court for *Live Like Pigs*, there was a punch-up at the Roundhouse. She sounds like my Mum.

On the day I am so keen to meet her I am 20 minutes late, i.e. I have started so early that I kill time by shopping at mad Martha Hills and then can't get across the West End. When I do get to the Nag's Head, which I can't find, there is no one in there who looks like the picture on the back of the Methuen paperbacks. Then I see John Arden and don't at all recognise the woman with him. I am able to pay for some drinks this time, so have time to turn away and think about this except that I trip and fall over, all 13½ stone and I feel like clearing off. He helps me up and they don't get funny.

She is thin, so thin, with dark hair. Big mouth, multipara face, and teeth in the Irish style – one missing at the side. Her eyes, which are light and very bright, look frightened . . . frightened? . . . and she sits back in her seat and talks down into her lap so that I can't hear what she says. I don't know what to make of her. John Arden says nothing and sits like a store Indian, shoved up into the corner.

elaine stritch

And then she smiles and her face changes so completely that it's almost creepy. She looks about 20, the eyes are full and clear, like a child, her face comes alive and she has the look of Tolstoy's sister-in-law, Tatyana Behrs, the model for Natasha. I ask the usual things, how they met, how did she get into this, who did what, how about the children, who is Margaretta?

The answer is she's an Irishwoman. She was brought up to the literary traditions of that country and Dublin, to the background of Synge and Yeats and Joyce and Beckett. Her father and her sister wrote, and she wrote plays from her childhood on. Then she trained as an actress and worked with and knew Aidan Higgins and John Beckett. She came to England and lived around Fitzrovia. She was working then with Valerie Hovenden and mentions some of the parts she played, including Peg Woffington.

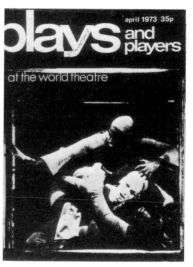

at the world theatre

John leans forward – 'She was fat then'. She would have looked all right fat but in those days you had to be like Jean Simmons. A woman with her sort of countenance would have baffled them. We sit there remembering the time when the theatre was Eliot, Fry and Rattigan and drink our Guinness, tomato juice and shandy.

So it was the work that brought them together. She found his work, and it had life and she couldn't believe anybody was writing like that. Also she had the Irish view of the English as 'damned imperialists' and it was only when she read Arden that she became aware of country people in England and working class people. And he, on his side, an architect by training, with a background of relations in Africa and India, moving through poetic imagination to middle ground. He began to write parts for her, but by this time they had married and she was pregnant.

We are interrupted by a man who comes up and then another, and they say to the Ardens that they would welcome a meeting to talk over the meaning of the play. And the Ardens nod and say 'Yes', and the man says, 'Is that all right?' and John Arden says

83

'Yes, I do think it a good idea, it is necessary. We need to get at the meaning.' And he nods his head and they seem happier and go away.

What's up?

And they say that the play isn't right, that John has been away three days to collect Margaretta and the children, and that on arrival she has been able to see the first run-through, with a fresh eye, and all is far from well. Even he notices differences after his three day absence – a bandit's simple beating up of a girl has become a whipping with his belt – 'all the difference in the world'.

'Oh it would go,' she says. They haven't got it, they both say. Not what they want. Not the life, nor the meaning. 'The music is all wrong' says Margaretta, 'it isn't near the stuff we heard in India. The sets are wrong'.

It is, in fact, exactly as John predicted the week before. And they are baffled. Because although they know they can't have the ad hoc changes of a fit-up company in the remorseless rolling stock of a company the size of the RSC, yet they feel that as living authors they have a right to as much flexibility as is technically possible. There is time to amend, they feel, if the will is there.

Margaretta says, 'The play is not alive.' John says, 'It's all very well, but I've been here from the beginning, how can I complain? I've been here. First it was too early for changes, if we don't speak up it's going to be too late.' Margaretta feels that if they can't be allowed to convey the meaning of the play they might as well not be there, but John is firm – he wants his play done, with the resources of this theatre, and something near to its intention. I sit there thinking that the only place they'll ever get this is in their own theatre, and that they must know this . . .

We go back to their working together and he then says something that surprises me very much, and that is, that he likes to work 'with people around'. Margaretta says, 'It would be almost impossible not to be totally immersed in the writing of a play with him since he writes, as it were, in public. He likes to read aloud, he writes aloud. In fact when we were in India, the Indians used to come and sit around and listen to him shouting his rhythms. I'm sure it's right, public, outward facing, group work is the way for the theatre.'

Surely the fact that the cast want to meet to discuss the meaning of the play is good? We are leaving, and the Ardens are abstracted. They are worried that in a permanent company there will not be the same tension, the need for one play to come through intact. What will they do if the management is imperialistic and the company won't listen? 'Go away.' Where, I ask, and they say they have a lot of work to do, and there are plans.

Serjeant Musgrave's Dance, Armstrong's Last Goodnight, The Workhouse Donkey, Left-Handed Liberty . . . you would think it would be enough. Where is their theatre?

No doubt there will be an Arden Theatre. And a Margaretta d'Arcy Playhouse. The books will be written and the rows picked over. When they're safely dead.

POSTSCRIPT. John Arden rings. David Jones, the director of *The Island of the Mighty*, has refused them permission to call a meeting of the actors to discuss the meaning of the play. There are to be no changes in the music, none to the set. Everything must be as planned, despite, says John Arden, 'verbal assurances to the contrary, and expressed willingness from some of the company to encompass change.' The Ardens, as members of the Irish Society of Playwrights, are fully affiliated to Equity. They intend to withdraw their labour from the play, approach the actors to do likewise in support, and, at this moment of writing, to picket the theatre, should that be necessary.

POST POSTSCRIPT. The Ardens have received a letter from David Jones acknowledging their 'resignation' but not, they say, accepting that they are 'on strike'. The letter, they say, states that they sought to take over the production. In fact, they maintain, they have demanded only the right to discuss freely all possibility of change with all concerned. 'We admitted ages ago,' says John Arden, 'to David Jones our fears that the RSC (being an established company, supported by the Tory government) would not be able to mount a play that is an attack on imperialism because actors and directors are all working in an imperialist atmosphere. We feel that imperialism has been exposed by David Jones's intransigent misinterpretation of our demands, just as in 1967, the Civil Rights demand in Northern Ireland was assumed to be an IRA takeover or communist inspired'. The Ardens relate the situation to Heath's policy re the Industrial Relations Act forbidding workers to strike except under conditions *recognised* by the government, and feel themselves, in this present situation, to be in the same position as the Impressionists quarrelling with the academics in the 19th century for the right to interpret their vision as they see it.

'But we have changed emphasis. We have given up the idea that it is possible for the artist to be a free creative individual. The artist is a worker linked with other workers (i.e. actors) who must all together demand rights from management. The whole issue is the refusal of David Jones to give us freedom of speech with the actors. This is also the whole Conservative policy. We do *not* intend a personal attack on David Jones who is himself caught up in the system. We had an *objective* view of the play and its relation to actors and the theatre. David Jones's attitude, and the attitude of the actors has always been *subjective.*'

DAVID JONES, the play's director, was in the final stages of rehearsal at the time we contacted him and was able to make only these three points.
1. I have never at any time refused a discussion between the Ardens, the actors and the production team. The company were asked if they would like a meeting and by an overwhelimg majority, they rejected this offer.
2. John Arden himself was present at six weeks of rehearsals and approved every stage, including design and music. Only when Margaretta D'Arcy arrived from Ireland did his attitude totally reverse. At that time, the play was near to opening and clearly the actors were against any radical change to what had been rehearsed over six weeks with Arden's approval.
3. In my view, John Arden and I have the same idea as to what the play is about.

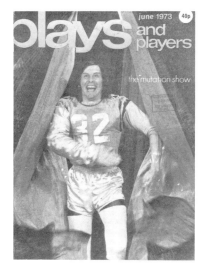

Angela Lansbury in   London's Gypsy

Green Room

*David Mercer or the haunted
playwright*

Those playwrights who are not left reeling with incomprehension after the Arden/RSC dispute – and indeed those who are – should perhaps by now be turning their minds to the questions raised, in more general terms. This particular case, with its charges, denials and countercharges, was less illuminating for what was allegedly revealed than for its vivid exposure of certain contradictions which have always haunted the politically conscious playwright. Certainly the playwright is a worker; but then how often have we heard those aggrieved and petulant voices ringing out from positions of relative wealth and privilege: 'We're *all* workers!' And one Tory Prime Minister at least has tried to have it the other way (in those long ago 'boom' years when people still spoke of the 'affluent society' in tones of smug conviction), when he said that we are all middle class. At any rate, one thing most playwrights certainly are not is *working class*, if one uses the term in its more strictly political, economic and ideological sense. He or she may identify with the class struggle, and this may be reflected one way or another in the work itself. None the less, in so far as the class transformation of society is concerned this is a political question – and one which does not ensure that other equally serious questions will wither away. These become quite tortuous, in a bourgeois society – where the Left is no less quick to pounce than is the Establishment Bureaucracy in a Stalinist society.

For one thing there is the undoubted problem of the play as one more commodity in a consumer-oriented economy. Its means of production are in the hands – or head – of the writer only so long as he remains in his study. Venturing outside with it, he relies on commercial management, subsidised theatre (cultural arm of capitalist/imperialists, as the ringing phrase goes), or some struggling and impoverished company which is trying to beat the system, subvert it, or demolish the concept of bourgeois theatre altogether. It is at this point, where the play becomes a production in the theatrical sense, that one is in the hands of those who own the means of production in the economic sense. Ideally, the play in its ultimate form, i.e. that of its *presentation*, is the result of the collective effort of many people, their ideas, skills and dedication. Sometimes this collective takes the play as a starting point only. Sometimes, the struggle is to realise as perfectly as possible the stated, implied, discussed, intentions of the author. The first is often a judgement or 'revelation' of the society as understood by those who undertake to do it; the second is more likely to be an event judged *by* society, whether the theatrical pundits, the box-office returns, or a mysterious combination of both. It hardly needs stating that there are interrelated permutations of both kinds or theatre – and here there is much murk and confusion.

'Art should serve the people!' is one of those mind-bending slogans heard loud in the din of battle; and one is tempted to slink away thinking: Yes. We know. And it's usually been the wrong people. And even if we think we know who are the 'right' people how do we get through to them? Back to the study, comrade! Brew a cup of Nescafé, and remind yourself that pessimism has its own role in life's huge dialectic. Which tends to bring on a paroxysm of impotent rage, mitigated only by that invidious form of self-treatment which whispers that *all* art is for *all* people and that it's one thing to write a play – another thing to strive for the

The haunted playwright: David Mercer.
(Photo: Irving Teitelbaum)

elimination of capitalism, the bourgeoisie, the whole interlocking structure of values and institutions which one would like to see go up in smoke. How gratifying it would be if one could say, like James Joyce (albeit in another context): *Non serviam*! To relax into a stubborn, if somewhat glazed, posture that whilst the world passes through the seismic convulsions of History – the thread of individual consciousness may still weave its spidery way across a page or two. Or through a book or two. And anaesthetise by thinking that when they blow the trumpet down here, I'll be here. To do which would, of course, be betrayal of others and corruption of oneself.

On the other hand to speak of withdrawing one's labour is a pitiable notion indeed. Write the plays and stick them in the bottom drawer? We simply do not have the industrial power, presence or weight of the miners, the dockers, the engineers, the technical unions. Except at the level of petty bargaining what have we learned to expect from Equity, the Writers' Guild? Political sell-outs, assertions of empty principle utterly divorced from political and economic reality, abandonment of our duty to the massive confrontation of forces shaping up in our society. There

87

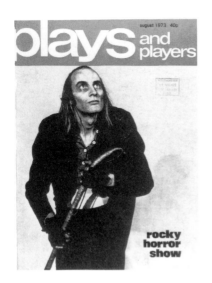

plays and players
august 1973 40p

rocky
horror
show

have been minor concessions to be sure: a wages deal here, a fee-structure deal there, bleats of protest on Czechoslovakia, the persecution of writers in the Soviet Union, the fate of Jews, Crimean Tartars and other items on the long, long list of iniquities being perpetrated right across the face of the planet. Yet the large contradictions still remain. Can we write, act, design, light and produce our work and *also* credibly exact our due from the forces of management, be it commercial or nationally subsidised? Can we find some real alignment with industrial power and solidarity? One has only to imagine some form of Playwrights' Union attempting this to be daunted by the scale of the tragicomedy. This is not to say that other unions would not come to our help; it is to visualise a wrangling body of individuals stretching across a spectrum from – let us say – the sceptically indolent entertainers in the West End, to the ideologically raucous innovators at various points on the 'fringe'. Political unity would be a chimera. Opportunistic unity for purely professional ends would simply promote the continued existence of the system such a union could only justify itself by denying.

So is one left alone then, feeling however gutless and gloomy, with the pen or the typewriter – leaving the field to the hustlers and the profiteers? Is one to observe that the whole thing is a churning mess and turn one's back? Many writers have done this or something like it, at varying times in history. Others have sunk their work to a level of crude polemic so sterile that it eviscerated their talents, such as they were, whilst at the same time degrading even the revolutionary objectives and concepts – let alone actual men and women – of their supposedly genuine intentions. At such people, in his own time, Trotsky pointed a derisory finger; and in a letter to André Breton reaffirmed the position of a great evolutionary on the matter:

> 'The struggle for revolutionary ideas in art must begin once again with the struggle for artistic *truth*, not in terms of *the immutable faith of the artist in his own inner self*. Without this there is no art.'

And again, in *Literature and Revolution*:

> 'Our Marxist conception of the objective social dependence and social utility of art, when translated in the language of politics, does not at all mean a desire to dominate art by means of decrees and orders. It is not true that we regard only that art as new and revolutionary which speaks of the worker, and it is nonsense to say that we demand that the poets should describe inevitably a factory chimney, or the uprising against capital! Of course the new art cannot but place the struggle of the proletariat in the centre of its attention. But the plow of the new art is not limited to numbered strips. On the contrary, it must plow the entire field in all directions.'

A far cry from then to now? By no means. Only the historical configuration has changed. And we must not supply ammunition to reaction by falsely identifying the nature of the conflict. In the case of the RSC it is ludicrous to speak of an 'autocratic bureaucracy'. The plain fact of the matter is that *those who do the work*, from artistic direction to stage crew, have never been anything other than honestly involved in trying to present an interpretation of the works of living playwrights in full collaboration with the authors. Disputes are inevitable – they are also healthy and proper. Collective discussion has been there for the asking, whatever the apparent rights and wrongs of the Ardens' experience. One suspects that in the latter case there have been more misunderstandings and mistimings of communication, than wilful disregard of the authors' demands and rights. To what extent that may be so, it would be arrogant of the outsider to judge and must be left to the parties involved themselves. But no one should be deluded that the enemy is the artistic management of the RSC. The real enemy is the social structure within which such an establishment has its uneasy existence. Finance, boardrooms, and all the way down the drain to the politicians themselves and their hirelings in the cultural life of the nation. It is they who buy and sell us, hire and fire us. And once the playwright's personal act of labour has been achieved and subject to contract, the subsequent act of withdrawing labour during production as an 'employee' of the theatre can trigger a vital public debate – but it can also *confuse* the strategic thinking of the Left in general. The very idea of democracy itself becomes a pot into which can be thrown the carcass of almost any sort of animal. There is nothing new in that, and democracy is all things to all thinkers. Those who lose out in *any* version of the democratic process may be tolerated or obliterated . . . live on to fight or be hauled from the scene. The labyrinthine notion of democracy adopted by our own society would seem also to allow for a policy of opting out and settling either for study vigilance (raps on the knuckles from Bernard Levin), or self-contemplating resignation with a touch of rhetorical nostalgia for more stable times (? John Osborne). Both courses reject any formulation of the dialectics of change. Both are seductive in various ways. Neither is an answer for what I have called the politically conscious playwright. He or she is bound to follow that 'truth to the inner self' but without regarding this as an individualistic principle. The incubation of the play, and its final realisation, often seem mysterious. Unless intentionally didactic, the arrival of characters, images, events on the page can be a bewildering experience.

This does not mean that the act of writing is divorced from the realities of living in a particular society. What is mysterious is not necessarily a mystery. Plays do not arrive from some metaphysical hinterland, but are the accumulated interaction of the subjective and the objective. They are as much the result of personal psychopathology as analytical and evaluative scrutiny of the environment in which the playwright just as any other living member of the species has his being. What is mysterious is the complicated interplay of these factors and the themes and obsessions which they throw up. Early formation, subsequent choices and decisions, commitment to or recoil from, the great issues of the time – all intermingle and join unconscious to conscious. One is either addicted to the psychology of people and

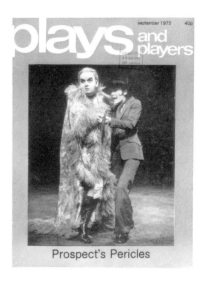

plays and players

september 1973   40p

Prospect's Pericles

situations or one ignores it in favour of a theatrical convention in which the deployment of power and the relations of social forces seem more important than the 'root-motivations' of those involved. It is like the question of whether great men make history or history makes great men.

The answer is, surely, both. Does one reduce Trotsky's assassin to an impotent psychopath and Hitler to a paranoid megalomaniac – or does one place such figures in the context of what one might call the historical machinery of their possibilities? It seems clear, for example, that capitalist reaction in Germany in the late '20s was ripe for a Hitler; but at the same time a wholly different man or group of men would have advanced the cause of fascism, since once the power of the working class had been first demoralised and then smashed – the industrial and ruling interests of the nation required the victory to be total. So the political playwright hovers uncertainly between the peculiar demands of his imagination and an overpowering sense of the imperative of relevance. He cannot crawl into the protective womb of his 'sensibility'; yet neither can he apply himself didactically *in the theatre* to his political convictions. He must *act* politically – which includes public self-declaration, allegiance to *viable* forms of union struggle within an ideological framework and the relation of class to class . . . system to system – and at the same time, *write* as he must.

Once more Trotsky (in a mood of wry paraphrase concerning the opposition of philosophical idealism and materialism): 'In the beginning was the Deed – the Word followed as its phonetic shadow.'

MAY

1973

Scofield in Style

Paul Scofield talks to Peter Ansorge

Kenneth Tynan has denied the frequently touted allegation that Peter Daubeny's World Theatre Seasons have had a decisive influence upon the repertoire of the National Theatre. *Plays and Players* thought it worthwhile to pursue the question of the WTS's actual feedback upon our own theatres in a specific way – namely, by talking to an actor who has given up a part of his career to playing a range of 'foreign', as opposed to exclusively anglo-saxon, roles. There are surprisingly few such animals in existence at least amongst those who earn a living on the English stage. There is one striking exception to this rule – an actor who can be counted amongst our few genuine theatrical titans. I'm referring, of course, to Paul Scofield whose involvement with cross-Channel theatre began with a British Council sponsored trip to Moscow as Hamlet in 1955. In the early '60s Scofield undertook another momentous tour of Eastern Europe playing the tortured lead in Peter Brook's production of *King Lear*. But, more decisively, Scofield has actually found an interest and involvement in playing parts which have often previously turned up in their authentic foreign form at various World Theatre Seasons. In the mid-60s Scofield brought his bravado sense of comedy to bear upon Gogol's *The Government Inspector* in Peter Hall's RSC production at the Aldwych. In 1970, for his year at the National, Scofield provided the central interest in productions of *The Captain of Kopenick* and *The Rules of the Game* which were both plays that

Christopher Hampton's *Savages* at the Royal Court with Paul Scofield. 1973.

had been seen at recent international get-togethers at the Aldwych.

For an actor who is understandably doubtful about the point and purpose of interviews, Scofield was remarkably willing to talk about the influence of the WTS on his own career. I caught him during a break in rehearsals of Christopher Hampton's *Savages* at the Royal Court in which he is playing the part of an English diplomat kidnapped by guerrillas in Brazil. He immediately points out that whilst he is involved in a new play and part, previous roles become distinctly 'foggy' and unreal to him. You soon discover that such remarks are deeper than the normal anxieties raised by actors when called upon by journalists to 'explain' their individual ways of creating a role. When Scofield starts to talk seriously he seems to draw upon tremendous reserves of concentration and mental energy – as if the words were surfacing from the deepest of wells. It strikes me that this is also an effect embedded in his performances – men like Lear or Thomas More in *A Man for All Seasons* who harbour a secret intelligence or

91

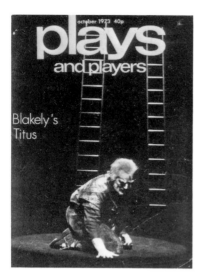

october 1973 40p

plays
and players

Blakely's
Titus

knowledge hidden deep beneath their granite-like features, like the souls scratching for survival inside Michelangelo's statues. But about the World Theatre Seasons, Scofield is clear and incisive:

'*The Rules of the Game* definitely derived from the work which Peter Daubeny brought to the World Theatre Seasons. I wanted to do it because I'd seen the Giovanni's Italian production at the Aldwych. *The Captain of Kopenick* was slightly different in that I never saw the German production which came to the Aldwych. The play had been sent to me previously by a German friend. But even so in a kind of way our production derived from Peter Daubeny's seasons. He has greatly enlarged the imagination of the theatre through the seasons. I think it's true to say that *The Government Inspector* was done at the Aldwych as a direct result of Peter Hall having seen the Moscow Art Theatre's production of Gogol's *Dead Souls.*'

I asked Scofield if his first visit to Moscow in 1955 had been an eye opener in any respect: 'I think we all found it a revelation. We were the first classical English company to go to Russia since before the revolution. A completely new world opened to me in watching the Moscow Art people at work. In 1955 we only saw a production of Tolstoy's *Fruits of Enlightenment*. I didn't see their work in Chekhov until Peter Daubeny brought the Moscow Art Theatre to Sadler's Wells in 1958. It was absolutely fascinating for me to see a company which had a rhythmic way of working that came from a concentration and awareness of the interior lives of the characters in relation to a Chekhov play. The actors had a sense of give and take, a flow of relationships between each other regardless of the text. They conveyed relationships which were outside the scope of what they were actually saying to each other. Their extraordinary detail and exactness never seemed mechanical or pedantic, but completely spontaneous. I think it came out of the experience of working together over a long period of time. The fact that the younger parts were played by actors who were too old didn't matter to me at all. They had a kind of spontaneity that could only come from long practice with each other. That might sound like a paradox but it gave them a freedom to be spontaneous. I'd never seen anything like it before – ever, not even in the best things which had been done in London.'

Did Scofield think that Chekhov productions in England were too laced with our own sense of fading middle-class values, rather than the comic fervour of the Russians? 'In Russia there is no real parallel to our English middle-class concept of Chekhov. I suppose we have no other way of interpreting the plays. It's no good doing it in English and pretending we're Russians. We've got to find some relation to the lives of English people even though we're calling each other by Russian names. But very few English productions of Chekhov have successfully conquered the manner of acting in translation. So often it just feels like translation – actors express themselves differently than through words which were originally written in the English language. All the cadences, the inflections have a kind of "translatese" in effect.

'But it's easier for the English actor to portray the Russian temperament than it is for them to portray the Italian temperament. The volatility, the sudden explosions, the immediate switch from a kind of anger which brings tears to laughing, becomes very melodramatic and exaggerated if done by an Englishman. Yet it's perfectly natural in Italian. For an Italian, Pirandello is very unvolatile and intellectual – so he's a little different. But even so I don't think I was the ideal actor for *The Rules of the Game* as that character should have appeared physically very Italian. Given the choice I would rather have done his *Henry IV* – but seeing the Italian production I thought *Rules of the Game* would be marvellous to try.'

Had the WTS encouraged Scofield to view a play like Zuckmayer's *Captain of Kopenick* in its social context – the Germany of post-World War One? 'I didn't go to Germany while preparing for the part though the director, Frank Dunlop, did. When it comes to studying a play I'm inclined to rely entirely on the text. Even when I played Thomas More, for instance, I never read Chambers' *Life of More* until after I'd played the part. In *Kopenick* I was fascinated by the "shifting sands" speech – the sense that the social background behind the play was very unstable. The lives of all the characters were based upon something very shaky indeed – something that was constantly moving and shifting. But I only got that idea from the play itself. It was something Zuckmayer talked to me a lot about afterwards.'

This kind of sensitivity was underlined when I asked Scofield about the varying reactions of audiences on his *Lear* tour. Instead of distinguishing between West and East European audiences, Scofield found differences between *East* and East: 'After half an hour of a performance an audience begins to unify – whatever it's getting from a play it's sharing, and the minute it begins to share it becomes, in a sense, like talking to one person. You begin to get a very strong sense of an audience's personality. This became particularly charged during the *Lear* tour. Bucharest, for instance, provided a strong emotional feeling. It was a very highly-strung warm, temperamental audience. In Poland they were very reserved, very intelligent, very listening. In Hungary there was a kind of melancholy attentiveness, there was something very sad about the Hungarian audience. The visits of English companies have a kind of diplomatic relevance in those countries. We're usually only invited during a thaw. Although it was before the agonies of 1968 there was a chilly feeling about the Czech audience. It came from a certain feeling in the culture, of their capital city Prague. It's difficult to define exactly what gives an audience the sense of being a unified personality. I think that it's something to do with the common experience between people. You felt that you had given a different performance in Warsaw from the one you had given in Prague. The emphasis shifts according to the response you're getting.'

It's a typical Scofield paradox that respecting 'common experience' goes hand in hand with uncovering varying audience reactions and levels of sensitivity. He agrees that a tragedy like *Lear* can travel and adapt to different nationalities more easily than comedy – as 'humour is so very national, the joke is very difficult to translate'. He cites the uniform joke in *Kopenick* as an instance: 'The Germans were so impressed by uniforms at one time that perhaps the other side of the coin is that they can find them funny.' But in the light of Scofield's enthusiasm about the Moscow Art company how does he think that English theatre compares in the ensemble stakes – particularly with the work of the RSC and National over the past decade?

'We don't have ensembles. It's idle to talk about either the RSC or the National as having ensemble work. They don't. They employ the same actors some of the time whereas a commercial management gets an entirely new group for every production. That's the main difference. I've worked several times with the RSC and once for the National. Each time I've worked at the RSC there has been, with one or two exceptions, a different company. During my year with the National there was a sense of continuous change – people were coming and going all the time. There's nothing wrong with that except that it doesn't make for a permanent company.' Apart from the free-lance economic set-up of English theatre, Scofield agrees that one of the obstacles to forming a permanent company is the lack of any specific style – a context for continuity: 'An English style doesn't exist. With Shakespeare or Sheridan you can produce something which resembles a style. But it's a style which comes from the dramatists rather than the organic creation of a permanent company. We have nothing for instance which is comparable to the French classic theatre. A style has limitations but also strengths. In this sense an English actor starts in a void each time he creates a role. But then you *have* to start from scratch on a new play – there is no basis from which to start but yourself and the text. I hate to think there is any hangover from any previous performance of mine when I begin a new play. I suppose that's death to the idea of establishing a style of ensemble work in England. Perhaps that's another point about Daubeny's seasons. He's given us a glimpse into the states of mind behind the different international styles. We've had a lot of gates opened to us if we only care to go through them.'

Now, Mr Hansen –
Hauser.
Sorry, Hausen. You are the Artistic Director of the Meadow Players, otherwise known as the Oxford Playhouse Company.
I am.
This is an Arts Council-supported Regional Theatre, an example of all that is finest in the British theatrical scene, a training-ground for young actors who in the fullness of time will add their tributary streams to the broad river of talent that empties itself ultimately into the majestic lake of London.
Well, I wouldn't put it that way –
I do not for an instant wish to denigrate the excellent work, on its own provincial level, that companies such as yourself no doubt often achieve. However, we are not here to make odious comparisons, but to investigate why, ignoring the advice of wiser heads, you have elected to challenge the collective wisdom of the Arts Council, a body renowned through the civilised world for its even-handed administration of justice and imperturbable self-approval, and perpetrate an act of what can only be termed self-immolation.
The basic reason was the Arts Council's decision to cut back its annual grant from £57,000 to £50,000 –
Hold hard there, my good man. The Arts Council deny there has been any cut, and you will find it difficult to refute their denial. The mere fact that the 1971–2 grant reached the figure of £57,000 and the current year's grant reached the figure of £50,000 does not mean there was a cut.
What does it mean?
It means that the latter figure was not as high as the earlier figure. And please, let us have no whingeing and whining about the rising costs of mounting productions. We all know that the price of timber has doubled in the last three years, that plywood alone will have gone up 100 per cent this year, that salaries, casual labour wages, lodging allowances and so forth are eagerly straining to achieve new summits – nay, and achieving them. You may well claim that your present grant figure leaves you worse off than you were seven years ago. But a Company must expect to move. That is Arts Council policy. 'Things change,' they have said, and if they don't change for the better they must change for the worse. You don't deny that they have their reasons.
There was something about the catchment area –
Precisely. The catchment area. You understand what they mean by that?
The number of people living within easy reach of the theatre.
Good. And what is the Oxford catchment area?
About half a million, I should think.
And, say, the Nottingham catchment area?
Perhaps four million.
There you have it. I'm not saying that these people ever go to the theatre. I won't deny that your own record of attendances is reasonable. But if your half-million came to the Playhouse every week, they would only fill it 100 times over. If the Nottingham catchment area came, they would fill it 800 times over. You see, you just aren't in the same league.
But does it make no difference how many people actually do come?

Green Room

Frank Hauser, for the preceding 16 years Artistic Director of The Meadows Players at Oxford Playhouse, investigates the end of the Company (with apologies to Frank Sullivan)

None whatever. We are dealing with figures, not reality. Now, let us pass on to the question of standards. Without wishing to denigrate anyone or anything, would you not agree that over the past three years your standards have slipped alarmingly?

Well, those years do include *Kean* and *The Misanthrope*, and *Romeo and Juliet* and *The Banana Box* –

I am not talking about your successes. No less a person than J. W. Lambert, Chairman of the Arts Council Drama Panel, has said that he had heard that there had been a report that some of your productions were not up to par.

The only two he actually saw were *Kean and The Banana Box* and he was very flattering about those.

Please, sir, we are not interested in what he liked. We are interested in what he was told he would not like. Were you 100 per cent satisfied with every show you put out over the last three years?

Of course not. Nor with every show over any three years.

Say no more. If you, the Artistic Director, cannot vouch for the total artistic success of every show you do, how can you expect an extremely busy man like Mr Lambert to see shows he might not like, or, what is worse, might actually approve, in direct contradiction to the report of his own Panel members?

I hadn't thought of that.

Perhaps you hadn't thought of the level of local subsidy either. Or perhaps you had thought, and decided that the local authority grant of – what was it, £3,000 a year? – was sufficient.

It wasn't. The local authorities recognised this last year when they raised it to £8,000.

Why did they raise it no further this year?

Because there was no one to do it. Local government is in the middle of a massive reorganisation, and this particular year the new officers have only just been elected.

Excuses, excuses. Why, before rushing into an over-dramatised hara-kiri, did you not suggest to the Arts Council that if they wished to make . . . not a cut, but, let us say, a move in the opposite direction . . . they should delay it until next year?

We did. They wouldn't.

I cannot believe my ears. Are you saying that a body which is the envy of the civilised world deliberately chose the one year to . . . institute their reform . . . in which you could not be rescued by the goodwill of your local authority? Please weigh your answer with care.

We did offer to postpone any thought of closing if they would postpone their . . . change of policy . . . until next year. They refused.

Then there must be some other good reason. As I recall, The Guardian *newspaper gave it. Perhaps you have forgotten?*

No –

I thought so. Then let me quote: 'The Arts Council also point out that Meadow Players only operate for 17–21 weeks in the year.' Perhaps that will refresh your memory.

The average number of weeks played over the past six years was 39, apart from last year, when we were required to pay back a backlog of debt in one season.

39 weeks is a very different average from 17–21 weeks. Are you suggesting that The Guardian *deliberately printed the wrong figure?*

The Guardian reporter says he phoned the Arts Council. Someone there gave the figure.

Sometimes I despair of getting a straight answer from you people. How did you accumulate this backlog of debt?

Largely through our association with the Arts Council's DALTA touring scheme.

Which collapsed because your productions were inadequate.

Which collapsed because it was ill-planned, poorly advertised, and involved *all* the drama companies that took part in headaches and losses.

As a result of which you gave up touring.

As a result of which we returned to our earlier touring pattern and made no further losses.

Evasions, cover-ups. It's another Watergate. Let me ask you one final question: in view of the undisputed facts that there has been no cut in the grant, that standards have dropped appallingly, that your catchment area is pitiful and your local authority non-existent, can you deny that your current season is a total failure?

I'm afraid I can. It appears to be the most successful ever.

To what do you attribute your so-called success?

Primarily the company. With people of the calibre of Alfred Burke, Judi Dench, Barbara Jefford, Leo McKern, John Turner and Edward Woodward appearing or about to appear –

Thank you. That brings me back to my original observation. Yours is a company which, in a small way, has done much to encourage such young actors as those you have listed, and set their feet on the path to higher things. It is, however, obvious that although the public may be flocking to see them, and you have already begun to indulge in the regrettable ostentation of 'House Full' boards, you and your company have lost that sense of earnest endeavour and limited aspiration which alone merit the seal of Arts Council approval. To put it in language which even your restricted intelligence should be able to grasp: if you weren't what they said you were, would they have done what they deny they did? You are silent. I thought so. Thank you.

1973 Awards

voted for by the London Theatre Critics

Best new play: *Savages* by Christopher Hampton; *Sizwe Bansi is Dead* by Athol Fugard

Best new musical: *The Rocky Horror Show* by Richard O'Brien

Best performance by an actor: Nicol Williamson as Coriolanus

Best performance by an actress: Angela Lansbury in *Gypsy*

Best performance by an actor in a supporting role: Frank Grimes in *The Farm*

Best performance by an actress in a supporting role: Frances de la Tour in *Small Craft Warnings*

Most promising new actor: Peter Firth in *Equus*

Most promising new actress: Mary Sheen in *The Mother*

Best production (director): John Dexter for *The Misanthrope*

Best production (designer): Tanya Moiseiwitsch for *The Misanthrope*

There were no less than 11 nominations for the 'Best Play' category this year indicating some measure of uncertainty in this department. In the event *Savages* tied with *Sizwe Bansi Is Dead* (via an editorial vote which took account of two further votes for Fugard's *Hello And Goodbye* which gave the South African *five* first choices in all). Howard Brenton received two votes for *Magnificence* and *Brassneck*, while both *Habeas Corpus* and *Equus* were at the top of three voters' lists.

Rocky Horror seized the prize from *Gypsy* with a total of eight votes over the American musical's five supporters. Nicol Williamson won six votes as best actor with his nearest rival, Alec McCowen, receiving four champions out of the 17 voters. Angela Lansbury (four) pipped Elisabeth Bergner (three) to the post as best actress (even though it wasn't *in* the best musical!) for *Gypsy*.

Best new musical: Richard O'Brien's *The Rocky Horror Show* premièred in the Royal Court Theatre Upstairs. 1973.

Frank Grimes (left) won a performance award for his supporting role in David Storey's *The Farm* at the Royal Court. 1973.

For the supporting players, Frances de la Tour made a clean sweep in her category picking up 8½ votes for *Small Craft Warnings*. Mary Sheen came out as the most promising actress with three votes as opposed to her nearest rivals' two mentions. Frank Grimes and Peter Firth emerged as secure winners in the masculine versions of these awards. With 11 out of 17 votes John Dexter found few rivals for the best director award. The only issue was over the best Dexter production with *The Misanthrope* (6½) finally winning over *Equus* (4½). His Moliere revival was also the front runner in the choice of best designer.

1974

As Watergate finally brought about the resignation of the American President, he was succeeded by Gerald Ford who thereupon granted Nixon an absolute pardon. The decline of Franco in Spain and the bloodless coup of April 25 in Portugal opened the door for a return to democracy in Iberia. President Makarios of Cyprus was overthrown but later returned after fleeing to Britain. The Greek military junta resigned, bringing Karamanlis back from exile to win a sweeping victory at the polls. There were food riots in India. Solzhenitsyn was deported from the USSR.

In the UK the second of two General Elections in the year (February and October) gave Labour under Wilson a slender majority. In the theatre, The Norman Conquests *ingeniously kept the Ayckbourn industry on view and focused attention on a rising star – Penelope Keith – as did the Beatles musical from Liverpool,* John, Paul, George, Ringo . . . and Bert *with the newly arrived Antony Sher as Ringo. And Tom Stoppard's latest,* Travesties, *had an award-winning performance at its centre from John Wood.*

Green Room

*Arnold Wesker on the playwright
as director*

It is not questioned that a composer can conduct his own music or
that a film director direct his own film; it is inconceivable, though
physically possible I suppose, that someone else should paint the
painter's canvas; the novelist and poet, of course, have complete
control of their material.

The arguments against the playwright directing his own play
seem to go like this: (1) The dramatist cannot be objective about
his work. The play as written has one dimension, but for staging
it requires the kind of objectivity that will permit a new dimension
to be added – which can best be achieved by a director: 'The
author imagines all his words are sacrosanct, and besides, doesn't
always understand his own play.' (2) The playwright only *writes*
the play. He has no appreciation of the technical problems
involved in mounting it: 'What works on the desk is one thing, the
stage is another.' (3) Actors are inhibited in front of the writer
and cannot experiment or play around with the roles in different
ways. Handling the actor, understanding his problems, demands a
different temperament from the one normally found in the writers:
'The writer may know what he wants but he doesn't know how
the actor must reach it. We're instinctive, the writer is
intellectual.'

Having attended the rehearsals of all ten of my plays on stage,
four again on TV, one again in the film studio, and having directed
five of them myself – one in England, unhappily, and four abroad
– I'm in a position to comment on these objections which are,
except for one, most curious.

One: Objectivity is presumably the ability to detach oneself – from the love, concern, fears, emotion and intellect invested in the play – in order to be critical about it. This, it is said, the writer cannot do. The objection suggests no understanding of the creative process, a process in which many drafts of a work may be written, *each draft being the result of the writer's objectivity about the previous one!* Every new version cuts, tightens, deepens, rearranges; a critical faculty is constantly in use. Why should that critical faculty, that objectivity, cease to function the moment the play enters rehearsal – the one period when the writer can most clearly see and be shown the play's faults? The objection has no logic.

A new dimension, it is true, can be brought to the production of a play by a director. But are all *new* dimensions inevitably *good* dimensions? There does exist the danger of an *incorrect* dimension. Perhaps the phrase 'new dimension' belongs more to the *often* performed play which is so familiar to theatregoers that a 'new dimension' can bring fresh light on the play's meaning, whereas a *new* play on its first exposure should be allowed to emerge with the *author's* concept of its dimensions – warts and all!

Or let's ask this question: if the world première of a new play were given simultaneous productions in six of the best reps in the country, would all six stagings communicate the *same* new dimension? Obviously not. Therefore wouldn't the author's interpretation be at least as interesting as those other six? Or is it suggested that, however mediocre, the six productions would all be better than the author's because there is some magic about an 'outsider's' view?

And then, what precisely can this 'new dimension' of the outsider's be? The play is – hopefully – already one man's new dimension of his experience. Can it be that a director is adding a new dimension to the new dimension? There could be dangers in that. The danger of censorship: The added dimension to the new dimension blocks out the new dimension! (I've deliberately allowed the absurdity to blossom). Or the danger of confusion of vision: 'I too have a point of view you know!' Or of trivialising: 'You must be more comprehensible.' Or of defusing: 'To be more acceptable.'

But these dangers are easy to counter. Much more insidious are the suggestions for change in text, characterisation, emphasis or rhythm which seem perfectly sensible but which are wrong for *reasons the author has forgotten*! Plays, though they appear simply an effort to put words into the mouths of recognisable characters who are involved in an engaging plot or set of relationships, are in fact very complex structures.

An author sometimes spends hours balancing six sentences in a monologue to ensure (1) they belong to the character uttering them; (2) they have an intellectual or emotional dynamic that is both compelling and valid; (3) they have rhythm; (4) they appear at the right and inevitable point in the scene, and so on. Sometimes he achieves all this instinctively and without effort, but usually the reasons or instincts he's brought to bear in the achievement are, odd though it may sound, often forgotten. It is very easy, then, for a director to deflect an author from his

plays and players

january 1974   40p

Vanessa Redgrave in Coward's Design For Living
LONDON CRITICS 1973 AWARDS

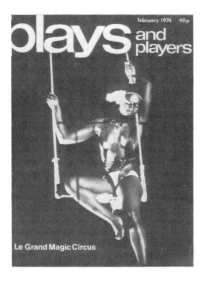

plays and **players**

february 1974 40p

Le Grand Magic Circus

intentions especially in the heat of rehearsals when 'the actors mustn't be disturbed now' or 'this is the wrong psychological moment to bring it up' (and then it becomes too late to bring it up!) or 'they're producing something else, isn't it magnificent?' or 'they're working so hard for you now, you can't tell them they're wrong, go away.'

The need, I think, is not for a 'new dimension' but for something much simpler and more necessary: an opinion. I owe many changes in my plays to the opinions of friends but it's not unreasonable that a certain moment is reached – by most play-wrights – when they've used up the present supply of 'objectivity' and require recharging by an opinion authoritatively founded in theatrical experience – a director's, an actor's, a set-designer's. For this reason I also owe certain changes in my plays to John Dexter. But, and here is the interesting point, though changes were made to *The Old Ones* under Dexter's direction in London, yet other changes were made to the play under my own direction in Munich. The conclusion could be that it is the *possibility* for change which encourages change, not the person. Give an author the chance to direct his own play and he will change as crisply and perceptively as any director.

Two: 'The desk is one thing, the stage another.' I've tried hard to consider that this objection might have some justification. But can it really be true for the serious, professional writer? On the contrary, alone at the desk one has all the time in the world to persuade oneself that *all* one does is wrong.

Most people at work in the theatre would agree that it is neither possible nor desirable to write in the stage directions for every shift of limb, flick of eye or intonation of voice, but I'm very conscious of the physical relationships of characters to one another, of particular actions while speaking, of the emotive effect of colours and textures, the visual impact of structure, the choreography of movement, the speed of delivery. All these are elements woven into the fabric of the play. Far from being indifferent to complex theatrical possibilities many writers are fearful that their inventiveness and craftsmanship will be missed or ignored by conservative actors and directors in a hurry.

It is possible to have made impossible demands of the theatre, rehearsals show one what those are; but the greater danger is for the playwright's innovations to be crippled. The best playwrights make not impossible but unfamiliar demands upon the theatre, they stretch its preconceived limitations. If the desk *is* one thing and the stage another then all the more reason for a playwright to come closer to his material.

Three: The actor/director relationship touches upon what is central to all productions. Two preliminary points: actor/writer relation-ships have a long history, longer than actor/director; and if they fail it may have to do only with a clash of personalities and not because it is a bookish old writer failing to understand the delicate, vulnerable actor – the evidence for which lies in the ruins of many actor/director relationships.

'We're instinctive, the writer is intellectual.' Sometimes yes, sometimes no, sometimes both. But in any case, what of the many directors who come from the intellectual disciplines of a university? And how to describe those writers who have come from the anarchy of a varied-work existence? Such writers could say 'we're experienced in real life, the actor is cloistered'.

As for the actor being inhibited before the author – I've rarely experienced it, except in the early days of rehearsal when actors are just as likely to be inhibited before each other.

Very often it's the actor who wants to deliver emotional lines emotionally and I've found myself having to force him to fight against my text. As director I've always patiently encouraged actors to twist texts inside out, act against them, try saying tragic lines with humour, lyrical ones vulgarly. Far from inhibiting or tensing an actor I've found my presence relieved him because he felt the one person who could give him an answer to his questions was right there.

But that a difference exists in temperament between actor and writer is true, and could fairly be offered as a reason why the playwright should not direct his own play. It is worth looking at. The craft of the actor is a complex one, and an article as brief and tentative as this would not presume to be exhaustive about it; but to further this defence of the playwright as director here is an observation which has perhaps not been sufficiently considered before.

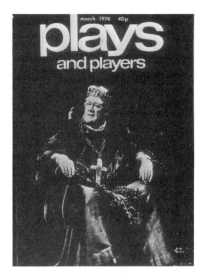

Paradoxically, basic to an actor's fear is his vulnerability to the accusation of 'acting'. He's vividly aware that society normally uses the name of his profession as the name of an abuse: 'Oh, ignore him, he's just acting.' 'Just acting' is the actor's *raison d'être*, his means of livelihood. He asks an audience to forget that acting is to pretend to be what and who you are not – which is rightly frowned upon in everyday encounters. What is despised in a person *off*-stage the actor asks us to praise *on* stage. In the audacity of this request lies his terror. This is why he fights; sometimes his fellow actors, sometimes the director, sometimes the set-designer, costumier, author, audience; sometimes all of them, sometimes the wrong ones. Any one of them might be leading him to make a fool of himself. The terror is absolutely understandable. No profession can be so racking as that where a person exposes himself to the ridicule of disbelief and the attendant ignominy of dismissal, the humiliation of being 'seen through'.

Who succeeds? Most actors will agree – very few. (See Gordon Gostelow's excellent letter in *Theatre Quarterly* 11). They are constantly 'seeing through' each other. But those who do break through the brittle and sour barrier of scepticism perform a miracle. To experience them is to witness men possessed. We all kneel before them. It happens rarely, however.

What is it the actor must do? Personally I believe the skill rests not in him being able to 'pretend' better than the next, but in *not caring* that he is pretending. The bad actor is usually one so worried to be caught pretending that he plays to be loved, or he plays what will easily amuse – and so be forgiven for pretending. One can sense his uneasiness, he communicates it to us through self-consciousness. Either he walks clumsily or he puts on 'a voice': 'see, I know I'm pretending really, so don't hurt me.' Or it produces that school of acting where the actor's style is one of pretending not to pretend; yet even that approach degenerated

into cosy mannerisms, despite some fine performances by Brando. But the great actor is – or appears to be – so intensely indifferent to the existence of the audience that, again the paradox, only through such total indifference does the audience feel he is really performing for them.

Now, the responsibility, for guiding an actor and helping him shape the performance in which he will not make a fool of himself, is an awful one. In taking on directorship the author divides his loyalties between a responsibility to his play and a responsibility to his actors. Sometimes they are in conflict because, too late to change, it is discovered that an actor does not have the correct set of registers and ranges to fulfil the part for which he's been cast. It's not a question of an inferior range, simply a *different* one. That scene will now never reach its intended mood, this speech will now never ring in its true pitch, that argument will now never be fully understood, that 'moment of truth' will now never be revealed in all its terror. But the play and the actor will be doing what he is not equipped to do and the function of the writer/director at that moment is to ignore the demands of the play and look for an *equivalent* approach from out of the resources the actor *does* possess.

It is not always easy. But then what is? What talent doesn't mature through experience or involve exposure to mistakes? A craft must be learnt. And even so, directors who've had all the experience in the world have suffered nervous breakdowns.

My argument is this: there is no mystique inherent in the craft of directing, the craft can be learnt. The learning may not make a great director but *it can be learnt*. And if the author has the wish, the inclination, the patience he, like the director, can command the craft through experience. More, *if* it can be learnt then the combination of the two talents in the one man is formidable and, potentially, thrilling.

Postscript: Of oblique but important relevance to the question of the playwright's estrangement from his work is the overall phenomenon of the creative artist's isolation by all those who have to interpret, present, represent and comment upon his work. Three encounters have brought this home to me in the last months.

One of our finest novelists recently returned from a lecture tour of the United States where she was fêted by her publisher in New York. 'You have no idea' she said, 'of the extraordinary sense of redundancy one feels among all these publishers, editors, agents, journalists. As though they'd been gathered together to meet each other rather than oneself.'

It was not a paranoiac complaint about rejection but an observation concerning the artist's alienation, measurements of regard. Impressed on her was a sense that her work was a commodity to be weighed, evaluated, speculated upon rather than esteemed for its literary merit or warmed to for its powers of perception. It was assumed she'd have no further interest in her 'commodity' nor understand the process which 'of necessity' had to take it over.

Then came the report from a friend, a young professor of literature, who'd just returned from an international conference organised by one of the new universities; the conference had themes to discuss such as: Relation between ideology and literature; The need for historicism; The study of literature as an aspect of the study of 'operations of cultural communications'; The extrinsic and intrinsic approaches to the sociology of literature with particular reference to Dickens's *Oliver Twist!* She, the young professor, lamented how not only was the conference arid because no living artist was present but, worse, his presence would have been superfluous. In fact, she observed wryly, a real artist might have embarrassingly gotten in the way! All that was important was theories about criticism, and responses to those theories, and responses to those responses.

The third encounter was with a young painter whose gallery takes 50 per cent of his earnings from sales (most galleries take an outrageous 33⅓ per cent). Not only that, but no regular account was rendered to him of *what* was sold, he had no way of checking for *how much* a painting was sold, he was not informed *who* bought the paintings (for fear he'd go to them privately to sell his work thus bypassing the gallery), and occasionally paintings were 'lost'. The attitude of the *entrepreneurs* reduced him to feeling an intruder and believing that favours were being done for him.

FEBRUARY
1974

The Party at the Old Vic

reviewed by Alan Brien

Centre Stage, a bed. On it, a couple of pale entwined bodies, shelled crayfish on a platter, in the red darkness of a Chamber of Horrors. Above their writhing bodies, tilted at a dangerous angle, a huge massy mirror, adding a new terror to love. Around this restless tableau, like photograph frames on a dressing table, screens on which are flashed portraits of revolutionaries, with quotations from their thoughts. I doubt whether anyone in the audience could take equal interest in both activities. At first, I thought that this must be some kind of test of our seriousness as playgoers. Was there a spectator of spectators monitoring the direction of our pupils to separate the Goodies who sternly pursued their Brechtian course of self-education by slogan, from the Baddies who indulged themselves in bourgeois culinary titillation with peeping-Tomfoolery? But then I realised that not every one at the Old Vic had my choice. Whether deliberately, or through an insecure appreciation of the laws of optics, the director John Dexter had confined the reflected sex-play to those who sat in the centre front stalls – a piece of class discrimination somewhat at variance with the egalitarian politics of the text. And it became clear that we were expected to follow the progress (or rather regress) of the coupling. Otherwise we would have missed the point that the man (Ronald Pickup) was as impotent, physically, as he later became politically. This is not an easy piece of exposition to signify without dialogue as no naked actor, in my experience, has ever been able to simulate a credible erection even when impersonating the most virile of studs. For those deprived of the sight, the message was conveyed by the somewhat obscure objective correlative of Mr Pickup exiting with a fit of coughing while his wife (Doran Godwin) kept on asking him if he 'wanted to talk about it'.

I have dwelt on the opening scene of *The Party* for several reasons. Partly because, even in these days of stage nudity and mimic intercourse, such an episode still requires some strong dramatic justification for its sensational presentation. Partly because it is one of only two flurries of actual action which occur throughout the oratorio of talk and argument that evening in 1968, in this London flat, during the Paris revolt of students and workers. Partly because it throws some background light on the central character which nevertheless fails to illuminate his psyche much better than his physique. How is he so rich, for example? A TV drama producer – he has a living room the size and style of an airport lounge, a garden large enough to lose a drunken playwright in, endless supplies of booze and spare rooms, and enough cash in hand to back his unreconstructed working-class brother in a small business.

What is his secret sorrow, evoked with such Chekhovian melancholy by Mr Pickup, with the dented smile and neglected hair of an old paintbrush left behind by the decorators? It can't be just inability to make it with his wife – and why does she care, since she spends most of the night out with her boy friend? Or is it that he has been seeing too many of his own productions of TV plays about the Northern prole ridden with guilt at having severed his roots and fallen in with leftist big-city trendies? Nobody up there asks him, and so nobody down here is ever told. The nearest we get is his first wife repeating the complaint of his second that he just won't talk. Considering the loquaciousness of his three chief guests – Denis Quilley as a caricature smoothy of a sociology lecturer with the self-satisfied smile of a Hallowe'en mask. Frank Finlay as a boozy, bawdy, obstreperous dramatist out of (possible even inside of) David Mercer, and Laurence Olivier as an indomitable, dying Trotskyite rather over-heavily drenched in sentimentality which only a massive conflagration of acting genius can burn off – it is perhaps just as well. All three are monologuists rather than talkers (Olivier has an aria lasting 18 minutes) and what they say is always interesting, at least to those of us interested in the semantics of Revolution, sometimes disturbing, often funny. But it tells us little about anybody except the speaker, and not always that.

One of the more gnomic messages on the walls of the Sorbonne in 1968 insisted – 'When the National Assembly becomes a bourgeois theatre, all bourgeois theatres must become National Assemblies.' I wish our national assembly had speeches of such eloquence and intelligence, but a trio of them does not make a substitute for bourgeois theatre, let alone a play for the National Theatre. The others present are cyphers. The reformist-Marxist lecturer claims that the proletariat is no longer the only revolutionary force today – and cites the blacks, the students and the women. But the token black, the statutory student and the obligatory woman say little except 'Right on' and 'What about us?' And even the proletariat is represented by those on the ultra-left belonging to minor cults of whom no actual worker, polled in an Elephant and Castle pub next door, would be likely to have heard.

The 'Revolution' of May 1968, in which 10 million French workers took part, was an unexpected upsurge of revolutionary action, unparalleled in Britain in 1926, or France in 1936, or even Russia in 1905. Two months later De Gaulle was back with an absolute majority. Such a subject demands more than a Shavian rehash of what was said at the time by those who stayed in Britain wondering what hadn't hit them. Either we need a multi-media, documentary post-mortem with first-hand evidence and all the stereoscopy of hindsight. Or we need to see how the event affected people here and then how *they* affected other people here. The author, Trevor Griffiths, has said that 'nearly every major character in the play is me or is the scintilla of me'. It is an honest, and quite brave, admission of creative egoism. But I'm afraid it shows: for despite the dozen or so characters, and two outstanding performances. *The Party* remains a one-man show.

Why did you take on the job of Director of the National Theatre?
When I left Stratford in 1968 I had a very firm conviction that I would never, under any circumstances, run a theatre again. I'd had it. I felt it was a dreadful strain, which is obvious, but more than anything, it was a liability on someone who's trying to be a director of plays. The unfortunate fact is that when you're directing a play is always the moment when news comes that the Arts Council grant cannot be increased or some member of the press accuses you of doing dirty plays or some actor finds he cannot honour his contract. One is very vulnerable. So I thought from now on I'm just going to be a director – swan around the world doing this and that. But it was a reaction against a central action. Whether I'm any good at running a theatre or not is for other people to say. I certainly don't know. But I do know that for 21 years my main motivation has been to try and create working conditions for other people which I myself can test and enjoy. It's selfish, but also altruistic. I think the two things go together. And the fact that the National has this extraordinary new building proved absolutely irresistible. I don't mean that buildings make theatres – I don't think they do – but good facilities are a considerable help in making good theatre. They're no guarantee of it. They can be a seduction. They can be a difficulty indeed. But I think the South Bank has three beautiful spaces. And it was a bit like being asked to go back to Go, and start again, with better resources and better opportunities. And it was therefore impossible to say no.
If the building had been less attractive, would you still have been interested in the idea of running the company?
No. If the building had been like most modern theatres that I've seen round the world, or indeed if the building was not there and if one was going to stay at the Old Vic, I would not have done it. No, I want to run a theatre again, but I want it to be one with good working and rehearsal conditions.
Are you aware of a certain feeling around that people are going to miss the Old Vic a lot when the National Theatre leaves it?
Oh yes of course. I mean the Old Vic is a very beautiful theatre to sit in, but hard to work in. It's nice to *act* in, but not to rehearse

MAY
1974

Towards the mountain top

Peter Hall talks to Robert Cushman about his plans for the National

plays
and players

august 1974 40p

COLE at the Mermaid

in. The actors never create their work on the stage where they're going to perform it. They are in dreadful rehearsal rooms which any factory worker would walk out of. I've spent many fine evenings there, as I'm sure you have, and it will be sad, it will be a pang, to leave it; but the National Theatre has reached its end point in Old Vic terms. It can't have enough activity, I think, to be a National Theatre while it remains there.

Now, why is the National Theatre different from other new theatre buildings?

Well, first of all, it was designed by an architect who listened to the brief of a group of theatre people. Denys Lasdun *used* the knowledge of the theatre that was available. The building committee of the National Theatre – I don't think there has been anything like enough comment or interest taken in this – under the chairmanship of Sir Laurence Olivier, was a very extraordinary cross-section of people, including Peter Brook, Michel St Denis, George Devine, Bill Gaskill, Michael Elliott, Jocelyn Herbert, Tyrone Guthrie for a short period. It was a very wide section of theatre opinion, and things were really hammered out. It wasn't a question of A's prejudices against B's prejudices. We really set ourselves the task of defining what is the best possible theatre at this moment. That was the brief, and that's what was given to Denys Lasdun. So a number of very crucial decisions were taken. We concluded that although fashions in staging may come and go, the one thing that does not alter is the scale of the human figure. We decided that if any member of the audience is more than 65 feet away you have a dilution of experience. So we said 65 feet is the maximum, and that is a very very high standard of communication indeed. The back of the stalls at Stratford is I think 83 feet – a lot further. And we thought of servicing the actor, so that he could work in one place, not in a draughty rehearsal hall on the other side of London, but actually work on the stage with his props and actually create his work for the place where he was going to present it. These may seem luxuries but they make for better work.

Isn't there a more general disillusion with institutional theatre?

Yes, and that is a swing of the pendulum. I think it's grossly exaggerated and wrong. I'd like to know what kind of life you'd lead as a critic if the institutional theatre did not exist.

I'd lead a dreary life. You said yourself, about a year ago, that you thought all three of the institutional theatres had got to a stage where they were very predictable.

Yes, I agree. I still do. I think everybody is looking for new paths. I don't expect that I'll find it and I don't expect anyone'll recognise I've found it until we're in that new building. I believe that the National must have a repertoire of plays which mean something to the moment – in other words I don't think there's much virtue in having a repertoire of classic revivals for scholastic or representational reasons or to show that we've all got a catholic taste. I think that you've got to believe that the repertoire should represent the collective obsessions of the actors and directors who are working in the National Theatre because they believe that the play will speak to their audiences. Our theme seasons in the Lyttelton will investigate areas of the repertoire which are entirely neglected.

Which areas?

Well, German expressionist drama is totally unknown in this country. It's just something we pay lip service to. I would think twice about doing a Toller play or a Kaiser play in the Olivier repertoire, but if I were going to do three of them together for a short season in the Lyttelton called German Expressionist Drama, with a few films at the NFT of German expressionism, some pictures in the foyers and a few talks about German expressionism, one could get something going. A further responsibility is obviously new writing and that will come from the writers who want to write for us. Pinter is there, he's an Associate Director. I hope he will write for us. We've commissioned plays from Howard Brenton and from David Hare of the younger dramatists, and all the heavyweight dramatists have been asked if they would like to write a play for the new National Theatre. They may or they may not. That's up to them.

Isn't a National Theatre in a tricky position when another company has the first right to the national dramatist?

I don't think so, there are 37 plays. The Stratford tradition is something which I honour and obviously have a terrific love for, and it will go on because the Stratford festival will go on. I believe that the National Shakespeare is going to take a little time to emerge. I know what it is and what we intend to do, but I'm not going to tell you because it has got to happen, not be talked about. We're not in competition with the RSC in any kind of 'Hands off *Hamlet*' spirit.

The National's Shakespeare has after all had 10 years to emerge already.

Yes, but you see one of the interesting things about that is that they haven't done enough Shakespeare.

That's one thing I'm getting at, they haven't done enough.

Well I think we will do quite a lot but in different terms from the RSC situation. You're pushing me, and I don't want to be pushed. But I mean I take your point that the National can't ignore Shakespeare or it can't say 'Thank God we don't have to do Shakespeare, there's the RSC', because actually inescapably the centre of our theatre tradition, whether you like it or not (and I do), is Shakespeare.

Well, I wouldn't be interested in the theatre if it wasn't for Shakespeare.

Nor would I, nor would I, you know, but on the other hand I would hate to run a theatre again whose main external purpose was Shakespeare. If you've got to do six plays a year they come round with great regularity.

There's too much received opinion trotted out. Too much of a feeling that if it's old, it must be boring. The reception of *Spring Awakening* was generally very good and the audience response has been splendid, it's packed and all that and there's a lot of young people there, because I think with reason young people find it a play which is about authority over the young, you know; but so many critics simply said 'In this permissive age, who needs a play about sexual liberation?', which is exactly like saying 'In an age where countries are not ruled by hereditary monarchs, who needs *Hamlet*?'. I mean that's really not the issue.

I quite agree, but I think one reason why they've been driven

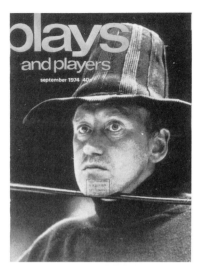

towards it is a feeling shared within the profession itself. Are we all a bit too hung up on relevance?

I think we are. That's the cant of the last 10 years which has hardened into a kind of dogma.

Do you find anything odd in the idea of writers like Trevor Griffiths or David Hare writing for an institutional theatre representing a society to which they are fundamentally opposed?

Well, who says that these institutions represent their society in that sense? I feel certainly that I'm running a theatre which is supported by the society that I live in at this moment. But the society is not telling me what I shall do and shall not do. I had a great argument with Trevor, whom I'm very fond of and think very highly of, not very long ago when he said to me 'Yes, I'll maybe give you the play after next, but I'm not going to give you the next play because it wouldn't be good for you, you wouldn't do it'. And, as I said, that is the biggest bloody impertinence. If you say I won't do it, you are turning me into the sort of theatre that you want to turn me into and you're not giving me the chance to be anything else. Now why will I not do it? And he said, well you wouldn't, it would be too controversial. I said, well you're frightened I'll say *yes*, and it would then upset your dogma. We had a terrific carry on. It was good. If a dramatist is absolutely seeking to change his society, it seems to me he can decide either to use the institutional theatre in order to get the message across, or not. It's up to him isn't it, not up to me. But certainly this particular runner of an institutional theatre is not going to silence argument or controversy or unpopular opinion. I won't. Obviously there's going to be a good deal of this sort of discussion and argument. The last thing I want the National to do is to trendily run after the most insulting and revolutionary dramatists and do them in a desperate attempt to show that we are broadminded. I really think that would be odious in the extreme.

How broad would you say your tastes were?

I think they are getting a little broader. I managed to get through the period at the RSC without doing a single restoration play. As I was leaving we did *The Relapse*. Restoration drama has been for me for years something insignificant. Now I'm beginning to understand it. I must say for many years I have thought of Shaw as a sexless pamphleteer with very little passion. Over the last years I've been rereading and rethinking Shaw and I want to do a Shaw play very much now. Where the boundaries of my own taste lie, I don't know, they change a great deal. I suppose that I could be seen as a working class scholarship Cambridge-warped, media-altered, lefty trendy of the sixties and that's my period, I suppose. But I refute that, I'm beginning again. The excitement of the seventies for me, is going to the National. I feel all sorts of new currents in myself. I'm excited at the prospect of working again in a theatre which must be part of the community. So I won't be labelled: it makes me indignant.

Opposite: **Albert Finney as the Prince in Peter Hall's production of *Hamlet*. 1975.**

1974 Awards

voted for by the London Theatre Critics

Best new play: *The Norman Conquests* by Alan Ayckbourn

Best new musical: *John, Paul, George, Ringo . . . and Bert* by Willy Russell

Best performance by an actor: John Wood in *Travesties* and *Sherlock Holmes*

Best performance by an actress: Claire Bloom in *A Streetcar Named Desire*

Best performance by an actor in a supporting role: Arthur Lowe in *Bingo*

Best performance by an actress in a supporting role: Penelope Keith in *The Norman Conquests*

Most promising new actor: Michael Feast in *The Tempest*

Most promising new actress: Kate Nelligan in *Knuckle*

Best production (director): Lindsay Anderson for *Life Class*

Best production (designer): Patrick Robertson for *A Streetcar Named Desire*

Everyone agreed that 1974 had been the toughest theatrical year ever for voting in almost every category of *P&P*'s annual awards. Only the choices of Best and Most Promising New Actresses were clear from the start, perhaps indicating our new-found wealth in this department. Claire Bloom in *Streetcar* and, more overwhelmingly, Kate Nelligan in *Knuckle* (the latter with an unprecedented 12½ votes) achieved obvious dominance over their rivals. For the first time since these awards began no clear leader emerged among our directors – a sign of a movement away from the great directorial theatre of the 1960s? Eventually Lindsay Anderson pipped the other contenders to the post by a mere 3 votes for *Life Class*.

In the new play and best design stakes the West End entered the critical arena with new-found confidence – the awards going to Alan Ayckbourn (admittedly, the *Norman Conquests* began in a subsidised theatre) and Patrick Robertson (*Streetcar*) coming out with 4 votes as opposed to Carl Toms's 3 for *Sherlock Holmes*.

Daniel Massey (for *Bloomsbury*) and John Wood (for a year's work at the Aldwych) were neck and neck in the Best Actor race with Wood finally inching ahead for both *Travesties* and *Sherlock Holmes*. The final result was 7½ votes for Wood against 5½ for Massey's portrait of Lytton Strachey. Clearly, Arthur Lowe (with 4½ supporters) was the obvious choice for Best Supporting Actor in providing the comic relief as Ben Jonson in *Bingo*. Penelope Keith claims the award as Best Supporting Actress by a mere ½ vote but she also came up as a nomination in the Best Actress department for *Norman Conquests*. As ever, some suffered from being chosen in several different categories – particularly Michael Gambon who was nominated as both Best Supporting Actor and Most Promising Newcomer.

Best new play: Alan Ayckbourn's *Norman Conquests* starring Tom Courtenay (left). 1974.

1975

A year of political killings and attempted coups saw King Faisal of Saudi Arabia assassinated by his nephew who was subsequently beheaded in public. President Tombalbaye of Chad and Sheik Rahman of Bangladesh were both murdered. Two attempts were made on the life of President Ford. Right wing coups in Greece and Portugal were foiled. Chiang Kai-shek died at 87, former Emperor Haile Selassie of Ethiopia at 83 and General Franco at 82. Prince Juan Carlos assumed power in Spain. Isabel Peron, President of a troubled Argentina, took a month's leave. The Suez Canal was reopened. Mrs Gandhi was found guilty of electoral malpractice.

In Britain Mrs Thatcher became leader of the Conservative Party and North Sea Oil began to flow. The untraceable Lord Lucan was found guilty in his absence of the murder of his children's nanny. In the British theatre, Pinter's new play, No Man's Land, featured the actor/knights Gielgud and Richardson and Simon Gray's new work, Otherwise Engaged, had Alan Bates in the lead. Lindsay Anderson and Joan Plowright set up the Lyric Theatre Company in the West End, Albert Finney gave his Hamlet for the NT at the Old Vic and some regional companies showed up strongly with Mike Stott's Funny Peculiar (Liverpool Everyman), Trevor Griffiths's Comedians (Nottingham Playhouse) and Paul Scofield's Prospero (The Tempest, Leeds Playhouse).

Harold Pinter's *No Man's Land* with John Gielgud and Ralph Richardson. 1975.

The latest in the line of Pinter's 'rooms' is a large, spacious area decorated with a plenitude of bottles and books. The windows are huge, gradually and symmetrically curved and they are, for most of the play, concealed behind plush, heavy curtains. It is night time and one old man pours a drink for his guest. The friendliness of the gesture is deceptive, for this is no casual occasion. Hirst (Ralph Richardson) is an alcoholic literate of fading reputation who, apparently, has encountered Spooner (John Gielgud) in a Hampstead public house. Spooner senses a security, a still safety in the room that his host refuses to acknowledge. Hirst, padding around his stiff-backed, centrally located chair is moving, spiritually, on another plane, where time is running out. 'Tonight you find me in the last lap of a race I had long forgotten to run,' he announces floppily after half an hour. Spooner wishes to attend on this lap, accompany it to its conclusion, play the honest boatman. Like Eliot's Prufrock he is 'deferential, glad to be of use, politic, cautious and meticulous'. The offer of friendship and loyalty is not completely unwarranted or, indeed, flatly refused. The men have some knowledge of each other and at times together represent a last-ditch resistance to some unspecified, barbaric onrush. The room is a lighthouse (the metaphor is stated by Foster, the younger of two confident, nasty manservants) around which beat the ugly waves. Light is banished by Hirst – one of many extraordinary physical eruptions in Richardson's performance comes when, having identified Spooner the succeeding morning as an old chum from Oxford and having improvised with him an outrageously hilarious sequence of nostalgic accusations, he swallows his drink, leaps to the curtains, savagely pulls them shut and announces his intention of coming to a conclusion.

Spooner sees the situation differently, more simplistically. There remain the English language, a memory of bucolic life, the grandchildren. These are worth clinging to, he feels, worth cherishing. The responses of Hirst at this stage in the play cut sarcastically through the caressing Spoonerisms (which are, in themselves, little Betjemanite pearls) and Spooner, impervious, builds to a jeering salutation of what he takes to be Hirst's admission of sexual impotence. But still the helping hand is disdained and Hirst suffers a sudden 'drop attack'. He staggers to his feet only to fall again and creep, on all fours, from the room. This is astonishing acting. I can imagine no actor other than Richardson achieving so truthful and riveting a demonstration of a cataleptic fit. Suddenly I wondered whether, perhaps, Pinter was writing about the total experience of alcoholism. Immediately before his first fall, Hirst's brow furrows and his eyes turn glassy. He haltingly declares: 'No man's land . . . does not move . . . or change . . . or grow old . . . remains . . . forever . . . icy . . . silent.' This is dead-end street, the freezing of sensibility, the craving for limbo that could belong to a dead soul or a tired alcoholic. Or both; until the play, at its last gasp, lurches strangely and metaphysically to its final tableau.

If communication is no longer possible, if the past is unsure (though evidence remains in photograph albums) and if that past may not bear investigation as to whether or not it 'properly existed' (the words are Hirst's on returning for his first drink after the falls and professing no knowledge of Spooner's identity), then

No Man's Land at the Old Vic

reviewed by Michael Coveney

words, it seems, may bend and govern the present. Hirst proposes that the subject be changed for the last time. Foster and the other, burlier, servant, Briggs, hover at his chair and ensure that the subject remains unchanged. A last, half-hearted attempt to unravel the significance and colours of a dream fails. Spooner, who for much of the play has tried to insinuate himself both in the past and the future as well as the dreams of Hirst, recites again the bleak characteristics of 'no man's land'. Hirst raises his glass ('I'll drink to that') and the curtain falls. If the final line is intended as a deflationary device, it fails. It is not half so effective as the surprise curtain Pinter springs at the end of Act 1, nor even worthy of the writing in the play as a whole. As Martin Esslin and others have often reminded us, Pinter's unique and muscular style of dramatic prose is rooted in a playful and poetic use of colloquial language exactly used with syntactical elegance. As a conclusive dramatic device, the gag is over-extended. Suddenly we realise that the two thugs, despite the impressive performances of Michael Feast and Terence Rigby, have been in no way geared to the development of a theatrical statement. Rather lazily Pinter concretises Hirst and Briggs only in anecdotal form. The anecdotes, needless to say, are their own, and involve tales of Oriental travels and the difficulties of escaping from Bolsover Street.

The play as an idyll is considerably less successful than was *Old Times* (1971), Pinter's last full-length play. But, in the end, most of the audience will enjoy this excuse for seeing Gielgud and Richardson in simultaneous harness once again. Theirs is an inspirational partnership, as we last saw in David Storey's *Home*. Not least remarkable this time is Gielgud's delineation of character. He bears an uncanny resemblance to W. H. Auden, with crumpled shirt collar and unruly fringe. His long protestations of devotion are, as you would expect, expertly phrased. If Pinter's dramatic scheme has for once gone awry, the prose is as masterly as ever. And when spoken as it is here, by what must surely be the funniest double-act in town, I would only willingly compare it with that of Congreve or Shaw. Peter Hall has directed brilliantly and John Bury provides one of his very best designs.

Everyman in Good Humour

Michael Coveney reports on the achievements of an outstanding company in Liverpool

Last year was the tenth anniversary of the Liverpool Everyman, an event appropriately marked by the success on Shaftesbury Avenue of *John, Paul, George, Ringo . . . and Bert* by Liverpudlian playwright Willy Russell. The show won a couple of awards (including top prize in *P&P*'s Best Musical category) and focused, somewhat belatedly, a degree of national attention on the cosily ramshackle premises that squat defiantly in the shadow of the city's new Catholic cathedral. Hope Street, Liverpool 8, was the mecca of the sixties for poets, musicians and various unaffiliated bohemians who trailed in the wake of the Merseyside explosion. Hope Hall, as it was then known, was the haunt and platform for such groups as the Scaffold and the Scene, such poets as Brian Patten, Roger McGough and Adrian Henri.

The musical was directed by Alan Dossor, who has just retired as Artistic Director after five years during which the overall audience attendance has grown from 30 per cent to 68 per cent. In addition, those five years have seen the transformation of a young peoples' theatre run by three talented, ambitious university graduates into a home of serious new drama for the people on the doorstep. One Friday night in the middle of June, as creaking revivals played to meagre handfuls of unimpressed tourists in the West End, a party of miners and factory workers among a full and enthusiastic audience cheered a new play by C. G. Bond about the Fisher-Bendix occupation at Kirkby.

Under New Management documented, partisanly but unpatronisingly, the history of blatant mismanagement at the local Fisher-Bendix factory that produces cookers, washing machines, sinks and gas fires. In ten years, prior to occupation by the workers in 1972, the plant had 12 general managers, the work-force was diminished from 2,000 to 800. The play lies, obviously and buoyantly, in an Everyman tradition stemming from a production by Dossor in 1970 of a play about Bessie Braddock, the popular and nationally renowned Liverpool Member of Parliament. Up to this point, the theatre had concentrated on productions of Shakespeare, modern classics and literary comedies. And that point had been reached after much struggle and achievement by the founding trio of Terry Hands, Peter James and Martin Jenkins.

Alan Dossor took up his appointment, however, with a very different idea of what the theatre should be doing. 'I felt that the work of the theatre should be directly concerned with Liverpool, that there should be a high proportion of new plays and that the "student-experimental" image should be ditched. Nobody came to see the first few new plays. *The Braddocks' Time* got a huge amount of publicity but still nobody came. At first I didn't understand it, but, of course, there was a certain amount of resentment that these arty outsiders should be doing a play about a local heroine. Well, we stuck to it and, as a result of seeing that show, John McGrath wrote a series of short plays under the generic title of *Unruly Elements* (1971), and that was the first time the audience looked as though it might be beginning to sit up and take notice. John learnt about the audience from that and went on to write *Soft or A Girl.*' The play was the fifth new play to be performed in Dossor's first season and a half and, in terms of audience figures, a massive breakthrough.

'I always felt that any sort of theatre that we were going to make work in Liverpool would have to contain the sort of elements contained in Joan Littlewood's work: music, jokes, vulgarity and colour. I also knew that it would have to be very clearly based in the city and its class history. The thing that John brought into that mixture, I think, was his particular skill with family situations. He takes politics and manages to make them real in terms of cornflakes over the breakfast table.' In the next year, 1972, McGrath wrote *Fish in the Sea*, a play of greater complexity and seamless construction. The Maconochie family are involved in a factory occupation, but whereas C. G. Bond's play is a saga based on the actual, journalistically researched words and spirit of the workers themselves, McGrath considered an industrial and social situation as reflected in the truthfully observed behaviour and fortunes of a fictional family. The pattern for the theatre was set and, at the same time, measures were being

plays and players

january 1975 45p

London Critics 1974 Awards

Twiggy's Cinderella

hatched which were to democratise the company and its operation. 'For the first three years I worried about how to keep the company spirit going. Everything revolved around me and certain token gestures towards democracy such as company meetings. Then, about two years ago, I began to feel that I was getting into a rut and, as a result of a whole series of conversations with various people, I actually tried to put into practice what I'd been talking about for several years – which was *actually* sharing power. There are two company members on the board, which gives the company more voting power there than me – although the three of us, in the instance of a vote on anything, would almost certainly vote as a threesome. Because before every board meeting there is a company meeting, and that meeting discusses the agenda of the board meeting in order to determine its own attitude towards that agenda and to instruct its representatives how to vote, or what to say. This covers every issue from ticket prices to choice of plays. That means, therefore, that the director and the company have to reach an agreement at those company meetings unless they want to appear split in front of the board – and no director in his right mind would want that. But, most important of all, we've removed that mystique of "corridors of power" by conducting the board meetings themselves on an open basis. Anyone – ASM, cleaner, actor – is entitled to attend the board meetings. For reasons of time everyone isn't allowed to talk; that's reasonable and why the two company members are deputed on their behalf.

'These changes have really been felt over the past year, and I would say that the company I have now is the best I've had in five years. Their unique quality derives from the fact that, for a year, they have, genuinely, been in control. They've known everything that's gone on; and they've been able to change things. They've run the theatre, really. My artistic position, as a result of this, has been made much stronger; it's impossible for me to select a person from the company and fire him because I take a dislike to him. If I talk as a director in rehearsal, I'm talking as someone with certain skills which are of use to this collective. But I'm *not* talking as a boss. So, that waste of time that always results from petty resentments and so on is just not there.' There is no other established repertory theatre in the country with so apparently democratic a system of operation. And the board has been totally co-operative in its formation. There had, until two years ago, been one member of the company on the board in addition to Dossor, and when the company said they felt they ought to have two, the suggestion was discussed and then agreed to. In the very early Everyman days battles had been fought on the theatre's behalf by Alderman Harry Livermore, a solicitor of cultural bent. As a spokesman and champion for the Everyman, he was as instrumental as anyone in ensuring the future of the project. He retired as Chairman last year and his departure (as Sir Harry) coincided with the introduction of a second company member on the board and the open meetings.

'Sir Harry's departure meant that there was no one left who was using the board as a means towards personal prestige. Livermore was one of the old-style city politicians. I do not wish in any way to undervalue his contribution to the Everyman's history. The trouble is that the kind of person a theatre desperately needs on its board in order to maintain standing and influence in the community is not usually very good at understanding the day to day problems of those running the theatre. It would be good if there could be a sort of Publicity Board that could fight the theatre's battles in the council; but those civic bosses so easily come into conflict with actors and directors, people whose values are probably very different from their own.'

Dossor himself, after university and drama school, worked as an actor and director with John Neville at the Nottingham Playhouse. There was no tradition of theatre in his family. 'I didn't see a play until I was 17. And that was *Look Back In Anger*. I went to see it on tour in Hull (with Frederick Jaeger playing Jimmy Porter) because I'd read about it in *Picture Post*. I came out thinking "what a medium!" The idea of being able to stand up and say those things. It was *really* happening and I thought that all theatre was like that: seats being tipped over, people shouting, arguments in the foyer. The excitement of that night was something that turned me on to plays, and at first made me want to act.

'As far as acting goes, I can act well enough to know what it's about. And I can't do it. I can act as well as about 60 per cent of the people who earn their living from acting – and I think what they do is dreadful. Just copying mannerisms; I can do that sort of acting and it's rubbish. It's about 90 per cent of what actors are made to do on the television and a good deal of what they are often encouraged to do in the theatre. A percentage of actors in this country, though, are incredible, and that's why I want to work as a director. When you watch actors like some of those who've worked at the Everyman – what they can communicate in a gesture, a movement, is so exciting and so illuminating about human beings and their potentialities. If acting is about celebration – and I believe that all the theatre is about a celebration of values – it celebrates, ultimately, being alive. To celebrate a human being's quality of "aliveness" is a huge responsibility and it takes a great talent to do it. I don't mean to sound contemptuous of a lot of actors when I say that they just can't do it. But that gift is not given to many.' And not to many writers, either. The influence of McGrath's plays on Willy Russell and C. G. Bond was important not in a very direct way – both have very individual voices – but because the combination of McGrath and the kind of actors he wrote for at the Everyman opened up all sorts of possibilities. Russell's Beatles' show was umbilically linked to the audience it addressed in Hope Street, while *Under New Management* was a documentary report on the situation affecting many lives in the city. 'To enter such a situation and behave as a reporter is, I feel, a very difficult thing to do. Even more difficult is to behave as a politically *helpful* reporter. What that play did, two nights ago, was to get the convenor of a real factory in Liverpool discussing with a theatre director in Liverpool and a worker from the factory and his wife (that's very important, that, his wife) how they should pay the workers in their co-operative. That's never happened to me before. We were tremendously conscious, from the moment we started work on it, that we were dealing with real people's lives. And I think we've been successful. They, as a result of that play, are looking afresh at their situation.

plays and players

march 1975 45p

Ashcroft in BORKMAN

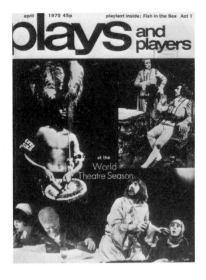

april 1975 45p   playtext inside: Fish in the Sea Act 1

plays and players

at the World Theatre Season

That, for me, is as much, and more, than I ever thought the theatre could do. I distrust theory in the theatre and I think it's a great strength of the English theatre that we don't take all that stuff too seriously. What I like doing, and what I do best, is helping actors who understand human behaviour to repeat it in order to express themselves. I use no techniques in rehearsal, nothing. Every scene, every page, presents a new problem and creates its own demands. I hate (although I *can* do it, if pressed) having to teach an actor how to drink a pint of beer or how to walk into church or betting shop. I like to work with actors who learn from ordinary people and who are in love with the body and the mind. You don't have to teach those actors; they teach you. You just watch and help.

'Popular Theatre (to use that awful term) requires actors who both understand the people they are addressing and are able to explore that understanding over a period of time.' In May, Willy Russell's first play since the Beatles' show opened at the Everyman. *Breezeblock Park* (the title refers to a particularly grim housing estate in the city) drew a savage and uncompromising picture of life among the aspirant, materialistic lower middle classes. Much fun was had at the expense of a desperately pathetic mother who believed that an intimate vibrator given to her as a joke Christmas present by her insufferable brother was, in fact, a device for stirring cocktails. Less obviously crafted than Alan Ayckbourn's *Absurd Person Singular*, the model was nonetheless clear. Russell used it, however, to unleash a disturbing and depressing comedy of bad manners and domestic cruelty. Dossor takes issue with those middle class critics who reacted in a worried way because they felt that the play, in some way, was insulting to the working or lower middle class.

'At no point was that feeling shared by the working class people who saw the play here. I know working class people who wept during that play while, all around them, middle class people roared their heads off. The play taught me a great deal that I haven't properly digested yet. It is strong and raw and makes absolutely no obeisance to middle class liberal standards. The people who thought the Beatles' show was a bit rough would go hysterical if you forced them to watch *Breezeblock Park*. The play wants to say that living in Liverpool can be fucking awful and it just says it. It does not say that there are some who rise above that awfulness and take books out of the library. So Popular Theatre may not always coincide with our developed notions of Good Theatre. That play was difficult and often uneasy to sit through. But that was not the fault of the play. It is a very good play indeed; of course, locally, Willy had a very bad deal indeed as there were plenty of knives out ready to hack him down to size after the success of the Beatles' show.'

The Everyman is about to undergo radical structural improvements, initiated by Dossor together with the Board and the theatre's genial General Manager, John Gardner. The floor is to be raised to the circle level (this has been done many times on a temporary basis, most recently for Geoffrey Reeves's absolutely stunning production of *Coriolanus*). No seats will be lost, as sight lines in the horse-shoe shaped circle will no longer be a problem and the whole seating potential will be released. There will be an increase, too, in the flexibility of staging shows: an arena stage, theatre in the round, a raised stage at one end – all will be possible. Dossor will continue to live in Liverpool and hopes to be able to do the occasional production for his successor, John Roche. He is not sorry to have a break from the daily grind and awesome responsibility that running a theatre involves. 'When things go badly it's a ridiculous job to have. Because usually, unless you hit a very exceptional situation like *Under New Management* you are really peripheral to what's happening in the country and the society you inhabit.

'When things go well, or even normally, you are just as cut off from everything else, as well as from areas of your own life. I haven't really read anything for about four years. I have missed the first five years of my daughter's life. I now intend to have two or three years of reading and talking and going for walks as well as directing. Then, after that two or three years, I'd like to take another theatre, one of the really big ones, to see if it's possible to make that work as a forum of ideas and beliefs in the way that the Everyman has. I'd like to try that in one of the big industrial cities such as Newcastle, or Glasgow or Manchester. Every time there is a major national or international crisis then there is material, important material, about it in those cities. What I've left, I think, is a theatre that is at the centre of what goes on in the city. If something important happened in Liverpool, I would expect to see it discussed and treated at the Everyman within a few months of it happening. I'm sure that will be the case, and I for one will be there, in the audience, contributing towards that celebration.'

'Improvisation' is not a very popular word among English theatre-goers. For the most part it tends to conjure up the prospect of dated Actors Studio exercises or, even worse, experimental evenings organised by keen young drama students for the purpose of fluttering sensitively about an empty stage in ballet tights. It comes as something of a surprise, therefore, to learn that Mike Leigh has evolved around 15 improvised plays for the theatre. Relative neglect by the critics has been compensated in part by Leigh's growing reputation as an innovator within his profession. His film *Bleak Moments* won accolades in Berlin and Paris even though it has yet to receive a proper distribution in this country. His Play For Today, *Hard Labour*, produced by Tony Garnett, is generally regarded as a minor television classic. Earlier this year an improvised studio play for BBC 2's Second City Firsts series, called *The Permissive Society*, enhanced his reputation as a television director. Even the theatre critics began to stir when his play for the RSC, *Babies Grow Old*, turned up at the ICA in February. 'The improvised play,' says Leigh rather wryly, 'is starting to spread'.

That's a view shared by Mike Bradwell, who runs the Hull Truck company which is currently touring the land with its latest improvised offering called *Oh What!* (due to arrive at the Bush for the whole of November). Bradwell played the part of Norman,

Making up the well made plays for today

Peter Ansorge on improvisors Mike Leigh and Mike Bradwell

may 1975 45p   playtext inside: Fish in the Sea Act.2

plays and players

Robert Stephens in Murderer

the folk-singer from Scunthorpe who will only admit to coming from Doncaster, in Leigh's *Bleak Moments*. That role provided part of the impetus for founding his own company in 1971 although Bradwell emphasises that Hull Truck is no carbon copy of Leigh's style of theatre. Talking to both Leigh and Bradwell, it became obvious that improvisation, rightly guided, can produce as varied a diet of drama as the typewriter. 'People think we make it up as we go along,' says Bradwell, 'that's nothing like how it really works.'

Mike Leigh's first professional contact with the art of improvisation arose during a class he attended as a student at RADA in 1961. 'Peter Barkworth used to run a technique class there. He had a thing going which he called, Think-Move-Speak. It immediately trapped you into a certain style of acting. We were taught all kinds of other things – how to move, how to walk, how to kiss, how to open a box of matches, how to learn your lines. But one of the lessons was called Improvisations. Barkworth would pick out two actors and would send one of them out of the room. He'd then give the actor who stayed a piece of information and send him out. Then he'd brief the other actor and bring the two of them back together. Then the improvisation would begin. Now that's exactly what I do now. But it was the sum total of my experience of improvisation at RADA. After that I went to Camberwell Art School. Suddenly I was sitting in a room having to create a drawing or a sculpture – something entirely new – out of my own experience. That never happened at RADA. There was no opportunity for student actors to take that kind of initiative then.'

Between 1965 and 1969 Leigh worked as a director at the Studio Theatre of the Midlands Arts Centre, at the RSC as an assistant, at East 15 and at the Manchester Youth Theatre. During this period he directed a total of nine improvised plays with titles like *The Box Play*, *My Parents Have Gone to Carlisle* and *Individual Fruit Pies*. Interestingly, he also directed the first (six-hour-long) production of David Halliwell's *Little Malcolm and His Struggle Against the Eunuchs* at London's Unity Theatre in 1965. That play certainly provides a clue to several of the obsessions which lie behind the early improvised works. There's a fairly constant regional background, a sense of living out a fairly repressed adolescence and of artistic ambitions failing to find a healthy outlet. More importantly, there's a suggestion in Little Malcolm's monologues of improvisatory anxieties – the difficulty of being able to talk to other people coherently. 'There's an organic relationship in that play,' says Leigh, 'between its theme and its method of production. On one level it is a play about people talking to themselves through monologues. On another level it was the concept of the artist having to remain solitary to achieve his ends. These themes were very much in my mind during the early plays. For instance, *My Parents Have Gone to Carlisle* was about a sixteen-year-old girl who decides to throw a party when her parents go away for a few days. I had the girl suddenly breaking away from the party in order to talk to her absent parents. Telling them what a good time she was having – though of course she was miserable.

'The concept of having characters soliloquise began to evolve in a different way. This was the idea of the actors being on their own in order to find a character *before* going into rehearsal with the other actors. That's how I work now. The actors base the characters on people they know but initially they always rehearse on their own. I never allow actors to base their characters on themselves or on other actors. It must start from a character they know – which implies some objective measure of truthfulness.

'There's a difference between plays which discuss politics and plays which cause an audience to think about people's real situations. In that sense all my work since *Bleak Moments* has been political. *Babies Grow Old* posed a number of political questions – mainly about the role of doctors in society. It was done quite specifically over the argument about the use of antibiotics. Like everything else, medicine is a victim of its own progress. Since there is no way of curing people, it's inevitable that doctors can't be expected to do the things we expect of them. But it would have been impossible for me to have been interested in a play which just concerned itself with a discussion of doctors. But *Babies Grow Old* also included a pregnant woman, an old lady suffering from rheumatoid arthritis, a soldier who's had his leg shot off – a microcosm of decay, deterioration and illness. It's against that background that the problem of doctors is examined.'

Leigh is in fact the son of a Manchester doctor. At times he seems to adopt a very scientific approach to the material which he watches developing in improvisation. He's currently completing a Play For Today, which he filmed in the countryside of Dorset and will then direct a series of six five-minute dramas for Tony Garnett (combining the art of cartoonist with that of dramatist).

'I like audiences to come away with a lot of new information from a play. All the stuff in *Babies Grow Old* about aspirins was true. So were the stories about the bloke who blew up in an oxygen tent and the awful bug that's contained by the World Health Organisation somewhere in the foothills of the Himalayas. The same is true of the latest Play For Today. On one level audiences will have placed in front of them a lot of facts about the environment. Those things provide the substance of the world in which the play occurs. But what it's really about is the problem of being a human being. The two things are not always compatible.

'My work is not primarily about what happens when actors improvise. It's about galvanising actors to improvise and then distilling what happens when they do. That isn't the same thing as actors improvising. There's a lot more to it than making up a lot of characters, doing a lot of improvisations, and then organising what happened into a play.'

In some ways it's easier to characterise the work of Hull Truck than it is to define the texture of Mike Leigh's plays. After working with Mike Leigh and Ken Campbell (he left the latter after a stint as an escapologist in an abandoned circus), Mike Bradwell decided that 'it was about time I pulled my finger out and did something. Otherwise I was going to end up as an employed stooge.' Having played Norman in *Bleak Moments*, improvisation came quite naturally to him as a method of working. 'I got the idea with Hull Truck of doing plays about people you

June 1975 45p playtext inside: Horowitz's Measure for Measure

plays and players

Gingold in Night Music

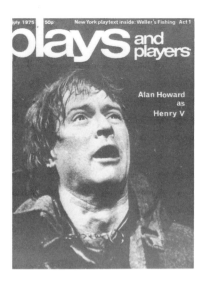

July 1975 50p New York playtext inside: Weller's *Fishing* Act 1

plays and players

Alan Howard
as
Henry V

normally don't see in the theatre. Mike Weller's *Cancer* was quite a turning point for me in this respect. Weller came down to rehearsals of *Bleak Moments* and I got talking to him about it. My character in *Bleak Moments* was a statement about a lot of people I'd come across over the years. Norman was based upon several people whom I used to know in Scunthorpe. They were people who used to hang around the folk scene. They used to come into the pub and play "Freight Train", very badly. Half of them didn't play at all but would turn up and cheer a lot. I wanted to continue doing plays about that area of country.'

Apart from the current *Oh What!* Hull Truck have presented three improvised plays since starting out – in total poverty – four years ago. The titles give a hint of the area of concern – *Children of the Lost Planet, The Weekend After Next* and *The Knowledge*. They have just completed a half-hour TV play for Second City Firsts called *The Writing on the Wall*. All the plays are set in Hull and the character list of *The Knowledge* is not untypical of the other plays: a liberal schoolteacher, an acid casualty devotee of the Mahara Ji, an incipient fascist lorry driver and an ex-merchant seaman yobbo mechanic.

'I'm interested in the kind of people who get classified, generally speaking, as hippies or students but who may not in fact be either. They're between the age of 19 and 30, they might have long hair or not, they neither wear duffel coats nor caftans nor whatever it is they're supposed to wear. When the costume lady at the BBC learned that one of the characters in our play was a student, she immediately came forward with a college scarf. That's very much the BBC's mentality regarding students. They wear college scarves and say "Right On Man" and sit down in public. They're rarely seen for what they really are.

'I got interested during the mid-sixties in the fact that a lot of hip philosophies – whether political or oriental or dope or whatever – and all of it was coming from America. I remember going to see the Living Theatre at the Round House. I had a smashing time and began to think that here was where it really was at. Then I went backstage to meet them and they turned out to be a real bunch of shits. The show they were doing was all about communication between human beings and Paradise Now – but when you met them they turned out to be aggressively exclusive hippies. They were the international hippie jet set. I became concerned with the people who became subjected to taking acid, smoking dope, macrobiotics, meditation and International Socialism – all that kind of caper – and actually having to go on leading ordinary and boring lives. Talking about Timothy Leary wasn't really where these people were at all – they still had to work during the day and talk to their mums. That sort of triggered off Hull Truck.

Both Mike Leigh and Mike Bradwell are fairly belligerent themselves about the critical reception given to their work to date. Bradwell finds the classical piece of misunderstanding in the notices for the first (stage) version of *Bleak Moments* which was presented late-night at the Open Space. 'They more or less said, "Take a bunch of actors. Let them loose on a stage alone and they're bound to come up with halting nervous conversation". They couldn't see that the character I was playing was a *nervous guy*. They thought it was the actors being nervous about being on a stage and not knowing what to do. They don't get our stuff by and large, the critics. They say, with exceptions, about *The Knowledge*, for instance, that people don't talk like that, they don't think or behave in that kind of way. For Christ's sake – if you're a theatre critic, what kind of a scene are you knocking about in! I mean *who* are you meeting?'

It is Simon Gray's very special gift to write about intellectuals in such a way that very non-intellectual audiences can understand their thought-processes and enter sympathetically into their dramas. Perhaps this does not seem such a rare thing to do. But while one can think of quite a lot of plays in which we are told that one or more of the characters may be regarded as intellectual – they are academics, philosophers, writers, something of the sort – in practice we might just as well be told they are stockbrokers or lavatory attendants for all the difference it makes to our experience of them: being intellectual is something they do off-stage to earn a living, but seems to be left in the wings. What, for instance, do the principal characters in Peter Shaffer's *Shrivings* ever do or say to convince us that we are witnessing a confrontation in the order of Bertrand Russell at grips with Robert Graves? Precious little. Not only do they not behave in a more intelligent way than the rest of us (that one would hardly expect from an intellectual), but their habits of mind seem equally woolly and undirected.

Now at least in *Butley* and *Otherwise Engaged* the central characters (and several of the peripheral) function as though exercise of the brain actually means something to them, is a natural way of dealing (as best one can) with the problems of life rather than merely being assumed for special occasions like fancy dress. There is an obvious temptation (especially given the coincidence of principal actor and director in the new play as well as writer) to suggest that *Otherwise Engaged* is a sort of *Son of Butley*, but that is not quite fair and not altogether true. It has elements of truth, but Simon the publisher in *Otherwise Engaged* is a very different and much more mysterious character. With *Butley* we can see the form of his escape from his problems – into indiscriminate destructiveness, into the world of nursery rhymes from that of T. S. Eliot, a deliberate self-lacerating rejection of the values which appear formally to shape his life. Simon clearly has his own form of escape, which is not Butley's; what remains mysterious is whether we should regard him as someone who has achieved a philosophic calm, or one who has declined into the passivity of a dead object.

He is accused at one point of being indifferent. 'Indifferent?' he inquires. 'As one might speak of an indifferent wine?' (he is very good at wittily pointing out grammatical and other ambiguities in the conversation of his visitors; also, as here, at turning aside wrath by creating a seeming ambiguity where none in fact exists). Towards the beginning of the play he appears to be a very decent sort of chap amiably putting up with a succession of bores and boors and creeps when all he really wants to do is listen to his new

1975

Otherwise Engaged at the Queen's

reviewed by John Russell Taylor

Ian Charleson and Alan Bates in *Otherwise Engaged* at the Queens Theatre. 1975.

recording of *Parsifal*; by the end of the play our image of him has changed considerably (though he has changed hardly at all), as we gradually incline to the belief, expressed most explicitly by his wife, that he can put up with all this just because he hardly notices and what he does notice he does not care about. He is indifferent (*not* like a wine); he is impregnable (but then, what is there left to penetrate?); he may seem to be otherwise engaged, but in all probability he is merely switched off. This means that there is a progression of a sort in the play, but not so clear and satisfying as that in *Butley*. Butley does, after all, get his come-uppance; for the first half of the play he attacks and insults and undermines everybody with seeming impunity, then in the second half we see them all gradually getting their own back in a series of neatly calculated, cumulative dramatic surprises. The craftsmanship in *Otherwise Engaged* is just as scrupulous, but the play is built on a series of internal rhymes (the invented suicide in act one; what sounds like a quite real suicide in act two; the carefully balanced reappearance of three of the characters and the matching of the two female characters), and is laid out in terms of an 'and then . . . and then . . . and then' succession of comings and goings. It is the perennial problem of how you can progress when you have a still centre, a character who does not really change from beginning to end.

But is that in fact quite what Mr Gray intends? There seem to be hints that Simon is still, if only just, a suffering human being who is keeping his cool with some difficulty rather than because it just comes naturally to him. The moments when uncontrolled, or hardly controlled, emotion breaks through are odd and unpredictable – and all the more striking for that. The moment when the insufferable lad from upstairs comes in wanting to borrow some Nescafé as an aid to seduction, and, failing that, Simon's expensive, cherished coffee-making apparatus, and Simon suddenly becomes – about that, of all things – perceptibly irritated beyond endurance is very strange and true. The moment near the end when his blustering, drunken critic friend accuses him of having blabbed to the police and got him arrested for drunk driving, and he promptly throws his drink in the friend's face demanding just what sort of person he thinks he is, is more clear cut but less easy to define – as played by Alan Bates, and therefore presumably as written, it seems rather a staged, deliberately histrionic gesture; his mind working again rather than his emotions getting really out of control.

Still, in the final analysis it does not seem to matter very much. Whether in theory the play should work or not, it triumphantly does. Simon is vividly present as a character, and so are the others – the sadly downtrodden brother, desperately eager for the assistant headmastership of a very minor public school; the loutish critic, with his diatribes against Australian writers taking over the world; the sexy but totally awful girl who tries to put the make on Simon in aid of her forthcoming book and gets wittily and unarguably turned down (though the book may be another matter); and, perhaps above all, the extraordinary man who is handed the central scene of the play, the 'plop' (slang of the old school he and Simon went to, meaning drip) who exacts from Simon an admission that he has on one occasion fooled around with his daughter, shows a surprising degree of prurient interest in the deed, then confesses that it is actually the girl he platonically lives with and goes into a complete recital of his ploppish life, from masturbation (with the youthful Simon, apparently, as his favoured image) to matrimony to monogamy. This whole scene (the act-break comes right in the middle) is a miracle of progressive dramatic revelation and knife-edge balance between comedy and drama, decorum and disintegration. It is marvellously played by Alan Bates and Benjamin Whitrow, and directed with that nervy precision which seems to be Harold Pinter's forté as a director. But if this sequence is the most spectacular instance of the play's way with its audience, it is symptomatic of the whole – scarcely an actor puts a foot wrong the whole evening, or is for that matter given a chance to by the script and direction. At first it is surprising to hear a regular audience laughing so heartily and continuously at what would seem to be rather rarified jokes, depending often on niceties of grammar and definition. But obviously, as in *Butley,* it really didn't matter if you had never heard of T. S. Eliot, so here it doesn't matter if you fail sometimes quite to get the point of what Simon is saying, because you get the meaning of the overall human gesture. Simon Gray's intellectuals are always unmistakably intellectuals, but the games of power and passion that they play are the games we all play, and can all recognise. If we do not altogether understand Simon, and cannot sympathise with him (he would be the last man to wish it) at least, in the theatre and afterwards, we have no doubt at all that he exists.

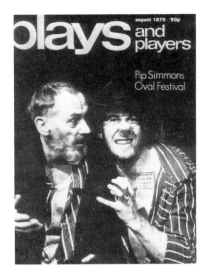

As we came away from the Royal Court after the first night of David Hare's *Teeth 'n' Smiles,* there seemed to be one name on everyone's lips – John Osborne. Wasn't it just like early Osborne, old Courtiers were saying. Didn't it carry you back to *The Entertainer* and those first, electric nights of *Look Back in Anger*? To which the answer, strictly and properly, should have been no, not really. I've never been among those who find it helpful to think of Bucharest as the Paris of the Balkans, nor would it strike me as flattering to call David Hare, or anyone else, the Osborne of the '70s. Still, because it was obviously shorthand and well-intended, I said yes, I saw what they meant. There had been an air of nostalgia about the evening, and it was good to see a new regime at the Court with a whopping hit on its hands, a play plugged deep into the rusty, defective socket of contemporary England, popping and sparking with anger at the connection.

The image is Hare's, more or less. For its first half hour or so, *Teeth 'n' Smiles* revolves slowly around an unconnected electric plug, centre stage. It powers, or ought to be powering, the amplifiers of Maggie Frisby's travelling rock-group, contracted to play at a Jesus College May Ball in Cambridge, 1969, and already ninety minutes late. But the group say it's not working, and none of them will touch it. The college porter comes and shakes his big silver watch at it. The ball's undergraduate organiser, incoherent with politeness and desperation, almost lays hands on it himself. But no. It may not be touched. Artists do not handle equipment ('You don't ask Heifetz to go out and strangle the cat', explains Smegs, lead guitar) and Inch, the road manager, is out investigating an offer of oral gratification by some groupies at the backdoor. So the plug lies there useless, artfully gathering to itself a charge of mounting irritation from both sides of the footlights.

The British disease? Demarcation dispute? No, this is a skirmish in the latest battle of an older, undeclared war. When the plug is finally connected, musical aggro sprays itself over the theatre with a roar like machine guns. *Teeth 'n' Smiles* is about the challenge of pop music in the '60s to the way privilege has regrouped itself in Britain since 1945: to the citadels of meritocracy, the playing-fields of competitive education, the boys and girls from good, book-lined homes who climb effortlessly from grammar school to Oxbridge to the executive jobs advertised, alongside Heal's furniture and the latest biography of Virginia Woolf, in the columns of the *Sunday Times*.

The Osborne play it brought to my mind, backhandedly, was *West of Suez*. That was the one, if you remember, which ended with an elderly, distinguished British writer being denounced for his witty, graceful literacy by a foul-mouthed American yob and then gunned down by rampaging Caribbean guerillas. 'They've shot the fox', pronounced his son-in-law, and cultivated members of the audience were left to pick up the inference that, when British taste and style have been dragged down to the rest of the world's level, civilisation will no longer have a pacemaker or standard to pursue and the new Dark Ages will have come. Myself, the message I took away from the occasion was that the Court and its house-playwright had travelled full circle. Jimmy Porter had turned into his father-in-law, the old Indian Army ramrod who couldn't understand why his world had fallen to the

Teeth 'n' Smiles at the Royal Court

reviewed by Ronald Bryden

Opposite: *Teeth 'n' Smiles* by David Hare at the Royal Court Theatre with Helen Mirren and Hugh Fraser. 1975.

barbarians. Well, in the new Court regime's first production, the barbarians are within the gates, stamping, singing and doing unmentionable things to the flags *West of Suez* ran up over Sloane Square. It's a happy spectacle.

Not that David Hare is naïve enough to suppose that the pop generation won the war, or even the particular battle of the '60s. He calls *Teeth 'n' Smiles* 'a history play' and its ending is as disillusioned and scathing an epitaph for the Beatle decade's army of mercenaries as any Osborne could devise. But he understands what the battle was about and mourns for its lost cause with a harsh tenderness which sometimes touches poetry. There's the moment, for instance, when the deferential college porter takes the band's orders for food. 'Hamburger and dill pickle', commands Maggie Frisby. 'And relish and french fries. Coca-cola. And a banana pretty. And a vanilla ice with hot chocolate sauce. Chopped nuts. And some tinned peaches. And tomato sauce for the hamburger. With onion rings. And mayonnaise. And frankfurters. Frankfurters for everyone, OK? With french mustard. And some toasted cheese and tomato sandwiches. With chutney. On brown bread, by the way. I'm a health freak.' The porter's face as he takes in the Wimpy Bar catalogue, and the underlying declaration that Maggie spits on the college's chicken and champagne for food of her – his *and* her – class, is a small victory.

It is almost Maggie's last, however. She knows the battle of pop has been lost and drowns her knowledge in whisky, deliberately wrecking performances which have become no more for her than ego-trips. Before the ball ends, she manages to burn down the wine tent. But that is small consolation for the lost dream of a popular culture which would overthrow the educational ladders which bear the fortunate few upward to their glittering prizes; which would turn the losers in the meritocratic race into winners. She can no longer bear the devotion of Arthur, the drop-out songwriter who launched her on her career, because he still half-clings to the dream and, the rest of the time, fashions an Auden-cum-Gershwin style from his despair. 'He's become a little over-earnest for me, don't you think?' she tells Laura, the group's faithful, long-suffering press rep. 'I mean, if there was going to be a revolution it would have happened by now. I don't think 1970'll be the big year . . . Gimme the bottle.'

The play's main flaw is that it is as much Arthur's as Maggie's. Maggie is Hare's thought: his recognition that the pop millenium never arrived, never had the political stamina to do so, but turned instead into a generation of self-exposers flogging lost, frenzied hopes for a few years of cash and glitter. Arthur represents his emotions, and the university cleverness which has turned against itself, which makes him the more lifelike and interesting character. With his melancholy, self-mocking jokes and imitations of Astaire and Cole Porter, he almost softens Maggie's anger to a Coward-esque sigh of stylish regret at how impotent cheap music turned out to be. Maggie is in fact cleverer than her Svengali, and often funnier. 'Why would I rather be American than English?' she tells a student journalist. 'Because America is a crippled giant. England is a sick gnome.' She just isn't so believable. You can't swallow a joke like that from the Janis Joplin of the Home Counties. It's the voice of David Hare.

This may reflect the fact that, while Jack Shepherd brings Arthur all the depth and inventiveness of his considerable talent, Helen Mirren is dashing but miscast as Maggie. She has all the attack and magnetism necessary for the middle of the role, but she can't convince you of its extremes – either that Maggie has the microphone magic to become a 'minor cult' or that she has a tougher brain behind the whisky haze than anyone else on stage.

But then, everyone in the play is a little too clever, too funny, too articulate, to be true. Even the group's stone-hearted manager Saraffian turns out, in Dave King's beautifully understated performance, to be a shrewd, self-loathing epigrammatist whose class-hatred has been undermined by a taste for vintage ports and vintage futilities. The evening works too well as theatre, allows itself too much dazzle and enjoyment, to put over satisfactorily the serious point it is trying to make. This may account for its last-minute attempt to wrench its mood on to another level with a quietly savage song by Tony Bicât, 'Last Orders on the Titanic'. ('The ship is sinking, But the music remains the same.') In effect, this turns out to be another stroke of excessive ingenuity and overkill. It might have been better to let the broken promises of the pop decade speak for themselves in the title song, printed in the rehearsal script but discarded in performance, to 'the most cheerful music you ever heard':

>   Mama, don't you know where your boy has gone?
>   He's gone to be a rock-and-roll star.
>   He's got a new set of teeth and a Chevrolet
>   And the cheapest kind of bass guitar . . .

One can see why, in the bleak and austerer chapels of the theatrical Left, Hare is mistrusted for his excessive brilliance and success. Also why he himself would perhaps find it necessary to school himself to the Brechtian impersonality of *Fanshen*. There is a kind of over-willed, show-off quality to his writing, an intrusion of himself on his creations by trying too hard to be magisterial, which distorts *Teeth 'n' Smiles* even more than *Knuckle*, and brings to mind the young Auden of *Dog Beneath the Skin*. All the same, I hope he will follow the direction of the two latter plays rather than that of *Fanshen*, excellent though it was. It is the personal tensions in his talent, the tug between popularity and politics, display and distaste for his own cleverness, which make him one of the most interesting playwrights of the '70s so far. It is they which have made *Teeth 'n' Smiles*, for all its impurities, a success. Rage as it may, the far theatrical Left has nothing to teach him until it has realised that, without success, political purity is as impotent as cheap music.

1975 Awards

voted for by the London Theatre Critics

Best new play: *Otherwise Engaged* by Simon Gray

Best new musical: *A Little Night Music* by Stephen Sondheim and Hugh Wheeler

Best performance by an actor: John Gielgud in *No Man's Land*

Best performance by an actress: Helen Mirren in *Teeth 'n' Smiles* and *The Seagull* and Diana Rigg in *Phaedra Britannica*

Best performance by an actor in a supporting role: Dave King in *Teeth 'n' Smiles*

Best performance by an actress in a supporting role: Anna Massey in *Heartbreak House*

Most promising new actor: Jonathan Pryce in *Comedians*

Most promising new actress: Lynne Miller in *City Sugar*

Best production (director): John Schlesinger for *Heartbreak House*

Best production (designer): Michael Annals for *Heartbreak House* and *Otherwise Engaged*

Twenty critics voted this year and there was a clear conflict between those who supported the smooth elegance of Simon Gray's *Otherwise Engaged* and others impressed by the rougher qualities of *Comedians* by Trevor Griffiths. In the event, *Otherwise Engaged* polled eight votes to the seven gathered by *Comedians*, other mention being made of work by David Hare, Stephen Poliakoff, Michael Frayn and Howard Barker.

Two runaway winners this year: *A Little Night Music* in the Best Musical category gathered an overwhelming twelve votes *(The Black Mikado* managed three); and John Gielgud had nine supporters for his remarkable performance in *No Man's Land* – his nearest rival, Donald Sinden in *An Enemy of the People* at Chichester, commanding three votes. For Best Actress,

Most promising new actor: Jonathan Pryce in Trevor Griffiths' *Comedians*. **1975.**

Helen Mirren and Diana Rigg fought an exciting duel, each in the end receiving six votes. Miss Mirren, of course, is allowed a full vote when nominated for either *The Seagull* or *Teeth 'n' Smiles* and only one vote when both performances are mentioned. Billie Whitelaw in *Alphabetical Order*, Peggy Ashcroft in *Happy Days* and Susan Fleetwood, in *Comrades* and *Playboy*, each netted two votes.

Where votes are split, a full vote is allowed for each nomination. Jonathan Pryce just pipped Stephen Read to the post as Most Promising New Actor (eight votes to Read's six); but justice was probably done as Pryce received nominations in two other categories. No obvious choice this year for Most Promising New Actress – Lynne Miller in *City Sugar* had three votes to the two collected by Jacqueline Pearce in *Otherwise Engaged*.

Heartbreak House was a clear winner as Best Production, having six supporters: in second place was *Fanshen*, with three votes. Michael Annals received votes for designs of both *Heartbreak House* and *Otherwise Engaged*.

1976

Jimmy Carter was elected President of the USA and Cyrus Vance replaced Kissinger as Secretary of State. The Lockheed scandal broke implicating, among others, Prince Bernhard of the Netherlands. José Lopez Portillo was elected President of Mexico and the deposed President Isabel Peron was replaced in Argentina by General Jorge Vidella. In India Mrs Gandhi arrested hundreds of political opponents. Mao Tse-tung died at 82. There were severe earthquakes in Italy, Chile and Turkey. Queen Elizabeth reached 50 and went to the United States to join in the celebrations of 200 years of independence.

In Britain Prime Minister Harold Wilson unexpectedly resigned to be succeeded by James Callaghan. Jeremy Thorpe resigned as leader of the Liberal Party after allegations concerning his private life. Former Minister John Stonehouse MP was gaoled. In the London theatre world the event of the year was the National Theatre Company's move into its own home on the South Bank. The NT took its leave of its temporary quarters at the Old Vic with a tribute to Lilian Baylis but the future of the historic theatre she turned into a nursery of talent remained in doubt. Elsewhere, Trevor Nunn's studio production of Macbeth *with Ian McKellen and Judi Dench excited great interest at Stratford-upon-Avon.*

Green Room

Ronald Bryden on critical
conditions for the British theatre*

Let's assume for purposes of argument that the British theatre will survive. It's only an assumption, of course. Theatres can die and theatres have – anyone seen any good new Greek tragedies lately? The myth of the Fabulous Invalid, always on the brink of mortality yet always miraculously recovering, is only a myth: a Broadway producer's way of reassuring himself that, whatever he does to kill any chance of another O'Neill, Arthur Miller or Tennessee Williams appearing in the American theatre, there'll always be another *Hello, Dolly* to pay for next winter's vicuna overcoat. No: the invalid the British theatre brings to mind this winter is General Franco. Take away the blood transfusions, heart-pacer, kidney-machine and intravenous feeding-tubes, and what you have left is a corpse. In which case, is all the trouble worth it? The question is *how* the patient will survive. If you can't provide a cure, shouldn't you let him die? Myself, I think the British theatre will survive the current economic crisis. I can't see any government, Labour or Conservative, quite bringing itself to turn off those feeding tubes. Not entirely, anyway. The political balance of pressures and motives will keep them pumping, just. As the crisis deepens in the next year or two, I expect there'll be cries on the Left to turn the trickle of subsidy toward some industry whose need is greater. As unemployment continues to soar, Northern MPs will point out that the millions needed to keep open Covent Garden, the new National, the Aldwych and Royal Court for a handful of privileged south-easterners could save a coal-pit, bicycle factory or other local industry – things which affect the lives and jobs of ordinary Labour voters, whose votes were not and never have been votes for the arts.

They'll be defeated, when they divide the Commons on the issue, by the 250 former presidents of the Oxford Union sitting on both sides of the House. By them, and the Government acting on Treasury advice. Oh, yes, the Treasury will vote to save the theatre. Our meritocratic mandarinate in Whitehall like a bit of Chekhov and Wagner. They are also recognising belatedly that to turn off the lights of Shaftesbury Avenue would be as false an economy as for Blackpool Council to cancel its illuminations and close the piers. Until North Sea oil pays off the longer-standing of our overseas debts, Britain will need every tourist dollar, mark and yen she can lure here. And what lures tourists here, Whitehall is beginning to realise, is theatre, just as food lures them to France, sex to Tangier and opera to Vienna. The last is a pertinent parallel. Vienna's operatic tradition has survived the loss of empire, inflation, *anschluss*, bombing and occupation. Austrian governments and their mandarinate recognised it as the last of their national treasures, alongside the Vienna Boys' Choir and the white Lippizaners of the Spanish Riding School, and kept it alive with subsidy. Today, if you want to see Mozart, Johann or Richard Strauss performed as sumptuously as they were under Franz Josef, you go to Vienna for it. That's what I'm afraid of. I'm afraid of the irony that, precisely at the moment when the theatre has at last become a matter for politics, the trend of politics seems likely to doom it to death-in-life. I'm afraid of the balance of motives which will lead to a decision to go on feeding it through those slender tubes of subsidy. Just enough to sustain life, of course. Not enough to offend the mass of voters who regard it as a

*Ronald Bryden was formerly drama critic of *The Observer* and then dramaturg for the Royal Shakespeare Company.

wasteful luxury for an elite of south-eastern culture snobs. Not enough – this is the terrible danger that worries me – to prevent permanent brain damage.

The Government will decide to sustain the theatre because it is a national treasure, one of the last things Britons can pride themselves they do better than other nations. They will try to sustain it as a National Treasure Theatre to which tourists will pay National Treasure prices. Such a theatre is politically safe. When rebellious and desperate Northern MPs force a vote on its subsidies, the 250 former presidents of the Oxford Union will demand indignantly whether they mean to vote against Shakespeare, Congreve, Sheridan and Shaw, and cow them into the appropriate lobby. In times of crisis, you can always frighten people into clinging to the pillars of traditional national culture. These are the times when anxious parents, seeing schools understaffed and university grants cut, will do without meat or cigarettes to keep up, for their children's sakes, payments on imitation-leather libraries of Scott, Dickens and Trollope. You can always raise votes for Shakespeare. There are no votes in Edward Bond, Joe Orton or Howard Brenton.

A National Treasure theatre at National Treasure prices will be a vicious circle. The higher the fewer: the more prices of theatre seats rise, the fewer plays playgoers will pay to see. They will only justify the expense of theatre-going to themselves for a once-a-year or once-in-a-lifetime experience – Olivier as Othello, Glenda Jackson as Hedda, Frank Sinatra flashing the old blue eyes for positively his last appearance on any stage until his next farewell tour. To lure the customers in, that means you have to provide the theatrical equivalent of imitation leather and gilt lettering, of Trollope, Dickens and Scott. If that were all British publishers could afford to print, would anyone claim we still had a living literature?

The awful irony is that this ought to be the most hopeful moment in our theatre's history. Its survival is now for the first time a political issue. It cannot survive without subsidy, and it has become too expensive for the Treasury to pass over that subsidy back-handedly out of its hip pocket without Parliament needing to notice. In order to keep it alive, governments from now on will have to ask their supporters whether they want it, whether they are prepared to pay its cost. This ought to be the moment when the answer comes back: No, not in its present form. Not unless it becomes a majority art, a theatre for the nation, not just for its university graduates. This ought to be the moment when a genuine popular theatre is forced to reincarnate itself for Britain. Instead, we seem doomed to a decade of Francoesque half-life which could lock the theatre forever into its present class structure. By preserving a theatre of the Hundred Essential Masterpieces to maintain desert-island morale through the coming economic hurricane the Government will in effect preserve the bourgeois theatre of the nineteenth and early twentieth century. It will, all too fatally, preserve the Britain we know so well: a culture of inequality.

Most of our masterpieces come from the great age of bourgeois art. The reason is simple. The bourgeoisie invented the notion of

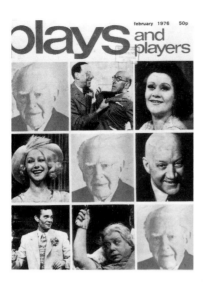

olays and **players**

february 1976 50p

the masterpiece. It was their equivalent of the heirloom. Aristocrats handed on to their children land, gold, family portraits by Van Dyck and Gainsborough. The new professional classes of the nineteenth century, whose power was knowledge rather than real estate, redefined wealth as wealth of the mind and handed on to their children treasures of art. The nobility were welcome to keep their crumbling rural palaces and murky Knellers. The Age of the Bourgeoisie had replaced them with a new scale of values whose wealth was *Middlemarch*, *Madame Bovary*, *War and Peace*, engravings by Doré and Daumier, the piano music of Chopin and Schumann. And the theatre, of course.

We still live in the shadow of their achievement. They created a perfect symbiosis between their art and world which we, struggling to replace both, can only envy and marvel at. If only we knew how to build a popular, majority culture whose arts had the perfect reciprocity with their audiences that nineteenth-century piano music had with the drawing-rooms where it was played; that *Madame Bovary* had with the bourgeois wives who read it on their horsehair sofas; that Ibsen and Chekhov had with those liberal, intellectual art-theatre audiences of the '80s and '90s!

Our dramatists, striving to escape that three-walled, cushioned cage where corseted wives tipple brandy and burn manuscripts, where strait-jacketed husbands are taunted into heart attacks, destroy it symbolically night after night. The archetypal twentieth-century play is set in a house whose servants rebel, whose children rage and run away, whose walls in the last act sag inward, revealing bomb-smoke and heaped corpses in the ruined garden outside. But the house and its bourgeois audience are there again the night after, ready to be assailed and destroyed again from within by the modern mutations of bourgeois intelligence and bourgeois guilt. The typical experience of a twentieth-century classic is elation at watching a bourgeois world laid waste in miniature combined with depression that all this leaves is an empty stage.

The new mass culture has created its own symbiosis, equally narrow and claustrophobic, with television: ten million families in front parlours laughing at families identical with themselves quarrelling in front parlours identical with their own. The children run away from that infinitely-duplicated house too, but not to the theatre – who wants to see the heirs of the bourgeoisie smash its heirlooms and, by doing so within a proscenium, create new ones? To find an art which fits a world larger than the British class system, they turn to science fiction, pop singers of universal harmony and the cinema of nakedness and catastrophe. To destroy the world they want to escape needs stronger images than sagging stage-flats – earthquakes, burning ships and skyscrapers, giant sharks rising from the ocean floor. That's the territory – melodrama, comic-strip primitivism, naïve prophecy of a global imagination – that our theatre needs to explore in order to attract the young, majority audience whose flag is the Apollo photograph of Earth hanging in space. And not with camp giggles and titters, as in *The Rocky Horror Show* and similar attempts to sophisticate pop culture for audiences of meritocrats. The exploration needs to be truthful, with a sense of wonder and poetry, as it was once long ago in *The Tempest*.

There are playwrights beginning to do this on the fringes of British theatre. They are young, disaffected and not in the heirloom business. They will not fill Art Treasure theatres with Art Treasure tourists. Any subsidised theatre which puts plays by them into its main auditorium will lose money it cannot afford under present circumstances and be told by the dispensers and watchdogs of its subsidies that the Government does not care to see money earmarked for preservation of cultural monuments used to gamble on radical nonentities. But unless the theatre can gamble on them, it will emerge from its present emergency survival operation as dead as Franco in his ghoulish pyramid. Surely one thing we know about our plight is that it is a crisis of under-investment; of once-healthy industries lacking capital to retool, to plan beyond next month or produce new models to compete in world markets. The theatre was one of our healthiest industries a couple of years ago. Already we can see it playing safe, retreading last year's models, packaging them in mock-morocco and imitation gilt as cultural totems and tourist souvenirs. If the present Government really wants a culture of equality, it ought to want a theatre which is not just a museum of bourgeois masterpieces but a stage of conversation, journalism, popular debate and millennial visions; a theatre of hope for the whole nation. In which case it should turn off the feed-pipes, kidney-machine and heart-pacer today. And bring the patient a tray of solid food, quickly.

The Government, of course, is not wholly to blame for its view of the theatre as a bourgeois museum. It depends for its theatrical information, like most people, on London's critics. As one of their number until five years ago, I've hesitated before now to criticise former colleagues. As an employee of one of the larger subsidised companies, I've avoided antagonising the main source of publicity for our productions. But now that I'm moving on to new pastures and new shores, I feel I can unburden myself of a conviction which has grown on me steadily during my years with the RSC.

To a great extent, the present crisis in the British theatre is a crisis of criticism. Everyone who works in the theatre knows it but is afraid to say so because their livelihood and the theatre's depend too heavily on what the critics write. With one or two honourable exceptions, the present crop of British theatre critics is a bad one which is damaging and retarding the theatre's development.

The conventional reply to charges like this is that criticism is purely a matter of opinion and therefore cannot be disputed. There is no common ground in criticism, only subjective taste, and therefore no standard by which criticism can be judged. This is false. There is common ground which all critics who pass judgement on a play have to cover, or ought to if their criticism is to be taken seriously. This is the basic work of attending to the play and its production, reading it with the ears, grasping the statement it makes and learning enough about the skills involved in staging it to evaluate them.

In the past five years, I have watched a dozen or so new plays through their various stages of preparation and rehearsal and their first nights. The following mornings I have read their reviews and

Ian McKellen: Stratford's Romeo writes inside

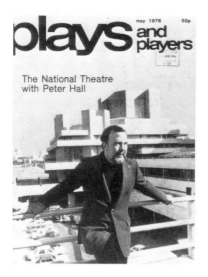

plays and players

may 1976   50p

The National Theatre
with Peter Hall

felt like a schoolmaster forced to mark a particularly dispiriting batch of essays on a set subject. It wasn't that particular critics didn't like plays I'd admired enough to recommend for production. I knew the tastes of my former colleagues sufficiently well to predict roughly, when plays were chosen, which critics would respond to what. The depressing thing was the elementary failure of attention: to keep eyes, ears and mind sufficiently open to see, hear and comprehend the play before them. The temptation was almost ungovernable to snip out reviews and return them to their writers scrawled over in red ink: 'Lazy, careless, inattentive work. Try harder next time'.

Of course, I knew by then how unfair it is to expect a critic to pick up from two or three hours of rapid playing the kind of understanding of a play those involved in presenting it acquire in six weeks of rehearsal and several months' intimacy with the script. The rush of red ink to my imagination might have been less had critics shown any inkling of this themselves. But no. Far more depressing than the inadequacy of their accounts of the plays they'd seen was the confidence with which they delivered their judgements of their own fragmentary readings. It was as if the less they had understood the readier they felt to be dismissive, slighting or outright vindictive. The critic has missed the point, therefore the play's to blame. The trouble, I think, has two simple causes. First, the majority of our present critics entered journalism in post-war years of the rise of the meritocracy, when Fleet Street seemed the pinnacle of meritocratic ambition – what career could appeal to a meritocrat more than one which enabled him to display the superiority of his intelligence by passing judgement on the rest of society daily? In that tournament of Lifemanship, theatre criticism was the Centre Court. Where else could the former star of the junior common room remain forever One Up, perpetually aloof and presented nightly with fodder to score off, wither and riddle with scorn? That is what the profession of theatre critic was made in the late '40s and '50s: an opportunity to display education at the expense of the less educated.

Second, since the '50s, a second wave of Welfare State meritocrats has come out of the universities. But instead of going into Fleet Street, they have gone into the theatre. Today, the average intelligence of the people producing plays in this country is considerably higher than that of the people reviewing them. This makes for worse than misunderstanding. In the terms of Fleet Street meritocracy, it makes for antagonism. The majority of present Fleet Street critics are against intelligence in the theatre, because the intelligence they find there is greater than their own.

Particularly, they are against the generation of intelligent university meritocrats who have turned against meritocracy and challenge its assumptions. The kind of theatre *they* want to make in Britain strikes at the foundations of meritocratic lifemanship; the distinctions between the urbane and the vulgar, the knowing and the innocent, the In and the Out, on which its system of scoring is based. The critics miss the point of their productions because they do not wish to hear these distinctions attacked. They want a theatre for the élite to which they belong, which recognises their élite status and continues to provide them with opportunities to display it. And doesn't go beyond them and show them up.

Some kind of British theatre will survive, I think. It won't be a living, popular theatre until it gets a new and better generation of critics.

A playwright's task is to stun an audience awake, to make it see what life forces it to forget. Edward Bond is one of the few English playwrights with the cunning and craft to meet this challenge. He is obsessed with man's death-dealing in a society whose myths of justice and fair play make it numb to its own brutality. Bond's sense of outrage has turned him, at times, into the Ancient Mariner of the English stage, buttonholing his audience and hectoring it with gruesome and generalised images of suffering *(Lear, Bingo)*. But in his superb new play, *The Fool: Scenes of Bread and Love*, Bond attains a new theatrical maturity. Luring his audience into the robust and violent rural world of John Clare, the farm labourer turned poet, at the beginning of England's industrialisation in 1815, Bond creates a pageant of exploitation which demonstrates how imagination as well as manpower were victimised by the ruthless pursuit of profit. 'Wrote first poem when I were a boy picking up stones in your field', Clare explains to the lord of the manor, Lord Milton, in his East Anglian dialect. 'Took a stone in me hand an a poem come in me head'. *The Fool* follows Clare's sad career from his life on the land to literary celebrity and finally, estranged from both land and literature, into madness.

Shuttling uncomfortably between action and contemplation, the writer is a mercurial figure. Rarely the activist, the writer fashions himself in the centre of experience. With characteristic boldness, Bond dramatises this aspect of Clare by first showing him on the periphery of events, dimly aware of the violence around him. Act I scarcely acknowledges Clare's calling, introducing him, instead, as part of the tatty band of farm labourers turned mummers who knock on the manor door at Christmas time to perform a rollicking song and play for small change and a hot meal. Bond shows the peasants collaborating in their oppression, their resilient good spirits contrasting with the condescending patronage of the gentry who stroll on to the porch and applaud them. The festive charade is spoiled when one surly performer, Darkie (played with seething mockery by Nigel Terry), objects to the holiday platitudes and earns a lecture on economics from Lord Milton. 'Civilisation costs money like everything else', says Lord Milton. 'Put too much in your own pockets and what's left to pay for our institutions? Well now you have something to think about.' It's always those with the fullest bellies who tell people confidently to tighten their belts. Hunger is not debatable, and Darkie scoffs back: 'Six day a week I goo t'work in the dark an come home in the dark – for what? Ten shillin. Even Judas got thirty – but he come from a good family and wouldn't work for less.' With brilliant economy, Bond sets up the extremes of his debate and places Clare in the middle, assuaging Darkie who refuses Lord Milton's food: 'Can't afford t'feel like that boy. Spite yourself . . .'

The Fool at the Royal Court

reviewed by John Lahr

Clare's mind has learned to avoid politics and concentrate on country pleasures. While Darkie fumes, Clare plays. As Tom Courtenay plays him, Clare is a lusty, dreamy, endearing character sneaking away from his fiancée, Patty, to touch up Lord Milton's servant, Mary; and later, screwing Mary in full view of Lord Milton's gamekeepers who now patrol the peasants' wood which is being cleared to make fields. 'Hungry?' Mary asks, sharing a crust of bread with Clare. He answers: 'Allus hungry'. Scavenging for life, Clare prefers to imagine himself in an abundant Eden. 'Well built gall like you', he says, touching her breast as she eats. 'Like t'live in this forest. The two of us. Tread the reeds and creep in.'

Edward Bond's *The Fool* with Tom Courtenay in Peter Gill's production at the Royal Court. 1976. (Photo: John Haynes)

The poet feeds on dreams; the woman survives by her wits. 'Damp,' she answers. 'Gypsies know better'n that'. After their happy meeting, Clare never sees her again. Mary becomes one of Clare's obsessions, the symbol of love and liberty to be pursued in poetry.

Clare is hunting for her in the wood the night Darkie and the other peasants loot the estate and strip the local parson. The

140

parson stands naked and quivering while they ogle at his white skin. 'My baby', says one woman. 'My baby ont got proper baby skin like that. Look how soft that is. Like silk lace. My baby's born hard – hev animal skin like summat live in the road. Look at that. Comes away in handfuls.' Bond's language rings with anguished poetry as Darkie, too, pulls at the parson's skin. 'Where you stole that flesh boy? Yoor flesh is stolen goods. Yoor covered in stolen goods when you strip . . .'

Darkie's rancour never touches Clare. Darkie and his cronies are sent to prison for their abuses of private property. Clare is present in Darkie's cell when all the sentences of death by hanging are commuted except for Darkie's. Revenge in the hands of the powerful is called justice; in the hands of the impotent, crime. It is a terrifying lesson, and Clare seems to learn nothing. In time, Clare, like Darkie, will be silenced for insisting on the truth. But in the prison cell, when mention is made of possible publication of Clare's poems in London, Darkie suggests: 'Write about this place. What goo on.' Clare answers: 'Who'd read that?' Amidst Darkie's death watch, Clare is thinking of Mary and laughing. He exits from the cell with the green coat Darkie refuses to wear to the gallows. ('Kep us in rags,' Darkie says. 'Ont dress up for em when I die. Ont their circus.') But Bond dresses Clare in Darkie's green jacket in Act II which begins with Clare performing in London's literary circus.

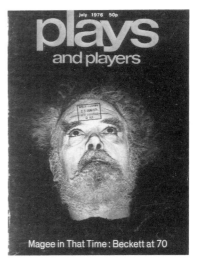

Magee in That Time: Beckett at 70

Act II opens with the startling image of a boxing match, the sound of flesh filtering through the shouts of the backers. In the foreground, Bond stages Clare as the centrepiece of London's literary arena. Like the boxers, Clare is surrounded by his avid supporters who are turning him into a property. Peter Gill's magnificent production makes the most of Bond's irony. Clare has finally understood his past. He hears his angry couplets quoted back at him:

> . . . Accursed wealth . . .
> Thou are the law that stops us being fed
> And takes away our labour and our bread . . .

A Chorus Line

But, having transformed the chaos of life into well-wrought and marketable art, Clare finds himself a victim of the market-place. Like any entertainer, he must please to live; and he finds his vision at the mercy of his customers' sense of reality. Clare meets Admiral Lord Radstock (played with amusing bluster by Bill Fraser) who is one of the poet's most important subscribers. The Admiral expresses nervousness about the 'radicalism' of the political verse and the vividness of his love poetry. 'The people you criticise', he says, advising Clare to adjust his style to the fashion, 'are only the ones who can afford books. The only ones who can read. I ordered twelve. Now I can't give them to my friends.' How punished is Clare by these encounters with the bourgeoisie? Bond offers tantalising hints. At the end of the scene, Clare approaches the bleeding and defeated Irish boxer whose backers have disappeared leaving him to beg money from Clare. 'Did he hurt yoo boy?' Clare asks the astonished Irishman. 'Yoo kip comin back.' The fighter has taken his beating to earn the allegiance of a backer Clare knows bet against him. The

Irishman exits with his betrayer just as Clare follows behind his English patrons who will soon abandon him.

The image of the fighter, like those of Darkie and Mary, haunt Clare as his mind starts to give way. 'Set up boxin'' Clare thinks out loud to his wife as a drastic measure to earn money for the family. 'They get paid for bein knocked about. I get knocked about.' Clare is five years older and battling vainly to sustain his craft. He has been rejected by London. His books don't sell. His wife, Patty, wants him to go back to the fields to 'sweat the scribble out of you'. Clare is a writer without access to an audience and with no means of reproducing his work. 'I wish I couldn't write my name' he tells Patty. 'But my mind git full of songs an I ont feel a man if I ont write em down.' Bond builds Clare's punishing isolation with consummate skill. A London patron visits him, bringing bags of unbought books. 'Your – scribble has to be decoded and accessible to polite society', she explains, suggesting he sell them himself. The unread books are like epitaphs to a stillborn spirit. Clare sees his predicament too clearly. He rejects the world that has destroyed him. He turns inwards, haunted by the ghost of his friends and his talent. Lord Milton accompanies the patron to Clare's cottage to inspect his condition and to see if medical attention is necessary. He asks Clare to read a poem. 'I hev – but yoo ont know how t'listen. Ont write for you. Ont be a poet then.' Clare continues in one of Bond's most eloquent laments:

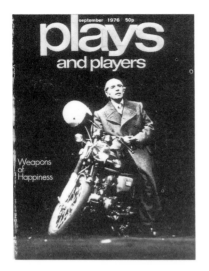

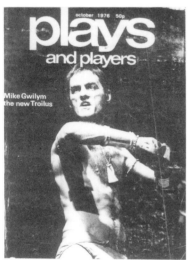

> I waited an no one come, or give tuppence without a grudge. An what I wrote was good. Yes. Worth readin. Shall I step in line now? No. I ont labour in yoor fields n'more. Labour in my fields. Yoo cut yoor fields up so yoo could eat em better. I've eat my portion of the universe I shall die of it. It was bitter fruit. But I had more out of the stones in yoor field than you had out of the harvest.

Clare is dragged from his home to an asylum surrendering his sanity and his family to the smug, understated violence of an intractable gentry. Bond shows Clare in the silence of old age, robbed of everything, called 'Poet' only by other inmates of the madhouse where everyman's heroic fantasy is indulged.

Bond, even more than most, has known the terrible frustration of writing well and being dismissed by those who have never dared journey as far as himself. He is a big talent; and Peter Gill's strong, clear production makes the scope and depth of Bond's humanity an astonishing spectacle. Every sentence, every sound has a gorgeous clarity. Gill has edited Bond's excesses which previous Royal Court productions have indulged. Together, Bond and Gill bring a whole society alive in a play as scrupulously well acted as it is well written.

To moans from the fringe, the regions, the disabled and cherub fanciers, the National Theatre opened its doors on 8 March – or at least the doors of the Lyttelton – not with a fanfare but with an almost audible sigh of relief, and a saturation of publicity. Denys Lasdun, backed up by Peter Hall, had promised – nay, protested – that, with people in them, the auditorium, the foyers, the terraces of his concrete palace of infinite variety would 'come alive'. But would they? Do they? Praise be, they do. Not since the old days at the Royal Court have I had any desire to arrive at a theatre before the last possible moment or to hang about afterwards. By my third visit to the new National I wanted to do both.

Crossing the threshold for the first time on a rather cheerless Monday afternoon one felt anxious, willing the thing to come up to scratch. The wind along that South Bank stretch can pulverise the kneecaps even when they are fainting with heat over in the Strand. In *Monty Python* fashion a one-man welcoming committee was sitting at a table in the middle of the road turning people away from the unfinished car park. He was livid with cold. 'Peter Hall should be doing that job,' someone said. 'Bloody right,' said the man with a dismissive sniff. 'He bloody thought up the whole bloody thing, didn't he?' Past the box office, more like a booking hall really, and through the front door. The entrance foyer has a warm, tiled floor. Spacious, businesslike, it's a place to leave your coat and exchange those vouchers that prematurely raised the blood pressure of non-theatregoers who write letters to newspapers. This space gives on to the ground floor Lyttelton foyer – carpeted, ingeniously and flatteringly lit, masses of space. As the two-week launching continues, it turns out to be easy to get a drink, a cup of coffee, a sandwich, or to stroll, and the book stall – selling programmes, magazines, softbacks, hardbacks and the evening papers – does a brisk trade. At night the scale of this foyer seems custom-built to accommodate anticipation: chatter, jeans, jewels, wheelchairs, lovers and, of course, the view. London, across the black river, in lights. For a moment it is hard to believe that things are as bad as we are told they are.

Up the snaking stairs there are two more floors of bars and buffets, more views (though on the first floor the panorama is partly obscured by a wedge of terracing, and I'll bet the bar takings suffer). That first afternoon the top floor – light and lemony – was taken over by a press reception, or bun-fight. One multi-lingual reviewer was proprietorially swiping bottles of wine from the bar to place before a tableful of Swedish radio reporters. Another, after vociferously lamenting the non-appearance of free sandwiches, all but shoved them up her jumper when they were borne in. The air of celebration rapidly went rancid; most of this international gathering of critics, correspondents and hangers-on looked as though they had been unwillingly rounded up for a matinée of *The Mousetrap* in a church hall. So, it was even more heartening that one's spirits rose again in the theatre proper. Here, too, the rough concrete softens as the audience comes in. The scale *is* intimate. Sight and sound in the stalls are remarkably direct (and it's good to know that the actors also feel this from the stage), although there have been some unsubstantiated grumbles from parts of the circle. By the third visit I was beginning to miss

Crossing the Threshold

Helen Dawson at the opening of the new National

143

an aisle. Sitting in the middle, especially when there are two intervals, is a nuisance if most of the others in your row don't smoke or drink but stay put. I suppose I miss it for traditional reasons as well, and for the fleeting sensation that perhaps we are going to be shown a film instead. But, otherwise, it seems about as fine as a proscenium auditorium can be, and both sets and actors look notably better on its stage than they did at the Old Vic.

The Olivier, of course, is the challenge. Further delays seem inevitable and impatience will have to be tempered. Meanwhile, and equally inevitable, there are snags to be ironed out, changes to be made. Many of the actors are unhappy about the dressing rooms. Backstage, all is technically far from well. The restaurant sports the same awful net curtains that blight the view from the staff canteen. One friend praised the salami sandwiches; I maintain that salami is theatrically anti-social. Another protested that *Plunder* was preceded by the National Anthem. A dwarf complained that the telephones were too high.

Never mind, it is there. Not, by a long way, in full working order, but as the poster says, the New National Theatre is *yours*. And, already, it feels that way. Could it be, just this once, that we have got something right?

JULY
1976

Yesterday's News

Ned Chaillet reviews the latest Joint Stock production

A careful examination of the physical events of *Yesterday's News* in the Theatre Upstairs would be helpful. The reports of the production's austerity, though accurate, are misleading: the play's seven actors do sit on chairs and talk to the audience about the British mercenaries in Angola but much more happens than that. To begin with, the actors enter the room after the audience arrives. The journalist enters with the audience, a professional voyeur among the paying spectators. Not until she takes a seat facing us is she distanced from us, and then only slightly, as in a classroom. Four performers follow her on and take seats beside her, radiating confidence, incomprehension, conviction and nervous pride as befits their roles. The first player to speak is Keith Jones, a 17-year-old mercenary portrayed by Will Knightley. As a survivor of the mass execution of British mercenaries by their own comrades, Keith was momentarily a national figure, now relegated with the events themselves to back copies of newspapers. He recounts his life story, his version of what occurred in Angola, and tells us of his readjustment to civilian life after his brief encounter with war. His recitation is broken up by a careful rota of speakers who talk of the effect of the events on their lives, but his is the central story with the war as the bleak highpoint in his life, surrounded as it is by little failure and no expectations of a brighter future. Knightley, even when not speaking, stares straight ahead as though looking at the horrors he recounts so calmly. It is a most alarming, convincing action.

The second speaker is a stockbroker played by Tony Mathews. His life is full of highpoints, but his well-mannered shiftiness and easy evasions of ideas suggest that he is haunted only by different visions of success. He trained at a monastery school; he enjoyed his brief time as an army officer; though he achieved only minor success as an actor, he longs to try again; the events in Angola make African investments insecure and he advises us not to invest in South Africa. A giddy, sincere girl speaks next, giving a public-house consideration of Angola, suggesting that the news would never have intruded on the weekly round of punch-ups and dancing if her lot hadn't known Keith. The character is made convincing by Linda Goddard's performance, and though she is seen as having been affected by the first false reports of Keith's death, it is clear that others weren't so affected, accepting death in Angola like the latest bomb in Belfast as a remote headline. Belfast is tied closer to events in Angola by the fourth speaker, Roche, an English recruiter of mercenaries, reasonable expositor of mercenary philosophy and occasional gun-runner played by Philip McGough. He had served with the armed forces in Northern Ireland but found it unsatisfactory because, having been 'brainwashed to kill', he was expected to practise psychology. In his new profession he feels greater job satisfaction, he has covert friends among the police and seems to feel that he is serving democracy.

These bits of information are given to us in starts and stops as speakers yield to other speakers, receding into a meditative privacy with each character unaware of the others speaking and totally unaffected by other monologues. During their silences the actors' retention of character is astounding. The first four speakers are encompassed in the broader view by Gillian Barge's journalist who tells how, by ingratiating herself with Keith's family, she was able to obtain an exclusive interview on his return. Her journalism (she always knew it would suit her temperament) is of a particularly repellent kind, manipulative, depending on (there is no other apt phrase) feminine wiles. And though she may have got her final exclusive story, Keith points out that he never said what she quoted him as saying.

This is the third production by the Joint Stock Theatre Group and is said to have been 'researched and edited by the group and Jeremy Seabrook'. There is more to it than that, a major element of invention somewhere, and the role of the directors, William Gaskill and Max Stafford-Clark, clearly extended to the shaping of the material. It would be useful to know just what sort of research produced the two mercenaries who, midway through the peaceful recitations, intrude: ominous, slightly paranoid, examining the space for possible dangers. Their relaxed military gossip justifies 'Colonel Callan's' massacre, presenting it as a slightly harsh, perhaps necessary, form of discipline. War for them is a continuing condition where only the places change.

Humour is present throughout the play but used more sharply and to greater insidious purpose by Paul Kember's ex-para-trooper. He jokes about death and conditions of war and from him we get a genuine English flavour to the fighting with rhyming slang introduced and explained as with 'Bacon Tree' from 'Ham Bush' and that from ambush. Always on the edge of violence, he again points up the Northern Ireland connection and praises his fellow mercenary (David Rintoul) as coming from the most élite group of fighters in the world, the SAS. Rintoul's characterisation is less convincing, with the character too reluctant, too soft-

Heathcote Williams's *The Speakers* adapted
by William Gaskill and Max Stafford-Clark.
Heathcote Williams (left) watching Tony
Rohr. 1976. (Photo: John Haynes)

David Hare's *Fanshen* with Gillian Barge,
Paul Freeman, Will Knightley, Robert
Hamilton, Bruce Alexander, David Rintoul
and Tony Rohr. 1976. (Photo: John Haynes)

spoken, altogether too private to be on stage. But the part has none of the damaging weaknesses of the stockbroker who is too much given to saying such things as 'one of my best friends is black'.

This play is a work consistent with Joint Stock's two previous plays. Like *The Speakers* and *Fanshen* it gives a voice to those who are denied access to the mass-communication media. The company could be seen as endeavouring to give all ordinary people a Speakers Corner. In each play the company illuminates through empathy, establishing in *Yesterday's News* sympathy through laughter. By joining in the laughter at racist jokes and military atrocities, the audience comes to see the characters as individuals. No wonder mercenaries are said to have liked the play, for it never criticises, just connects. There is still some way to go before these connections become useful, but William Gaskill and Max Stafford-Clark have developed consistently, along clearly defined lines, and could be well on the way to establishing the most significant English company of the decade.

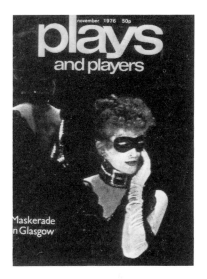

1976 Awards

voted for by the London Theatre Critics

Best new play: *The Fool* by Edward Bond

Best new musical: *A Chorus Line* by James Kirkwood, Nicholas Dante, Marvin Hamlisch and Edward Kleban

Best performance by an actor: Ian McKellen in *Macbeth* and *The Winter's Tale*

Best performance by an actress: Janet Suzman in *Three Sisters*

Best performance by an actor in a supporting role: Philip Locke in *Hamlet*

Best performance by an actress in a supporting role: Angela Pleasence in *The Bitter Tears of Petra von Kant*

Most promising new actor: Paul Copley in *For King and Country*

Most promising new actress: Julie Covington in *Weapons of Happiness* and *Jumpers*

Best production (director): Jonathan Miller for *Three Sisters*

Best production (designer): Frantz Salieri for *La Grande Eugene*

Best performance from Ian McKellen with Judi Dench in Trevor Nunn's Royal Shakespeare Company production of *Macbeth*. 1976.

1977

The year the Argentine Commission for Human Rights claimed that upwards of 30,000 had disappeared and 2,300 had been killed under the Vidella regime was the year Mrs Gandhi lost her seat and Morarji Desai became the new Indian PM. The USA and Cuba resumed official contact after an 18-year suspension. It was also the last year of the original Orient Express. President Geisel of Brazil assumed emergency powers. Jean-Bedel Bokassa crowned himself Emperor of the Central African Empire in a ceremony costing £14 million. Elvis Presley died and the Laker skytrain service began operations to New York.

In Britain the Queen celebrated her Silver Jubilee and Red Rum won the Grand National for the third time. Foreign Secretary Anthony Crosland died suddenly to be succeeded by Dr David Owen. Roy Jenkins left the Westminster political arena to become President of the EEC. A £300 million underground extension to Heathrow was opened. Gay News *was fined £1,000 for blasphemy and its editor gaoled.*

In the world of the theatre there was an anticlimax on the South Bank after the fanfare of the previous year's opening. The company was embarrassed by the cost of running the new building and labour problems which closed it for a time in the Spring. Prospect moved successfully into its former home, the Old Vic. The RSC had a good year with the opening of a second studio theatre in London, the Warehouse, and two transfers to the West End, Peter Nichols's Privates on Parade *and Alan Bennett's* The Old Country *which brought Alec Guinness back to the West End stage, provided talking points.*

Privates on Parade

Charles Marowitz reviews Peter Nichols's hit RSC comedy

Peter Nichols's newest play is full of solid, old-fashioned virtues. There is a maze of story-line; a lot of sympathetic, clearly-delineated characters; an unmistakable sense of location; tenderness, conventional morality, comedy, high-spirits and human reassurance. Set in the environs of Malaya during the so-called 'emergency' period and following the fortunes of a squad of performing militia-men (the south-east Asia ENSA brigade), the show strongly resembles the war-films from which so much of its nostalgia is derived. In those larky capers of the '40s, a sense of impregnable camaraderie managed to resolve all conflicts indirectly attributable to 'the enemy'. That is, if 'spots of bother' developed among the principal characters, it was always because they had been hauled out of civilian life and forced to bear arms against an implacable enemy which threatened the tranquillity of their domestic lives.

These films were invariably filled with colourful characters who, despite their outward flippancy, were cast in the heroic mould. One knew that although they talked crudely and drank rather more than they should, when the chips were down, they could be counted on to defend democracy and resist the encroachment of Nazi tyranny. They were as distinct as Commedia dell'Arte types. There was the prude, the bully, the goofball, the sad-sack, the pathetic young man whom one knew early on was bound to get killed before the last reel; the 'hero' through whose eyes we comprehended most of the action; the inflexible sense of hierarchy: the big brass, the NCOs, the enlisted men. It was a universe as ordered as Shakespeare's; as circumscribed by Christian values as the Elizabethans were by the chain-of-being. And as suspect. It was a genre of film in which the ordinary bloke, the doughboy and the GI Joe had modest ambitions, an identifiable occupation, a specific regional location and a girl back home. He exemplified the bed-rock virtues of the Empire that was shortly to crumble. He was the antithesis of 'the enemy' who were trying to foist a way-of-life inspired by Genghis Khan or Ivan The Terrible (i.e. Joe Stalin, Mao Tse tung). But no matter how diabolical his cunning, he would prove no match for the doughboy, or GI Joe whose common decency would always, given the propaganda-imperatives of such war-films, win out in the end.

Nichols's play is rooted in that kind of simplicity, and to pretend that it is questioning the British presence in South East Asia or delving into the deeper issues of the emergency years is unadulterated bunkum. It isn't, nor does it need to. Mainly it is demonstrating a kind of playwriting which hasn't been around for a very long time, which, indeed, has fallen out of fashion, and which, when it was in fashion, was the mainstay of those uncomplicated movies which are regularly revived to oohing-and-aghing audiences at the National Film Theatre. As a piece of comic engineering, one must salute the ingenuity that could construct such a play in the 1970s. To be so profoundly tuned into the ambience of another time and to be able to work it to your advantage, is no mean feat. Although it is not uncritical of those halcyon years, it is palpably affectionate about them, and to encounter a play motivated by affection rather than social loathing or class prejudice is itself a rarity these days. It falters only in the second half when it gets bogged down in jungle-safari plots and begins to reiterate itself. *Privates On*

Peter Nichols's *Privates on Parade* directed for the Royal Shakespeare Company by Michael Blakemore.

Lindsay Kemp's SALOME

Parade is a displaced Ealing comedy; a delayed legacy from the Boulting Brothers. It is 'the play of the film' and if nostalgia, now waning, ever gets a second wind in England, it could be Lew Grade's next big cinematic block-buster. In so being, it will have found its most natural form.

The show is full of acting opportunities and Michael Blakemore's well-drilled and well-assembled cast has realised most of them. It is heartening to see Joe Melia, so frequently wasted at the RSC, finding a role that fully taps his talents. As the unfortunate Corporal Len Bonny (Nichols's single casualty, the one sacrificial victim in an otherwise jolly charade), Melia shuttles between the preposterously deadpan and the irrepressibly manic. His rasping nasality (a sound like a Kango cutting through concrete) makes the most of every joke, and when he is called upon to sing and dance, he sidles with ease into music-hall conventions which seem to be as natural to him as breathing. Nigel Hawthorne, playing this kind of deadly British officer whose historical prototype is Haig and whom Guinness played to perfection in *Bridge on The River Kwai*, is the very embodiment of county values, militarily displaced. In a highly eccentric but entirely appropriate drawling rhythm, Hawthorne doodles little details around this Blimpish Major whisking him away from caricature just long enough to remind us the type is rooted, not in stage-history, but in the country manors of England. It is a beautifully-observed, precisely-escalated characterisation.

As the fruity compère who directs the stray band of military mummers, Denis Quilley is invited, in almost every scene, to go whistling over the top; an invitation he discreetly declines, producing instead a delicately controlled performance which perfectly balances comment and caricature. From the first moment he flounces on stage, it is clear that the English audience is reuniting with an old and dear friend, the Jolly Queen who is both flip and predatory. It is to Quilley's credit that he never overstays his welcome and that every hoary old camp-joke in the Index is received as if it was a newly-discovered North Sea oilfield.

Most of the evening is seen through the eyes of Ian Gelder's recently arrived recruit. Although a remorseless straight role without the comic rewards offered to his colleagues, Gelder plays it with unflinching earnestness and unwavering sympathy.

Emma Williams, being the only full-fledged female in a group much given to female impersonation, tends to play with too much unrelieved attack, although when she is singing or dancing, the unabated energy nourishes the role. In the quieter moments, she never quite drops down into a deeper level of characterisation. It remains highly-competent musical-comedy acting even when something more naturalistic is called for. Dennis King's music is so faithfully pastiche, it effortlessly accommodates actual numbers from the period, and Michael Annals's prefabricated set is the essence of dinkiness; utterly economical and stylistically flawless.

On the surface, Mander and Mitchenson are a couple of retired actors, who share a house full of old programmes and photographs and dip into these every so often to produce a coffee table book of theatre history. In fact, as far as the recent past goes, they are responsible for the very existence of that history. They have chronicled careers, productions, and the life-stories of theatres with a catholicity eschewed by more academic historians. Dame Sybil called them 'the actor's passport to posterity'. The Boys add, 'Trust old Syb to sum it up', before rattling off a story of how, opening an exhibition in Birmingham, Dame Sybil was waving her arms about so excitedly that she knocked her own hat off.

If the sweep of their work has been broad, their thoroughness is nothing short of lustful. And so by telling the story of, say, musical comedy with the same scholarship as they apply to that of *Hamlet*, they help create in the profession's corporate mind a sense of substance when it is all too easy to feel ephemeral. Actors and actresses talk so obsessively about who did what in which show when, as a way of contacting their own history, almost to make sure it is still there when all the external pressure suggest theatre doesn't quite have an existence in the real world. Raymond and Joe legitimise this green-room activity. They have given walls to our memory bank, and then expanded it.

In *Lost Theatres of London*, brought out in an opulent second edition earlier this year, they detail and illustrate the stories of 23 theatres which have functioned in London during the past hundred years but since disappeared without trace. Uncovered, amongst others, are the crop of tiny club or 'subscription' theatres which staged exotic pieces between the wars in defiance of the Lord Chamberlain. You can read of the Knightsbridge Torch and the Grafton in Tottenham Court Road, or of Mr Peter Godfrey, whose interminable struggles to keep open the Gate Theatre ('the Gate to better things'), make a strengthening, sobering read for the present-day Fringeophile. This volume, one of 16 by Mander and Mitchenson, is the follow-up to *The Theatres Of London*, which did the same job on playhouses whose buildings survive. The programme of just about every theatre in the capital has reprinted its own entry from this earlier work: The Boys get everywhere. Their own books, and more than 600 by other authors towards which they've contributed the illustrations or research, are only the tip of the iceberg. In the Collection, The Boys keep constantly updated files on each of the West End theatres, that on Her Majesty's being three feet deep already. They have similar records on the careers of directors, musicians, actors, designers, and even impresarios, and these complement their own prodigious memories. When I arrived to interview them, the Players' Theatre had just phoned up for help with a gala night which was to be attended by Princess Anne. The theme was to be jubilees, and Raymond Mander had started composing the requested programme notes without looking up a thing. 'Sir Arthur Sullivan wrote a ballet for Queen Victoria's jubilee, and in it Queen Victoria was depicted at her coronation; it was more a scene than a *tableau vivant*. Depicting Queen Victoria on stage was banned for years, and everyone thinks the ban was first lifted in 1935 when the Duke of Windsor let them put on Houseman's *Victoria Regina*. But it wasn't, it was this thing of Sullivan's at the Alhambra of all

The Boys' Own Collection

Jim Hiley

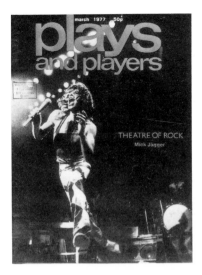

places. Well, she would lift the ban for her dear Sir Arthur, wouldn't she?'

Each room of their lanky old house, overlooking Sydenham's unsalubrious railway station, is furnished and cluttered by the Collection. But system governs its contents, not whim. They own shelves of rare theatre criticism, including one privately-published Agate, donated by the grand old man of letters himself with thanks for their putting him right on a little point. They keep prompt copies, and own a heavily-annotated edition of Shaw's *The Devil's Disciple* made by the author. When Jack Gold was directing a revival of the same play for the RSC last year, he spent a whole day at Sydenham poring over this particular gem. They have the original design drawings for *The Apple Cart,* and for *The Mousetrap*, and all of such material is made generously available to the profession. They have innumerable picture postcards and photographs, which they lend out to television programmes, films, and exhibitions, so that hardly any theatre occasion of note goes by without a contribution from The Boys of one kind or another. They have also been unofficial co-authors on several stars' autobiographies. 'Cathleen Nesbitt, when she was writing hers, used to ring up and ask "Who was with me in such and such a production?", and when we told her she'd say, "Was he really? Oh, I've got another chapter there!".'

Apart from royalties, their income derives from 'fivers and tenners' for the loan of material, and consultancy fees. They're the invaluable aides of many a television research team. When, for example, the guest of *This Is Your Life* is from the theatre, they'll dig into his or her past for any association with famous names who can then be invited to lend their glamour to the programme. They've contributed to 50 editions of *Looks Familiar,* and in the pop music history series *All You Need Is Love,* nearly every 'still' in the music hall edition comes from Mander and Mitchenson. Their only complaint about telly is that the BBC tend not to include their names in the end-of-programme credits, as if it would be advertising. For 12 months they were on the payroll of impresario Peter Saunders as he put together his ill-fated bio-musical on C. B. Cochran. 'He'd ring up every week with a list of queries. At first, the project was so secret he used a code-name, we weren't allowed to say "*Cockie*".' They explain all this, not exactly talking simultaneously, but each bursting in before the other's quite finished, as new facts are recalled. 'We christened Peter "The Mousetrap Man"; at first he thought it was silly, but ended up using it for the title of his life story. We can rib Peter a bit, not many people can.' The fact is, their personalities are irresistible. They are camp, always friendly, high-powered, polite, and the cascade of talk is so well worth keeping up with because they combine a professor's seriousness with the enthusiasm of a star-struck teenager. This has undoubtedly helped give them what they call their 'roving commission', their access to every state in the theatrical federation. They are a two-man grapevine, the confidants of managers, the friends of designers, the mollifiers of prima donnas. They *represent* the profession in a particular manifestation, and nowhere more so than in their friendship with the actress Judi Dench.

Shortly after her early success as Juliet at the Old Vic, Ms

Dench struck up an acquaintance with The Boys that has gone from strength to strength. 'We introduced her to theatre society; she had no idea, really, that the West End knew her. One first night we took her to – it was Tyrone Guthrie's Canadian company at Her Majesty's – she said, "Isn't that Emlyn Williams over there?", and all I had to do was go like this . . .' Joe Mitchenson crooks his little finger in a beckoning motion '. . . and Emlyn came over. Afterwards, she couldn't believe it, all he'd wanted to talk about was how good she was as Juliet. Later, when she was in *Cabaret* at the Palace, she had a dressing room with a window at street level, and told us she'd never get swell-headed because she could hear what the public were saying on their way home. Whenever she needed cheering up, we'd go and stand outside near the window, and chatter away, making favourable comments about her performance. We love Judi, she's the only one, now, who comes near to old Syb.' And when the memorial service for Noël Coward was held at St Martin-in-the-Fields, The Boys were the ushers outside the church. Really, there were no other candidates for the job. They'd been close friends of the Master, but in addition were the only ones who could guarantee to recognise, and be recognised by, all the fading stars.

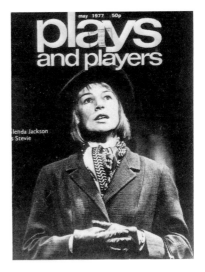

The only date about which they quarrel is the date of their first meeting, but eventually they settle for St Valentine's Day 1939, when both found themselves appearing in *The Merry Wives of Windsor* – at the Dockland Settlement Theatre, incredibly enough. By this time they'd enjoyed busy, if not startling, careers as actors. Joe and Alec Guinness each made their West End debuts in the same production of *Libel*, and Raymond was in Ivor Novello's *Henry V* at Drury Lane, playing a part Shakespeare didn't write. 'It was a pageant production, and everything had to balance out visually. The French court had a herald, Mountjoy, but the English court didn't. So they invented a herald for the English scenes, called the Duke of Norfolk, and that was my part.' Before Joe was called up, and again after he was invalided out, they produced their own shows, playing parts and painting the scenery, and touring everywhere, (including Berlin in 1945 with *Pygmalion* for ENSA). While Joe was conscripted, Raymond began to broadcast on theatre subjects. They'd each had collections before they met, and these continued to grow, so that after the war they were mounting theatre exhibitions as well as touring with shows. Then, in 1946, disaster struck their producing venture, though they tell it somewhat enigmatically: 'We lost our backing at Croydon' says Joe, and Raymond adds, 'Because we'd been used to employing ourselves as actors, nobody thought of employing us. We couldn't get jobs'.

More than 30 years ago, then, Raymond moved in with Joe, they gave up the profession proper, and the merged collection 'took over our lives'. People had already started sending contributions and they've never since had to ask for a thing. The relatives of deceased pros liked things to go to The Boys, and their friendship with producers has helped too. 'Binkie' Beaumont gave them all the front-of-house photographs by Angus McBean from H. M. Tennent's golden era and when Peter Saunders recently bought the Vaudeville, he discovered scrap-books containing every review of every show the theatre had housed. These

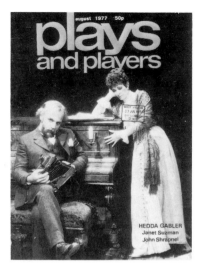

HEDDA GABLER
Janet Suzman
John Shrapnel

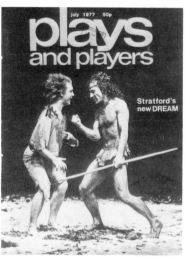

Stratford's new DREAM

were naturally sent down to Sydenham. Somebody else donated an escutcheon carried at David Garrick's funeral ('That was the year *School For Scandal* was first produced') and the complete outfit worn by Irving as Cardinal Wolsey. They won't accept personal mementoes, but made an exception when the Master died. Cramped up in a cupboard with Anna Neagle's Queen Victoria costume, are three of the famous Noël Coward dressing gowns. These aren't, they claim, as rare as you might think. 'Lots of actors got dressing gowns' said Raymond Mander. But there are two unique and deeply cherished gifts, which they always take with them on First Nights. Joe was left a silver match box, given to Coward by Gertie Miller ('then the Countess of Dudley'), and Raymond has a gold cigarette lighter that was a gift from Gertrude Lawrence on the first night of *Words and Music*. It is inscribed:

> Love to Noël from Gert, September 16th, 1932. Can't afford it, but I'm mad about the boy.

Cliché as it is, The Boys started writing almost by accident. Somebody they now prefer to forget enlisted their help on what was supposed to be a series comparing changes in the style of Shakespearean production. The collaborator dropped out at an early stage, taking the publisher with him, though not before The Boys had amassed a pile of material on *Hamlet*. They didn't want to waste their efforts and decided to plough on, finishing a book and finding a new publisher themselves. *Hamlet through the Ages* came out in 1952, and they returned to work on the Collection. They had been approached to do what should have been for them a routine job, to catalogue an exhibition of theatrical paintings. But the collection belonged to W. Somerset Maugham and contained remarkable works, some of which weren't even identified. 'It was the most fascinating job we've ever done, such a challenge, we spent over a year on it and then thought – "What we've come up with's too good for a catalogue, let's make it a book". We asked Willie Maugham, and he said he'd write a foreword to the book if we found a publisher. So we were a bit cheeky and went to Willie's own publishers. Within an afternoon, we'd signed a contract.' But the launching of *The Artist and the Theatre* in 1955 was hardly auspicious. It was overshadowed by an announcement that the National Theatre board had commissioned plans for a theatre, and this was anyway at the time of a newspaper strike so only *The Stage* and *The Tatler* covered the occasion. To make matters worse, Joe Mitchenson confides, a little hiatus occurred between them that was to rear its unhappy head in later years too. 'There was a famous picture in *The Tatler* of me and Raymond with his hand right in front of my face. I don't know why, he sometimes tries to do that. We were on television last year, and when they came to take the publicity stills I saw that hand of his coming up – but I was ready, I pushed it down again and kept my face in!'

Fortunately, the collaboration survived, and, having become friendly with Maugham, they were soon working on a 'theatrical companion' to his work. 'Maugham could be terrifying, though he was very nice to us. He invited us for lunch at the Dorchester and we had scrambled eggs before the roast beef! When the book was coming out, we gave him lunch at Gow's, that's near the London Coliseum, it's Flanagan's now. Well, Willie don't like women, except for Fay Compton, and we didn't intend to invite any. But we had to have the publisher along, and his wife insisted on coming. Willie didn't say much to her and she knew he wasn't happy she was there: Toward the end of the meal, Willie got a little choking fit, and this lady, hoping to make things easier, hurried to pour a glass of water. He lifted his chin, looked down his nose at her and said: "Water, madam? Wine!" and helped himself. Poor woman!' They also did companions to Shaw and Coward, and by the early '60s, with the publication of *Theatres of London*, their reputation as authors was made.

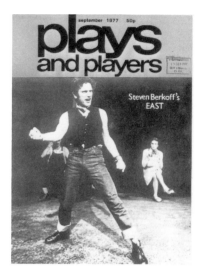

Their first love and greatest preoccupation, however, is the Collection. Until this year they've been caught up in a harassing web of legal politics over what is to happen to it when they die. It's typical of them that they should want to get all this clearly worked out, their simple ambition being to bequeath it to the nation. But as long as it officially comprised private belongings, the risk was that half the contents would have to be sold to meet death duties. Only this year have the Treasury and the Charity Commissioners agreed to regard the Collection as a work of art and said they can form a Trust which will ensure the Collection's kept intact. Judi Dench is one of the trustees. And only last month did the Borough of Lewisham announce that, there not having been room as originally hoped at the new National Theatre, the Collection would eventually be housed as the centrepiece of an arts centre being created in a mansion in a municipal park. This is one story of an institution that has a happy ending.

Having got posterity sorted out, their conversation remains peppered with references to the old plays they appeared in and saw, and of course each reference is given with details of cast, author, and who was in the film version. 'Jean Forbes Robertson was in a play called *Berkeley Square*, she was "associated" with it as they say, that means she did it three times. It had this idea of a man sitting on a hill, watching a river in the valley. One part of the river may be the past, another the present, another the future, but the man on the hill sees it all as one. We're like the man on the hill. Everything's theatre history to us, tonight is as much history as a long time ago. 'Of course, you regret giving up acting, but you don't make a fuss about it. We've seen·parts of the business we'd never have seen as actors, we're trusted. You know what it's like in the profession. There was a strangely obsessive play called *Thunder in the Air* by Robins Miller – that's with an "s" – where the dead son of this family appeared to different characters in the play. To each one he was totally different, there was no such thing as the son as he had been, he didn't exist, there was only how he was remembered by each of the different people, how he was talked about. We talk about people, we keep them alive. Once you're not talked about, that's when you're dead'.

The Mander Mitchenson Collection is scheduled to be transferred to Beckenham Palace in 1987.

Bedroom Farce at the Lyttelton

reviewed by Sandy Wilson

There can by now be few theatregoers who are unfamiliar with the plays of Alan Ayckbourn and, after the recent massive burst of publicity, with the way he produces them. But, just in case one needs to be reminded, the whole process is revealed once more in a chummy little interview which takes up most of the Lyttelton Theatre's programme: the announcement of this year's Ayckbourn to the faithful Scarborough fans who promptly troop to the box office and book every seat for the entire run, followed by a period of agonised suspense on the part of the cast and stage management, during which the maestro resists every effort to drag him towards his typewriter, and then, in the nick of time for rehearsals, a few fevered hours of creation, and, lo and behold, another opening, another show, and another transfer to the West End – but not of course for the Scarborough company, who can sit back and relax with Ibsen, Pinter and such until next year's Ayckbourn is announced and the whole process begins again.

Although it was commissioned by the National Theatre, *Bedroom Farce* was produced in the statutory manner and written, according to Mr Ayckbourn, 'during three or four sleepless nights a couple of years ago'. But clearly the actual writing of these plays is only a small part of the work that goes into them. Take the present one for example. It occurs in three bedrooms in three different houses ('Why three?' asks the incautious interviewer. 'I like threes. It's a comic number', replies Mr Ayckbourn. '. . . Besides I couldn't get more beds on the stage at Scarborough.' Nor, I imagine, on the stage at the Lyttelton, wide as it is) on 'one long Saturday night' and the ingenuity that keeps the eight characters bobbing around from bedroom to bedroom is prodigious, especially since, despite the title and although several couples get into bed, nobody has any sex.

The first bedroom – and to my mind the funniest – is occupied by an ageing pair, Delia and Ernest, who are celebrating their wedding anniversary, the second by Malcolm and Kate, who are giving a house-warming party, and the third by Nick and Jan, who are friends of Malcolm and Kate, Jan also being an old flame of Delia and Ernest's son, Trevor. It is the fourth couple, Trevor and his wife, Susannah, who cause all the fuss on this particular night and who end up, ambiguously, in Malcolm and Kate's bed. But a bare outline of the plot gives very little idea of the ludicrous and yet always quite credible predicaments into which Mr Ayckbourn manoeuvres this octet. Highlights for me were Nick (Michael Kitchen), who is confined to bed with a strained back, attempting to retrieve a book and ending up immobile on the floor. Malcolm (Derek Newark), a do-it-yourself enthusiast, constructing a 'surprise' piece of furniture for his wife at 3 a.m. and, best of all, Michael Gough and Joan Hickson, as Ernest and Delia, retiring to bed for pilchards on toast and a reading of *Tom Brown's Schooldays*. The cast is uniformly excellent, but these two – he the incarnation of a Thurber-esque downtrodden husband and she the sort of lady whose instinctive reaction to her daughter-in-law's desperate plea for help in her sex life is to offer her a cup of tea – show particular accomplishment. Peter Hall and Mr Ayckbourn himself have directed them all with an expert eye for timing and detail and Timothy O'Brien and Tazeena Firth's three wittily contrasted bedrooms, lit to a split second by Peter

Radmore, provide appropriate backgrounds to all the goings-on. The audience laughed and applauded throughout.

Why then do I find it impossible to say that I liked it? Because I didn't. I certainly laughed more at this than I did at the last play of Mr Ayckbourn's that I saw, *Absurd Person Singular*, at which I barely smiled. But sense of humour is a tricky thing and I don't think it has anything to do with my feelings of distaste for *Bedroom Farce*. And, to be sure, nothing distasteful happens on stage, even though I thought at one point that Mr Ayckbourn was about to land us in a Freudian situation, when Susannah (Maria Aitken), who has confessed to Lesbian urges in a previous scene, finds herself forced to share a bed with her mother-in-law – but she indulges in nothing more unnatural than several nightmares. No, I think the trouble is that to me Alan Ayckbourn, with all his gifts of timing, observation and construction, seems to lack one thing entirely: heart. 'You gotta have heart', sang the baseball players in *Damn Yankess*, and I find myself obliged to agree with them. I don't know where he finds his characters – in fact their geography and occupations are never indicated in this case – but, whether they are based on real people or spring from his imagination, of one thing I am certain: he dislikes them. I would even go so far as to say he despises them. With the possible exception of Jan (Polly Adams), the cast of *Bedroom Farce* are an unappetising bunch: second-rate, self-centred, inadequate creatures, victims of suburban standards and prejudices, and preys to trivial disquiets and dislocations. The farcical nature of their involvements is observed not with joy but with contempt, and I was aware that with a flick of Mr Ayckbourn's pen our laughter could all too easily have turned to disgust. In his interview he remarks that, whereas he writes his successul plays to make money, his less successful ones are written from a 'deep subconscious urge to change the world for the better'. It seems to me that a commission from the National Theatre must have given him an ideal opportunity to satisfy that urge. But he has failed to take advantage of it.

AUGUST

1977

Touched at the Royal Court

Paul Allen reviews the George Devine Award-winning play

The theatre, and the entertainment industry generally, has been inclined to regard the Second World War as a vehicle for the heroics of fighting men or a canvas for roseate memories of a Home Front which was all Vera Lynn, good old Winnie and we-all-pulled-together-in-those-days. Stephen Lowe, who shared this year's George Devine Award for *Touched*, may not have written the great war play but at least he has helped put paid to that dismal tradition.

Touched is set in a Nottingham suburb between VE Day and VJ Day and, put blandly, tells the story of three sisters coping with the prospects of peace after surviving six years of war, counterpointing the public triumph with the drained exhaustion of private life. Mr Lowe is, above all, interested in good old-fashioned dramatic ironies and paradoxes of which that is only the biggest. It is echoed in the story of the most interesting sister Sandra, who undergoes a form of hysterical pregnancy and then –

Stephen Lowe's *Touched* with Marjorie Yates as Sandra. 1977. (Photo: Gerry Murray)

when she is 'well again' – has such a bleak vision of the world that she kills herself. It is echoed again in the fate of her small son, never seen, who survived the bombs but was knocked down by a car in the blackout; again in the rigid morality of her stronger sister, Joan, who believes it is all right to sleep with the allies ('Keeps their morale up') but is enraged at the idea of what her husband may be doing with conquered Germans; yet again in the romantic dream of the younger sister, Betty, who has got engaged to a Pole who will take her to his big house, surrounded by water back home. 'There is no Poland,' says Sandra right at the end, and it is – to the audience's knowledge – almost a literal truth as well as a philosophical one.

But there is nothing veiled about the way Mr Lowe sets his scenes. We meet the sisters in the backyard of the adjacent terrace houses where two of them live. The backyard is faithfully re-created by designer William Dudley, who serves the play well throughout its shifts of time and place. Mr Lowe admits to having been born two years after the war ended, but he leaves us in no doubt from the first scene that this was what it felt like to be alive in Nottingham in 1945, waiting stolidly for the war to end. The mood is of relief, half-sceptical. Sandra celebrates with a packet of Weights, saved specially, but has to be persuaded by the more robust Joan to leave the washing: 'Bugger the washing, bugger the world'. It is never quite clear whether there is some form of private angst driving Sandra or whether the world in general is intensely dismaying. This is the serious fault which eventually flaws the play fatally, making it settle down into a downbeat case history. Mr Lowe is aware of the paradoxes and ironies, but if he has made a connection between the public and private worlds he doesn't pass them on. This is in spite of using recordings of Richard Dimbleby describing Belsen, whose horrors were then being discovered, and in spite of occasional political references which are in fact the unhappiest points of the play as written, pinpointing ironies but ones which Mr Lowe has grafted forcibly onto his theme. For instance, in an almost all-female society the only man we see much of is a young epileptic who is also, gratuitously if not impossibly, made mentally retarded. It seems heavy-handed to make him the street's principal Labour canvasser and give him the line: 'They say I'm just the sort of chap the Labour Party needs.' There is also a sort of comic revolutionary chef who appears in order to voice the Labour dream of 1945 and remind us again that the new Jerusalem has in fact been postponed.

As it happens, both these parts are excellently played by Mick Ford and Brian Glover. The whole of Richard Eyre's gritty production is well played and full of sustained integrity. But in these cases the acting underlines the awkwardness of the way Mr Lowe is using the characters, whereas in other cases they illuminate marvellously Mr Lowe's clear-eyed view. Marjorie Yates gives an outstanding performance as Sandra, summed up by a truly memorable scene in which she is briefly persuaded by the ever-practical Joan (Susan Tracy) to abort the phantom child. Faint, unsteady with the gin Joan has been forcing down her by the cupful, she strips off and steps into a tin bath with more scalding water than the regulations permitted, is converted to the idea of having the child by the romanticism of Betty (Kay Adshead) and steps out again, insisting on getting out into the sunlight. There is nothing coy about Miss Yates at this point, just simply dignity and truth and a kind of beauty transcending the fact that she is vulnerable and apparently ridiculous. It is at that point that Joan gives the play its title: both Sandra and Betty are 'touched' – but she is the one who, trying to be sensible, is 'painted black'.

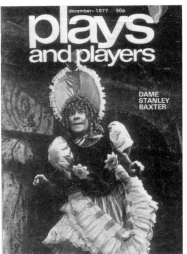

It is the high moment of the play, and if Mr Lowe lets the evening slip away from then on he has already given evidence of a firm theatrical grip of which we shall surely see more. There is clearly a real writer at work here whose vision goes beyond the mere naturalism to which, in the end, he seems to limit himself.

1977 Awards

voted for by the London Theatre Critics

Best new play: *The Old Country* by Alan Bennett

Best new musical: *Bubbling Brown Sugar*

Best performance by an actor: Alan Howard in *Wild Oats, Henry VI* and *Coriolanus*

Best performance by an actress: Alison Steadman in *Abigail's Party*

Best performance by an actor in a supporting role: Timothy West in *Hamlet*

Best performance by an actress in a supporting role: Mona Washbourne in *Stevie*

Most promising new performer: Ian McDiarmid at the Royal Shakespeare Company

Most promising new playwright: Mary O'Malley for *Once A Catholic*

Best production (director): William, Gaskill for *The Madras House* and Terry Hands for *Henry VI, Parts 1, 2 and 3*

Best production (designer): Hayden Griffin for *The Madras House*

Twenty-one London critics vote this year, playwright Ted Whitehead having succeeded Kenneth Hurren on *The Spectator* while Mr Hurren moved across to edit *What's On in London*. Runaway winners this year in the categories for Best Actor (Alan Howard registering seven votes for three mammoth performances), Best New Musical (although there were as many abstentions as votes cast for *Bubbling Brown Sugar*), Best Actress (six votes for Alison Steadman in *Abigail's Party* as well as a couple for her in the Newcomer category), Supporting Actress (six votes for Mona Washbourne in *Stevie*), and Most Promising Playwright (Mary O'Malley scoring six votes for *Once A Catholic*, now a fixture in the West End).

Our new playwright category is introduced for the first time this year and the former categories of

Best actor: Alan Howard with Norman Rodway in *Wild Oats* revived by the Royal Shakespeare Company. 1977.

Promising New Actor and Promising New Actress combined into the one. *The Old Country* had five supporters as Best New Play, closely followed by David Edgar's *Destiny* with four and Robert Bolt's *State of Revolution* with three. Behind Alan Howard, Michael Hordern received two votes for *The Ordeal of Gilbert Pinfold* at Manchester, as did Donald Sinden for *King Lear* and *Much Ado* with the RSC and David Schofield for *The Elephant Man* at Hampstead. *The Elephant Man's* opening marked the closing date for the period under review, initially set for 5 November but stretched to accommodate that opening on 7 November. As almost every critic observes, it has been a

rich year for new plays and most found it hard to avoid mentioning the prolific Barrie Keeffe, while Stephen Lowe (*Touched*), Pam Gems (*Dusa, Fish, Stas and Vi*), John Byrne (*Writer's Cramp)* and Bernard Pomerance (*The Elephant Man*) each received two nominations. There was no clear winner in either production category: William Gaskill and Terry Hands receive three votes each for *The Madras House* and *Henry VI* respectively; while the National made all the running in the design stakes, Hayden Griffin (with five votes) warding off challenges from Timony O'Brien and Tazeena Firth (four votes for *Vienna Woods*) and John Bury (three for *Volpone*).

Mona Washbourne 'best supporting actress' with Glenda Jackson in *Stevie* at the Vaudeville Theatre. 1977.

1978

*It was the year of the three Popes –
Paul VI, John Paul I and John
Paul II (the first non-Italian Pope
for nearly 500 years). Mrs Gandhi
began to make a remarkable
come-back in India where an Air
India jet exploded off Bombay
killing 213. In South Africa Prime
Minister Vorster resigned to be
succeeded by P. W. Botha. Carter,
Sadat and Begin were brought
together at Camp David.*

*In the UK Warwick Castle was
sold to Madame Tussauds for £1.5
million and President Ceausescu
of Romania made a short State
Visit. In the theatre Peter Brook
returned to the UK to direct
Glenda Jackson in* Antony and
Cleopatra *but it was Riverside
Studios under Peter Gill that most
excited the critics – particularly for
his* Cherry Orchard *production.
And although Tom Stoppard
offered* Night and Day *and David
Hare* Plenty *it was Tom Conti in
Brian Clark's* Whose Life is it
Anyway? *that got the general
public excited.*

Green Room

Clifford Williams's Diary of a West End director

January. Haven't been in Palmers Green for years. Stevie Smith's house, in Avondale Road, remains untouched. John Gunter takes photographs but resists the temptation to knock on the door. We already have photos of the interior, and anyway *Stevie* doesn't purport to be a documentary play. Rather an attempt to lift gently the veil on the secret life which lies behind the face of every unknown person we pass in the street. Stevie Smith moved obscurely from home to office, and office to home, and few could have given her a second glance. Even at home she wrestled with her *daemon* in upstairs privacy. Of course, one mustn't overstate the case. She wasn't like one of those French peasant ladies who are discovered in their eightieth year, living in the Dordorgne, surrounded by scores of their own *naif* paintings. Her *Novel on Yellow Paper* was published when she was 33 and was followed by a slow but steady output of further novels and poetry. She was recognised, if only by the cognoscenti, as an interesting but elusive writer. She could be found in the corner at cocktail parties. But finally the tiny bird-woman flew home thankfully to the blessed anonymity of Palmers Green. There she moved about her home, went shopping, cooked meals, looked after her aunt, and outwardly was no more remarkable than any other resident of Avondale Road. The play seems to be about these other residents just as much as about Stevie. It's a little hymn in praise of the creative spirit lurking in everyone.

> Here lies a poet who would not write
> His soul runs screaming through the night
> Oh give me paper, give me pen,
> And I will very soon begin.

February. Go to see Michael Holroyd who is half-way through a ten-year stint writing the official biography of Bernard Shaw. I hope to pick his brains and also get him to write something for the programme of *Man and Superman* which I'm to direct for the RSC at the newly-revived Malvern Festival. He tells me that he hasn't had time to prepare properly for our chat and then shoves a folder in front of me which seems to contain pretty well everything that Shaw could have written about the play. Particularly interesting are a series of letters which Shaw wrote to Harley Granville Barker, J. E. Vedrenne, William Archer and to actors and others concerned with early productions of the play. Very direct, practical and fairly acid! Holroyd has found a lot of unpublished Shavian miscellanea stashed away in American universities (I didn't realise how obligatory it was for these seats of learning to possess their quota of Shaviana, Joyceana, Yeatsiana and so on), but the piece which really took my fancy was a published letter which Shaw wrote to Charles Ricketts:

> William Morris used always to say that plays should be performed by four people in conventional costumes, the villain in a red cloak, the father in a bob-wig, *etc, etc, etc,* and I have always loved Harlequin, Columbine, Sganaralle, *etc,* in eighteenth century Italian Comedy and French Champêtre painting. If only we could get a few plays with invisible back-grounds and

lovely costumes like that in a suitable theatre, with fairy lights all round the proscenium, there would be no end to the delight of the thing . . .

PS Shall we do a pantomime for Christmas at the Savoy – a real pantomine?

Later, just after rehearsals started, seeing Shaw's prompt copy of *Man and Superman* confirms Shaw's directorial insistence on finding 'the music in the piece'. The margins are decorated with *p*'s and *ff*'s and *presto's*.

March. Carte Blanche is not going too well at the Phoenix Theatre. Ken Tynan and I spent over two years preparing a blockbuster, but it teeters along with all the force of Minnie Mouse on the rampage. The cast are gallant beyond the call of duty as we try cutting, rearranging, rewriting, role switching. Conferences nightly into the small hours as we face up to the fact that the show has simply not caught on. (They must be laughing down the road at *Oh! Calcutta!* but I don't have the courage to go and find out.) Our three-headed management (Michael White, Richard Pilbrow, Hillard Elkins) remains incredibly calm, patient, helpful and hopeful as we launch into a final gamble. As the Memo says – *As from Tuesday 8th March* Carte Blanche *will be comprised in one act only with an altered running order and content, as set out below.* As the curtain rises, our company manager hisses in my ear – 'Version 18!' As the curtain falls it seems to me that the show is not only more compact (inevitably) but it has also acquired a tighter, friskier rhythm. But its nature hasn't changed, and that is what will sooner or later kill us. The revue is possibly prettier, suaver, cooler, more sophisticated than *Oh! Calcutta!* but we have failed to embed within it a talking-point, a *scandale* which would make *tout Londres* sit up and take notice as moving frontal nudity had done seven years earlier. Now I wonder what that *scandale* could be?

April. A cruel month. Rupert Rhymes of the English National Opera and myself have been commuting to Newcastle-on-Tyne in order to conduct an enquiry on behalf of the Arts Council, Tyne and Wear and Northern Arts into the state of play, or rather the non-state of play, of the University Theatre. The UT has run into heavy financial weather, and its company has been disbanded. Our job is to advise whether a re-commencement is possible, and to comment generally on the provision of theatre in the area. Although we mean primarily to address ourselves to the future, and not to conduct a post-mortem, there is no way in which we can refrain from asking searching questions about the past. Everyone we question – theatre workers, councillors, union representatives, journalists, patrons – respond more in sorrow than in anger. There is praise and criticism for the policy and administration of the Tyneside Theatre Company, but no sugges-tion other than from a handful of politicians – that Newcastle should be permanently deprived of a repertory company. So far so good. But we need also to look at the broader implications of a general theatre policy which concerns itself with touring (dramatic and lyric), the future of the Sunderland Empire, the funding of

plays and players

march 1978   60p

INGRID BERGMAN
at the Haymarket

several community theatre groups, as well as the provision of a resident repertory company. Above all, since the crisis at the UT has expressed itself most clearly in financial terms, we feel we must suggest ways and means of ensuring sufficient funding and proper fiscal control in the future without inhibiting creative enterprise. The deeper Rupert and I go into the problems the more we feel we could spend the rest of our lives scurrying from office to office and interview to interview. A few more weeks and there'll probably be two men following us around. Shades of Kafka. The Arts Council are pressing, understandably, for an early report, for every month of closure is felt to aggravate the situation. On the other hand, Tyne and Wear, on the spot as it were, suggest we ought to try and see everyone who has anything to say on the subject. In any case, nothing can be done till after the local elections!

June. Alan Howard must leave *Wild Oats* for his Stratford commitment, and Lewis Fiander is to take over the role of Rover. Tim Wylton is off to Stratford as well, and some of the smaller parts are being changed, so a solid piece of re-rehearsal is necessary. With the best will in the world all concerned may find this an onerous business. The new incumbents will rightly not wish to rubber-stamp their predecessors' work. The old hands may find it difficult to rehearse during the day with the incoming group and play at night with the outgoing. The director finds himself working overtime trying to keep everyone inspirited and on the mark. Of course, it's pleasant to know that one is re-rehearsing because the production has been successful, but – if honest – I think everyone would admit it's a bit of a chore. All the same *Wild Oats* has been one of those plays which knits a group together in special joy. Unknown to begin with, tricky to rehearse, the outcome genuinely uncertain. After the first night back in December, Alan Howard, Norman Rodway, Joe Melia, myself and our respective wives had dinner together in unparalleled gloom. In vain did the wives try to comfort their spouses. Disaster was in the air and *we* knew it. Happily we were wrong. Heinemann published the play, and the only real blot on the proceedings was that the Notes which I compiled and which give the sources of the many quotes in the play, remain incomplete. I haven't been able to trace any of the following:

'Ay, to foreign climates my old trunk I bear'

'Himself in one prodigious ruin'

'I say my sister's wronged, my sister Blowsabella, born as high and noble as the attorney – do her justice, or by the gods, I'll lay a scene of blood, shall make this haymow horrible to Beedles'

'Only squint, and by heaven, I'll beat the blown body 'till it rebounds like a tennis ball'

'Sir, to return to the twenty pound'

'But by the care of standers by, prevented was'

'More music in the clink of her horse's hoofs than twenty hautboys'

'Oh, such a sight! talk of a coronation'

'I was thinking of a side-saddle'

'Why, you fancy yourself. Cardinal Wolsey in this family?'

'A bowl of cream for your Catholic Majesty'

'You get no water, take the wine, great Potentate'

'Go, go, thou shallow Pomona'

'Verily, I could smite that Amalekite till the going down of the sun'

'A Blow! – Essex, a blow!'

'Thou worm and maggot of the law'

Any offers?

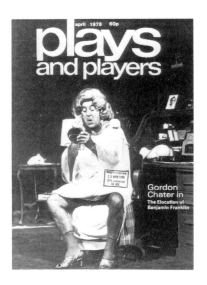

July. I've been working in the theatre for over 30 years but I can never get over the feeling of being a beginner. I fancy everyone else knows everyone else whereas I seem to know very few (*know* in the sense of *worked with*). Well, here goes with Bruce Bould, Faith Brook, Heather Canning, Alec Guinness and Rachel Kempson in Alan Bennett's *The Old Country*, produced by Michael Codron, John Phillips – I do know, from *Too True to be Good*. And John Gunter, the designer of *Stevie*. John G and I hanged about each other's necks in sheer terror at the first rehearsal. Sir Alec lifted one eyebrow ever so slightly and we sprang apart! I haven't really done much of what I suppose is known as West End work apart from *Sleuth* and musicals/revues. But now I'm in at the deep end. How the devil do I start? I can't begin by delivering a lecture about the play since everyone – bar me – seems clear on that score. (They aren't, of course, but that's what terror does for you!) Michael Codron is looking at me like a man covering up the deepest alarm with encouraging nonchalance. I glance at John Gunter in despair, and he promptly knocks over the model of the set. I hear myself faintly murmuring 'Well . . . let's have a . . . bit . . . of a read'. We have a bit of a read. Wonderment. Sir Alec totally – beautifully – brilliantly – embodies the core of the play. We all mutually and harmoniously agree certain areas which require a modicum of rewriting. Alan B staggers off looking cheery and sick as a dog, at one and the same time, to tackle the said modicum. John Gunter has managed to glue his model together again, and we gather round to confirm that it does look both like S-rrey and R-ssia. The stage management make tea, and Alec produces vodka and caviare. After refreshment I decide that I've had enough for one day and am pleased to find everyone agrees with me. We pull ourselves together, clear up and file out on to the pavement. The Thames glitters on our left. Chelsea makes noise on our right. The first day is over.

August. A quiet month except for the 16th when *The Old Country* had its first performance at Oxford and *Man and Superman*

opened simultaneously at the Savoy. I don't propose to say anything further about the 16th. The rest of the month passed by less dangerously in peering over Jeremy Brooks' shoulder as he beavered away at his translation of Ibsen's *Rosmersholm*. Every new production I do – especially when it's of the calibre of *Rosmersholm* – serves to remind me that history was never my strong suit. Off to the London Library for a crash course in nineteenth century Norwegian politics. Odd to realise that this play which signals Ibsen's retirement from the political world, and which prepares the way for his last great plays (moving like *The Tempest* into a metaphysical world), nevertheless employs as its mainspring the precise political climate prevailing in Norway in 1885. Ibsen assumed that his audiences would know about that intimately. But today, of course, they don't. How shall we deal with this? For once, a programme note seems essentially in order, but do theatre-goers read their programmes? Sharp division of opinion on this. I begin to assemble some material relevant to the play – not only on its political content but on its psychological precocity. Quotations from Michael Meyer's splendid biography, from Strindberg and Freud (a fascinating analysis of Rebecca West), from Ibsen's letters and from Halvdan Koht's *The Life of Ibsen*. In particular, I wanted to include in the programme a speech which Ibsen made to a workers' procession in Trondheim not long before he wrote *Rosmersholm*. In the event, we manage to include the Trondheim excerpt and a bit of the Freud.

September. An even quieter month. For the first time in years I spend the whole of a rehearsal period (*Rosmersholm*) actually working on stage. To begin with I think of it as a luxury, but second thoughts occur. Where on earth do I station myself? If I stay on stage with the actors then I can keep in touch, but it seems unnatural to be perched alongside a pros, and if I go anywhere else I find myself in danger of falling off the stage during unguarded moments. If I retire to the stalls I feel hopelessly cut off and obliged to charge up and down perpetually (much barking of the shins). I elect to sidle up and down between the front row and the stage which increases my acquaintance with the company's ankles if nothing else. Are there patrons who actually *choose* to sit in the front row? Amazing. They should be paid! Or at least, it would be sensible in most theatres to make the first couple of rows or so cheaper than further back. There are other snags to rehearsing in theatres. The midweek matinée chops unmercifully into one's time. All those good souls who have business about the theatre during the daytime cannot completely silence their vacuum cleaners and hammers and bottle-crates however hard they try. In the end, I think I prefer the shabby halls we are all used to. Some of them are perhaps a shade too dingy, and pretty cold in winter, but they're mostly quiet and one can concentrate.

October. Time to wonder whatever happened at Newcastle? Rupert Rhymes and my *Enquiry into theatre in Tyne and Wear* was circulated in June. Parts of it, critical of Northern Arts, were immediately 'leaked' in the Northern press. Northern Arts riposted: (a) They didn't like our *reporting* local dissatisfaction with aspects of their administration. (b) They found the *Enquiry* too brief. I suppose that longwindedness can be equated with thoroughness but, as far as Rupert Rhymes and myself were concerned, the need was for speed and direct speaking. I imagine the content of our *Enquiry* must be widely known in the North-East by now but not elsewhere. Basically, we recommended that a body should be formed with overall responsibility for professional theatre activity at the Theatre Royal, the University Theatre and at the Gulbenkian Studio, and that a repertory company should be re-established and enabled to produce both at the University Theatre and the Theatre Royal. We recommended that this body should maintain, through its officers, close liaison with, and offer positive help to, the area's community theatres. Our basic recommendations were reinforced by suggestions as to how they might be practically realised. We have no knowledge of what discussion went on, if any, between the three parties which commissioned the enquiry after they had received it. We do know that shortly afterwards Tyne and Wear withdrew its support from the Tyneside Theatre Trust (which was the governing body of the company operating the University Theatre) and the Trust was disbanded. The UT was occupied, and Equity have now formulated proposals for running it pro tem. It is pretty clear that here is a situation in which there are wheels within wheels. It is also clear that no enquirers would expect their recommendations to be accepted hook, line and sinker. But I cannot conceive of anything odder than engaging professional opinion and then running smack against it. Or is such procedure common?

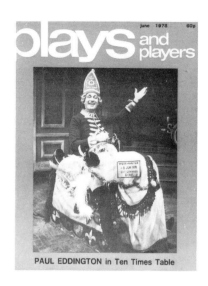

PAUL EDDINGTON in Ten Times Table

November. Some long faces to be seen about the West End. Audiences have fallen in the past week or so. Is this because of the cold weather, the power cuts and the usual pre-Christmas doldrums? Aggravated by the tourist migration? London theatres this year have certainly benefited from the huge crowds of foreign visitors. More than once, standing in a theatre foyer or bar, and listening to the polyglot babble, I've wondered just what would happen to the metropolitan theatre (and some regional venues as well) if tourists were to withdraw their patronage. Catastrophic? I can only speculate for I don't have any figures on how audiences across the board break down in terms of nationality. Has anyone researched this recently? For that matter, has the question of *who* goes to the theatre in London been examined in any scienfitic fashion? I know of several repertory theatres, at home and abroad, which have analysed their audiences according to age, sex, occupation, income, regularity of attendance, etc. But has any exhaustive statistical survey been carried out in London? I've never heard of one. Surely it would be invaluable to have some factual information instead of the ragbag of received notions we exist on.

   Who? leads to *Why?* or, more importantly, *Why not?* It is clear that, for a variety of reasons, many people avoid the theatre like the plague. They may find it too expensive, or too snobbish, or too inaccessible, or too frivolous, or too serious, or they may simply prefer doing something else. Equally clearly, if you work in the theatre you can't help wanting to convert people to it. When the Tory MP Norman St John-Stevas says that 'the market for culture in Britain may well be as low as 3 per cent' we want to change that figure. We want to capture new, fresh, wider audiences, and we don't want anything to stand in the way. We may – or we may not – want to put a bomb under the contemporary theatre scene, and start all over again, but whether we do or do not, wherever our theatre work takes us, whatever we do in the theatre, whatever type of theatre we believe in, whichever way we believe the theatre should be structured in our society, we are united by a common belief in the pertinence of theatre to life. Jean-Paul Sartre said that when we choose for ourselves, we choose for everyone. When we commit ourselves to the theatre we are committing humanity as a whole to the theatre. A little grandiloquent? I don't think so. But the ways and means of developing that commitment need to be explored unceasingly and, to return to my earlier point, a few facts and a little less speculation would be helpful.

MAY
1978

Whose Life is it Anyway? at the Mermaid

reviewed by
W Stephen Gilbert

I recall being told some years ago of a man, a professor in fact, who was stopped in his car by the police late at night. The professor was sober and driving perfectly correctly. He wound down his window for one of the cops to stick a slab of face through. 'Where of yew bin?' demanded the cop. The professor regarded him steadily. 'I beg your pardon, constable,' he said. 'Where of yew bin?' insisted the cop. Again the prof rejoined, 'I beg your pardon, constable'. The cop had a ponder and then began again. 'Excuse me, sir.' 'Ah, that's better,' said the prof. 'Now what can I do for you?' The point of the story is, of course, not (or not entirely) that cops are thick-headed, oppressive yobs; rather that this particular specimen didn't perceive that, according to the way of the world, different orders of humans require different approaches.

It was Brian Clark's play at the Mermaid that reminded me of the anecdote. It's his first major stage play just as, back in 1972, it was his first major TV play, a fact not disclosed in the Mermaid programme. Interestingly, the play has been received with wild delight by the theatre critics, some of whom have expressed pleasure that an 'issue' should be dealt with in the contemporary theatre much as it might be on TV. The TV version, though praised, caused half the fuss.

I think the fuss is misplaced for the reasons implied in the anecdote. The play treats of one Ken Harrison, paralysed from the neck down in a road accident. He wants to be discharged from the hospital, whereupon he will certainly die in a few days. The medicos, represented by Dr Emerson, the senior consultant, oppose his wish and the law is called in to arbitrate.

Broadly, the revival is timely, questions of euthanasia, 'brain death', individual rights and so on exercise the press a good deal just now and the play suggests a link with those questions. What the play doesn't do, however, is pose a dilemma. As written and played, there is no question where audience sympathies are expected to be placed. Around the question of the title is a piece of pure 'General Hospital' – coy gropings between a trainee nurse and a chirpy orderly; brisk efficiency on the part of matron. But the centre of the play is 'General Hospital' too, an issue made nice, clear, bright and no contest.

For Ken Harrison is a classic West End hero. He's a sculptor, for God's sake – so he's artistic, independent, sensitive, denied the use of his hands. And he's a know-all, he has all the lines, all the anticipation and the gumption (though of course it's a disguise for the horror) to joke about his plight. No one else can match him. The play reminds me of nothing so much as a good-hearted *Otherwise Engaged*.

Which is a pity. Clark is a serious, diligent writer, a self-effacing reporter and researcher of people faced with the vagaries of authority and bureaucracy. He could easily have made the central character an oik; then the play would have been the richer, much as the anecdote about the cop would be the more resonant for a confrontation with an oik rather than a supremely self-confident professor. As it is, the play is knocking on the West End transfer door precisely because it's a portrait of an archetypal wit triumphant over gadflies.

It's fair to wonder, then, how fair the play is to the medical profession. A week or two before seeing the play, I had occasion to visit a kidney unit where patients go through a long and demanding routine on the kidney machines so that they may stay alive. Missing the twice-weekly stint on the machine is effective suicide for the body soon silts up with poison. Some patients elect to do away with themselves; others are too old or too incompetent to avail themselves of the sophisticated treatment. I talked to the consultant in charge of the unit. For him death was a fact of life. Not every patient could be readily accommodated. Some, then, would die. Such was the price of disease, of the complexity and expense of the treatment.

Clark's consultant, on the other hand, behaves as if death is something the hospital has never encountered before. The saving of Ken Harrison's heavily circumscribed life is the only course he can countenance. He has little to offer on the subject – merely that Harrison's wish to die is symptomatic of passing depression. The rest of his staff is itself paralysed by the resultant bottleneck and attempts to jolly the patient along while he sets the legal option in motion. Clark's surest touch is, interestingly, with Harrison's attempts to exorcise his lingering sexual instincts, and he's much assisted by Jane Asher's sharp performance as the doctor who copes with Harrison's wanly witty banter.

Tom Conti, for a mercy, is compelled to act merely with eyes, head and a curious nasal, occasionally Scottish, whine. We are spared the hands through the hair, the shrugs and double-takes, the gamut of expansive gestures. We still get the full frontal assault of calculated charm, however. I don't find him capable of delivering a witticism and didn't laugh (I smiled at Trevor Thomas's lithe casualness as the orderly). Indeed, were I the consultant, the question about his survival would have been different: I should have throttled him before the interval. Ian McShane took the part for Granada in 1972 and, if memory serves, played it rather more crossly and consequently to more ambiguous effect.

Michael Lindsay-Hogg, a highly gifted director of studio tele-drama, is imported to realise this production, perhaps in view of

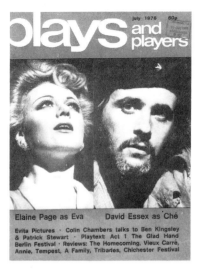

Elaine Page as Eva   David Essex as Ché

Evita Pictures · Colin Chambers talks to Ben Kingsley & Patrick Stewart · Playtext: Act 1 The Glad Hand Berlin Festival · Reviews: The Homecoming, Vieux Carré, Annie, Tempest, A Family, Tribades, Chichester Festival

Julia Foster and Susannah York in
THE SINGULAR LIFE OF ALBERT NOBBS

Dorothy Tutin talks to Gordon Gow · Michael Bogdanov: Young Vic · William Raidy: New York · Bergen Festival · Reviews

his totally successful work on Trevor Griffiths's teleplay *Through the Night* which is the precise complement of Clark's play and therefore will never play the West End. But there's something visually cumbersome about this production, caused most by the necessity for much walking around to preserve the illusion of a multi-storey hospital. Conti's room gets far too crowded for comfort, merely for the sake of keeping to wall-lines on the stage floor.

1978

Green Room

Edward Bond on Us, Our Drama and the National Theatre

It's said that the National Theatre was finally built when we no longer needed one. Over the last few decades there has been a theatrical revolution. Most of its important battles were waged at the Royal Court and on the fringe. Now there is a new theatre: light, mobile, adaptable. There are many young, very talented writers, a new way of acting is being developed and new audiences are being sought. All this means that the grey mammoth by the Thames is not merely irrelevant but dangerous: it soaks away money needed by the real new theatres and the theatrical companies.

I disagree. Our new theatre is not a theatre of experiment, it's a theatre of application. The techniques of theatre have been experimented with for a hundred years and now we can understand our craft better. What we have to do is apply that craft to interpreting and understanding our age and our society. That's why although the NT won't replace the new theatre it can assist it and be part of it. It has resources of space, time, skill and technology that we can use to strengthen our work and relate it more closely to our age. We use advanced technology to travel to our jobs and to bake our bread, and there must also be times when we use it to create those images of ourselves which are essential to culture and human nature. The stone age artist used the advanced technology of his time, and we must use ours. We must not merely occupy the fringe but the centre.

This won't happen unless the NT uses new writers more than it has done so far. It can't even produce the classics well unless it does this. Our age, like every age, needs to reinterpret the past as part of learning to understand itself, so that we can know what we are and what we should do. But we can only do this by, at the same time, confronting the problems of the present – and this is precisely what the new, younger writers are doing. There are no acting or directorial solutions to the problems of doing the classics. A more radical reinterpretation is needed, a reassessment of our intellectual and moral understanding. Actors and directors can only discover this reassessment by working on contemporary plays. And unless the NT produces these contemporary plays it will be parasitic on the new theatre – or a museum of the present.

Whether we like it or not we live in times of great change. New technology has destroyed the structure not only of our society but also of our subjective selves. So we had better learn how to rationally guide this change. Many new dramatists are helping to do this by writing new kinds of plays. The bourgeois theatre set most of its scenes in small domestic rooms, with an occasional picnic or a visit to the law courts. It thought it understood the world and believed that nothing in it needed to be changed very much. Things merely needed to be adjusted from time to time with the right word of advice, the right letter or the right sympathy. But we need to set our scenes in public places, where history is formed, classes clash and whole societies move. Otherwise we're not writing about the events that most affect us and shape our future. The Olivier stage is ideally suited to this sort of theatre. It's like a public square or the meeting of several roads or a playing field or a factory floor or a place of assembly and debate. And one truth leads to another. This open space demands a new sort of acting. At the first run-through of *The Woman* at the NT I was astonished at the way the acting forced the play into the ground, buried it in irrelevant subjectivity. Much of the acting still belonged to the nineteenth century. The company were acting emotions, hugging feelings to themselves, gazing at themselves, speaking to themselves even when they shouted. They were private performers on a public stage, still part of the bourgeois theatre. How damaging it can be to an actor to spend years trying to pump emotions into the classics, years of reducing acting to funny voices and freak gestures.

You cannot act an emotion, you can only act an idea. You *reproduce* an emotion. But this isn't the heightened action that is the basis of acting. A murderer's fear must be more heightened, more emotional, than an actor's copy of it. How could this 'copying' reveal anything or tell the 'truth' art is said to be about? An emotion reproduces itself and changes nothing. This is the decadence method acting has been reduced to. Its weakness often passes unnoticed because it's usually seen close to, where it can overwhelm with its primitive force. In the Olivier it's seen for what it is: not just right acting in the wrong place, but a lie. A lie because it cannot tell a story. Telling a story is an essential part of epic theatre – the theatre of change, the only theatre that can analyse and explain our condition.

Chekhov's characters watch history from the windows of their decaying mansions or the shadows of their dying trees. Life passes by and their only reality is their emotions. There are no pauses in Shakespeare but Chekhov is full of pauses – indeed each play is a pause. Chekhov knew this and that's why he wanted his plays produced as if they hadn't been written by Chekhov. His plays have no beginning and no ending, all they have is a middle. But we have to do that highly subversive thing: tell a story with a beginning, a middle and an end. Our theatre is still largely the theatre of Coward and Rattigan, and so it doesn't yet always know how to deal with this. But unless a story has a beginning, a middle and an end its events can't be fully understood and it can't lead to an action that results in change. Telling such a story, describing history, needs a new sort of acting. Put roughly and briefly, it's this. A concept, an interpretation (of the situation, not the character) must be applied to an emotion, and it is this concept or interpretation or idea that is acted. This relates the character to the social event so that he becomes its story teller. When this is done emotions are transferred to the surface. Instead of being hidden in the heart or the gut (or other corners of the bourgeois

september 1978 60p

plays and players

Derek Jacobi and Eileen Atkins in
THE LADY'S NOT FOR BURNING

Jack Shepherd talks to Ned Chaillet · Festivals: Stratford and Hamburg · Playtext: Michael Hastings' Gloo Joo Act 1 · Picture Reviews: Boo Hoo, Man of Destiny/Dark Lady of the Sonnets, A & R

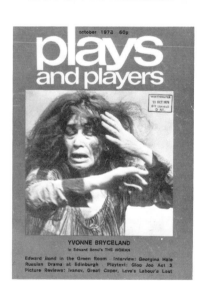

october 1978 60p

plays and players

YVONNE BRYCELAND
in Edward Bond's THE WOMAN

Edward Bond in the Green Room · Interview: Georgina Hale
Russian Drama at Edinburgh · Playtext: Gloo Joo Act 2
Picture Reviews: Ivanov, Great Caper, Love's Labour's Lost

november 1978 60p

plays
and players

DINSDALE LANDEN and POLLY ADAMS
in THE PHILANDERER

David Mercer in interview . Orton on theatre . Edinburgh Festival
Belgrade Festival . Playtext: Werewolves Part 1 . Reviews: The
Changeling, Inadmissible Evidence, Gloo Joo, Celestina, Mary Barnes

december 1978 60p

plays
and players

Alan Howard and Glenda Jackson in
ANTONY AND CLEOPATRA

Vanessa Redgrave and Michael Elliott interviewed . Dublin Festival
Playtext: Werewolves Part 2 . Reviews: The Lady From The Sea
Threepenny Opera . The Merchant . The Double Dealer

soul) they go to the hands, feet, face, head, and become living, creative energy. Then the actor is freed to interpret the situation. For example, he should think of his voice as a commentary on an action; or of his actions as movements in a silent film on which he dubs his voice. All that he does on the stage is disciplined by one end: the elucidation of the truth of the story. To do this properly his various skills must not become trammelled up together as if he were an unconscious automaton propelled by a self-sufficient mechanism. He must freely choose how to deploy each skill.

Usually only part of the Olivier stage is used. A smaller stage is used. A smaller stage is built on to it so that the rest of the stage is hidden and wasted. This symbolizes the way we often lazily waste our chances to create a new theatre. I used the whole stage not because I was sure how to use it, but because it was important that the company and I faced the challenge, and took the opportunity, of using it. It's a stage that can help us to create the new sort of acting we need to demonstrate our world to audiences. It needs broad, unfidgety acting that moves from image to image, each image graphically analysing the story. When the audience's attention has been won in this way it's possible to do very small, subtle things. This combination of large and small, far and near, is a visual language of politics.

Sometimes I write plays with 80 or more characters, but I never write parts for small actors, for rent-a-crowd. My scenes describe situations not characters. The smallest element of a situation is obviously as important as the largest. You can think of one of my scenes as a sheet being held open by a group of actors round the edge. If one actor drops his part of the sheet the whole sheet sags. So a line, a gesture, a sound, a position is often vital, and if it's badly done the whole scene is wasted and becomes untrue. I need a group of players who can shape an event. Sometimes, of course, the group becomes a crowd, just as this happens in history. Then the actors are united by a common purpose and become a crowd. There is such a crowd in *The Woman* (Act 1, scene 12). A crowd of poor people forces some rich people to back up a flight of steps and then takes a statue from a temple. I tried to show their common purpose through their hands. First their hands are flat and extended, the hands of beggars; when they come closer to their enemies their hands become fists; when they carry out the statue their hands are weapons, claws and flails; and when they're united in one moment of choice (to give the statue to the Greeks) their hands swing in the direction of the harbour like the leaves of a tree turning in the wind. Critics said I hadn't 'differentiated' the crowd enough. They don't want the poor or oppressed to have a common purpose. It's nicer, safer, when they're picturesque individuals. In the second half of the play the group is used for a different purpose. An island is occupied by foreign troops. In rehearsals the actors discussed the ways in which they could react. Some wanted to resist, others to quietly comply because they saw their situation as hopeless. Of those who wanted to resist, some wanted guerrilla action and others wanted an open attack, because guerrilla action would provoke reprisals. All these reactions are recorded in performance. As the pressure mounts the reactions change and develop until at the end – at the moment they are

freed from their enemy – they move in one united movement to face the sea – and then back to face the audience. Here, conversely, critics said I hadn't controlled the crowd in the way a more experienced director would.

Interesting. Some critics don't like the crowd when it's united in a common purpose and complain that it's lost its picturesque individuality. But when the crowd is a group of reflecting individuals – showing that they can think – they want them to be passive spear carriers.

I ask: isn't a spear the last thing that should be carried passively?

Susan Fleetwood and Yvonne Bryceland in Edward Bond's *The Woman* at the National Theatre. 1978.

1978 Awards

voted for by the London Theatre Critics

Best new play: *Whose Life is it Anyway?* by Brian Clark

Best new Musical: *Annie*

Best performance by an actress: Diana Rigg in *Night and Day*

Best performance by an actor: Nicol Williamson in *Inadmissible Evidence*

Best performance by an actress in a supporting role: Dorothy Tutin in *The Double Dealer*

Best performance by an actor in a supporting role: Michael Bryant in *The Double Dealer*

Most promising new performer: David Threlfall in *Savage Amusement* and other work at the RSC

Most promising new playwright: Brian Clark for *Whose Life is it Anyway?* and Nigel Williams for *Class Enemy*

Best production (director): Harold Prince for *Evita*

Best production (designer): Tanya Moiseiwitsch for *The Double Dealer*

Summing up yet another year 'at the British theatre' the majority of the London critics (nineteen in all this time) agreed that the most exciting new venue was the Riverside Studios, staging both home-grown productions of exceptionally high quality as well as hosting controversial British and foreign companies. At the same time concern is expressed about the Open Space's, the Bush's and the Roundhouse's fading profiles. Some critics, while acknowledging valuable work by a great number of talented young dramatists point out the failure of some of our established writers (Pinter, Gray, Stoppard, Bond, Mercer) to satisfy the naturally high expectations.

Best New Musical, *Annie*, at the Victoria Palace Theatre. 1978.

Dorothy Tutin (right) 'best supporting actress' in the National Theatre's revival of *The Double Dealer*. 1978.

Harold Prince's 'best production' — *Evita* with Elaine Paige in the title role. 1978.

1978 is regarded by many as the year of one-man shows (Alec McCowen in *St Mark's Gospel*, Leonard Rossiter in *The Immortal Haydon*, Gordon Chater in *Benjamin Franklin*, James Earl Jones in *Robeson*, Dave Allen at the Vaudeville) and a year – although a generally flourishing one – with an unusually high rate of disasters, those most frequently referred to being *Dracula, Woman Pirates, The Rear Column, Kings and Clowns, The Travelling Music Show* and *Beyond the Rainbow*. However diverse their opinions in many fields, according to the results of our Awards, the critics seem to be remarkably united on three issues: in their choice of the Most Promising New Performer, The Best New Play and the National's production of *The Double Dealer*, which pocketed three awards.

David Threlfall (winner of the Most Promising Newcomer Award) will, we hope, not be intimidated by the enormous trust our critics have expressed in his talent. He won eight votes, followed by Elaine Paige and Jane Wymark with two each.

Whose Life is it Anyway? received an astonishing six votes in the Best New Play category, while other new plays like *The Glad Hand, Night and Day* and *Plenty* got two each only. Dorothy Tutin (Best Performance by an Actress in a Supporting Role) and Michael Bryant (Best Actor in a Supporting Role) received the awards for their remarkable achievement in *The Double Dealer*. This production also won the Best Design award for Tanya Moiseiwitsch (she first won this *P&P* Award for her *Misanthrope* at the National in 1973), closely pursued by David Mitchell (for *Annie*), who received only half a vote less. Dorothy Tutin with three votes was followed by Suzanne Bertish (*Three Sisters*) and Barbara Atkinson (*Molly*) with two each. Michael Bryant received as many as eight votes while Robert Stephens had four in the same category. Diana Rigg (for *Night and Day*) shaded out Jane Lapotaire (for *Piaf*) by one vote as Best Actress. Other likely candidates included Vanessa Redgrave and Kate Nelligan. (Miss Rigg shared our 1975 Award for Best Actress with Helen Mirren.)

Nicol Williamson's victory is slightly more realistic, with his five and a half votes against Tom Conti's (for *Whose Life?*) and Brian Cox's (for *The Changeling*) three (Mr Williamson was voted the Best Actor in *P&P's* 1973 Awards for his *Coriolanus*.) Although *Class Enemy* received no votes whatsoever in the Best New Play category, its author, Nigel Williams, shares the prize of Most Promising New Playwright with Brian Clark.

Surprisingly, it is not *Evita* but *Annie* running off with the laurels as Best Musical, having nine votes as opposed to *Evita's* seven with one abstention only. Still, Hal Prince won the Best Production (Director) Award with five votes. Peter Gill must be counted terribly unlucky not to win in this category since his two productions, *The Cherry Orchard* and *The Changeling,* taken together, polled half a vote more than the actual winner.

Pam Gems's *Piaf* with Jane Lapotaire as 'best actress' in the title role in the Royal Shakespeare Company production at the Warehouse. 1979.

1979

The Shah and his family having been forced out of Iran, Ayatollah Khomeini returned from exile in France to lead the Islamic revolution. Students invaded the US Embassy in Tehran to take 63 hostages. An IRA bomb killed Earl Mountbatten in Co. Sligo. Pope John Paul II visited Ireland, the USA and Turkey. Emperor Bokassa of the Central African Empire was overthrown and former President Bhutto of Pakistan was executed. Tripartite agreement on Rhodesia was at last reached. Suarez returned to power in Spain.

In Britain Mrs Thatcher became the first British woman Prime Minister. Airey Neave MP was killed when an IRA bomb exploded in the House of Commons car park. Jeremy Thorpe was acquitted of conspiracy to murder Norman Scott. Robert Runcie succeeded Norman Coggan as Archbishop of Canterbury. Anthony Blunt was revealed to have been the fourth man in the Burgess, MacLean, Philby spy ring. In the theatre although Ayckbourn's Joking Apart *and Dick Vosburgh's* A Day in Hollywood, a Night in the Ukraine *attracted some attention,* Shaffer's Amadeus *starring Paul Scofield in Peter Hall's production was to prove to be a blockbuster and fat dollar earner for the National.*

1979

Green Room

Ian McKellen is on the road with the Royal Shakespeare Company

Ever since the Middle Ages, when the earliest drama, growing out of the liturgy, left the Church to parade on carts outside, actors have been on the road. Four hundred years ago, when Shakespeare was a boy, professional actors were touring regularly through Stratford-upon-Avon. In the eighteenth and nineteenth centuries, the great actor-managers depended financially on frequent progress through the provinces (as the regions were then called). Henry Irving died on tour in Bradford. Many living actors, like myself, were first introduced to the theatre by the Old Vic or West End companies travelling the Number One circuit of Moss Empires and of Howard and Wyndham, en route from one London success to another.

In our time, the rise of first-class repertory theatre (where many actors learn their trade), competition from television (where most of them practise it) and the ever-increasing costs of travel, all these have discouraged touring at home and abroad. It just doesn't pay like it used to when Donald Wolfit was alive and barnstorming. Despite the recent innovation of touring allowances, living in digs and away from home for long spells, isn't always congenial.

And for a complex organisation like the Royal Shakespeare Company, firmly based in Stratford and London, travel is particularly unsettling. So the old pattern of touring has faded and the Number One circuit is up for auction. But the RSC, committed by its charter to our greatest playwright and subsidised by our taxes through the Arts Council of Great Britain, has national responsibilities. Indeed, for its own healthy development it needs constantly to reach new audiences. What, nowadays, are the best ways of touring?

Recently *Henry V* travelled the traditional route of weekly stays in large cities. A quicker and cheaper way of reaching the nation has been the televising or filming of stage successes. *The Wars of the Roses, Antony and Cleopatra, Hedda Gabler, The Comedy of Errors* played to millions more at a single viewing than ever they could in the theatre. So will *Macbeth*. These single plays don't however, convey the scope of the RSC's work. And so for the last two years the company has played a Spring season in Newcastle-upon-Tyne: four or five Shakespeares plus the contrasting small-scale productions from The Other Place, Stratford's tiny second theatre. These, augmented by visits to schools, by recitals and late-night shows, constitute a modern version of touring. The RSC has leased a northern home to match Stratford in the Midlands and the Aldwych Theatre in the South-West.

But from arts association officers and theatregoers outside these areas, there have been increasingly urgent requests not to be ignored. So, the RSC planning committee was asking itself in 1977, what about elsewhere in the country? And what about those who didn't miss the RSC because they didn't know it existed? A tour should be planned for them. In November 1977 I was asked to plan it, starting from scratch – scratch being Trevor Nunn's promise to direct a play and mine to act in it. My joy in playing Macbeth, and Face in *The Alchemist*, at The Other Place had convinced me that I wanted to continue examining the classics in intimate surroundings, hopefully shunning the rhetorical style encouraged by the size of the big theatre at Stratford. A tour that was small – on the scale and in style of The Other Place needing minimal scenery and props – ought to be portable and flexible, suited to visiting areas of Britain away from towns already served by repertory or touring theatres. John Napier agreed to design a wooden platform, roughly twenty feet square and four feet high, with a simple cloth backing.

All touring companies aim for the highest standards – hence the planned democracy of the Actors' Company and Prospect's hope for a stable home-base in London which can compensate leading actors for the rigours of touring. I was determined not to lead a 'B' company round the regions. We had to be accepted as the RSC itself. The entire staff were old hands from Stratford, recruited by Jean Moore, who left The Other Place to become our administrator. (She had previously worked for the RSC's Theatregoround – a touring company of shock troops abandoned eight years ago for lack of funds.) Half our actors, too, were RSC stalwarts. The productions were planned exclusively for the tour and will now never be seen in London, despite the enthusiasm of the national critics. Between July and October, *Twelfth Night* and *Three Sisters* augmented by an anthology entertainment about the English devised by Roger Rees, one of the company, these three played twenty-six towns in England and Scotland.

Negotiations to get to Northern Ireland where theatre is a maimed victim of the troubles, were frustrated by the shaky response from the Province to whom we seemed too expensive. Travelling fifteen actors and eight staff (not to mention four dogs) cannot be cheap, particularly when for the first time in my experience, they are not expected to subsidise themselves by receiving less than adequate living allowances. Money came mostly from the Arts Council's Touring Fund. Hallmark Cards, BP and some local firms (principally in the South-West) bought themselves prestige by their additional patronage.

Often, on tour it's difficult to tell which town you're in. Main streets, redeveloped into massive shopping centres, are these days, almost identical. Woolworths and Boots and John Colliers, Birmingham is Leeds is Manchester. But get away from the Number One circuit of the number one cities and Britain's local variety is revealed. The coal-black town hall at Dewsbury looks out over green moorland. The music pavilion's stage-door at Exmouth opens straight on to the seashore. The converted pub 'The Plough' is on the main street of rural Great Torrington that seems forever Ambridge. At Canterbury we shared the university campus with the Lambeth Conference and now know what the actress said to the bishop: 'I'm sorry, it's full; you should have booked earlier!' We played schools: comprehensives in Devon and Yorkshire and private ones at Blandford and at Horsham where we opened the tour. There the resident stage-crew were schoolboys. During the final technical rehearsal for *Twelfth Night*, the teenage stage director announced a dinner-break in the early evening which lasted all of twenty minutes. Work then resumed and carried on through the night. We often played two towns in a week – sometimes three when the group turned off the main route for a Sunday in Glastonbury, Rotherham or Great Yarmouth. So on this tour we could always tell where we were but not often remember where we'd come from! Split-weeks meant rushing too fast through the countryside although I'll never forget a blessed

Diana Rigg in Night and Day
BEST PERFORMANCE BY AN ACTRESS

Inside: London Theatre Critics' 1978 Awards

POLLY HEMINGWAY in A RESPECTABLE WEDDING
Colin Chambers talks to RSC director Bill Alexander . Part 2 of David Rudkin's Hippolytus . Reviews: Saratoga, Strife, Flashpoint, Action Man, The Millionairess, Hang of the Gaol

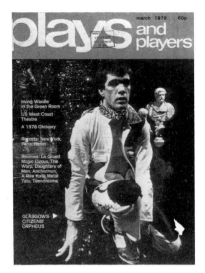

sunny Sunday in the Trossachs and a couple of afternoon strides along the Cornish coast.

Otherwise life concentrated on work and late-night Indian and Chinese restaurants. I did manage to catch the first half of the 11 a.m. 'Sooty Show' in Great Yarmouth when I was falsely and publicly accused of stealing Sweep's jam tarts. At Poole (the newest theatre complex) I was allowed to watch Leslie Crowther's closing spot from the wings of the large theatre adjacent to our own and with which we shared a bar and green-room.

In Edinburgh our matinée-laden fortnight at the Festival prevented our seeing anyone else's shows but we did meet the Malaya Bronnya Company, whom I'd seen rehearsing and playing in Moscow. On their last night here we found them drinking together in their digs, round a table littered with sardine and caviare tins. Perhaps they had too little sterling or too much exuberance to consider celebrating at the genteel Festival Club. Via the interpreter, we got our notes on *Three Sisters*, which they found a little old fashioned in its emphasis on naturalism. Their own *Cherry Orchard* explores the variety of Chekhov's styles – characters for instance, address the audience directly, all dressed in white on a composite set surrounded by white net curtains which gently billow in tune with the play's emotions. Following their example, I'd discovered that I could make sense of the sisters' brother, Andrei, by letting him soliloquise in a Shakespearean way and thereby share his deepening misery with the audience. Ironically, my Toby Belch was more appreciated as being 'truly Russian'. The Russians caricature English acting as restrained, understated and precise, and any flamboyance was a welcome surprise to them. Our evening ended with one staggering Muscovite accusing his best friend of pontificating like a 'Russian Lenin'; but, eventually, restrained by his embarrassed colleagues, his anger mellowed into lust as he crawled about the floor weeping 'I want a woman!' We pledged eternal friendship in the sentimental way actors do on these international situations and we left feeling a little less English and a little more prepared for our remaining Chekhov performances.

The worth of our tour can best be measured by the warmth of the welcome and the evident gratitude of our audiences and of our hosts, the local organisers. Let me give one example of how that response justified our hard work and headaches and replaced them with excitement.

Andrew Campbell, the deputy stage manager, had just bought a second-hand Fiat and on its maiden journey, I hitched a fifty-mile lift from Exmouth to Camborne, one of Cornwall's few industrial boroughs. At 6 a.m., Thursday 5 October, we drove through the dawn to within two miles of the Carn Brea Leisure Centre – a complex of swimming pools, cafés, squash courts, saunas and everything sportif. In a by-road, the engine failed. I breakfasted on blackberries and completed the journey in the stage carpenter's Dormobile, our lighting designer/operator asleep in the back. We'd always known that this would be a tricky date, technically. But the sports hall, where we would play for three nights; was still a shock at 8.55 a.m. It was enormous: one hundred and thirty feet square with unfaced brick walls and a glass roof too expansive to be blacked out for the next day's matinée. The Leisure Centre's staff (swimming instructors, masseurs) were not used to a 'get-in' which meant their unloading our pantechnicon and then building our stage on its trestled support and erecting lighting scaffolds at the four corners of our makeshift auditorium defined by local bleacher seating. These half-dozen Cornish lads, tracksuited as befitted their normal jobs, joked about the imminent arrival of free-and-easy actresses from London and were suspicious of having to accept directions from our female administrator. No blame: there is no professional theatre resident in Cornwall.

Demand for tickets had been overwhelming. Despite our prior agreement about an intimate auditorium, the spaciousness of the hall had deceived the box-office into accommodating every request for a ticket – Shakespeare was oversold by one hundred and fifty per performance. I spent much of the day checking each seat for sightlines and general comfort.

Always low on our priority list was backstage comforts. But the communal dressing-room, a badminton hall, was roomy and near the stage. The hall's echo wasn't impossible. In the afternoon I met the county drama organiser. John Trelease is a proud Cornishman overwhelmed at playing host to the RSC. He welcomed the actors at 5 p.m. unforgettably. 'Your visit is the theatre event of the decade – your audience will sit on the floor or stand for three hours – anything to be here.' In four shows we played to nearly one per cent of the entire population of Cornwall.

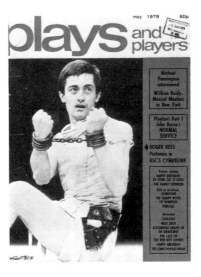

Next day we held a morning workshop for four hundred kids bused in from local schools for the daylight matinée of *Twelfth Night*. We showed them how actors learn to breathe properly and to relax. Edward Petherbridge led them all in a mass improvisation. We answered all questions and talked about the Elizabethan theatre where, like in Carn Brea, that afternoon, there was no scenery and no lighting. With the audience as well-lit as the actors during the show, there was a rare atmosphere of making-do and of sharing. Emphasis was thrown on to the words, as Shakespeare intended. Although protected by a roof, we were back with conditions akin to the Globe c.1600. Most of our audience were new to the play.

We contracted the auditorium for the two remaining Chekhov performances. Both these were watched throughout by two tracksuited crew. They had never seen a play before.

Of course many of our adult audiences regularly travel to first-rate theatre in Bristol, Exeter and London, even. But as elsewhere there was added appreciation in seeing our plays so close to home. Rather like a circus coming to town. Judged by my original hopes of a small-scale tour, Carn Brea and other massy non-theatres ought to have been a disappointment. But one was being reminded that professionalism and excellence are not dependent on ideal conditions and sophisticated technicalities, and that a play lives in so far as the actors and audience combine enthusiasm to appreciate it. In that sense, time and again our tour was triumphantly worthwhile. Personally it was constantly satisfying. It reaffirmed my belief that theatre people can best be welded into an association worth calling 'a company', if they are united by someone or something other than the plays themselves. Large theatre companies, on the inside, can feel too much like large business corporations. So the more they are divided into smaller groups, the more easily they may find a focal point for their identity. (Hence, perhaps, the recent reorganisation of the National's three theatres.) Our *raison d'être* was the constant reassurance that we were needed by the communities we played to. Their welcome grew from respect for the reputation of the RSC over the years. We trailed past glories of other people's work.

But I detected no unsophisticated acceptance of our shows. They were judged on their merits, yet always within the special context of a special event. Shakespeare and Chekhov alive in a sports hall on your doorstep. It seemed exciting to be there watching the plays. It was certainly gratifying to be acting in them.

Night and Day at the Phoenix

reviewed by Steve Grant

Tom Stoppard's latest stage work represents a marked shift of tone, style and subject matter. Apart from one crucial but small theatrical device it is the author's most authentically naturalistic piece: a well-made play on a topical subject (press freedom and press foibles) which has brought forth comparisons with Shaw and Rattigan and which throws up a considerable number of often contrasting and contradictory ideas not merely about our fourth estate, but about the very nature of 'freedom'. *Night and Day* is in some respects the logical outcome of much of the author's recent (and not so recent) output: *The Real Inspector Hound* and *Dirty Linen* contain uncomfortably accurate parodies of journalistic excesses; *Every Good Boy Deserves Favour* and his excellent TV play *Professional Foul* extend the ethical debate into the field of contemporary politics. Finally *Night and Day* is a less startling departure than was Hampton's *Savages* (a play which it resembles in several aspects) and yet it is the author's most perplexing and, in so many respects, least satisfying work.

Set in a mythical and recognisable African state called Kambawe, *Night and Day* focuses on two journalists and their brief, acrimonious and competitive relationship during a period of sub-civil war. Drawn together by the local political unrest, Jacob Milne (Peter Machin) and Dick Wagner (John Thaw) meet up at the smart neo-colonial residence of a British mining engineer and his intelligent, acerbic but bored-stiff wife. Though ostensibly working for the *Sunday Globe* Milne is a dashing young idealist whose refusal to join a strike on his local paper has led to his eventual resignation, and search for a promising foreign journalistic development. Wagner is more like the (un)-real thing: Australian; abrasive, ingratiating (when it suits); intoxicated (both with his job and his whisky); smugly witty ('Comment is free but facts are on expenses'); ruthless in pursuit of 'the facts'; and a 'solid' believer in the power of the NUJ.

Night and Day is an admirably elusive and antithetical piece: 'Wagner has engaged in a somewhat unbelievable night of sexual fun' ('I believe it's called debriefing') with the engineer's wife after a very chance meeting in London a week before. So too Mrs Carson (Diana Rigg) is deeply enamoured by the young 'scab' Milne, though her 'seduction' of the young pup at the onset of Act 2 is, I believe, conceived as a fantasy sequence and not as the *bona gropa*. Yet it is Mr Carson's telex machine and not his wife to which both men are drawn: a geographically unrepresentative instrument by which stories can be transmitted magically to London; by which Wagner can protest at Milne's non-membership of the NUJ and be wittily rebuked ('up-stick protest arsewards'), by which Wagner can learn that the so-important story on which he and Milne have reluctantly collaborated will not appear because of a protest strike; and (irony of many ironies) on which Wagner will send a communiqué to his London base following the death 'in action' of non-union member Milne. The play has three distinctly if uncertainly interlocking layers: (1) the Milne-Wagner debate on the press, which also concerns the once-hounded Mrs Carson who figured in a society-divorce shocker, and by Guthrie (William Marlowe), a McCullen-style photographer specialising in hot spots; (2) the 'romantic' involvement(s) of Mrs Carson and the private language of her debate with self, communicated to the audience by the means of anti-naturalistic asides, quotes and occasionally excruciating song clips ('Help, I need somebody . . .'); and (3) the internal politics of Kambawe, a third-world state ruled by an eminently sane, youthful, stealthy and Charter-house-educated tyrant called Nageeba (Olu Jacobs); I don't think he believes in unions either.

Though critics have talked at length about (1) and have taken the stance that one (including no doubt Mr Stoppard) would expect, very few have even bothered to examine the relation of the play's main thesis to its sub-structures. As a series of debates on free speech versus the closed shop, *Night and Day* is almost worthless without reference to (2) and (3). The Milne-Wagner debates are theatrically loaded (Milne finishes as the romantic hero – Wagner as the likeable but discredited slob) and, consider-ing Stoppard is seeking Shavian heights, riddled with polemical potholes. The play *feels* right: Stoppard was a journalist and has done much research during the play's composition. Yet it has a dramatic impetus which far exceeds, counteracts and finally overturns its credibility as polemical toing and froing. Milne, we are told, wouldn't join a strike on a local newspaper. The strike was about journalist-printer pay differentials. Milne then launches into an eloquent, witty and speciously credible onslaught on 'lego-set' journalism. Yet there is almost no information about the plight of local newspapers and local journalists whatsoever, and the glorified half-paragraph which accrues paints a distinctly unfamiliar picture. I have been a journalist long enough to know that the *Grimsby Evening Messengers* of this world are more often than not peopled by overworked, underpaid, and predominantly junior journalists working in semi-feudal conditions in what is one of the few profitable corners of the industry. It's a small point of presentation and detail. The play comes down distinctly and decidedly against the closed shop in journalism – and good luck to it – but the distribution of rhetorical weight is unequal and the conclusions which the audience are invited to draw are danger-ously specious. Why is the NPA more 'free', 'enlightened' or 'democratic' than the NUJ; if 'freedom' is neutral (the play's overriding thesis) isn't the NUJ free to choose to align itself to the Children of God if it so desires – as the *Sun* itself might have roared: 'Come Off It, Tom, You're Rumbled!'

Diana Rigg in Tom Stoppard's *Night and Day* at the Phoenix Theatre. 1979.

However this play is actually about *more* than press freedom – it is about freedom in general, and consequently has a more subtle and insidious effect than the debates on free speech, and the clever but run-of-the-mill parodies of journalese with which much of it is filled: (incidentally Hare, Brenton, Griffiths or Edgar could provide pastiches just as telling). The final emotional and ethical weight of the piece is carried by Diana Rigg's brilliantly characterised Ruth Carson: this really is a portrayal in a thousand, a mixture of isolation, grandeur, vulnerability and candour, laced with the wit with which all Stoppard characters seem almost cursed. It is Mrs Carson who speaks most eloquently about freedom and yet it is she who is least free of all the characters (even the glorified houseboy, Francis), enchained by marriage to a man whom she actually adores but does not love: by a self-style which denies her capabilities (capabilities which she makes admirably obvious); by life in a foreign country as the chattel and ornament of an anachronistic lifestyle; by an inability to indulge her sexual appetites without battering herself with rationalisations and doubts. Her disgusted reaction to Milne's death is a tour-de-force, both in the language and the delivery; a death not for truth or ideals or even facts but for the sports page, the crossword, the letters page – and for the macho-myth-mountain which represents and looms over much of our best (and that is the final irony) and most honourable journalism. Tom Stoppard the feminist? Maybe not, but this is by far the strongest and most potent part that he has yet written for a woman.

Night and Day has been rightly criticised for its stasis, but the final scene is another tour-de-force, a theatrical cliff-hanger in which Wagner gets a dream chance to meet the anti-Communist President Mageeba (who is most particular that he played Caliban and not Othello at Charterhouse). The aspect of third-world political strife has been unfairly underrated by most critics: it is to some extent the legacy of a colonial past reflected by the parochialism of our popular press and a chilling gloss to the comparatively academic debates on press 'freedom' familiar to post-colonial Britons. Mageeba's hilarious definition of a 'relatively free press' is a free press edited by one of his relatives. It's a fine joke followed up with a whack (literally). Milne the scab is killed; Wagner the 'solid' union man is clouted by the President. Minutes before, Wagner has been telling Mageeba that in the bad old days Northcliffe could sack a journalist for not wearing the right hat: on leaving, President Mageeba turns to the dishevelled and bloodied Wagner and says: 'I'm sorry if I was rude about your hat.' It's the same point that Brenton made in *Weapons of Happiness* – the difference being that Mageeba is a principled opponent of Communist jackals!

Peter Wood's direction is strong on the broad strokes and weak on details. Milne's much-vaunted exclusive interview with the rebel leader seems about four paragraphs long when he cuts it out of the paper; a radio picks up exactly where it left off five minutes before. The performances are largely splendid, particularly William Marlowe's denim-clad photo journalist Guthrie; Olu Jacobs's articulate and desperate Mageeba; Peter Machin's green but eager Milne and of course Ms Rigg's superb Ruth Carson. Unfortunately I cannot share in the overwhelming support for John Thaw as Wagner: he looks perfect with all the furred durability of the Fleet Street 'fireman', but his Sydney accent is bloody terrible – why didn't Stoppard make Wagner a Cockney for Thaw's benefit?

A perplexing, partial, exhaustive but unsatisfying evening which is still far better in quality than most things London's commercial theatre can offer, and which it would be silly to underestimate or to classify. Then again that may be Stoppard's problem: occasionally his talent is like some Jumbo jet coming in to land on the narrowest of fences. Recently he has been pilloried shockingly by the Left: for writing about European dissidents; for being 'trendy' *and* popular, for allowing his plays to tour South Africa; for sexism in *Dirty Linen*; for everything short of poisoning Chairman Mao. It seems finally to be getting to him and (in part) this latest work is probably the result: a pity. Tom Stoppard is well worth courting – any playwright whose final defence of a largely foul industry contains the remark that 'information is light' must be on the right track.

1979

Betrayal at the Lyttelton

reviewed by Martin Esslin

Is this a new Pinter? A Pinter free from ambiguities and dream-like uncertainties, elaborate speeches with oblique reference points, a wholly realistic Pinter? It might seem so. *Betrayal* tells a realistic story of adultery in London middle-class, intellectual circles: the world of publishing, literary agents, chic galleries and holidays in Venice, with the occasional foray to New York to pick up the promising first novel. It is all spelled out in convincing detail, down to the small flat taken under an assumed name in the back streets of Kilburn to consummate the affair during lunch-hours and early afternoons. There is only one unusual touch: the story is told backwards. It starts in 1977 with a meeting of the two adulterous lovers – Jerry, the literary agent, and Emma, the publisher's wife – two years after the end of the affair in a bleak pub; a meeting during which Emma informs her ex-lover that her marriage to Robert, the publisher and once upon a time Jerry's best friend, has finally broken up. And then we follow the whole affair into 1975 (the end of adultery), 1974, 1973, 1971 and finally in 1968, the scene when Jerry, drunk during a party, made his first pass at Emma. Would, as some members of the first-night audience asked themselves, the play work just as well told in the right chronological sequence from 1968 to 1977? The answer is: no. There is, it seems to me, much, much more in the play than meets the first casually observing glance. It is – like so many earlier Pinter – far more subtle than first impressions might suggest.

Above all, the story told in reverse order presents a new variation on one of Pinter's favourite motifs – the fallibility of memory. In other plays we are left to guess which version is correct. Here we are afterwards given the answer by actually seeing what happened. Thus the sting lies in the final scene, the beginning of the affair. Throughout the first eight scenes we might still have believed that it was the end of a great, tragic passion that we witnessed at the beginning. Here it is revealed that it arose almost casually, out of drunkenness, and, above all, that the husband who burst into the room just as it was happening not only remained blind to what was going on but actually encouraged the affair by taking the confession of his friend's affection for his wife as no more than politeness and withdrawing, leaving the two together.

It is also by seeing the story in reverse sequence that the theme of the play indicated by its title gradually emerges: who betrayed who? Is it Emma who now, more or less, confesses that she is having an affair with Casey, the writer whose agent Jerry, whose publisher Robert is? Or was it Emma and Jerry betraying Robert while they had their affair? Or was it Emma and Robert who betrayed Jerry by not letting on for two years that Emma had confessed her affair to her husband and was carrying it on with his connivance? Or was it Emma who had betrayed Jerry, her lover, when she became pregnant by her husband during a time when Jerry was in America on business? Or was it Jerry who betrayed Emma when, at the height of their affair, when she wanted them to divorce their respective spouses, he simply declared that he could not contemplate leaving his wife and two children?

So Pinter is in fact drawing a horrifying portrait of a society, a way of life based on an infinite number of mutual betrayals; or is

Harold Pinter's *Betrayal* with Michael Gambon and Penelope Wilton. 1979.

he, perhaps, saying that human life itself, of necessity consists of such a web of lies, deceptions and treasons? But it is not, as a number of reviewers have pointed out, all told in bland dialogue consisting of inane small-talk. Are not the characters left as mere surfaces so that we never penetrate into the world of their emotions, never are made to realise what they actually feel, actually see in each other, whether there is any special quality to their relationship? This is certainly true. But to me it seems the very point of the play, indeed its subtlest point: there is very little human emotion among these characters, least of all between the men and the woman. As Robert exclaims when Emma confesses her affair with his best friend, he probably liked Jerry better than her; and Jerry is more distressed about Robert having known about the affair than about anything that could have happened between him and Emma. But even this latent homosexuality – graphically expressed in the sexual connotation of playing squash together – remains purely physical male bonding. The human emotion between these characters, their relationship on a personal, intellectual, spiritual plane, is shown as totally arid, in fact, non-existent. That, to my mind, is the point the play is making. And it is by no means a trivial point. It is central to the sickness of our society.

189

So, in fact, this is a new Pinter and yet the old Pinter, the Pinter of oblique and indirect approach, the Pinter of hidden subtleties and deep layers of gradually emerging meaning. The play is beautifully written. Its only flaw seems to me a cliché Italian waiter in a restaurant scene, who is also very badly played by an actor with a fake funny Italian accent.

John Bury's set, centred around the screen which displays the all-important dates of the period of the proceedings, is a masterpiece of geometrical stylisation and also succeeds in narrowing the wide Lyttelton stage to the proper chamber-play dimensions. Peter Hall's direction is impeccable in its clarity and the elegance of his groupings. I was less happy with the casting: Michael Gambon is a splendid actor but he lacks the physical charm which alone would explain the motivation of the woman in the case, who is married to the infinitely more attractive Daniel Massey. If the point of the play, as I believe, is that these people's lives, lacking human values, have been reduced to the casual operation of mechanical physical impulses, then this seems a somewhat perverse bit of casting, however skilfully each of the two men plays his role. Penelope Wilton, on the other hand, is superbly well cast and gives a well-nigh perfect performance. We have all met this woman around NW1: bright, well-dressed, efficient in running her household and her art gallery; and yet strangely helpless, almost passive in the way she drifts into emotional or sexual adventure; intelligent, well-mannered and yet without passion, dried-up and immature; a victim of the men in her life, but perhaps not without reason, because at the core of her personality there is a void.

plays and **players**

november 1979   75p

John Dexter interviewed
Snoo Wilson on The People Show
Evita/Broadway
Bebes: William Raidy in New York

Playtext Part 1
Nigel Baldwin's MEN'S BEANO

GEORGINA HALE
LEE MONTAGUE in
LAST OF THE RED
HOT LOVERS

Reviews by
MARTIN ESSLIN
NED CHAILLET
COLIN CHAMBERS
JOHN COLDSTREAM
PETER STOTHARD
and others

Picture reviews
WHAT THE BUTLER SAW
AMADEUS AND SPREAD
RICHARD III
LAST OF THE RED HOT
LOVERS

Reviewed
AMADEUS
REED, HOLLY
THE ORCHESTRA ING
THE GUISE
SCREAST

NOVEMBER

1979

Amadeus at the Olivier

reviewed by Martin Esslin

Thematically Peter Shaffer's new play is bold and of profound interest: it deals with the mysteries of genius and of the creative process (as did *Equus*) and with the contrast between the overcivilised and the natural man (as did *The Royal Hunt of the Sun*), between sexual restraint and the free flow of self-expression through sex (as did *The Battle of Shrivings*). The historical anecdote around which it is built, the rumour that Mozart might have been murdered by a rival and fellow-composer, Antonio Salieri, has been treated before, by one of the greatest of all poets, Alexander Pushkin, in a brief verse-play *Mozart and Salieri* (1832). And in fact there are fairly striking parallels between Pushkin and Shaffer in the basic conception of Salieri's character as that of a man of modest talent, consumed by envy for one of the world's greatest natural geniuses. But where Pushkin's play is concise and explicit (his Salieri actually poisons Mozart), Shaffer's is complex and built on an epic scale. And here, I feel, lies its problem: neither the form nor the language of *Amadeus* is up to its tremendous subject-matter. To put a man like Mozart on the stage is, admittedly, the most daunting of all projects. How *can* genius be made manifest in the theatre? The writer of the play would have to be of equal genius to invent lines of convincing impact, otherwise the genius in question would become a mere lay-figure, a mere name being dropped. In the case of Mozart the difficulty is compounded a hundred-fold by the fact that in his letters Mozart reveals himself as an individual of earthy sexuality and scatological expressiveness. What a paradox: the most sublime spirituality issuing forth from a man who is capable of making endless jokes about shit and piss!

Peter Shaffer's *Amadeus* at the National with Paul Scofield as Salieri and Simon Callow as Mozart. 1979.

Here, I think, Shaffer made his big mistake: it is one thing to be scatological in letters to intimate relations (as Mozart was) another to make him use that kind of language in public, in polite society, at the very court of the Emperor. And this precisely is what Shaffer does: the result is a figure of grotesque inappropriateness, a veritable monstrosity, further enhanced by the acting of Simon Callow, who resembles nothing more than a buffoon, horse-faced and giggling, who seems to have escaped from one of the children's plays that one might still occasionally find around the country and which rely on characters like this one to provoke at least some mirth from the tiny tots. Mozart may have had a funny giggle, when amused, but he certainly would not have got away with the unnatural neighing sound which Simon Callow seems to have learned by rote and which issues forth from his throat mechanically and unmotivated, whenever the script indicates 'laughter'. The play is called *Amadeus* but with this Mozart certainly seems *Hamlet* without the Prince of Denmark.

On the other hand, Mozart is not really the main character of the play, which is seen from the point of view of Mozart's rival, Salieri, who tells his story in flashback, quick-changing from doddering elder into the dashing courtier of his prime and back again to salivating dotage. It is Salieri whose tragedy we see: the tragedy of the man of modest talent, musical enough to recognise (perhaps alone among his contemporaries) the true greatness of genius, but not talented enough himself to match it. Shaffer heightens this conflict still further by making Salieri, who had prayed to God for talent and fame, turn against the Deity for having let him down so badly. This Salieri cannot understand why the supreme music of all time should issue from a coarse and clumsy individual, rather than from someone polished and worldly-wise and virtuous as he himself feels he is. Having, Iago-like, determined to revenge himself on the God who betrayed him, Salieri devotes himself to the destruction of Mozart, not by the physical means of poison, but the psychological one of playing on his fears. Here Shaffer uses the old story (or chestnut) about the mysterious stranger who commissioned Mozart to write a requiem mass and whom Mozart came to regard as a messenger of his own death. In Shaffer's version of the story Salieri actually has his servant, mysteriously masked, convey the commission, and to haunt the dying Mozart by appearing before his window.

Paul Scofield has a whale of a part as Salieri and he pulls out all the stops in his vast register of voices and moods. It is a fine performance; yet the flatness of the language in which the part is written and the limitations of the potential of the character (who explicitly represents 'mediocrity' writ large) militate against its reaching the real heights of which Scofield is capable.

In fact, the only performances that I found wholly satisfying were Felicity Kendal's delightful Constanze (Mozart's wife): here the actress managed what would have made the Mozart of this play believable, namely the fusion of naïve earthiness with genuine charm; and Philip Locke's sallow, skeletal servant, Salieri's valet. Of the rest of the cast, the less said the better. In order to make the Viennese background familiar to an English audience, Shaffer uses the hoariest of devices, a chorus of two 'venticelli' (Italian for 'little winds', bearers of rumour and tittle-tattle) who speaks in unison or antiphonally in the manner of radio features in the infancy of the medium: 'Have you heard?' 'Have you heard?' and so on in that vein. They really ought to be cut out altogether.

And why is the Emperor Joseph II, the standard bearer of the Enlightenment, a gloomy intellectual, portrayed as a Restoration comedy fop by John Normington? And why are his courtiers (Basil Henson, Andrew Cruickshank and Nicholas Selby) reduced to pantomime grotesques? The set, by John Bury, is both beautiful and ingenious.

And, incidentally, a question to Peter Shaffer: What is a Chapel Master (the title Salieri sports)? If it is a translation of the German word Kapellmeister, let it be noted that while the word Kapelle *does* mean chapel, it also means orchestra – so that in fact a Viennese Kapellmeister, far from being a 'chapel master' is no more and no less than a bandmaster, the conductor of the orchestra.

1979 Awards

voted for by the London Theatre Critics

Best new play: *Amadeus* by Peter Shaffer

Best new comedy: *Joking Apart* by Alan Ayckbourn and *A Day in Hollywood, a Night in the Ukraine* by Dick Vosburgh

Best new musical: *Chicago* by Fosse, Kander and Ebb

Best performance by an actress: Jane Lapotaire in *Piaf*

Best performance by an actor: Warren Mitchell in *Death of a Salesman*

Best performance by an actress in a supporting role: Carmen du Sautoy in *Once in a Lifetime*

Richard Griffiths' 'best supporting actor' with Zoë Wanamaker in *Once in a Lifetime* in the Royal Shakespeare Company production at the Aldwych Theatre. 1979.

Best performance by an actor in a supporting role: Richard Griffiths in *Once in a Lifetime*

Most promising new actress: Lynsey Baxter in *The Lady from the Sea*

Most promising new actor: Alfred Molina in *Accidental Death of an Anarchist*

Most promising new playwright: Victoria Wood for *Talent*

Best production (director): Trevor Nunn for *Once in a Lifetime*

Best production (designer): William Dudley for *Undiscovered Country*

Our 1979 award honours were voted for by eighteen London theatre critics. Closing date for the period under review was set for 31 October but stretched to include the 2 November opening of *Amadeus* which anyway previewed within our period. In the twelve categories only one has produced an outstanding majority, that of Best Actor, Warren Mitchell for *Death of a Salesman* with ten votes. Other categories with easy winners are Best New Play, *Amadeus*, with seven and a half votes, and Best New Musical, *Chicago*, with eight votes. Our critics have voted five apiece for Best Production, director, Trevor Nunn for *Once in a Lifetime,* and designer, William Dudley, for *Undiscovered Country.* Our new category of Best New Comedy has produced some

interesting results as *Joking Apart* was also nominated as Best New Play and *A Day in Hollywood, A Night in the Ukraine* received for Best New Musical. However, in the final count they tie with three votes each. For the rest, lists of nominations were pretty diverse with thirteen actresses nominated for Best Actress in a Supporting Role and fourteen for Best Actress. Eleven actors were nominated for Best Actor in a Supporting Role and fourteen for Most Promising New Actor. Ten actresses were nominated for Most Promising New Actress and the fourteen writers nominated for Most Promising New Playwright includes work presented from fringe theatre to Shaftesbury Avenue. The 1979 awards represent a survey of quite considerable range.

William Dudley 'best designer' for the National Theatre revival of *Undiscovered Country*. 1979.

1980

It was the year that President Carter embargoed the export of US grain to the USSR in retaliation for the Russian invasion of Afghanistan. Carter's plans to rescue the American hostages in Iran miscarried humiliatingly and his brother was quizzed by a Senate sub-committee on his dealings with Libya. Queen Juliana of the Netherlands abdicated in favour of her eldest daughter Beatrix. The deposed Shah of Iran moved from Panama to Cairo where he died. President Bourguiba of Tunisia suffered a stroke and the Roman Catholic Archbishop Romero was shot dead whilst celebrating mass in El Salvador. President Tito of Yugoslavia died.

Following the suicide of its founder publisher Philip Dossë, Plays and Players *ceased publication with the June 1980 issue and did not reappear until October 1981 when it was relaunched with a new publisher.*

1980

Transformation

Ned Chaillet on the restoration of the Lyric, Hammersmith

It is the malaise of the times that there should be anything controversial about the rebuilding of the Lyric Theatre, Hammersmith. Before it was demolished in 1972 it had earned its place in London's theatrical history. As early as 1892, when the brothers John and Charles East began offering dramas and pantomimes in the theatre, it had made a city-wide reputation. Before it finally closed its doors in 1965, it had played host to the best players of the British stage, including Peggy Ashcroft, Alec Guinness, John Gielgud and Paul Scofield. It had even been the disastrous host to Harold Pinter's first full-length play, *The Birthday Party;* an event which would have kept the theatre alive however thorough the demolition of the building. But the demolition was not thorough. The elegant mouldings from the auditorium which Frank Matcham had designed in 1895 were preserved. Many Hammersmith residents had persevered in a fight to have the beautiful Victorian interior rebuilt as part of modern Hammersmith and their fight finally culminated in the reopening of the theatre, in a new building several storeys high, by Her Majesty Queen Elizabeth II on 18 October.

And there are objections, cogently put by such as Michael Billington, drama critic of The *Guardian*, and Sheila Hancock, an actress whose distinguished career includes work at the old Lyric. For Billington's part, there are two main objections: 'I seriously hope it works, my only doubt is this: all the successful new theatres built in Britain in the past 15 years have got away from the proscenium stage.' He lists an impressive number of stages, from Manchester's Royal Exchange to the Young Vic and the Olivier, and then considers the unsuccessful proscenium stages, among which he includes the National's Lyttelton. For that reason he finds it a 'touch perverse to reconstruct a Victorian theatre in Hammersmith in 1979'. And, while he finds it 'architecturally a marvellous piece of reconstruction', he feels that the presentation of architecture is not the best reason for building a theatre.

Fenella Fielding, who appeared at the old Lyric as a very young actress in Sandy Wilson's musical, *Valmouth*, found it hard to accept such arguments when I raised them. 'You might just as soon say that if you found an antique fragment in a tomb in Egypt, rather than preserve it or restore it you should turn it into something from Habitat.' Fielding will show her faith in the building's future by opening the theatre's thoroughly new and thoroughly modern studio theatre with a revival of the sell-out cabaret that she offered at a recent Edinburgh Festival. It is the old stage that holds the most charm for her, however; she first stood on the restored stage nearly a year before its royal opening, 'when they were still joining up old bits of plasterwork with the reproductions of it, and you could see the joins – marvellous'. Even then, 'climbing over bits of cement and through a modern foyer', the theatre felt 'absolutely right'. Unlike a large modern stage such as the Olivier, which she feels requires a lot of muscle from the performer, she admires the intimate feel of the Lyric. 'Also, there is that thing you get in those particular theatres, that group of theatres that are kind of theatres royal, where you've got your raked stage . . . and you've got the horseshoe circle, so that you are wrapped and they are wrapping you, and you can reach them and they can be reached. Which is nice all round.'

The intimacy between performer and spectator is a point that will come up again and again. Even the back row of the upper circle feels close to the stage, which in fact it is. There was a time when the theatre claimed to seat a thousand spectators, in 1888 when it was only licensed for marionettes, and an uncomfortable time it must have been. In the reconstruction there are 537 seats, comfortably spaced, without a bad sightline.

Michael Blakemore, who in 1980 will join David Giles as one of the two intermittently resident directors working with artistic administrator Bill Thomley, has spoken eloquently about the merits of the Lyric. One suspects that his great proscenium love was originally the Old Vic, where he was an associate director of the National Theatre with Laurence Olivier, but this enthusiasm for the form is infectious. 'I happen to respond to proscenium arch stagecraft,' he explains. 'I like the apparatus that a proscenium arch theatre has; I like the fact that you can fly with ease, you can have a revolve; I like the fact that audiences are seeing the events on the stage from the same point-of-view, largely. I like the possibilities for transformation and scenic surprises or for the absence of those things. And I like what it does for actors, the way it allows actors to organise their performances from a particular perspective. Some of the great actors, the great performances, Olivier particularly, you do think of within the frame of the Vic or the New Theatre stage.' He also feels that debates about auditoriums can be overstated: 'When people say come and see this building, it's absolutely marvellous, usually my heart sinks. Because it's a little bit like a cinema manager taking me into his cinema and asking me to admire this marvellous new screen he's had installed. "Look at it," he can say. "It's glistening white and it's got little holes in it and it does this with one of the pictures." And you say, "Yes, but what's going to be shown on it?" And in a sense the difficult thing, the paramount thing, in any theatrical work is to make something happen which is so interesting that it merits a lot of people gathered around, sitting on seats, looking at it for an hour and a half, two hours. That's the hard thing to do and that can happen anywhere.'

The Lyric, which altogether cost Hammersmith Council about £3.2 million, is not subsidised by the Arts Council and expects the bulk of its income to come from audiences. Like its multimedia neighbour, the Riverside Studios, it has come through the local council cutbacks relatively unscathed. That is unusually far-sighted of the council, but then Hammersmith serves an area roughly the population of Birmingham and amenities are important.

Despite the authenticity (*vis-à-vis* the original) the Lyric is a new theatre, rebuilt by the architect, Dereck Woolland, to capture the original charm, but fully modern in its stagecraft and, happily, air-conditioned.

1980

Rose at the Duke of York's

reviewed by Jeremy Kingston

After being dark for close on a year the Duke of York's has reopened stunningly refurbished, thanks to Peter Saunders and Capital Radio. [Peter Saunders had sold the Duke of York's to Capital Radio.] The notorious pillars have been removed from the auditorium, cream plasterwork is discreetly picked out in gold, and everywhere there is the gleam of dusky-pink paint and plush. This gives something of the sensation of sitting inside a smoked salmon. The play that marks the return of the Duke of York's to the world of the living theatre is a character study by Andrew Davies, originally called *Diary of a Desperate Woman* when produced at the Belgrade, Coventry. The new title will have more appeal but the first expresses the purpose and suggests the style of the play. Alan Dosser's direction places it on an empty stage painted purplish-black where items of furniture are brought on and removed by jeaned stage-management. Eight doors (four left, four right) allow the periodic appearance of reproachful figures. It is a style admirably fitted to the confessional type of play (cf. *Habeas Corpus, Forget-Me-Not Lane*).

Rose, the desperate woman (Glenda Jackson), is on stage throughout the 2¼-hour running time, addressing us or the unseen primary schoolchildren she teaches, or when present in scenes with other characters never with more than two at a time and generally only one: prim, huffy mother, monosyllabic husband, old college friend, current teaching colleagues, attractive school inspector. We do not learn much that is unexpected about these other characters, and on the two occasions that we do the disclosures are unconvincing. It did not strike me as probable that the mother (Jean Heywood) should let herself talk so intimately about her dead husband, nor that Rose's husband (David Daker) should abruptly reveal his undiminished love. The programme illustration of Rose drawn in detail against the grey silhouettes of the others is apt. Perhaps we do not finally learn much that is unexpected about Rose either but what we see of her is consistently interesting and appealing. Married to someone who has – manifestly, I should have thought – ceased to cherish her and won't rise to her attempts to communicate, she isn't a success in the staff room either. The headmistress (Stephanie Cole) is a battleaxe and the only other teacher we see (Gillian Martell) is soppy. Naturally, Rose's more lively classroom technique finds little approval there. Frustrated at home and frustrated at work, a brighter future seems to beckon when the young inspector (Tom Georgeson) appreciates both what she does and who she is. The scene at the school assembly ('A typical morning's opening,' Rose comments, 'Song, Story, Prayer and a Bollocking'), the two teaching scenes and the wineshop meeting with the inspector, Jim, are the best-written areas of the play. The author has endowed Rose with irony, a fondness for the direct statement and an adroit line in sexual badinage. All three burst forth while she sits nervously sipping her red wine, unable to let events take their own gradual course: the long, uninterrupted recital of how their affair is likely to get going is true and funny, and Miss Jackson impressively makes us see all this and at the same time presents herself as a bewitchingly attractive person. One can entirely understand Jim's fixed, fascinated gaze.

And why is she a desperate woman, precisely? She wants to be what she truly could be, it seems, and wants for herself and others the nerve to say so. People are frightened. In infants' story books the fluffy little animals who venture forth meet wild, alarming creatures and scamper back to the farm. 'That's not the world I see,' says Rose. 'All the wolves round here are on valium.' But

Andrew Davies's *Rose* with Glenda Jackson in the title role in the re-opened Duke of York's Theatre. 1980.

the character established by such trenchant comments is undermined by the story development. If she wants her husband's affection (and doesn't she?) and he wants hers, isn't that a happy ending? Well, evidently it isn't but the nature of Rose's desperation at the end has become unclear. The play is finally more a part than a play, an interesting part for an exceptional actress. But it is a play set in the truly here-and-now, where characters get thumped by the slings and punctured by the arrows of contemporary misfortune. On that score, too, it is to be welcomed.

Jonathan Pryce's most striking characteristics as an actor are not those of the traditional Hamlet. He naturally projects a hard-edged forcefulness and menace that have no place in the customary noble Prince who is paralysed by excessive thought. In approaching Hamlet, Pryce has not forsaken his modern virtues for more Romantic ones, but rather incorporates them into a character distinguished less by the depth of his thought and sensibility than by a formidable nervous energy. In the opening scene of Richard Eyre's production (the first scene on the battlements is cut), Pryce sits amid the court, tense and quiet, almost shy, clearly holding himself in check. But once left alone, the emotional energy begins to flow, and from that moment on the entire play is carried along by it. Only when Hamlet is sent to England in Act IV do the pace and tension slacken. The performance as a whole is bold and gripping, not subtle or tidy. Pryce concentrates on delineating Hamlet's different states of mind in vivid colours, rather than trying to wring every nuance of meaning from the play's poetry. He is by turns subdued, aggressive, witty, angry, exultant, bitter. Coolly vicious in one scene, he is tender or scared in the next. This Hamlet is not a coherent, compre-

MAY

1980

Hamlet at the Royal Court

reviewed by Colin Ludlow

199

hensible character with all the gaps and creases in his development carefully ironed out into a seamless whole. He is unpredictable and excessive. His prevailing characteristic is not melancholy but volatility.

The production adds a further facet to his shifting multiplicity by dispensing with the character of the Ghost. Instead of receiving the demand for revenge from his dead father, Hamlet pronounces it himself while in a state of apparent 'possession'. His body convulsed, eyes closed, head rocking back and forth, Pryce belches up the Ghost's words from the depths of his stomach in an agonising growl. It is a spectacular and mesmerising effect that completely overshadows the substance of the words themselves, but introduces a sense of mystery and power fully in tune with the animal vigour of the Prince. While other productions may have given a clearer insight into the mind of Hamlet himself, few, and certainly none I have seen, can have given a clearer insight into the meaning of Hamlet's behaviour to those around him. The most obvious example of this is in the closet scene where the absence of the Ghost means that when Hamlet suddenly breaks off from his dangerous and aggressive onslaught, goes into a spasm, starts talking to an empty space and growling in reply, he does indeed seem mad. The audience experiences the scene from Gertrude's point of view instead of, as usual, from Hamlet's.

Similarly in Act III Scene I, the uncertainty we feel about the reasons for Hamlet's behaviour brings us much nearer to Ophelia's position when Hamlet unloads his fury upon her. The perplexed and guilt-ridden sense of responsiblity that Harriet Walter manages to bring out in the short 'Oh, what a noble mind is here o'erthrown' soliloquy provides a fully understandable transition to Ophelia's subsequent madness, which for once seems a perfectly logical development instead of simply arriving like a bolt out of the blue. It is the strength of this production that the supporting cast make the most of these opportunities which Pryce's portrayal of Hamlet opens up for them. Jill Bennett is a tender and genuinely distressed Gertrude, Harriet Walter a sad Ophelia, and Simon Chandler a tamely conventional Laertes alongside such a protean Prince. As Claudius, Michael Elphick suggests a man genuinely weighed down by power who is at the same time ruthlessly determined to hold on to it. Such a potentially dangerous Hamlet as Pryce's certainly poses a threat to him, and Elphick conveys a wonderful sense of gnawing anxiety and unease as long as the Prince is around. He is at his best not in Claudius's big speeches, but in the business scenes about the court with Polonius and later with Laertes. Constantly looking over his shoulder, furtive and restless, sometimes weary, affectionate when Gertrude presents herself, occasionally revealing a hint of guilt, his Claudius is a splendidly various creation, giving a memorable insight into the corrosive nature of power and the obsessive insecurity that the struggle for it breeds.

A programme note emphasises that there is more to the play than the Prince, and it is appropriate therefore that the sharpest impression the production makes should apparently owe more to Claudius than to Hamlet. It is as a whole that the performances work, and Richard Eyre's direction, though given to occasional quirks (there is no apparent reason apart from fashion why Hamlet

should address the 'To be or not to be' soliloquy to Ophelia for instance), co-ordinates these admirably, putting the family drama into its political context without straining or overemphasising the point. William Dudley's set provides a valuable contribution to this by creating an environment full of unexpected doors which is thus much less secure and enclosed than at first it appears. The production has some ragged edges and disappoints, particularly in the players, but these in no way diminish its substance or reduce the excitement it offers. Long after the final curtain, it continues to exercise the imagination. The Royal Court is more than justified in turning its resources to a classic revival on this occasion.

Early Days at the Cottesloe

reviewed by Ronald Hayman

'Supposing some young writer were to come along,' wrote Arnold Bennett in 1910, after seeing Roger Fry's first exhibition of the Post-Impressionists, 'and do in words what these young men have done in paint, I might conceivably be disgusted with nearly the whole of modern fiction, and I might have to begin again.' He might conceivably have been disgusted, too, with nearly the whole of modern drama, and, seventy years later, it's striking that so very few playwrights have been prepared to begin again, to do away with the old methods of story-telling, to attach themselves to the modern movement, to experiment with form. Having been trained at an art school, and having trained himself to be a novelist, David Storey is more aware than most of his contemporaries, though no more aware than any artist should be, that what is done in one form may have bearings on what can be done in another. In some ways *The Changing Room* (1971) was like a dramatised painting: he made wooden benches, clothes-pegs, towels and rugby boots contribute on almost the same level as dialogue to the picture of the footballers' experience. The conception of *The Contractor* (1969) was largely visual, and in *Home* (1970) he built up a post-impressionist picture out of unfinished sentences, evaded confrontations, inaccurate memories. Like a folly on a steep hill, the play was built precariously on the side of madness.

Slighter, but still richly satisfying, his new play goes playfully back to the same method, but this time only one of the characters is verging on amnesia, unreason, childishness, senile delinquency; much of the action deals with the attempts of family, doctor, and well-paid male companion to restrain him from his more embarrassing pieces of bad behaviour – urinating against a wall, leaving abusive messages on telephone answering machines, manoeuvring to pitch his daughter into an adulterous affair with the doctor. It's an excellent part for the 77-year-old Sir Ralph Richardson, with his superb mixture of vulnerability and élan, excitability and peevishness, extrovert warmth and temperamental withdrawal. Ever so slightly larger than life-size, he's never been so much a star as a defiantly human full-faced moon, pulling in tides of affection from all over the auditorium, as we all think that he's just like us only more so. He always gives the impression of being so full of life that it's liable to spill over the front row, and the painful paradox of this play is that the man verging on death is more alive than the younger people, who have to stop him from spoiling the appearances they're trying so hard to keep up – the suave son-in-law, the tactful daughter, the frustrated catering manager standing in as manservant, the affable country doctor, the spunky, affectionate grand-daughter and her poet fiancé, self-consciously non-conformist, instinctively respectful.

One of the pleasures of the play is the central ambiguity about the extent to which the old man's lapses and confusions are voluntary. Presumably it's quite large. He's probably choosing to forget his son-in-law's surname, choosing to suspect the ex-catering manager of being a spy ('He reports everything I say to Moscow'), choosing to behave badly in order to cause trouble for the conformists, choosing to misinterpret his perceptions. ('There's a man beating his wife. Or is it a carpet?') But is he capable of choosing not to? Bored by inactivity and surveillance –

**David Storey's *Early Days* with Ralph Richardson in Lindsay Anderson's production
at the Cottesloe, National Theatre and at the Comedy Theatre. 1980.**

he is almost a prisoner in his son-in-law's home – he reaches rebelliously towards more dramatic events, partly to keep himself entertained, partly to keep us entertained. This kind of play can admit to being what it is. At the same time there are advantages in not having to tie up all the loose narrative threads. We're fed quite a lot of information about his political career, but we can only guess at the relationship between the roguishness we see now and the mistakes (whatever they were) in the 25-minute speech and the 15-second interview that spoiled his prospects of becoming party leader. We don't know and don't need to know whether it's only the imminence of death that encourages him to take such risks or whether his anarchistic streak has always been too strong for a careerist.

Lindsay Anderson's production gamely makes the risk-taking central. There's the constant risk that the play will seem too much like a game that playwright, director and leading actor are enjoying too much, but I suppose there isn't much danger that the audience won't join in. There's the constant danger that Sir Ralph – after playing so many small parts at the National he at last has a really large one – will fluff lines or deviate from script, but, I suppose, not much danger that this could unbalance the action. There is very solid support in the performances of Gerald Flood, Rosemary Martin, Michael Bangerter and Peter Machin, and it wasn't Barbara Flynn's fault that the rage against the old man seemed too abrupt and contrived. 'The name of your party, old man, is death.' David Storey was trying to say more than the situation admitted, but this is a mistake he made very seldom.

march 1980 75p

plays and players

Playtext Part 1
Andrew Davies's
ROSE

Glenda Jackson
Felicity Kendal
interviews

Irish Theatre in
London

Catherine Itzin:
Swedish Festival
report

William Raidy in
New York: Love...
the great disaster

JULIA McKENZIE
KEITH MICHELL
ON THE 20TH
CENTURY

Reviews by
RONALD HAYMAN
JEREMY KINGSTON
ANTHONY CURTIS
LUCIND CALDECOTT
and others

Future Reviews
BEFORE THE PARTY
ON THE 20TH CENTURY
THE BORMAN COMETH
TAKE AND ME

Reviewed
ROSE
TRIAL OSM
GREEK
APPEARANCES
THE WEAVERS

JUNE

1980

North of the Border

Cordelia Oliver looks at the contemporary Scottish theatre scene

In Scotland one becomes resigned to perennial complaints about the lack of a theatre aimed purely at serving Scottish players and Scottish writers past and present. The various abortive attempts to get such an enterprise off the ground would need a whole article to themselves. However, a recent move by Ewan Hooper to initiate a Scottish Theatre Trust seems likely to stand more chance of success than any of its predecessors if only because he has sensibly set a limit on his proposal, eschewing the idea of a prestigious Scottish National Theatre with the sort of exorbitantly expensive substructure such an institution implies. He aims to concentrate on building up a good company of stage touring productions of plays by new Scottish writers, and revivals of Bridie, Kemp, McLellan and others less well known, as well as Scots adaptations of such European classics as seem suitable.

As yet, Hooper's is an exploratory project with modest Scottish Arts Council backing but, if he can find enough financial support from the SAC and others, and if the thing really takes root, everyone is going to be happy. Indeed, taken in conjunction with that lusty infant the Glasgow Theatre Club, Hooper's Scottish Theatre Company may at last take some of the heat off Giles Havergal and his excellent Citizens' Company, whose only 'fault' (much magnified by the fact that his is presently the only rep theatre operating in Glasgow) is a frank admission that specifically Scottish-speaking plays are out with their terms of reference – and indeed their capabilities. To anyone but a fool it should be obvious that to ask the Cits Company to change their style would be like demanding that a fine painter should turn weaver.

In any case, so far as new Scottish plays are concerned, the complaints seem to me to be overdone. Out of some 16 productions seen during the opening season in Edinburgh, Glasgow, Dundee and Perth, no fewer than eight were by Scottish writers. True, three of these – *National Causes* by Tom Gallacher, *The Quartet* by Ronald Mavor and *A Waste of Time* by Robert David Macdonald – were written in standard English, but that would seem to be a reasonable proportion in a country where most of the middle-class population speaks just that.

Dundee Rep, the oldest in the country, is almost at the end of its miserable existence in the converted, and fast disintegrating, church building in Lochae Road. By next season the company ought to be established in the new theatre in much more accessible Tay Square; not before time, since the amenities which most theatre companies *and* audiences accept as normal barely exist in Dundee. Even so, that the company spirit and audience loyalty remain enviably high was obvious from the response to Robert Trotter's high-spirited reading of that comic fantasy, *Too True to be Good* (the flip side of *Heartbreak House*) in which the ageing Shaw wags an admonishing, but oddly indulgent finger at the post-war twenties generation with its eroded values and pleasure-seeking morés. It got off to a slowish start (partly the fault of the author, maybe) but ended up with a brisk, Shavian, all-comers debate in which the contemporary parallels were obvious. Andrew Melville and Anne-Louise Rose were notably well cast and capable.

Perth Theatre, a cosy, small-scale nineteenth century auditorium, has the edge on Dundee for comfort and period ambience to put it mildly, but Perth itself is a county town and, as such, extremely reactionary in its tastes. All the same, Joan Knight, with the able assistance of Andrew McKinnon and Patrick Sandford, manages to slot occasional interesting rarities (like the recent production of *The Cocktail Party*, which, sadly, I missed) and new Scottish plays among the farces, bedroom comedies and other recent London successes. Tom Gallacher's new comedy-thriller, *Natural Causes*, turned out to be an amusing piece with (surely?) an element of self-parody in the metaphysical strand that emerges early on with the appearance of Mr Kernahan (Martyn James), an Irishman of more than everyday significance, among the psychical researchers brought together in an isolated hostelry in remotest Galloway. It's a well-judged, satirical entertainment with a mordant after-taste; neatly constructed and briskly directed (by Joan Knight herself) in one of those sets where a sense of actuality rouses its own applause. When somebody looked out of the open door at the unseen landscape you could almost smell the sinister Solway Firth.

In one sense Edinburgh is better off than anywhere else in Scotland at present, with two auditoriums serving the Royal Lyceum Company and, of course, the inimitable Traverse. But the latter was forced to go dark between Christmas and March (just as the Citizens in Glasgow must now close between early April and September). Still, Marcella Evaristle's four-hander,

plays and players
april 1980   75p

Michael Gough
Andrei Serban
interviews
Thirty Years of
Greenwich Theatre
Co-Operative
Acting
Arrivals and
Departures:
William Rardy in
New York
Carnival in Venice:
John Francis Lane

JILL BENNETT
JONATHAN PRICE
The Royal Court's
HAMLET

Reviews by
DAVID MAYER
RONALD HAYMAN
HUGH ROBINSON
LEONIE CALDECOTT
MICHAEL RICHMOND
and others
Picture Reviews:
OTHELLO
HAMLET
MAKE AND BREAK
Reviewed
THE IMPRESSO
ON THE 20TH CENTURY
THE SUMMER PARTY
SCHOOLDAYS

Playtext Part 2
Andrew Davies's
ROSE

Hard to Get, was worth waiting for; full of laughter but tinged with *lacrimae rerum:* a couple of Glasgow's intellectual W1 meet, marry, talk endlessly, and discover – in painful stages – that chemical attraction doesn't rule out utter incompatability. That's basically it – but the situation is seen with a feminist slant that says more about sympathy with the human predicament than about female chauvinism, as such. This had performances by Peter Kelly, Maureen Beattie, Stephen Boxer and Maggie Shelvin which would bear the microscope in almost every particular. By comparison the Lyceum revival of John Byrne's *Normal Service*, with Patrick Sandford guest-directing and a group of able Scots actors imported for the occasion, was seen to be more or less plotless; a satirically – but never harshly – objective scanning of the human fish-tank – in other words, the multi-self-centred and chaotic design room at Caledonian Television. It's a place, this, where nothing much happens, but where the talk, leap-frogging non-sequiturs and all, is hilarious. Ideally this was one for the Little Lyceum (or better still, the Traverse) where most of the company's worthwhile productions have been staged, usually with Brian Howard directing, as in the thoughtful staging of *Miss Julie*.

When the Royal Lyceum board of directors decided to make a scapegoat of Stephen Macdonald – who, though admittedly he made mistakes in judgement, had a reputation which deserved a far longer development period, and whose genuine respect for theatre as an art was never in doubt – it seems to have been agreed that nothing should stand in the way of bringing in the crowds. Leslie Lawton was clearly engaged to do just that by fair means or foul. And it must be admitted that he has been largely successful in putting on plays to attract the elderly evening-outers. Only a proliferation of Aunt Ednas and Uncle Berties could have spent three weeks of happy evenings laughing so heartily at that octogenarian's snigger, *The Bed Before Yesterday*, in which Wendy Craig, imported as a draw from TV's soap opera *Butterflies*, had the grace to look uneasy. And *Equus*, more popular with somewhat younger audiences, was no more than a fair stab (based as always on John Dexter's original staging) at a shallow, showy piece which obeys the law of diminishing returns.

Summer sees the reps going dark, although the lively Wildcat Company and the slightly more demanding 7.84 Theatre Company, Scotland, will no doubt continue to tour the halls and smaller theatres with amusing and more or less polemical shows with or without drums, guitars, keyboards and psychedelic lighting. And the Borderline Company, based at the Harbour Arts Centre, Irvine, is touring a strongly cast revival of *The Bevellers,* by the late Roddy MacMillan. But the summer season, by tradition, belongs to Pitlochry, Kenneth Ireland's 'theatre in the hills', where 1980 will be the last before the major move to the new theatre complex. As usual, the repertoire for the coming Pitlochry season ranges widely to suit most tastes, from Oscar Wilde (*Importance of Being Ernest*) and Anouilh *(Dinner with the Family)* through *Gaslight* and *Filumena* to a new thriller by Scottish writer David Hutchison.

1981

The year Ronald Reagan was sworn in as the USA's 40th President (and later wounded in an assassination attempt) was the year the Gang of Four in China were given suspended death sentences. After 444 days in captivity, the American hostages in Iran were released. Suarez made a surprise resignation as Spain's Prime Minister and Antonio Tejero Molina led an abortive coup holding the cabinet and 350 MPs at gunpoint in the Spanish Cortes. Sadat was assassinated in Egypt. Mitterand was elected President of France.

In Britain it was the year of another Royal Wedding – that of the Prince of Wales and Lady Diana Spencer. There were two days of violence amongst blacks in Brixton. Bobby Sands's hunger strike in Belfast's Maze prison ended in his death. In the British theatre it was the year of the hit musical Cats *and the year Brian Friel's new play* Translations *moved from Hampstead Theatre into the NT repertoire.*

Plays and Players, *now published by Brevet Publishing, returned in October.*

1981

Green Room

David Hare, after a year in America, looks at the English theatre

I recently spent a year in America, because I was tired of this country. Eventually I came back, if only to see how the story is going to end. The visit had made me realise how lucky an English playwright is, for he works under the illusion that what he says may affect peoples' lives. This may well be an illusion, but it hardly matters. For me it has been an essential illusion. Without it I would rather sell shoes. Only a fool would maintain this illusion in New York, for there most theatre offers little but the chance for its audience to touch success. They are there to decide among themselves whether the show is a hit, not to embark on the time-consuming and laborious business of listening to what its author is saying. The way of life in the States gives people so much more self-confidence – or at least so much more need to appear self-confident – that only oddballs are interested in spending serious evenings in the theatre. The system, so the thinking goes, *works*. It would be bad magic to go anywhere near an evening of doubt.

Fortunately nobody believes England works. For the country this may be regrettable, but for the playwright it has long been excellent news. The door of self-doubt is already half-open, so it's not hard for the playwright to jam his foot in. Things are so bad that people will listen to any damn fool who comes along to tell them why they're so miserable; and the most conspicuous damn fools of the last thirty years have been the theatre writers. The usual objection to this line of argument – that uneasy times produce interesting playwrights – is that plays, we are told, should not be addressed exclusively to social questions, but that instead they should be concerned with things called 'the eternal verities'. People go remarkably hazy when you ask them to spit out exactly what these verities are. 'We are all going to die' is sometimes offered. 'Love never lasts' is apologetically advanced as well. My own view is that by abandoning these bloody verities the British theatre has managed to pass through a remarkable period. Earlier this year a little group of fans revived Christopher Hampton's early play *Total Eclipse* at the Lyric, Hammersmith, and people were generally pleased to find that the play was much better than they had first thought. This argued no special discernment in us, for the truth is that almost at random you could now pick out a whole range of post-war plays which are a great deal better than anyone realised at the time. Any management which mounted a season of, for example, *Occupations, The National Health, The Soul of The White Ant, Events While Guarding the Bofors Gun, A Patriot for Me* and *Savages* would be offering a group of plays of some breadth and power. *Christie In Love*, recently staged under the promenade in Brighton by the Sardonic Fish Corporation, looked as smart and funny as ever. Stephen Lowe's *Touched*, a failure at the Old Vic in 1976, revived splendidly at the Royal Court with the original actress in the lead.

I dislike the patriotic argument that the one area in which England still excels is the arts – as if all that Empire-building, nigger-killing energy had now gone into the gouache and the arts centre. It is simply untrue. Anyone comparing standards in the arts between now and, for example, the 1930s would have to deal with a great fact of Auden, quite apart from the lesser facts of Lawrence, Orwell, Eliot. The proposition is self-evidently ridiculous. This is not a specially distinguished period in what is called and taught as 'culture'. But if it has a single feature of any interest it is that from the early fifties public forms became those in which the most gifted writers chose to work. 'Literary' England, isolated, still has no sense of this, still prefers to read and propagate the truly dreadful old novelists and poets who represent the official culture. The best novels now written in the English language are by an Indian. In America and Australia great novelists live and work, while here it is in music, television and theatre that artistic life flickers, not often excellent, but broadly to the point.

David Hare. (Photo: Martha Swope)

The actress known for her appearances in my work used to complain a good deal about my craven love of a joke. 'I suppose' she would say, 'that we have just taken this four-page detour in the plot for the sake of this single *laugh* . . .', landing witheringly on the last word. 'Well,' I would say, 'I think it's rather a good line.' 'It was a good line when I had it in *Knuckle*. Now I've got it in *Plenty* I'm not so sure.'

Howard Brenton said the best thing about jokes in the theatre that I know. To the young playwright jokes are what hands and feet are to the young artist. They may not eventually turn out to be what he wants to spend his life drawing, but they are a skill he must acquire on the way. I am envious of other writers' jokes and would like to have written the line 'There's no taxi, you crackpot. Die with dignity, for Christ's sake.' But it was Peter Nichols. I am also particularly fond of 'All the observable phenomena connected with the train leaving Paddington could equally well be explained by Paddington leaving the train.' (Stoppard's).

For an actor laughs are dangerous because they give him a false idea of how the evening is going. Worse, they come to be the stepping stones of his own performance. Lonely up there and insecure, the actor is grateful when the audience wave their tiny flags of understanding. But the pattern of his playing may too soon become dependent on them. One unhappy actor (now dead) was famous not only for the conventional failing of needing to have his dialogue written on cigarette packets and the backs of chairs, but for insisting to the stage management that his moves be written down as well. He would look at his feet and taped to the floor would be the instruction 'Now go to the desk'. A whole evening's progress would be marked out in this way, and he would proceed as on some bizarre, personal treasure-hunt from one memory-aid to the next. Sadly, in comedy, actors' performances often add up to little more than this: lazy motion from laugh to laugh. It's the pursuit of laughs which has killed the West End, for managers have been encouraged to believe in a disastrous genre called 'light comedy'. For years they asked us to admire the art of making something out of nothing. Critics were impressed not by how much there was in a play, but how little. Nothing was more important to them than the skill with which the actors and writer had managed to disguise this, and the word 'soufflé' was always used approvingly. Coward, wrongly, was thought to be the supreme disher-up of nonsense, the man who could entertain you by breath and brilliance. It says something for the pervasive melancholy of the English that they accepted the idea that an evening out could only be a vacuum which needed the most painless covering over. What a perverse idea of theatre it was! Now the dead temples of this belief stand empty on Shaftesbury Avenue, smelling slightly of urine and disinfectant.

Does it matter that the commercial theatre is in such trouble? Michael Codron apart, managers have done so little for writers and actors, have been so unimaginative in the techniques of publicity and presentation, have lived so long off the vitality of the subsidized theatre that the general attitude seems to be one of good riddance, that they have failed because they deserved to. Actors no longer like long runs, and anyone wandering in to a West End play in its sixth month will know exactly why – though to be fair, *Nicholas Nickleby*, in the public sector, was by the end of its London run in a far more spectacular desuetude than any one-set comedy.

It's dangerous to moralise from failure, especially when in the subsidised sector we demand the right to empty houses, indeed defend them perhaps too vigorously. But comedies about nothing still seem to me not a good artistic manifesto. It would be good to see the West End prosper, because there *is* something bracing about working for a manager whose money is on the stage, who cannot hide from the results of his own actions.

The work of the Royal Court is now fashionably overlooked, and taking advantage of this state of affairs with indecent zeal, the Arts Council's Finance Committee has decided to see whether it can execute one of its celebrated economies. My own guess is that it will fail, for there is just enough realism in Piccadilly for the committee to sense that the consequences could be far-reaching. Of the two organisations, the Royal Court looks much healthier. Both the outstanding new plays of 1980 – *My Dinner With André* and *The Arbor* – were presented there, and I'm told that *Hamlet* and *The Seagull* both set higher standards than are usually met at the big state theatres. (As a persistent non-attender of institutional classics, I have no standards of comparison). No financial threats the Arts Council is making seem to be as ill-judged as the letter which its Drama Officer sent to the board of the Royal Court suggesting specific changes in the spoken text of *A Short Sharp Shock!*. A line here (I am understating) was surely overstepped. 'We think it would be better if . . .' is the naked language of censorship. It has always been a principle of arts subsidy in Britain that the funding body did not try to interfere in the content of a theatre's work, and the very fact that a Drama Officer thought he could doctor last year's most politically sensitive production suggested even then a prevailing mood of unbalanced axe-happiness inside the Arts Council. His suggestions were rightly rejected. Time and the bureaucratic waters have covered his blunder over. By drawing attention to it now, I would hope to prevent him trying again.

Robert Walker has seen a 'catastrophe' and it results from the way in which the British theatre has been confined in an aesthetic straitjacket. He argues that we now exist with a rigid theatrical style and method administered by astute, intellectual Oxbridge-educated directors. Its mode is naturalistic or realistic, its style puritan, isolationist, Brecht-influenced though not necessarily Brechtian. It has imposed its hold upon interpretation of both classical and modern dramatic writing and as a result affected the forms in which stage writers organise their plays. This approach tends to discard the influence of the related arts of painting, sculpture, cinema and music, and this century's tendency to move towards the abstract or expressionistic forms which attracted Ibsen, Strindberg and Pirandello in their latest phases. In this new-English dispensation, stage design and lighting are subordinate to the process in which actors and directors work in a relatively unadorned space, discovering and evoking the written text. The real and spiritual presence of the dramatist is thereby discovered without extraneous, sentimentalising clutter. The supremacy of the word and the actor's voice and his movements are crucial. It is a style occasionally challenged, though the Theatre of the Absurd has in England, if absorbed at all, been

Half Moon Man

Robert Walker talks to Nicholas de Jongh

taken through this reductive, naturalising process. The audience is left with the hard, stretching feat of responding to this austere communion of actors with a text.

Robert Walker, the director of the two Half Moon theatres in East London, three of whose productions have now transferred to the West End and are running concurrently, dissents from this prevailing orthodoxy, and works at several removes from it. He cites Giles Havergal and the Glasgow Citizens' work as one of the sole British examples of a school of theatre which is visually and aurally orientated, continental and sensual. It is no accident either that Walker's own career as director virtually began through Havergal's good offices.

'He started me off at the Glasgow Close theatre and gave me a company of six actors and the chance of directing them in plays. It was an incredible act of faith. But Havergal's a rare exception and the best theatre manager in the country. He should be running the National Theatre. He takes chances, runs risks. He's exciting. And he's not just a one-school of theatre man. He runs a broad church, but he's not stuck in a groove.'

For the rest of the British theatrical director-producer breed Walker has little time and less enthusiasm. 'I didn't go to Cambridge and I try not to have anything to do with anyone who went to Oxbridge. The cerebral approach of the Cambridge graduate directors and the fact that they control our theatres is a catastrophe. It seems to me that they've lost any sense of sensuality or spectacle. Theatre seems to me to be far more than just that. It's a fusion of the intellectual and the sensual. In my view the whole emphasis of Peter Hall and his school is solely on the text. They think the actor needs to stand there in a good light on barish stage – I went to see Hanif Kureishi's *Outskirts* at the Warehouse recently and I said to the designer "Where the hell is the set?" And he said "The director cut the set in rehearsals."'

Although there is probably an element of good natured caricature and exaggeration in Walker's theory, there are important elements of truth and insight in his criticisms. He cites the example of the People Show, that combination of surreal, non-linear, non-narrative, art-influenced methods, with an emphasis on sound, gesture, lighting and movement, as integral to his criticisms: 'The People Show are accepted all over the world. But only now are critics here beginning to see some merit in them. I read in Colin Chambers's book *Other Spaces* that a whole new school of writing was started by Buzz Goodbody. He omits to say that it was years before she got the chance to direct a play. And then she committed suicide. You can't (and he means he can't) get access to big stages here, because there's just a small ring of directors who do. They like nice young lads from Cambridge.'

Walker discerns a reason for the prevailing orthodoxy. He suggests that realistic methods of stage production involve and imply a 'conservative view of the world. They say that give or take a few moderate changes society is OK. But if you want to turn society on its head and think it ought to be swept away in its present form you have to find a theatrical method which is non-naturalistic or expressionistic. So that's why people like me have a little dilapidated theatre. In Germany we would get a large subsidy having proved ourselves. Here they draw back from resources for a big popular form of expressionistic theatre.'

Walker is particularly vehement in his attack upon designers, though they only fulfil the demands of the director. He sees them as the purveyors of the spacious clarity, the lucid, unadorned, perhaps representational set which easily slips apologetically away into the background. 'Take Jocelyn Herbert. Her great idea was to clear the playing area (for the actor). It was a great and liberating idea at the time, but the results have been disastrous'. Designers' functions have withered in the new process. 'Let the action and the acting fight against the set' he urges. 'Actors love that. It's what happened in the Half Moon production of *Arturo Ui*. Simon Callow certainly did. You see that's why design in Germany is light years ahead of here.'

Germany is the country which functions as his point of reference. It is to German theatre and its ways that his conversation returns and refers like a moth forever succumbing to some glamorous lamp light. It combines the traditions and methods, allied with a wealth of state subsidy, which he wants. It is also his second home: he was born in the East End of London and his father who was a teacher decided to live and work in Germany. As a result from the age of eight to sixteen Walker was brought up and educated there, and though in an English school over there, he learned the German language. At the age of 16 he came back to England with the dream of settling in some likely garret to become a great novelist. But he was at once converted, as quickly as the traveller on the road to Damascus. His parents had decided to take him to see John Gielgud's Shakespeare anthology *The Ages of Man*. Walker hankered instead after an East End show, written by a fellow called Brendan Behan and directed by a woman famous now as Joan Littlewood. It was *The Quare Fellow* and maybe it changed Walker's life. 'It had the Littlewood force, the idea that life's worthwhile and exciting. And the next day I went down to Stratford East and got myself a job working as a stage hand.' Joan Littlewood was on hand to be heroine-worshipped though such adolescent business was soon put to an end: the young, awed Walker dared one morning to suggest that she might be willing to read a play of his. She looked at him with contempt and said 'What d'you want? D'you want to be a bloody star then.'

Who does not? Walker came, in the end, to the Half Moon with an unformed if promising reputation and has made the place matter in a way it never had before. His directing falls roughly within four categories. There are the modern foreign revivals like his *Arturo Ui, Woyzeck*, Brecht's *Mahagonny*; the political farces such as *The Accidental Death of an Anarchist* and *Can't Pay? Won't Pay!;* the old American musicals, with *Pal Joey* and *Guys and Dolls* revived as tantalising miniatures, bathed in a retrospective of nostalgia, and the occasional non-doctrinaire works of which Bernard Kops's *Ezra* is perhaps the most remarkable. His production of *Woyzeck* gives a useful idea of how he works. The extraordinary, science fiction set by Mick Bearwish was the production's starting point. 'We decided that Woyzeck did not fit the world and that the set should reflect his idea of life. There would be no way he could fit. So there were edges, corners, ridges, unlovely, unfit for a human being. It became a futuristic

PLAYS & players
90p
OCTOBER 1981

DAVID HARE
GREEN ROOM

HUGH LEONARD
AT CATS

ROBERT WALKER
GOES WEST

213

set though we didn't want to root it in any specific historical period. We wanted it removed from historicity but to keep it in a plausible, hostile world where human kind was a mistake. That's what the audience should experience – that the world's not right for him. Then we thought about the objects in Woyzeck's world. The bed was important because of his lover. The curious oxygen tent represented his son – because he was alienated from him and that seemed an explicable way of describing alienation. Then the fairground had lights which resembled a machine, rather like a computer panel. The fairground in life should be cosy and comfortable, but for him it was alienating and hostile. There was the tank in which he drowned himself. We wanted to bring the experience of drowning on stage – to isolate that event.'

The arrangement of this astounding stage furniture at once altered traditional expectations. This jumbled, menacing, future world, the stuff of which memorable nightmares are made, corresponded to Woyzeck's perception of things. The devices served to tender in visual terms what is only implicit on the printed page. The method of acting, often terse, automatic, and fierce matched: 'You have to work drawing out the actors. It's not easy. In a naturalistic play you say to an actor "Now you get a cup of tea." It's a language they understand. This was different. You have to coax your actors on. Woyzeck even when walking was out of place, in a kind of agony, and you have to show it.' A virtual monodrama was opened out.

Mahagonny, the accompanying and matching piece, was done in its original form because Lotte Lenya would not allow a full-scale version. Walker transformed and modernised the bald text, the song-spiel, with an improvised story by Robin Hooper and Robin Soanes which roughly paralleled the original scenario. Here was an upper class dinner party where a group of gluttonous, artificial caricatured people spoke in fast monotone. 'Eating and consumption is very important in *Mahagonny*. In early Brecht there is an attack on the idea of theatre as a prelude to eating; the idea that you go to theatre as an hors d'oeuvre before a restaurant. So we had this mad dinner party. But there's still the basic Brecht idea of a guy who can't pay his bills.'

Ezra, one of Walker's most recent productions is a second example and perhaps the most outstanding, of Walker's ability to vivify and render theatrical what seems a word-bound, static text. Walker reckoned that at the core of the play was Kops's recognition of and response to a man who 'wrote like an angel on the page and yet was the most reprehensible person. He was a curious phenomenon.'

The play is set within the confines of Pound's demented, wandering mind while he was imprisoned during and after the Second World War. The set devised by Martin Sutherland was the liberating point for a play originally devised for radio. With its scaffolding-array of cages, high and low playing areas, it opened up the play for a large mind-voyage and made the play physical as much as it was verbal. 'We wanted the set to be like a piece of sculpture so that it would speak the play. We almost tried to get it to look like the inside of Pound's skull. There were two stage/cage areas. The stage in which he was imprisoned was a mouth. The two higher areas were his eyes and the projecting part of the stage was formed to be like his nose or a fascist salute. It was his interior landscape. Actors love to grapple with and fight against a set.' And the bizarre set of wire cages and wooden platforms became the areas for Pound's wandering, with volleys of echoing and reproaching voices.

With three plays in the West End it is hard to describe Walker as an absolute outsider. Yet his views make him one. A voice in the wilderness then? 'D'you think so?' he asks, sounding rather pleased with the description. 'Perhaps you're right. Only five theatre managers in Britain have ever offered me work'.

I have three cats, if the possessive verb is not an impertinence. Rover is a genial ginger tom whose party piece is to open a microwave oven single-pawed and is so absent-minded that I have twice seen him trip while he ambled upstairs. Dubh (the Irish for 'black', pronounced 'dove') is a sleek, amber-eyed puma who filches Dover sole from the hotel next door and lays them at our feet in lofty think-nothing-of-itness. And Oscar is 13 and so obese that when he lies on his side he rocks like one of those unknock-downable toy clowns with a weighted bottom.

I mention this by way of brandishing my credentials as one who, through the years, has run the gamut of catdom from Siamese to mog. There are no thoroughbreds on view in *Cats*, however. The setting is a junkyard; above it, stars glimmer and clouds flit across a fat yellow moon. Cats' eyes glare at us out of the dark, the circular stage revolves gently (as does part of the audience), and a horde of alleycats slinks on for a bacchanalia.

It is the most unlikely of ideas: 20 poems from T. S. Eliot's *Old Possum's Book of Practical Cats* set to music and staged in a manner that makes *Forty-Second Street* look like *Huis Clos*. Coming to it unprepared, I spent the first 15 minutes waiting for the plot to begin; then the message penetrated this thickest of skulls and I sat back to enjoy the Whiskas.

If I have a grumble, it is that Andrew Lloyd Webber often aligns his faster rhythms with Eliot's more intricate rhymes, and the words become a blur. The sense of it is there and the unfailing good humour, but as in the case of cats themselves, you recognise that there is a row in progress but miss the actual fishbone of contention. It is ironic that the show's progenitor – Eliot – should be its only near-casualty.

Given the static nature of the beast, Trevor Nunn has pulled out more stops than are imaginable. His performers – and of course the choreographer of British musicals is always Gillian Lynne, unless otherwise stated – leap, spin, tap-dance, roll, crawl, strut, tumble, purr and claw; they enter through the stage, from the roof, by trapeze and out of thin air. Bits of junk become a railway engine, and, in a rock version of the panto transformation scene, a car tyre with its feline cargo becomes jet-propelled in a pea-souper of dry ice.

The current fashion in musicals is for much style and rather less substance, for a score that is as featureless as a blancmange, with one hit song, like a dollop of jam, in the middle. Richard Rodgers

Cats at the New London

reviewed by Hugh Leonard

would whirl like a dervish in his tomb. The token hit of *Cats* is 'Memory', sung by Elaine Paige, who, as Grizabella, schleps in and is so bedraggled as to invite putting down. Miss Paige belts her one song superbly, but my own favourite was 'The Moments of Happiness'. The mark of a square, perhaps.

Andrew Lloyd Webber's *Cats* at the New London Theatre. 1981.

The show is, of course, a fat 18-carat hit and has a self-awareness to match. It seems to run on energy alone – often for its own sake, as if for fear that our attention might stray. Even so, the first half has its doldrums and most of the prime catnip seems to be crammed into Part Two. There is, for example. Stephen Tate's gently ga-ga recital as Gus the Theatre Cat: a beguiling piece of Clive Dunnery. And, of all people to meet under the unlikely big top of the New London Theatre, Brian Blessed is first-rate as the patriarchal Old Deuteronomy, with a smile that threatens to linger on – like another cat's – after the revels.

The most celebrated of Eliot's cats is probably the arch-criminal, Macavity, and here for once Mr Nunn's invention seems to falter. The fun revives, however, with Wayne Sleep – a name, which is here derisively inappropriate – as Mr Mistoffolees; and, among the ladies, Susan Jane Tanner must be the brightest new comic talent in town.

An immensely warm, friendly show, then – strangely, the essentially aloof nature of the cat is nowhere in evidence. Two bright bespectacled little girls in the front row were held spellbound until the last moggy vanished up the aisle: which, in itself, was a rave notice. It is a personal carp that behind the razzmatazz the substance of the evening seemed becalmed, but still I would not swap it for a Whorehouse of Annies.

Having insulted the Irish by putting on Howard Brenton's play, *The Romans in Britain*, which equated the Catholic population of Northern Ireland with naked, illiterate barbarian aborigines of a wild ancient Britain, the National Theatre has now redressed the balance: Brian Friel shows us a Gaelic-speaking community in County Donegal, around 1830, the members of which are able to converse in fluent Greek and Latin, quoting Homer and Virgil, proud of their native Irish tongue and despising English as a language particularly suited for the purposes of commerce, but without any poetry. The scene is a 'hedge school' one of those privately, and almost clandestinely established schools in which the rural population of Ireland endeavoured to keep alive with the country's ancient language and high culture.

How much more subtle and intelligent Brian Friel's approach to the Irish problem is than Brenton's clumsy pamphleteering! An ordnance survey mapping operation is being conducted in the school's area by English soldiers, Royal Engineers. One of the schoolmaster's sons, Owen, is acting as interpreter and helping with establishing the names of villages, hills and other features of the landscape. The English lieutenant in charge of this name-giving is unable to transliterate the subtle Irish sounds and so the region's place names are being radically and insensitively angli-cized – a wonderful metaphor that for the process by which a culture is being obliterated by conquerors. Yet that self-same lieutenant, George Yolland, is enchanted by Ireland, wants to learn Erse and has fallen in love with a beautiful local girl, Maire, with whom the schoolmaster's other son, Manus, is also, but unhappily, in love.

1981

Translations at the Lyttelton

reviewed by Martin Esslin

PLAYS & players 90p
NOVEMBER 1981

NED SHERRIN
GREEN ROOM

MARTIN ESSLIN
AT THE LOVE-GIRL

JOHN RUSSELL TAYLOR
AT ON THE RAZZLE

COMPLETE PLAYTEXT-
INSTANT ENLIGHTENMENT
INCLUDING VAT
BY ANDREW CARR

Brevet Arts
Magazines
Art & Artists
Books & Bookmen
Dance & Dancers
Films & Filming
Music & Musicians
Plays & Players
Records & Recording

In a subtle and beautiful scene – with echoes of Henry V and his Kate – George and Maire establish their mutual love for each other in spite of their inability to speak each other's languages, but are observed by a dumb girl whom Manus has helped to regain some ability to speak. She tells Manus that his girl is making love to another man; Manus is so devastated by seeing the scene, that he decides to leave the area. When George Yolland, the English lieutenant, disappears and must be presumed murdered, the next morning, suspicion is bound to fall on his disappointed rival. Some of the villagers know that the murder has in fact been committed by local Irish nationalist rebels. The English announce that unless the matter is cleared up the whole village will be dispossessed, the population evicted. As the play ends all we know is that the schoolmaster's other son Owen has gone to deal with the matter. Will he save the village by betraying the nationalists with whose cause he is in sympathy? We are left with that question.

It is this ending which, I feel, shows Brian Friel's subtlety and political intelligence: he has abundantly established the case for the Irish population's national feeling and yearning for freedom. He has also shown the undoubted mutual human attraction between at least some individuals on both sides of the national divide. And he brilliantly highlights the moral dilemma of those in Ireland who desire independence and national freedom but abhor violence in any form. If the perpetrators of the murder are denounced to the authorities the majority of the population will at least keep their homes. But we also know that their language, down to their very place-names, is being obliterated, that the new schools being established will ultimately eradicate the Irish language and the old culture of Gaelic Ireland . . . it is the same kind of dilemma that faces many in Northern Ireland to this day.

It is, of course, the ultimate irony of the play that it is written entirely in English, in a convention by which we must believe that the Irish characters speak Erse, the English English, and the translator between them suggests what he is doing merely by paraphrasing the same sentence in different (English) words – which is, in itself, an extremely funny and effective device, as it makes us see what the interpreter suppresses, how he reduces the pompous bureaucratic language of the officers into homely commonsensical speech. Similarly the love scene between George and Maire gains its humour and poignancy from our hearing both sides of this mutually incomprehensible exchange.

The performance – under Donald McWhinnie's unobtrusive but very sensitive direction – is on a very high level. Shaun Scott and Bernadette Short are a touching pair of young lovers; Tony Doyle as Owen, the man between the cultures, conveys both the down-to-earth pragmatism of the assimilated Irishman and the agony of his awareness of the moral choices his attitudes presents him with. Sebastian Shaw turns in one of his masterly portrayals of a lovable, unwashed old lecher who can quote Homer in Greek and revel in the erotic implication of the Greek poet's description of goddesses. Ian Bannen is the old schoolmaster: he, it seems to me, falls far too much into the old, discredited cliché of the drunken old stage Irishman. But I am not sure whether this is his fault or Brian Friel's. The long story this character tells of the time, in 1778, when he set out with all the volunteers to fight for freedom and the whole expedition petered out in a pub, seems to me perilously near that hoary stereotype. Is it really obligatory for every Irish play to contain it?

But this seems a minor blemish compared to the play's obvious merits: its political and moral integrity, and the subtlety of its construction, the ingenious way in which it modulates variations on the theme of language and communication between human beings: the speechlessness of dumb Sarah, for example, is sensitively brought in as another variation on the theme of language; and that it is her ability to speak that Manus has given her which destroys Manus's world is a masterstroke of dramatic irony, as, indeed, is the fact, that her shock at what she has done, again deprives her of the power of speech, probably for ever.

Translations is undoubtedly one of Brian Friel's best plays. It puts him in the very front rank of contemporary dramatists.

The Mitford Girls at the Globe

reviewed by Hilary Spurling

Jessica Mitford tells a story of how, when she was sent at 16 to learn French under the protection of a respectable Parisian lady, she met a middle-aged man at a party and asked if she might go out with him. '*Ma petite, il vous jeterà sur un divan et il vous violerà.*' said Madame philosophically ('My dear, he will dump you on a sofa and violate you'), but Jessica went all the same.

She escaped from the brothel in which the evening wound up by a combination of footwork and fast talk, only to have a fate worse than death catch up with her, metaphorically speaking, nearly 40 years later at the Globe. Madame's prophetic phrase admirably sums up an evening described by its authors, in a line characteristically cribbed from 'Other People's Babies', as 'Thirty years of Mitford hopes and fears/Hearing them laugh, drying their tears . . .'

Certainly the six Mitfords themselves laugh a good deal in the course of the evening, especially Patricia Hodge's Nancy who has a habit of winding up each speech with a musical titter part way between Mrs Thatcher's mirthless tinkle and a set of door chimes. Otherwise Caryl Brahms and Ned Sherrin have rather remarkably managed to eliminate all trace of humour from the many Mitford jokes (culled chiefly from Nancy's novels and Jessica's autobiography) strung together to form their text. The Brahms-and-Sherrin method, patented after many years of effort on the musical stage, is not unlike the notorious process of roller-milling, chemical bleaching, adulteration and emulsification that goes to produce a loaf of Mother's Pride.

Texture is removed, to start with, by casting the sisters as identical sextuplets (a thing impossible in nature), all roughly the same age, height and size, all wearing the same party frocks (each gets a new one half-way through), gloves, shoes and pearls, topped with the same glassy smiles and crimplene hair. Anonymous and eager as Bond Street sales ladies, these synthetic look-alikes make patent nonsense of references to individual characteristics such as Unity's great size, Diana's beauty or Nancy's wit. Nor are they in any position to re-create the notable eccentricity of the Mitford background and upbringing which (except for a

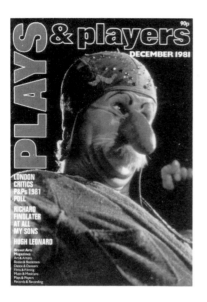

PLAYS & players 90p
DECEMBER 1981

LONDON
CRITICS
P&Ps 1981
POLL
RICHARD
FINDLATER
AT ALL
MY SONS
HUGH LEONARD

Newest Arts
Magazines
Art & Artists
Books & Bookmen
Dance & Dancers
Films & Filming
Music & Musicians
Plays & Players
Records & Recording

creditable effort, from Gay Soper, at mastering Debo's trick of imitating the strained look on a chicken's face while it lays an egg) seems here as sanitised and troublefree as Crawfie's royal nursery. The oddest moments come when faint traces of a more barbaric and peculiar original poke through the plastic sheeting: when three of the indistinguishable six, for instance, pretend to be young Mitfords in the Hons cupboard, perched on the trellis-work set and talking gingerly in genteely nervous voices about unmentionables like abortion, or why ducks copulate only in running water.

It is not until you see them so effectively demolished that you realise how crucially the flavour of Mitford humour – indeed of English humour at all levels – depends on habits of reticence and irony bred in the bone. There is nothing either amusing or alarming about the Mitford progenitor, Lord Redesdale – the dreaded Farve who, whatever else may or may not survive of the family myth, will surely go down in literature on a footing somewhere between old Capulet and Captain Hook – when he is played (as here by Oz Clarke), as precisely the sort of freshfaced, ingenuous bounder in a blazer that Farve himself most violently abominated.

It is not simply jokes that fall flat in the complete absence of the taboos and restrictions they were designed to sabotage. Any more substantial element of social or political awareness is similarly removed by treating the public events of the twenties and thirties – rise of fascism, capitalist collapse, Spanish civil war, Nazi upsurge – as so many offstage concert party turns. Hitler (who became Unity's mentor, and for whose sake she shot herself) comes on as a sort of Monty Bodkin, another blazered bounder with a swastika armband, while Oswald Mosley (who married Diana) spells nothing more, in this context, than true romance.

One cannot but concede a certain nerve, or wholesale ruthlessness, to Brahms and Sherrin when, having thoroughly processed their tasteless, textureless, bland and flavourless fakery, they next proceed to douse it (much as commercial bakers make wheatmeal loaves, by dyeing white ones brown) to saturation point in the more familiar sentimental melodies of the period. As to Patrick Garland's production, Stephanos Lazaridis' set, Lindsay Dolan's choreography and the eight piece band, they are all by current meagre standards comparatively lavish. But I doubt if even the Globe theatre – whose high points in the twenties and thirties ranged from Ethel M. Dell to Ivor Novello and *Murder in Mayfair* – has ever seen anything to beat the complacent vacuity of this musical.

After watching the American dream being dissolved into caution-
ary nightmares by crusading moralists and propagandists for 30
years, it's hard to imagine the shock-effect of *All My Sons* on
Broadway in 1947; and to exhume it in the West End so soon after
the National Theatre revivals of Miller's later and greater plays,
The Crucible and *Death of a Salesman*, was a manifest managerial
risk. Yet taking risks in staging significant contemporary work
was, once upon a time, a hazard occasionally embraced by the
better London 'commercial' managements, and the Omega Stage
Company again deserves applause for continuing this spasmodic
tradition by investing so much talent in a serious play of an
unfashionable kind.

Arthur Miller's first success, an Ibsenite morality-melodrama
written during the last war, is an often clumsily contrived text
about the fatal results of exalting family life and the ethos of
private success above public good and the sense of social responsibility. It may also be interpreted as an attack on the arms
industry, the capitalist system that it feeds and protects, and the
double-think of its apologists, especially in the aftermath of war.
Joe Keller has made a wartime fortune by selling airplane parts,
and has survived the sale of defective cylinder-heads which caused
the death of twenty-one men – a secret crime for which he let his
partner take the rap and go to jail. When his own guilt is finally
revealed, and he discovers that the suspicion of it had already
driven his beloved son to kill himself, Joe also commits suicide,
offstage.

Compared with *Death of a Salesman*, staged only two years
after the Broadway première of *All My Sons*, this play shows its
age and the forceps-marks of a playwriting-course Caesarean. The
plotting creaks with symbols and traditional trickery, of which the
stalest example is the flourish of an all-revealing letter. Yet, in
spite of its flaws, Miller's text combines a driving moral force and
grave social concern with a compassionate response to human
weakness for which one looks in vain to the didactic political
cartoonists of recent British drama. Joe Keller is not merely
paraded as an agit-prop villain, a handy historical scapegoat or a
puppet of the system: he is a man of complex feelings and motives,
as husband, father and boss. And Colin Blakely makes the best of
this subtlety, bringing to the role a concentrated yet relaxed
naturalism, a density of lived-in experience, an irresistible mastery
of understated but detailed characterisation that constitutes one
prime reason for seeing *All My Sons*. The fact that this mastery
does not extend to the convincing simulation of an appropriate
accent scarcely matters, in my view, after the first ten minutes:
the capacity of British actors to talk American has barely
improved since the war.

As I recall the 1947 London production, its Joe Keller (Joseph
Calleia) was – though incontestably American – inferior to this
one; and I preferred Rosemary Harris as Joe's wife, refusing to
acknowledge her son's death because that would mean recognising
her husband's guilt, to the mid-Western Lady Macbeth of Margalo
Gillmore in 1947. Miss Harris glows beautifully through the role,
helping to give the play and its family emotional coherence, in
spite of her problems (at the preview performance I saw) in
communicating with some members of the cast, who seemed to

All My Sons at Wyndham's

reviewed by Richard Findlater

221

Arthur Miller's *All My Sons* revived in Michael Blakemore's production at Wyndhams Theatre with Colin Blakely and Rosemary Harris. 1981.

have difficulty in looking each other in the face, or to be paralysed by arthritic intensity. (As the prime culprit was warmly praised by first night critics, these alienation effects must have rapidly disappeared.) I can't help feeling that Mrs Keller should resemble Mrs Portnoy rather than a Norse Madonna; but I succumbed to Miss Harris's all-conquering, myopic sweetness. Michael Blakemore controls the action inside Hayden Griffin's excellent back-yard set with a fine sense of the self-deceptions that seam the play, not only in Joe Keller's evasions and rationisations but in the illusions nursed by his wife and son, knowing them, in their hearts, to be lies. And now will Omega, or some other brave management, please let us see Mr Miller's plays from the past ten years?

1981 Awards

voted for by the London Theatre Critics

Best new play: *Translations* by Brian Friel

Best new musical: *Cats* by Andrew Lloyd Webber

Best performance by an actor: Alan Howard with RSC for *Good* and *Richard II*

Best performance by an actress: Penelope Wilton with National Theatre for *Much Ado About Nothing*

Most promising newcomer: Alice Krige in *Arms and the Man*

Most promising new playwright: Nell Dunn for *Steaming*

Best designer: Ralph Koltai for *The Love Girl* and *The Innocent*

Best director: Adrian Noble for *The Duchess of Malfi* and *A Doll's House*

In the best new play category, Brian Friel took a runaway lead with ten votes cast for his *Translations* which opened at the Hampstead Theatre Club and is currently in the National Theatre repertoire. Among the runners-up were Simon Gray with three votes for *Quatermaine's Terms* and Peter Nichols with two and a half votes for his *Passion Play* given in the Royal Shakespeare repertoire at the Aldwych. There was similar runaway voting in the best new musical category with the Andrew Lloyd Webber *Cats* attracting ten votes, with *One Mo' Time* taking five, *Barnum* three and both *Restoration* and *The Mitford Girls* collecting one each of the balance of the votes.

Voting was much more widely spread in the Best Actor and Best Actress categories. Alan Howard, given four votes, is nominated Best Actor for his performance with the RSC in *Good* and *Richard II*. A total of 14 Actors receive votes under this heading and Michael Bryant was a close second with three votes cast for his performance at the National Theatre in the revival of Calderon's *The Mayor of Zalamea*.

Right: Peter Nichols' *Passion Play* with Billie Whitelaw.

Helen Mirren in the revival of Webster's *The Duchess of Malfi* by 'best director' Adrian Noble. 1981.

Peter Nichols' *Passion Play* in a Royal Shakespeare Company production at the Aldwych Theatre with Anton Rodgers, Benjamin Whitrow, Louise Jameson, Billie Whitelaw, Eileen Atkins. 1981.

Three critics voted for Penelope Wilton as Beatrice in *Much Ado About Nothing* at the National Theatre. With a total of fourteen actresses receiving nominations this made Penelope Wilton Actress of the Year. Close behind her were Cheryl Campbell (in *A Doll's House*), Brenda Blethyn (in *Steaming*) Georgina Hale (also in *Steaming*) and Helen Mirren (in *The Duchess of Malfi*) all of whom received two votes each.

In the Most Promising Newcomer category a number of critics split their votes with double nominations. This made Alice Krige Most Promising Newcomer for her performance as Raina in *Arms and The Man* collecting four and a half votes. There were seventeen actors nominated in this category and a close runner-up was Tracey Ullman who collected three votes for her performance in *Four in a Million*. Eight dramatists received nominations in the Most Promising Playwright category with Nell Dunn collecting the award with five votes cast for her new play, *Steaming*. Hanif Kureishi (*Outskirts*) with four votes, Michael Wilcox (*Accounts*) with three votes, Ellen Dryden (*Harvest*) with two votes, Paul Kember (*Not Quite Jerusalem*) with two votes Jim Morris (*Blood on the Dole*) with two votes, Alan Williams (*In Dreams*) with one vote and Sarah Daniels (*Ripen Our Darkness*), one vote, were the runners-up.

Ralph Koltai for his set for *The Love-Girls and the Innocent* in the RSC repertoire at the Aldwych was Designer of the Year with a total of 7 votes cast for it, among runners-up were John Napier (three votes) Eileen Diss (two votes) and Carl Toms (two votes).

Voting was very close in the Best Director section and Adrian Noble wins this nomination with three votes cast for his work with *A Doll's House* and *The Duchess of Malfi*. Runners up were Mike Alfreds for Shared Experience's revival of *The Seagull* (two votes) and John Dexter with two votes (*Galileo/Shoemaker's Holiday*).

Sarah Daniels' *Ripen Our Darkness* **with Gwen Taylor. 1981. (Photo: John Haynes)**

1982

It was the year of the Falklands conflict resulting in the resignation of Foreign Secretary Lord Carrington and the sinking of the Belgrano *with the loss of 321 lives. The Pope visited both Britain and Argentina. The Prince and Princess of Wales had their first child, Prince William. Miguel de la Madrid Hurtado was elected President of Mexico and Felipe Gonzales, leading the Spanish Socialist Workers Party, became Spain's new Premier. Brezhnev died to be succeeded by Andropov. Lech Walesa was released and martial law was lifted in Poland. Helmut Kohl replaced Helmut Schmidt as West German Chancellor.*

In Britain miners accepted a 9.3% management offer recommended by their outgoing President Gormley. The De Lorean Motor Company went bust in Belfast. Roy Jenkins won Hillhead Glasgow in a by-election for the recently formed SDP party. The National Theatre had an interesting year with Hall directing The Oresteia, *Richard Eyre* Guys and Dolls *and Judi Dench appearing as Lady Bracknell and in Pinter's latest, the one-act* A Kind of Alaska. *Stoppard's new play,* The Real Thing *was put on by Michael Codron in the West End.*

1982

The Oresteia at the Olivier

reviewed by Martin Esslin

The performance of Greek drama, some two and a half thousand years after it flourished, presents problems far more difficult than, say, that of Elizabethan or Restoration plays. However little we may know about the style of performance of these more recent theatrical masterpieces, we do know the essentials: what was spoken and what sung and what the audiences expected from the plays, what they got out of them. In the case of Greek drama the situation is much more complex: we don't know whether the choral passages were spoken or sung, for example; and if they were sung, what kind of tunes were used; we don't know what kind of dance steps the chorus executed; and of the style of acting and speaking of the spoken passages we also know relatively little for certain.

A performance of a Greek play might well be analogous to a performance of an opera that might result if the producer had had nothing to go by except the libretto, without stage directions and without the music and did not even know whether there had been any musical score. Imagine a performance of a Wagner opera, with spoken text only, in in-the-round theatre. Some of the poetry of the lines might come through, some of the plot; but it certainly would give a very poor idea of what the author was after when he wrote and composed the work.

Peter Hall's production of the *Oresteia* at the Olivier is a daring and wholly admirably intentioned attempt to give us an experience as near to the real thing as present knowledge could allow us to achieve. For one, the shape of the Olivier is very similar to that of a Greek amphitheatre. Peter Hall, moreover, decided to let us have the whole of the *Oresteia* in one evening, which is also much nearer to what happened in ancient Athens in the fifth century B.C. And, knowing as we do, that Greek actors wore masks, Peter Hall decided to use masks very similar to the masks actually worn at the time. And, as only men performed Greek tragedy, the National Theatre decided to cast the play with men only. The masks easily allow them to impersonate women.

The chorus was the basis of Greek drama, solo actors only gradually emerged from the chorus. So Peter Hall decided to forgo the naming of the actors playing the leading solo parts. His soloists are part of the chorus; after having assumed the mask and costume of a named character, they often return in another scene as an anonymous chorus member.

All this is fascinating and of great interest as a daring artistic experiment. This performance of the *Oresteia* is undoubtedly a major event, and a unique occasion to evaluate possible valid contemporary approaches to Greek drama.

How successful is it? That isn't a question that permits a simple answer. The experiment is far too complex for that. Let me start by saying that the masks are beautiful (Jocelyn Herbert is responsible for the total design of the show) and so is the stage: the simple semi-circular playing area with two diagonal approachways at either side and a metallic back-structure, very similar to that in the original Greek theatre, which allows itself to be opened to provide the inside of a temple or palace, a gate, or high up the eyrie of a watchman.

But the masks, of course, present great problems to present-day actors: those are full masks, which means that, on the whole, movements of the mouth are not visible. Alas, some of the masks, have openings so situated on the face of their wearers, that one *can* see the lips move in the mouth-opening. This produces the odd result that some characters are seen to speak, while others are not and what is more: acting with such full masks is a very complex skill. In fact, the actor should be able by *other* gestures of the hand or head to indicate *that* he is speaking (Japanese Noh actors, who use such masks are superb masters of this technique). Some of the actors in the National Theatre obviously have not quite learned it. There are scenes, particularly in the second play, *Choephoroi* (the libation bearers) when Orestes, Electra and the chorus are engaged in an intricate dialogue, when, the voices of some of the speakers being very similarly tenoral, one simply does not know who is saying what. At such moments the performance becomes like a film that has gone out of sync. And this difficulty makes it very hard to get a sense of what is going on.

The choral passages have been, on the whole, divided up among the (usually twelve) members of the group. This helps comprehension (although here also not knowing *which* of the twelve is saying what is rather annoying) but it also interrupts the lyrical flow of these passages; there are always small pauses at the point of junction of the half-sentences or short speeches of the different *choreutes* and that produces a rather jerky and less than poetic effect. Some choral passages are sung. Some of these are very fine, and lyrical, but then the words are again far more difficult to understand.

This brings us to the vexed question of the language. Tony Harrison is a brilliant translator and a fine poet. But the idiom he has couched the Aeschylean text in, is very peculiar. He goes in for very Germanic sounding compound nouns – a husband is a *manlord*, a ruler a *clan-chief*, a bird of prey a *prey-bird*; moreover he calls a God a *He-God* and a Goddess a *She-God*, and so it goes on. Until you have grasped the principle behind this, it makes understanding the text difficult. On top of that somebody, translator or director, has made the decision to let the play be spoken in a kind of stage North-of-England hybrid Lancashire-Yorkshire

PLAYS &players 90p

JANUARY 1982

COLIN BLAKELY
AND ... OWEN
... ERVIEW
MARTIN ESSLIN
AT THE ORESTEIA
RICHARD FINDLATER
AT 84 CHARING X RD

Brevet Arts
Magazines
Art & Artists
Books & Bookplans
Dance & Dancers
Films & Filming
Music & Musicians
Plays & Players
Records & Recording

accent, with a hint of the Beatles. There is nothing wrong with that, except that it emphasises a striving for folksiness which also informs the wording. Aeschylus doesn't go in for shit, or pissing in wells and similar vulgarisms. He was the stateliest and most dignified of poets (at least in his serious plays; he also wrote satyr plays, but they used a totally different linguistic convention).

No wonder that the choral passages lack all of the great, overwhelming lyrical beauty which has made them famous and which constitutes the chief attraction of this trilogy. Add to that the fact that the chorus moves very badly and you have reached the central point of what is wrong with this production. The strong likelihood is that the Greek tragic chorus *danced;* the area of the stage where the chorus disported itself was called the *orchestra* which means the 'dance floor'. This chorus does *not* dance. It moves around, in supposedly choreographed patterns; but, quite frankly, these are a mess. The chorus of elders in the first play, *Agamemnon*, dodders and totters around like the most ragged chorus in a third rate opera company; and the Eumenides in the third play are equally slovenly and unconvincing. It is as if they had been told: 'at this point you all move around a bit' and had then been left to their own devices without any serious attempt at rehearsing any movement of precision and unified pattern. This is a pity: the choral passages are the heart of these plays; one ought to look forward to them, as deep lyrical and choreographic experiences. Here, they often merely hold up the action.

The music, by Harrison Birtwistle, is very effective. There is a lot of percussion, action underlined by drumbeats. And this is very effective. But the rhythmic quality of the performance does raise problems. The basic verse of Greek tragedy was the *iambic trimeter*, a six-beat iambic line. In English this is the most effective type of verse; Shakespeare's blank verse is based on an iambic rhythm, albeit a five-beat one. This translation, on the other hand, is mainly *trochaic* and also tries to bring in rhymes as often as possible. The effect of this is one of doggerel verse rather like that of nursery rhymes. Whether the basic rhythms of the musical score have anything to do with this strange choice seems to me a question that might be asked.

As regards the acting: The leading roles are played by members of the group of sixteen actors listed in the programme as responsible for the speaking parts. One can therefore merely cite the performance of individual characters. It may well be that the same actor plays a character that has seemed to me to be very well acted, and also another, that is far less successful. We shall never know.

Easily the best performance, in fact the only one that has, in my opinion, wholly solved the problem of acting in full mask is that of Clytemnestra. A very strong and individual character emerges from this: proof that it is possible to present a rounded, very interesting and psychologically profound personality, without actually using one's face. This Clytemnestra has a masculine voice, but she is nevertheless wholly convincing as a woman. The watchman who opens the play is also very well done: here the homely idiom fits; and he has a fine sense of humour. Very good also is the Herald in the *Agamemnon*. The Orestes of the two subsequent plays looks splendidly Japanese in his fine mask and costume and speaks well, but his movement is hopeless. Either he doesn't move at all, so that we don't even know whether he is speaking; or he jerks about mechanically as if merely moving because he has been told to move. The two Gods in the last play, the *Eumenides*, Apollo and Athena, are very unconvincing. Greek actors used the cothurnus, an elevated kind of shoe, that made them taller so that they could be seen better in the large arenas. Clearly that was unnecessary in the smaller Olivier, although I cannot understand why the actors should be barefoot in this performance. But surely the Gods ought to have been taller or otherwise superhuman. Here they appeared more like caricatures out of Aristophanes than like the high Deities (or as Tony Harrison has it 'He-God' and 'She-God') of Aeschylus. Which makes the solemn ending of the play less moving, convincing and effective. This is puzzling in view of the director's obvious intention on turning the ending of the trilogy into a genuine quasi-religious experience.

The audience is asked to stand while the actors – led by the Furies who have been changed into benevolent deities (which is the meaning of the word *eumenides* – well-meaning) file out and a solemn hymn is heard from the back of the auditorium. This is a great and moving moment. It would be far more moving if the Gods had appeared as truly awe-inspiring, transcendental beings.

Much of all this may sound like carping criticism. It is, of course, merely the result of taking this fascinating experiment really seriously. An experiment like this is, above all, a basis for discussion; it is an experience from which all concerned, director, actors and audiences must be able to derive benefit, learn something for further experiments. The Olivier has proved now that it is an ideal venue for Greek tragedy. We have seen that full masks can work extremely well and that they add a whole new dimension to the art of acting.

This, therefore, is an event not to be missed on any account. It is a performance which, without doubt, can prove a milestone in the development of our theatre towards opening up a whole hitherto much neglected area of classical drama, perhaps the greatest drama of all time. This performance has not only clearly defined the direction in which further work will have to be pursued; it is, in itself, a memorable theatrical occasion.

PLAYS &players 90p
FEBRUARY 1982

JAMES FENTON
BEING A CRITIC

RICHARD FINDLATER
AT MRS TANQUERAY

FRANK MARCUS
GREEN ROOM

In aspiring to turn a private correspondence into a public performance the theatre-wise adapter may balance the occupational risks of closed-circuit cosiness and static duologue against several potentially large assets. The greatest of these – apart from the cut-price economics of such operations – is that many good letter-writers give the illusion of being authentically *natural*, even when keeping an eye on posterity: they write as if caught in the act of self-revelation, talking aloud without inhibitions or fear or being heard, and in this direct address an audience may enjoy collaborative eavesdropping. Good letters have the freshness of good talk with the bonus of second thoughts: their self-censorship and self-portraiture (conscious and unconscious) may show up more enter-

1982

84 Charing Cross Road at the Ambassadors

reviewed by Richard Findlater

tainingly in performance than in print, satisfying the still-irrepressible current appetite for biographical fact or, better still, gossip.

Such assets have been skilfully and sensitively exploited by James Roose-Evans in making a surprisingly strong theatre-evening ('play' is a misnomer) out of a somewhat flimsy (though funny and endearing) book published in hard covers eleven years ago. *84 Charing Cross Road* is an exchange of letters over 20 years between Helene Hanff, a bibliophilic Jewish scriptwriter in New York's Grub Street, and Frank Doel, the manager of a second-hand bookshop in Charing Cross Road which supplied her not only with books but were grateful recipients of food parcels and warm, witty, apparently artless letters, carefully preserved by Miss Hanff. With the help of two excellent performances by Rosemary Leach and David Swift, Mr Roose-Evans – whose adaptation was first staged at Salisbury in July – has given West End playgoers the chance of an unexpected minor treat. Our thanks for an evening of rare pleasure are due not only to him but to the management, Michael Redington and Tillymic Ltd, newcomers to London. I hope their initiative and courage will be rewarded, so that they will stay in the West End, where such qualities are in perennially short supply.

84 Charing Cross Road lacks most of the conventional ingredients of commercial success, old or new, upmarket or down. There is no plot, no drama, no violence, no sex. The protagonists never meet: they merely write each other letters, at a distance of three thousand miles, and the letters are largely about books – the authors, prices and bindings of out-of-print volumes unobtainable a few blocks away at Brentano's but procurable, sometimes after very long delays but at prices that seem astonishingly cheap, by Marks & Co. Several secondary characters (mostly employees of Marks & Co) figure shadowily in the cast, but with no more dramatic purpose than to tell Miss Hanff a few facts about the shop and their own lives. The only 'development' is the thawing out of Mr Doel, whose insular reserve melts under the friendly, present-giving, postal zest of his lonely customer on the East Side of New York. The only 'suspense' (a surprisingly effective thread of linking feeling) lies in the uncertainty about whether Miss Hanff will ever find the time, the money and the chutzpah to make the London trip that she postpones for two decades (at the Ambassadors, rather less than two hours). Yet the only flaw in the play, which adheres closely to the text of the book, is when it peels away from it – in the attempt to round off the evening by showing Miss Hanff in London at last, entering the shop of her dreams when it is empty, and on the verge of closure, with Mr Doel in his grave. This is a mistake; but it lasts for a few minutes only, and it doesn't spoil the impact of what has gone before.

What helps to give *84 Charing Cross Road* its special charm and theatrical truth is its transmission of *enthusiasm* – most conspicuously, about books. Helene Hanff's interest in them is not that of a literary critic, a sociologist or an academic: it belongs to the vanished world of *John O'London's Weekly* and the *Saturday Review* rather than that of the *Times Literary Supplement* and the *New York Review of Books.* Her love of books is that of someone *hungry* for literature, longing to fill the gaps in her reading, searching for new friends among the old authors: it has nothing to

Rosemary Leach in the James Roose-Evans' adaptation of *84 Charing Cross Road*. 1982.

do with the sated sophistication of an erudite collector with private libraries at hand. Miss Hanff's hunger is part of a romantic passion for London, as reflected in the literature of the past, and for an idea of England that seems close to the chimera so long preserved among her more susceptible fellow-Americans by our Tourist Board. But it is expressed with a sharp, knowing, self-mocking Jewish humour, which checks her tendency to gush and whimsy without blocking the genuineness of her response – to people as well as books.

At the Ambassadors Rosemary Leach communicates these enthusiasms with splendidly infectious energy. Her incarnation of a New York loner, gleefully embracing such friends as 'Sam' (Pepys) and 'John Henry' (Newman), exploding in fury over the cutting of Donne's sermons, enjoying her own generosity with powdered egg and nylons, not only squeezes all the available fun, and a bit more than the available poignancy, from Miss Hanff's edited missives, but also makes the postal posturing more credible and more lovable. In Frank Doel's brief and muted responses David Swift has far thinner material for building a believable character, but he does it, oh so deftly, evoking with subtly suggestive brush-strokes an individual pain and pleasure behind the English stereotype. The only serious weakness of Mr Roose-Evans's production is the injection of miscued, intrusive music.

Together with its celebration of an unusual and ambivalent Anglo-American pen friendship (faintly shadowed by the approaching death of the old-style Special Relationship) *and* its celebration of second-hand bookshops – irresistible to those who, like this reviewer, secrete dream shops of their own creation, occasionally revisited in sleep on gala nights – *84 Charing Cross Road* exudes a gentle, kindly, sentimental nostalgia and (supreme pejorative of days gone by) escapism, sprinkled with laughter, which may well, given time, bring it success on both sides of the Atlantic.

There are two categories of theatre-critic: those, like J C Trewin, John Elsom or Irving Wardle, for whom the theatre is the central interest of their lives, and those, like James Fenton, Mark Amory or Milton Shulman, for whom it is only one, and perhaps not the most important, of a number of competing interests.

It is to the second of these two categories that I myself belong. Apart from the fact that I regard myself primarily as a novelist, I must be the only theatre-critic who became one, not by choice and effort, but by accident. My predecessor, Frank Marcus, fell ill and since I had both worked for the *Sunday Telegraph* for a long time as a literary reviewer and been a constant theatre-goer since my teens, the editor asked me to deputise for a single week. Soon, Marcus decided to retire and the editor had liked my one contribution sufficiently to ask me to replace him. Essentially, I am an amateur, in both senses of the word: I love the theatre passionately and I am not a theatre person.

Theatre-critics of each category have their advantages and disadvantages. Those in the first category possess a dedication and

Professional Amateur

Francis King, Sunday Telegraph *theatre critic contributes to* P&P's *second theatre criticism series*

PLAYS & players 90p

MARCH 1982

FRANCIS KING
THEATRE CRITICISM

SHERIDAN MORLEY
GREEN ROOM

HILARY SPURLING
AT LA RONDE

knowledge that those in the second cannot match; but those in the second are often better able to relate the one art to its sister arts and a little world to the larger one of which it is a metaphor. Once, on my way to Chichester by train, I found myself, the only theatre-critic of the second category, in the same carriage as three theatre-critics of the first. It was the period both of the Thorpe trial, to me an event of outstanding political and psychological interest, and of some kind of minor upset at Chichester, of which I knew nothing. I wanted to talk about the trial; but my colleagues, excited by the Chichester events, not only did not want to talk about it but seemed totally ignorant of its details.

Theatre-critics can be further divided into those who hobnob and those who refuse to do so. I never attend theatrical parties or press conferences and if a hostess holds out to me the bait of some theatrical celebrity ('I know she'd *adore* to meet you'), I at once glide away from it. I am intensely interested in plays and performances but I am not stage-stuck in the sense of wanting either to rush into a dressing-room and say 'Darling, you were wonderful!' or to act – as one of the most charming of my colleagues does so effectively – as confidant, psychoanalyst and adviser to people of the theatre. There are two reasons why I hold myself aloof in this manner. Firstly, I want to retain my illusions about those people up there on the stage and, ever since, many years ago, I guided Edith Evans for the British Council in Italy and was horrified by the self-centred trivialities that she uttered for want of lines by Congreve, Chekhov or Shakespeare I have learned that people like John Gielgud, Janet Suzman and Simon Callow are exceptional in not dwindling and dimming when being merely themselves, instead of filling a role.

The second reason is that I suffer from a morbid reluctance to give pain, and that reluctance is intensified if I have to give pain to someone known to me. I remember my horror when I travelled up to Manchester to see *The Dresser* and, as I entered the Royal Exchange, came face to face with Ronald Harwood, whom I both admire and like. What would I say to him, if I loathed his play? More recently, I had the same problem with Julian Mitchell, a friend of many years, at the first night of *Another Country*. Fortunately, in each case, the play proved to be one which I could praise with no insincerity.

This reluctance to give pain often leads me into attempting to hint at what is wrong with a play, a production or a performance, instead of coming out with the truth with no prevarication. Thus I find myself writing of a thoroughly nerveless piece of acting that 'The director should have encouraged X to adopt a rather more strenuous approach to his role' or of a thoroughly misguided one that 'Y takes a curiously unorthodox view of the character.' Of course, the actors are not fooled – any more than a patient at the dentist is fooled by being told 'This is not going to hurt' – and it would be better to be franker. A deficiency in me, I know.

Inevitably, what one writes is influenced by the organ for which one writes it – just as a performance is influenced by the audience for which the actor gives it. The *Sunday Telegraph* rarely allows me more than 800 words to review at least three and sometimes as many as five plays in a single week. The discipline of having to cut and cut and compress and compress has undoubtedly done my style more good than harm; but I regret that, as a rule, I have to confine myself to a judgement of a production or a performance, with no attempt to re-create it in words for my readers – as, for example, Irving Wardle and Benedict Nightingale, each with far more space, manage to do so vividly. A telegram can often have more impact than a letter; but none the less I should prefer to compose the latter.

Again, it has become clear to me from the correspondents who bother to write in to me, often at regular intervals, that the *Sunday Telegraph* readership is interested primarily in mainstream theatre. I, on the other hand, tend to be most strongly excited by the kind of production in which a young dramatist is still straining, often ineffectually, to get out all the things churning around inside him, the actors are struggling to overcome inadequacies of technique, and designer and director have had to contend with a tiny budget and, in many cases, a tiny stage. I love that sense of potentialities in the process of realisation. But clearly, if I am to satisfy my readers, I must devote more space to the latest witless comedy or mechanical thriller to arrive in the West End with its complement of telly stars aboard, than to a new play by a new dramatist in a club or a pub.

Both in literature and the theatre I have always differentiated between critics and reviewers. The former have both eyes on the object to be appraised; the latter have one eye on the object and the other on the readership, although, throughout this piece, I have used the word 'theatre-critic', most of us for most of the time are, let us face it, theatre-reviewers. Ours is not an absolute 'This is good' or 'This is bad' but a relative 'If you like this sort of thing, then you'll like this' or 'If you don't like this sort of thing, then stay away.' I should never choose to go and see *The Mousetrap* or *The Sound of Music* or *No Sex Please, We're British*, except for sociological reasons; but many of my readers would choose nothing else and I have to bear them in mind.

I find that many of my correspondents are people who once either worked in the theatre or were regular theatregoers but who now, for reasons of age, ill-health or residence in the country, can participate only vicariously. The fact that my memories go back to seeing Gielgud and Olivier alternate as Romeo and Mercutio (not Romeo and Juliet, as the *Sunday Telegraph* once mysteriously printed it), Katina Paxinou gave the most powerful Gertrude that I have ever seen and Elizabeth Bergner disport herself with androgynous but irresistible charm in Barrie's *The Boy David* means that, though I probably bore my younger readers when I find an affinity between, say, Donald Sinden and Godfrey Tearle or Michael Pennington and Ion Swinley, my older readers respond with gratitude. (I have never received more letters of protest than when I wrote that Anna Neagle had been a better dancer than Jessie Matthews).

I still find that my theatre reviews take far longer to write than my literary ones. Last summer J C Trewin kindly gave me a lift back from Stratford in the car that he had hired. 'Would you mind if I just stopped off and telephoned through my notice?' he asked. I resigned myself to a long wait. He popped into a telephone-box, I watched his mouth opening and shutting, and ten minutes later he was out again. When I read it the next day, the review proved

PLAYS & players
APRIL 1982

IRVING WARDLE: THEATRE CRITICISM
RICHARD FINDLATER AT HOBSON'S CHOICE
NICHOLAS DE JONGH: GREEN ROOM

to be a model of judiciousness and lucidity. Could I perform the same feat? I doubt it. But life might be easier if I were obliged to – since then I should be exonerated from tinkering away at each article throughout the week, until Friday arrives and then at long last, like a mother uncomfortably swollen with a ten-month baby, I am shot of it.

I like to think that over the years I have acquired an instinctive flair as a critic of literature in general and of the novel in particular – just as, over the years, even the dimmest of GPs eventually acquires an instinctive flair as a diagnostician of day-to-day ailments. But I am far less confident of possessing that instinctive flair as a critic of theatre. The result is that whereas, when a literary review produces a letter of dissent from the author or one of his admirers, it seldom persuades me to change my mind, a similar letter of dissent about a theatrical review at once has me agonising: Was I fair? Was I right? Did I miss the point? I have been reviewing theatre for little more than three years and it may well be that, in due course, I shall acquire for my theatre-reviews the same self-confidence that I have for my literary ones.

For lack of this self-confidence, I take great pains with my reviewing – being, to that extent, a complete professional and not an amateur. J R Ackerley, the best literary editor for whom I ever worked, once remarked to me that if it was a choice between a brilliant reviewer who never produced his copy on time and a sound one who was never late, he would always opt for the second. I am punctual on first nights and I do not leave before the end of a performance, however bored I may be; unlike at least one of my colleagues, I do not take refuge in sleep; I return the tickets that I do not intend to use; if available, I look at the text of a play before I go to see it; my copy reaches the office on time. That I am so scrupulous about all these things is an indication of that lack of self-confidence of which I am always conscious.

As a novelist, I am fascinated by the relationship between us drama-critics. Literary critics may rarely, if ever, meet each other – certainly they do not all sit in the same room at the same time reading the same book. But drama-critics spend more hours in each other's company than, in many cases, with their closest friends, cats or dogs. Yet, with a few exceptions, the relationship remains a wholly static one. A is the drama-critic who is always courteous, kindly and affable; B is the drama-critic who is always courteous, kindly and affable except when he is with a 'friend'; C is the drama-critic who is always courteous, kindly and remote; D is the drama-critic who one evening nods at one and the next looks over one's head; E is the drama-critic who invariably asks one what is on the next week, as though mysteriously all those press releases that rain down on the rest of us never come his way; F is the drama-critic who would sooner miss a first-night than a freebie . . . So one could go on, to Z, who never reviews one play for fewer than three outlets. The point is that, only in rare instances, does one see a colleague's home, meet his wife and children or learn anything more about him.

English drama-critics have some power but less than they would like to imagine and less than their counterparts in the States. I suspect that such power that we do have derives not so much from our actual reviews as from the quotations that can be extracted from them. As though conscious of this, some of my colleagues sometimes strike me as writing not with a column but with a newspaper advertisement or a hoarding in mind. 'Laughed till I cried.' 'Had me on the edge of my seat.' 'Sent me out excited, moved and exhilarated.' Can those phlegmatic and sometimes even somnolent people around me have really been reacting so intensely? In general, I find that the less my colleagues get quoted, the higher my opinion of them. Good copy is copy which swings between extremes of adulation and derision. Good criticism is something else. Three of the worst theatre-critics of the recent past were three of the most widely read and the most frequently quoted.

How little attention the theatre really pays to its critics has been demonstrated to me over and over again by a letter which begins roughly as follows: 'Dear Mr Marcus, I wonder if I can persuade you to come and see . . .' As I have already indicated, it is more than three years since Marcus retired from the *Sunday Telegraph* and I took over from him. In a moment of spleen, John Osborne wrote one of his by now notorious postcards to the *Sunday Telegraph:* 'King must go. Has he ever been?' I know exactly what he meant by that question.

APRIL
1982

As Times Go By

Irving Wardle, The Times *drama critic is this month's contributor to* P&P's *Theatre Criticism series*

As the editor of *Plays and Players* kindly reminds me, I have been stuck in the same job for over 20 years and am one of the few surviving reviewers who contributed to a series on this topic in the early 1960s.

I have forgotten what I wrote then, but I can imagine what it was like. I was a chippy ex-National Serviceman and demoralised ex-music student: I owned nothing, knew nobody, and it gave me quite a kick to be sitting in judgement on professional artists some of whom were definitely officer material.

I am now a middle-aged householder, fully loaded with all the fetters of family life, and I know a lot of people in the theatre whom I am reluctant to hurt. 'You aren't as sharp as you used to be,' one of them said the other day. He was right, and I don't regret it. As Ken Tynan once put it, there comes a time when there are more important things in life than driving William Douglas Home off the stage.

Not that he is often found there nowadays. If I have changed, so has the theatre. It is harder for class prejudice, philistinism, and sexual bigotry to get a hearing, and on the whole it is controlled by people with their hearts in the right place. Quality apart, I rarely see anything that makes the hackles rise as they once rose to the comedies of Hugh and Margaret Williams; and the whole business of theatre-going has become less artificial than it was in the West End of Moss Empires and the Littlers.

What has not changed is the widespread dislike for reviewers. For much of his life, the reviewer is cushioned against this by the simple fact that his favours are required as a source of free advertisement. Letters of invitation arrive by the sackful, all recommending their wares in the most respectful terms. Press

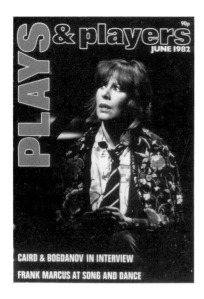

PLAYS &players
90p
JUNE 1982

CAIRD & BOGDANOV IN INTERVIEW
FRANK MARCUS AT SONG AND DANCE

offices are staffed by lovely girls who seem genuinely glad to see you no matter what you wrote last time. I am not questioning any of this. Press representation naturally attracts friendly people into a job that requires them to make friends. But the reviewer is making a mistake if he thinks anyone else in the theatre looks on him as a friend.

Here are a few comments about reviewers that I have picked up over the years from artists on the receiving end. 'Well, XYZ's a nice man, but he's in a shit's job.' 'Power? Certainly you've got power, like the Wizard of Oz.' 'Why should we put on a memorial meeting for Tynan? He was only a critic.' 'I don't care how long you've been at it, I don't believe in your occupation.' 'Being a theatre critic teaches you that being a theatre critic teaches you nothing about the theatre.'

These, I should stress, are considered opinions: not trigger-happy overnight insults. I have plenty of those as well: including the obligatory Osborne hate telegrams, formal cancellations of long-standing friendships, and – the ones that hurt most – sorrowfully bewildered messages, like one from the late C P Taylor beginning, 'What's all this? My old mate going on about "defects in structure" . . .'

When I took on my job with *The Times* there was a feeling that the new theatrical generation and the new young reviewers were all moving in the same direction, and it was going to be a ball. But it was not long before the strokes of midnight broke up the party and the old suspicions and antagonisms returned. This is not going to change until there is a total change in the system of public performance and public comment. A bunch of actors come together as a temporary community, working single-mindedly towards an opening night which can only succeed if they have developed a strong network of internal loyalties and belief in what they are doing. How can they feel anything but suspicious towards an outsider who has made no such investment in the work and whose first task must be to produce a readable piece of copy? If, on the other hand, a critic sits through rehearsals, he finds himself turning into the company's lucky mascot, and utterly unable to form any detached opinion on the work of all these talented and charming people. In the words of Tom Stoppard, who got out of reviewing at the first opportunity, 'I never had the moral character to knock a friend: or, rather, I had the moral character never to knock a friend.'

Finding oneself ranked with the enemy was at first a dismaying experience; but now I am rather glad of it. A salaried reviewer is in a most unfairly privileged position. As long as he gets his facts right he can say what he wants; he can make fun of hard-working artists, luxuriate in schoolmasterish moralising, safe behind his typewriter and drawing his regular money while helping to put other people out of work. It is quite right that he should get something back in the teeth from time to time. For one thing, it makes him think twice before going in for the invective, gleeful teasing, and narcissistic self-promotion on which reviewers like the dreadful James Agate built their reputations.

An acquaintance once asked Agate what kept him on at his job with the *Sunday Times*. Agate pondered conspiratorially and then stuck his stone-ball head in at the taxi window to confide his secret. 'Great fame!' he said. That attitude has gone, thank God. The breed Orwell characterised as 'verminous little lions' is now extinct. Thanks to the initiative first taken by the Royal Court, the theatre has stopped playing the old game of mock-subservience to its critics. There is now small chance of growing a swollen ego. We are always being told how obtuse, ignorant, flabbyminded, morally and intellectually blinkered we are. Fine. If that is how we seem, we have the chance to disprove it every night. If our occupation is held in contempt, it is up to us to practise it honourably.

The old suspicions are never going to dissolve, but at least – if you will forgive the cant term – the lines are open for dialogue. The form this takes will obviously vary according to temperament. Some reviewers are high status performers who prefer to write from a position of strength. My natural tone is low status. Whenever I raise my voice it immediately sounds false. If I have a style it comes from following a few home-made rules: such as trying to express adverse comment through irony, as I am no good at inventing jokes; and never writing anything about a man that I could not also say to his face. I wish it were possible to confine criticism to selective reportage, avoiding downright judgement and all the worn-out adjectives that go with it. However, I realise that readers look for the moment when a reviewer steels himself to decide for or against a show. However dead they may be for the writer, words like 'marvellous' or 'lamentable' still have their effect on the page. If they point the public in the right direction or please an actor, that is more important than preserving the chastity of the reviewer's diction.

At the time of writing, [*The Times* was not being printed at the time Irving Wardle was writing], I have no idea whether I shall ever review a show again. This will be no great loss to anybody else. If I had anything worth saying, I have had plenty of time to say it over the past 20 years. But, apart from the spectre of the dole queue and the alarming discovery that I am now too old for the job I fancied with the Express Diary, it will be a big loss to me never again to be stuck on page two with the office clock coming up to half past eleven.

This piece may sound dejectedly apologetic, but I am making no apology for criticism itself. Reading it and writing it have made me feel I had some business in the world. It is a great pleasure to see a man hitting a nail on the head; and doubly exhilarating when you are allowed to have a go with the hammer.

In my case, the original impulse comes from music. Listening to it always left me feeling frustrated: the better the music the greater the frustration. There ought to be something you could *do* about it; something you could pay back while at the same time making it your own. There was no answer to that, given my musical limitations. But the theatre offered an alternative means of completing the circle of experience; of receiving a piece of work and paying for it through an articulated response. And if that seems the act of a parasite, it is only the last stage of the whole parasitic process by which the writer steals from life and the performers then steal from the writer. We all want attention, we all want a bit of praise now and then; and if the reviewer gets it right, he is giving artists the food they need as well as bestowing

PETER NICHOLS: GREEN ROOM
PLOWRIGHT ON PLOWRIGHT
BENEDICT NIGHTINGALE ON THEATRE CRITICISM
ADRIAN NOBLE AND RICHARD EYRE IN INTERVIEW

some kind of permanence on a transitory event and satisfying his own appetite.

By 'getting it right' I mean taking possession of an event: grasping the unspoken intentions of a production, understanding why a play has been put together in a particular way, finding a phrase that precisely encapsulates a moment of acting (one reason for Olivier's popularity with critics is that he gives you so much that can be put into words). If you succeed, you also have the satisfaction of articulating what a lot of other people have been thinking privately.

For much of the time, of course, we achieve no such thing. Tynan used to describe himself as a lock into which a play might or might not fit. The opposite is true in my case. Success is tied up with the act of theft. I am out front like a burglar on a dark street, weighing up my chances of breaking and entering the brightly lit stage premises. On an easy night, the property is wide open to the critical intruder. Other properties are secure, and the eye scans their blank walls and locked windows seeking somewhere to insert a jemmy. If you do penetrate the defences you can possess the contents. If you fail to get inside, you have to make do with describing them. However, even this can be useful so long as it does not pretend to any bogus insights. Something legitimate can be said at every level of ignorance, provided you understand which level you are at.

Much of any reviewers' output will consist of snap-reaction routines no more worth remembering than the tricks of a performing dog; equally, much of the work he sees is soon going to be forgotten. Mediocrity on both sides is normal; and also essential. It is the unending traffic of ordinary theatrical craftsmanship and competent journalistic response that supplies the conditions for big events to take place. Whether we are up to recognising a big event when we see one is another matter. A man who spends every evening seeing shows is liable to turn into a shrewd guide to the second-rate, and blind to everything beyond it. In the past, every innovative playwright from Ibsen to Pinter was greeted with derision. Fearful of falling into that trap again, we now suffer from the opposite temptation. Pathfinding was and remains a precarious occupation, but it is the one activity that sorts out critics from reviewers.

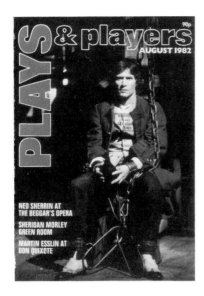

Richard Eyre's production of *Guys and Dolls* at the National Theatre with Bob Hoskins, Barrie Rutter and David Healy. 1982.

'Why,' ran the eternal question before this production opened, 'should our National Theatre be doing an American musical, a hit from the *commercial stage*?' Even at the time, there were ready answers to this, such as 'Why shouldn't they?' and 'In the cultural climate most of us hope for, there will scarcely be any such thing as the *un*commercial stage'. But the sight of the thing being done, on the broad apron of the Olivier, has banished theory in any case. *Guys and Dolls* is a terrific show, performed really well, and those who would rather it hadn't happened are revealed as wet blankets of the soggiest kind.

The process wouldn't have worked with any old musical. A National Theatre *Oklahoma* would necessarily have turned out as corn-fed pastiche with outbursts of lumbering 'sincerity'. But because *Guys and Dolls* is openly and proudly a low-life pastiche to begin with, it doesn't even matter that we realise the performers are not native Americans. In fact this enhances the affection in which we hold the show (which is not too stale an affection either, because there are some fine neglected numbers in the score). The first neon signs that come warmly roasting into view to establish the Manhattan landscape (settings: John Gunter, lighting: David Hersey) are 'Wrigley's Spearmint' and 'Maxwell House Coffee' – which suggest a comforting overlap of economies, if not of cultures, between ourselves and Damon Runyon's zoot-suited metropolis.

Vocally, we get the same overlap from the cast. After hard work, the accents throughout are a most honourable near-miss. Only Julia McKenzie as Miss Adelaide truly strikes the ear as a possible American import, and she has the advantage of the kind of song (a poissun can develop a cold) that practically can't be sung except in pungent Brooklynese. Bill Paterson, as Harry the Horse, has his own solution, a nasal delivery suggesting Walter Matthau in an adenoids crisis. It took time to work Harry out – a pleasant occupation even if Richard Eyre's hot-foot direction didn't leave you many spare moments in which to indulge it.

But it was the way Paterson *moved* that gave the real clue to the evening's success. This Harry the Horse doesn't walk, he treads – in a rubber-soled, bent-kneed, interior-sprung manner drawn straight from the early American comic papers and animated films. And looking around the ensemble, one realised that everybody had some speciality of this kind going for him. Larrington Walker, to take a single example, was a one-man Harlem at all times. I mean no slight on the dancing profession when I say that the one giant strength of this production was that everything was done by actors. Gone – completely gone – was any sense that a stiff-backed phalanx of principals was being eased through the strenuous part of the evening by a lithe *corps de ballet*. This is an authentic all-singing, all-dancing cast, and though everyone isn't equally good at everything, they're aiming to be, and they all count. The sense of unity achieved by David Toguri's staging was an exhilaration and a delight.

A programme note records Runyon as saying 'To Hell with plots'. People, he claimed, 'remember the characters'. This is certainly true of *Guys and Dolls*, whose plot could be comfortably inscribed on half a postage stamp. Almost its only working part is the bet contracted between Nathan Detroit and Sky Masterson, as to whether the suave, high-rolling Sky from Colorado (nice

Guys and Dolls at the Olivier

reviewed by Russell Davies

vocal distinction by Ian Charleson) will persuade Sarah the Salvation Army girl to accompany him on a binge/spree in Havana. Possibly because the process of theatre-going is in several respects emotionally akin to betting – as a show progresses one is constantly placing one's metaphorical money on the characters and shifting the investment about – the audience takes to this gladly, and requires little else in the way of propulsion through a 2¾-hour show.

But there is plenty of extra gas, and it comes direct from the music. Astonishingly – well, I wasn't aware of it – there are no weak numbers in *Guys and Dolls*. If there is a weakness in the apportioning of Frank Loesser's songs, it's that Nathan Detroit's musical share doesn't match his part in the plot; but this may have come as a relief to Bob Hoskins, whose singing isn't the best of him. Raucous even when *sotto voce*, he is very fine in the dramatic sequences, and probably the only member of the cast whose shape actually justifies a double-double-breasted suit. David Healy's Nicely-Nicely Johnson wears a perpetual beaming smile that isn't all the role. This is the very picture of an actor seizing, successfully, the part he was built for (come to think of it, I take it all back about Hoskins's exclusive right to The Suit).

Charleson's Sky, a Gary Cooper-style Western hero in better-draped civvies, rises to the songs with unexpected relish, and the climactic note he supplies to *Luck Be a Lady* tops off the superbly-set sewer encounter in the only appropriate way. He also blends very affectingly with Julie Covington in *I've Never Been in Love Before*, the first-half closer – and this is a stroke of luck, because Miss Covington's voice is of such a special timbre (described by a perceptive early admirer as 'like celery') that she isn't easily matched. Hers is easily the toughest role of the night: Sarah is the only character hinting at emotional depth. The plot dictates that her early entrances should put a damper on the gamblers' cavortings, which doesn't make it easier for her to establish herself; but she has nothing to worry about. The Havana scene – brilliantly stoked up by the opening solo from Bobby Orr at the drums – sets her free for what is, in the circumstances, a musically thoughtful performance. The blend with Julia McKenzie, in their pre-closer *Marry the Man Today*, is again excellent. Miss McKenzie of course, given a whole evening's opportunity to send up her own piercingly traditional skill in the old show-stopper game, is on a winner from the start. I thought there were moments when both ladies would have been helped by some lusher musical upholstery, but the decision not to have strings was apparently forced by budgetary considerations. It did leave the orchestrations leaning sometimes a bit too close to the Brechtian wind-band tradition.

Everyone agrees that *Guys and Dolls* is a 'perfectly efficient mechanism', but there is heart in it too. The book is full of gags that work, or woik ('His wife's havin' a baby. He's noivous, it's his foist wife'), and songs that are more various, musically, than anyone has a right to expect from a single source. Justice is done to the original author's style (*Take Back Your Mink, To From Whence It Came*), and though the tale is determinedly simple-minded, the talents of our National actors are nevertheless stretched in all available directions. I don't ask for anything more, apart from the chance of buying some more tickets.

Guys and Dolls at the National Theatre with Julia McKenzie and Bob Hoskins, designed by John Gunter. 1982.

Along with Camels and Coke and Miss Youth Form ('Aristocrat of Slips – Cannot Ride Up'), the neons of the National's *Guys and Dolls* have flashed one more name indelibly into the audience's mind: that of John Gunter. This year, in fact, he has the distinction of designing the biggest successes at both the major subsidised theatres: the ravishingly beautiful, and astonishingly adaptable, glazed conservatory for the RSC's Edwardian *All's Well that Ends Well* at the Barbican was also his work.

Gunter is an exceptionally thoughtful man who, one feels, could easily have been a gifted director or even a critic. Bearded and sensitive of feature, he suggests one of the more intelligent Shakespearean kings: Bolingbroke, perhaps. And he has a gentle, modest manner – so self-critical as to constantly belittle his own achievement – which sorts agreeably with his apparently effortless flow of precise ideas. When I interviewed him at the National he had just given a stimulating and superbly articulate talk to a visiting American theatre group; parts of that are incorporated in the transcript that follows.

I began by recalling the extraordinary variety of the productions of his that I'd seen: the evocation of New York in *Guys and Dolls* and the National's *Death of a Salesman;* the realism of the D H Lawrence trilogy at the Royal Court, or the suburban front room of *Born in the Gardens*; his two contrasting Restoration comedies at the Court, the sumptuous *Double Dealer* and the wittily impressionistic *Soldier's Fortune*; the hauntingly surreal, 'dead' colours of the forest and dacha in *The Old Country*; the black box in which he set *Rose*; that tent in *The Contractor*; and now *All's Well* (one of his few Shakespeares). Our conversation proceeded as follows:

As I run through all these in my mind, you seem so protean that it's hard to place you as a designer. I wouldn't have thought they were all by the same man.

That's probably my fault.

No. It's certainly no criticism. You don't always want the same style. But, unlike the work of most designers and directors I've studied over the years, those designs don't offer anything intellectually common to all of them . . .

Well, one has a choice, of course. One could regress and become a designer with a very strong style that is inevitably fashionable for a limited space of time . . . I really tend to see myself, sometimes, as a sort of hack. What I would like to feel I am doing is that every time I'm set a problem, I try and take a little step forward to understand more about my abilities as a designer, to try and set myself new problems. So there wouldn't particularly be a continuity with the rest.

Actually, I feel now that there *is* a continuity. When I first worked here, before my years abroad [Gunter spent, on and off, nine years in German-speaking countries, including both theatre and opera at Berlin, Hamburg, Bochum, Cologne, the Burgtheater in Vienna, and three years as head of design at the Zurich Schauspielhaus] I was probably very schizophrenic and confused in my approach to design. I came back understanding a good deal more. Perhaps, now, I take on too much. It's a funny way of working: the energy that's created actually creates the energy to design. Having not understood that first process – and who does?

A Guy Called Gunter

John Gunter, designer of the NT's Guys and Dolls, *discusses his progress from social realism at the Royal Court in the 1960s to Broadway musical at the Olivier in the 1980s in conversation with Anthony Masters*

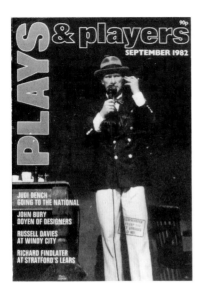

PLAYS & players 90p

SEPTEMBER 1982

JUDI DENCH
GOING TO THE NATIONAL

JOHN BURY
DOYEN OF DESIGNERS

RUSSELL DAVIES
AT WINDY CITY

RICHARD FINDLATER
AT STRATFORD'S LEARS

– you get desperately worried that if you take away what you think is the stimulus, the process may never work at all. And God knows there are others, actors included, who get so worried about trying to understand what actually makes them tick they cease to be creative and fall to pieces.

So, at this stage in my life, there is that awful fear that I *am* becoming just a hack. You reach a point where you've got a certain standing, a certain professionalism, being able to solve problems as a master craftsman, but you still want to feel that you have a creative spark, the sort of fire that a younger person would have who's determined to make a mark – in short, the capacity to say things in design that I would love to be given the opportunity to say.

You talk about being a hack, but what comes across strongly from you is a very sensitive receptiveness towards each work of art you interpret. What's wrong with that?

It probably comes from the way that I was taught at the Court . . . Yes, that is my philosophy of design. At times I flounder in it and don't live true to it, but then I don't think one should be tied down too tightly . . . But yes, I do believe that I'm not there to say, when the curtain goes up, 'Here's a John Gunter design'. I would love to feel rather, that by the end of the evening people say 'What a fantastic evening's entertainment I've had'. To me it's very exciting to go into a performance of *Guys and Dolls* and just feel that audience reaction, to which I've made as great a contribution as everyone else.

Our starting-point for *Guys and Dolls* – both the director Richard Eyre's and mine – was a love of musicals generally. I saw almost all of them, including the Broadway *Guys and Dolls*, when I was very young. I don't remember much about it. But designing it now had, for me, the quality of looking back with nostalgia; it drew on my love of shows like that and my love of New York. (I'm married to a New Yorker). It had more of a feeling towards films than theatre work – Richard Eyre has been working on films recently – though there are deliberate theatre tricks, using theatricality to its best advantage, like the trucking of the mission scene. There's nothing wrong with the obvious if it works . . .

I don't think any British production (some American ones *may* have) has used neon in the way we have. Nor has the Olivier Theatre's flying system been used quite like this before: people had actually said it wasn't working fully. Well, on one occasion things got stuck in and wouldn't fly up, but . . . I was interested in the architecture that neon produces – a seediness that certain areas of New York have, and then the neon gives you a pazzazz when you want it, which floods out the seediness. It's wonderful. When you have a very dextrous operator, as we have, you can do what you like with it. When you turn it down, the intensity of colour remains. You can have all the flashing and the winking and everything you want – a lot of fun.

It has been a strange production – with all the delays, and it was one of those projects that was constantly on and off, I had only a couple of weeks to produce it . . . it was suddenly a rush. The Olivier is certainly a daunting area of space, it's very hard to make it work. It's a stage for actors. Chichester, of course, is even worse: it's so flat, the audience is flat, it's difficult for the director to make sure that everybody's seen, for the actors to project, and for the designer to do anything at all. I was exceedingly unhappy with my work there . . . The Olivier, of course, has come from classicism. In a musical, fortunately, you can forget that, and just put as much as you can on the stage.

Guys and Dolls seems to be realistic – but, as you say, only up to a point.

Yes. At the Court, I got labelled 'social realist'. But that was partly the plays I did, like the Lawrence trilogy, which made you observe social/domestic situations on the stage. It is, really, rather dead, though I was obviously very grateful about what it led to. I think that you can take it so far, within the limits of those particular plays, but you can't make it, as it were, a house style. If you impose it on everything, that's when it becomes wrong.

Is it something that's built into some plays, the way they've got to be done? Supposing the National asked you to do a Lawrence or a play like that now, would you feel it had to be done like that and say yes or no accordingly, or would you – well, blow it apart?

This may be a laugh, now, but the people at the Court who advocated this philosophy now think that one's work has no remnants of it, but the philosophy of the Court was that it was a writer's theatre and respect should be given to that writer, so that the intentions he or she might have in a particular play should be explored.

Exactly.

And you explore them to the extent of seeing if they would then work within the play. Now I may have shut all that since, but . . .

No, of course you haven't.

Well, it's given me an attitude where if I were confronted, say, with doing a Lawrence again, I'd find it probably hard to approach it any other way but the way I approached it in the past. I must admit, I've seen Lawrences done in Germany where I tended to feel it was to the great detriment of the pieces, where the designs were so overwhelming . . .

That it lost the smell, as it were, of that time and place?

The particular domestic situation, the environment and what the people did for a living were very much an influence upon it, but what was essential was to see those reactions trapped within that confined space. So you looked at it, like under a microscope. Of course, the Royal Court as a theatre allowed you to do that. But, whichever way you do it, I can only work out of what I find in the script, dig in it and mine it for what I find interesting. I'm not a designer that can easily think of a concept that is very spectacular and make it work.

Now in Shakespeare, in most 'classics', it's different, in that you don't necessarily find a particular milieu of time and place that it's appropriate to give the full Zeffirelli-type treatment to, but what you do find is a particular emotional climate and work from that. Surely that is much harder, and more interesting.

Yes. I've done very little Shakespeare. *All's Well* was my first in a long time. I was very fortunate in the work that we did on the script with the actors. But we had set out, quite deliberately, our own choice of social environment, and we did the most dangerous thing possible – to force the glass slipper of Shakespeare on to the Ugly Sister's foot to get a fit. Certainly, luckily enough, there

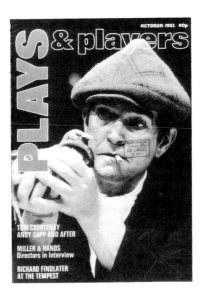

OCTOBER 1982 90p

PLAYS &players

TOM COURTENAY
ANDY CAPP AND AFTER

MILLER & HANDS
Directors in Interview

RICHARD FINDLATER
AT THE TEMPEST

PLAYS & players

NOVEMBER 1982 90p

RICHARD FINDLATER AT
THE IMPORTANCE
OF BEING EARNEST

ROBERT CUSHMAN ON
THEATRE CRITICISM

EMLYN WILLIAMS
IN THE
GREEN ROOM

were within that script so many references that it was absolutely cast-iron, there was no work at all. And of course we had a particularly worrisome piece to bring across to an audience, to make them believe this extraordinary tale and this extraordinary deviousness to make the whole magic work. And the result was that we went back to a perhaps too overploughed field, the late nineteenth century. But it fitted, and one identifies so much more with people wearing trousers and modern shoes and so on.

Yes. In some second-rank Shakespeare plays, social delineation like this can help a lot.

I don't know how I would approach one of the first-rank Shakespeare plays. Obviously I'd have to use the equipment I've got already.

You've never done one?

No. I feel now I'd love to tackle them. But I'd be very frightened . . . *All's Well* was actually designed with the Barbican in mind. It's a wonderful theatre, the only trouble is that the acoustics are so good. That means one can hear every tiny scene change. It always seems to be worst when Dame Peggy is on. She says I'm deaf . . .

You know, the scene changes, the rhythm of the play, is vital. I did things in *All's Well* I would never have risked on my own, major scene changes I would never advocate on the greater Shakespeare plays.

This is something at the heart of a lot of John Bury's concepts being able to perform each act virtually unbroken.

Of course, don't forget what play you're doing. In some operas they were quite prepared to go away for a meal between scenes. But it's only in the last couple of decades, really, that we've acquired this particular sensibility. It's been people like Peter Hall – and thank God he did – who, in a way, put his own neck in the noose and said that these great stretches of Shakespeare had to go without a break.

But the rhythm is *your* business. Recently I did an opera where the composer (now dead) was criticised because the scenes seemed to pause and be chopped about; and I knew I had helped that criticism on its way. No one ever said anything, but I knew that in myself. It's certainly up to us not to show the faults, to try and cover the patches that in our minds we know are wrong . . . I'm just about to do *Plenty* in New York for Joseph Papp and discussing it with David Hare – of course, he's written some huge scene changes. What is interesting is that *Guys and Dolls,* because it comes out of that particular time and place with Manhattan's keen interest in financial viability, is beautifully written, there's no wastage at all. When you look at those scripts, they are perfect. Perfect.

We are always told so. I disagree.

Well, I will say that they make my life a great deal easier. You instantly see how they fall, so to speak. It doesn't necessarily show, but once you get inside one of those scripts, it flows, because it's been hacked to pieces in Baltimore and then in Boston and then somewhere else.

Well, you certainly have a box-office success with it, of proportions that the theatre can hardly handle.

Yes. To be unkind, the system of the National, like all repertoire houses, allows only for an artistic success, not a popular success.

What do you think makes a successful designer?

Ouf! When you look back over the past, it's always to do with a personality – not money (which may follow if they're lucky). You have to find a personality charismatic enough to attract writers, directors, designers, everybody, to want to work within a situation . . . The enjoyment I have is in collaborating with everyone else on the production. If I'd wanted an ego trip I'd have been a painter or sculptor (and no disrespect to them – it's a much, much harder thing to do). But it would seem pointless to me to go into design for your own sake alone. That isn't the work – the work is to work with others.

No such personality as that immediately comes to mind. Perhaps it's a wrong way of thinking, but I think there'll have to be, it's inevitable. Look at the examples of the past – somebody like Joan Littlewood.

It looks as though she's going to cast quite a long shadow over these design interviews . . .

When I was at college I used to go down to the East End regularly, just to be in and around that atmosphere, because there was something very exciting that spun off. And they had no money at all at Theatre Workshop. But there was a preparedness, an idiotic dedication, a determination to fight for that cause. Inevitably it burnt itself out, rather too rapidly . . . But I think that's what's required: a director and perhaps a writer who can together create an atmosphere. Joint Stock is a good example. And David Hare, when he was talking about *Fanshen*, felt that that was the end of the working process in that style. So that there is always a climate. It's very easy to say there isn't a climate. Having worked with young designers over the last seven or eight years [as head of the Theatre Department at Central School] the thing that worries me most is that they are so disillusioned with what is happening and yet are not creating something themselves, not determinedly going out.

It's very difficult to know what to do . . .

Sure, the designer can't do everything himself. And the atmosphere of their surroundings, in Britain now, inevitably colours their opinions. With the current depression and lethargy, it's extremely hard to think at all positively. Indeed, I think that's why *Guys and Dolls* has come at the right time; the public needs it, as it needed that kind of thing in the thirties.

What has happened over the last few years didn't just happen through Thatcherism. For one thing, the writers have started to go away. There *are* some young writers, very interesting ones, who are still feeding the system, but it's not the same. Writers used to learn their craft, but there's no necessity for that now. God knows, it's by no means finished, there are exciting acting talents and directing talents, but there needs to be another Joan or even Bill [Gaskill]. Joan has given up and Bill has seen too much of the realities . . .

You have to have, perhaps, a wonderful naïvety to go out and conquer. The social climate of the time means that many of the young don't feel they can actually succeed. And I'm afraid George Devine used to say 'If there isn't a theatre, you have to go and make or find it yourself'! That's as true now as it ever was.

245

1982 Awards

voted for by the London Theatre Critics

Best new play: *A Kind of Alaska* by Harold Pinter and *The Real Thing* by Tom Stoppard

Best new musical: *Andy Capp* by Alan Price & Trevor Peacock

Best actor: Bill Paterson in *Schweyk*

Best actress: Judi Dench in *Alaska* and *The Importance of Being Earnest*

Best director: Richard Eyre for *Guys and Dolls*

Best designer: John Gunter for *Guys and Dolls*

Most promising newcomer: Kenneth Branagh in *Another Country*

Most promising playwright: Terry Johnson for *Insignificance*

Above left: Harold Pinter's 'best new play' *A Kind of Alaska* with Paul Rogers, Judi Dench and Anna Massey at the National Theatre. 1982.

Left: Tom Stoppard's 'best new play' *The Real Thing* with Roger Rees and Felicity Kendal. 1982.

Above: Terry Johnson's *Insignificance* at the Royal Court Theatre with Ian McDairmid and Judy Davies. 1982.

The year 1982 in fact stretches from the beginning of November 1981 (when last year's poll finished) up to November 25 this year – the copydate for the January issue. Twenty-one critics voted in 8 categories – Best New Play, Best New Musical, Best Performance by an Actor, Best Performance by an Actress, Best Designer, Best Director, Most Promising Newcomer and Most Promising Playwright. In the Best New Play Category there were 14 nominations with Harold Pinter's *A Kind of Alaska* and Tom Stoppard's *The Real Thing* taking the award with 3½ votes each. Runners up included *Top Girls* (Caryl Churchill's new play at the Royal Court) taking 2½ and *Noises Off* (Michael Frayn's play now at the Savoy) collecting 1½ votes.

Under the Best New Musical Category, there were 11 nominations with some of the critics expressing their disappointment with this year's new musicals by voting for 'old' musicals – *Guys and Dolls* and *Pirates of Penzance* and with one critic offering No Vote. But *Andy Capp* at the Aldwych took the Award with 5½ votes. Runners up included *Windy City* (4½ votes) and *Yakety Yak* (2 votes).

246

There were 13 nominations in the Best Actor category with Bill Paterson as Schweyk at the NT collecting the Award with 5 votes and Runners up included Michael Gambon (3 votes for his King Lear at Stratford), Antony Sher (2 votes for his Fool in the same production) and Jonathan Pryce (2 votes for his performance in *Talley's Folly* at the Lyric Hammersmith).

The most clear-cut voting came in the Best Actress category with Judi Dench collecting 10 votes for her performances at the National Theatre in *A Kind of Alaska* and *The Importance of Being Earnest* and emerging as Actress of the Year. Runners up amongst a total of 11 nominations included Mary Maddox with 2½ votes in *Rocket to the Moon* at Hampstead and at the Apollo in the West End.

Voting was similarly clear-cut in the Best Designer category with John Gunter collecting 11½ votes for his *Guys and Dolls* set at the National and emerging as Designer of 1982. Runners-up in 9 nominations included Grant Hicks with 2 votes for his set for *Talley's Folly* at the Lyric Hammersmith and Ultz with 1½ votes for *The Twin Rivals* seen this year at The Pit in the Barbican.

There were 11 nominations in the Best Director category with Richard

Eyre being nominated Director of 1982 for his work at the National, notably on *Guys and Dolls* and *Schweyk*, giving him 6 of the 21 votes cast. Runners-up included Adrian Noble with 4 votes (for his *King Lear* and *A Doll's House* revivals at Stratford), Jonathan Miller for his *Hamlet* at the Warehouse collecting 2 votes and with Trevor Nunn (also with 2 votes) for his *All's Well That Ends Well* revival seen again this year in London at the Barbican. In the Most Promising Newcomer category there were no less than 16 nominations with Kenneth Branagh taking the Award with 3½ votes cast for his performance in *Another Country* at the Queens. Rupert Everett was closest runner up in the same play with 2½ votes cast.

Finally in the Most Promising Playwright category, Terry Johnson for *Insignificance* at the Royal Court was the clear-cut winner with a total of 9 votes. With 8 nominations, closest runners up were Tony Marchant with 3 votes for *The Lucky Ones* and *Raspberry* and Stephen Fagain with 3 votes for *The Hard Shoulder* at Hampstead. Critics who voted two ways in any category were reckoned to have cast ½ vote in each case.

1983

It was the year the Pope visited Central America and the year that Joshua Nkomo fled from Zimbabwe to London fearing that Prime Minister Mugabe planned to kill him. It was also the year that the 13 members of OPEC were compelled to cut oil prices for the first time in 22 years.

Mario Soares was sworn in as leader of a new coalition in Portugal and Bettino Craxi was made the first Socialist President of Italy. The French expelled 47 Russians for alleged spying and Klaus Barbie 'The Butcher of Lyons' was extradited from Brazil to France to be tried for war crimes. Menachim Begin resigned as Premier of Israel and Lech Walesa was awarded the Nobel Peace Prize. A suicide terrorist killed 229 US servicemen in Libya.

In Britain the general election returned Margaret Thatcher and the Conservatives with 397 seats to Labour's 209 and the Alliance's 23. Later in the year Neil Kinnock was elected the new Leader of the Labour Party.

In the theatre the RSC recovered from the trauma of the move from the Aldwych to the Barbican with a strong season in which Antony Sher attracted much attention for his Fool in King Lear *and his* Tartuffe. *The RSC and the National competed on the musicals front – the RSC fielding* Poppy *and the National launching Richard Eyre's stunning production of* Guys and Dolls *in the Olivier.*

The Rivals at the Olivier

reviewed by Richard Findlater

Having extolled the design of the still-untested Olivier in the inaugural 'guide' to the National Theatre, transferring my loyalty from the venerable cause to its so-belated home, I have ever since felt especially apprehensive before each visit to a new production on those wide open spaces where the warmth and even the life has drained away from so many plays that seemed to be draughtily camped in a theatrical vacuum. The Olivier *can* be made to work splendidly when designer and director work together in a partnership as effective and imaginative as that of Jocelyn Herbert with John Dexter, or that of John Gunter, recently, with a number of directors. He has now followed his New York for *Guys and Dolls* and his Florence for *Lorenzaccio* with Bath for *The Rivals*, directed by Peter Wood. It is a wonderful design which ensures the success of a generally admirable cast in an excellent production, making the Olivier and the National's resources serve Sheridan by connecting his play with a contemporary audience in a way that no commercial manager could now afford but is far more than the decorative revivalism of the Tennent tradition which its *appliqué* surface effects (like the final all-together-now dance) sometimes recall.

Geraldine McEwan and Michael Hordern in Peter Wood's production of Sheridan's *The Rivals* at the National Theatre. 1983.

When you go into the theatre you see the city on the stage. The recognition is exhilarating not only because this crescent of tall Georgian façades, these demi-urban perspectives beyond the obelisk, have a tangible architectural reality, but also because John Gunter has captured the *personality* of the place that is embodied in the play's subtext and goes on tugging people back to what is still the least vandalised and the most classically beautiful of British cities. Looking at this set I hoped for the best, and I got something very near it. My initial pleasure was alloyed only by the suspicion that *The Rivals* was going to be one of those productions in which the designer hogged the leading role and the cast could not live up to and into his sets. I quickly and happily found I was wrong. As the buildings are pushed, pulled and turned around to reveal skilfully detailed domestic and public interiors – the inside as well as the outside of Sheridan's society – they reduce the stage enough to combine spaciousness with intimacy, to the benefit of the cast. With so much scene-shifting, atmospheric lighting change (Robert Bryan), singing, shouting and sedan-chairing, Peter Wood's production is at times a bit over-busy, but the overall result justifies the superfluity of means.

Most of the obvious liberties that Mr Wood has taken with the text also seem justifiable in the context of the production as a whole. The most conspicuous of these is casting the agelessly seductive Geraldine McEwan as that 'old weather-beaten she-dragon', Mrs Malaprop. We can do without the joke of the 'harridan's' age and ugliness (although its absence makes nonsense of her abrupt rejection by Sir Lucius and Bob Acres at the end) when the joke of her dictionary dyslexia is so brilliantly restored and sustained in laughter that ripples on throughout the play. With changing subtleties of facial play and vocal timing Miss McEwan makes an astonishingly high proportion of Malapropisms (some of them unknown to Sheridan) seem infectiously funny, largely because she gives their originator – the standing joke of the play – a convincing new identity. She plays Mrs Malaprop as a would-be bluestocking striving to keep up intellectual appearances in Bath society, not as entirely sure of her 'parts of speech' as she pretends. With carefully lowered eyes, a watchful air and a genteelly confiding social manner she pauses for a split second as she picks her way daintily – time and again – towards the wrong word, and adds it knowingly to her pile of finds.

I am puzzled why Lydia Languish should seem quite so notably older and graver than the dewy, dappy, romantic ingénue who usually appears under that name. Anne Louise Lambert is an actress of promising resource and authority, but she is scarcely convincing as the 17-year-old beauty of Sir Anthony's lecherous paeans or as an attitudinising addict of sentimental fiction. What her manifestly mature performance does help to do, by diminishing the romance of the Jack-Lydia relationship, is to underline a little the play's social realism about Jack's need for Lydia's money and her quick acceptance of this commonsense view of marriage. Julia, too, seems a bit older and more hockey-stickish than the text suggests, but Fiona Shaw acts with controlled strength.

Here my main reservations about the acting are ended. It is uncommonly good and, for the National, unified. Tim Curry's Bob Acres is a sturdy, wide-eyed, wide-smiling, irresistibly cheerful innocent abroad, not a caricatured rustic oaf, and we see him being coaxed through the urbanising pressures of Bath by tailors, hairdressers and dancing masters. Niall Buggy gives fresh (and tuneful) life to that bellicose Irish silhouette Sir Lucius O'Trigger. Edward Petherbridge as Faulkland – played as a pensive Scot in a bottle-green coat with a faint look of Stan Laurel crossed with Byron – achieves the most difficult feat in the production by making this self-tormenting bore not only credible but interesting.

Barry James serves the play well as a nimbly resilient not-too-campish Fag. Patrick Ryecart holds the plot together by the attack, charm and presence of his appropriately actor-ish Jack Absolute. And to complete the pleasures of *The Rivals* there is Sir Michael Hordern's Sir Anthony. Nodding, grunting, winking, beaming, growling with rage or randiness, this blue-coated old tyrant limps his way through the play with occasional textual lapses but consistently comic effect. Listen to his inventory for Lydia's charms ('Then Jack, her *neck*, Jack'); watch his use of the cane, which plays a leading part in his performance; see him at breakfast, scoffing his boiled egg, stuffing himself with fruit, as he gently mutters that he will never, never, never, never see his son again. Writing about Sir Michael, Miss McEwan and most of their colleagues makes me want to see *The Rivals* again soon – and wait in high hopes, for the next production to be designed by John Gunter.

The Trojan War will not Take Place – Lyttelton

reviewed by Hilary Spurling

There can be no doubt that Giraudoux's *Tiger at the Gates*, which opened in Christopher Fry's translation with a star-studded cast at the Apollo in 1955, represented for anyone with the faintest hint of cultural pretensions a high point of pre-revolutionary pre-1956 playgoing in this country. 'I do not believe that anyone could emerge from *Tiger at the Gates* unaware that what had just hit him was a masterpiece', wrote Tynan in a tremendous puff redeemed from rank hyperbole only by sly digs at the costumes (this was the play in which Diane Cilento's Helen wore what Tynan memorably described as a Freudian slip) and the precipitous decor ('enough to make a chamois nervy').

The play, now reissued in Fry's version under Giraudoux's original title *The War of Troy Will Not Take Place*, seems an ideal case for treatment under the National Theatre's current revisionist policy of reconquering the forgotten (indeed until recently forbidden) heartlands of the commercial West End in the middle years of this century. The case for revival is further strengthened by roping in Harold Pinter as director; and Pinter, 25 when the original production seemed to the more ambitious members of his generation the embodiment of theatrical magic, has done an uncanny job of re-creation. His Troy turns out to be a split-level, concrete wilderness designed in the neo-brutalist, Festival-of-Britain style by Eileen Diss with the great gates of war – flung open as the curtain falls – looking like nothing so much as the mock-bronze, fake-classical doors of the classier kind of fifties cinema.

The mediterranean sky is a lowering roof of banked black lighting rafts, the sea a band of blue cloth heaving queasily between the breeze blocks. The Trojans from Hector downwards are got up (costumes by Robin Fraser Paye) like old-fashioned fairies in short-skirted, pastel-shaded tunics with gold embroidery, gold hairbands, gold boots, belts and bracelets. Their women trip on and off in chitons more like Grecian cocktail frocks with wedge-heeled sandals, bouffant Grecian hair-dos, rather too much rouge and mascara. No wonder all concerned adopt the pained looks and stilted delivery – disdainful simperings, smirks, moues, knowing winks and nudges – of people required to stand about in uncomfortably skimpy clothes for hours on end with nothing to do but look as though they were listening (not all of Pinter's large cast manage to bring this off) to dialogue which sounds, nearly 30 years on, not so much glittering, crystalline or doom-laden as simultaneously leaden and inflated.

This, so far as I remember, was very much what the West End theatre all too often looked and sounded like before Pinter and his contemporaries set about taking it apart; and I don't believe that anyone could emerge from his NT production still thinking this banal and self-admiring play a masterpiece. Martin Jarvis's Hector, looking as peculiar as he no doubt feels in a hair ribbon and pale blue skirtlet, has none of the conviction, let alone the weight and passion, that made Michael Redgrave in this part seem a demi-god to Tynan. Julie Legrand's Cassandra nags away with a waspishness more appropriate to fear of finding a parking ticket on her windscreen than a foreign army invading her home town, while Annette Crosbie's superlatively genteel Hecuba is clearly too preoccupied with her own deportment and elocution to spare a thought for impending war. The only characters to emerge from this charade with dignity are Brewster Mason's majestically ironic Priam and Barry Foster's vigorous Ulysses.

Nicola Pagett, playing Helen as a pea-brained film starlet, takes her cue from Giraudoux's description of the old men of Troy lining the walls to look up her skirt. But probably the only way to restore any sense of feeling would have been to set the play in its historical context, namely Paris in 1935. The programme contains a photo of the original Hector and Helen dressed for a quite different, far more elegant, French pre-war cocktail party; and it is hard not to feel that something of this spirit might have given an authentic frisson to all the bluster about doom and destiny in Giraudoux's Trojan world of vapid socialites and worldlings, warmongering chauvinists, peacemakers desperately aware of their own impotence, potential collaborators at every turn.

'What's your new play about, Mr Ustinov?'
'It's about what might happen if Beethoven came back to life in a music critic's house in London.'
'Why does he come back?'
'Does it matter? Aristotle said: "Better a probable impossibility than a possible improbability."'
'Does Beethoven speak English?'
'I thought about that. I put an intellectual Viennese au pair girl in the house so that she can interpret for him.'
'A whole *two hours* of interpreted dialogue?'
'All right then. Beethoven learned English after he died.'
'A probable impossibility . . .'
'Exactly.'
'Wasn't Beethoven stone deaf?'
'Sure he was. But he can have a hearing aid. We'll have an E, N, and T man fix one in his ear. That'll be good for a laugh or

AUGUST

1983

Beethoven's Tenth at the Vaudeville

reviewed by David Benedictus

two. We can make the doctor a jogger too. Joggers raise a smile.'

'So Beethoven will be able to hear his own music?'

'On the music critic's stereo. That's the whole idea. Brilliant.'

'What's Beethoven *do* beside listening to music?'

'Goose the au pair. Eat. Quarrel with the music critic. Explore London and be confused by the horrors of a modern metropolis.'

'Satire.'

'Why not?'

'What about his relationship with the family he crashes in on?'

'That's easy. They've got problems. Father and son problems. Husband and wife problems. Son and au pair problems. And Beethoven sorts them out. That's what strangers always do to quarrelling families in West End plays.'

'Good.'

'You don't sound enthusiastic.'

'It's just that there doesn't seem to be much passion.'

'I know. But I thought I'd bring back Countess Giuletta Guiccardi, and the man she married, Count Gallenberg, too. Beethoven called her "a fairy, a young beloved" but she was not of his social class . . .'

'Like the au pair and the music critic.'

'Hmmm.'

'So you're going to have a sort of fantasy scene in which Beethoven's past is reactivated?'

'That'll get us through the second act.'

'You've never liked second acts much, have you?'

'Shaw and Stoppard got bored with their characters too.'

'So you are bored with the characters?'

'Not with Beethoven.'

'And you'll be playing him.'

'Yes.'

'It'll be all right then.'

'Yes.'

But it isn't. The whole play is too self-conscious, too contrived, too undramatic, and, although Peter Ustinov is predictably wonderful as Ludwig Van, he can no more carry an entire play than Robert Morley could (in such as *Hippo Dancing*) or Wilfred Hyde White. I saw Alastair Sim carry a whole evening on his back and hurl it into the air where it dispersed in a sparkling shower of golden rain, and I saw A. E. Matthews bumble his way joyously through a whole evening of rich eccentricity. But such occasions were very rare, and, while Ustinov might manage it as a raconteur – for he is brilliantly funny and much loved – he can't manage it as an actor in his own play.

There are compensations. In the scene in which Beethoven listens to his own music for the first time and Dilys Laye (as the music critic's mousy wife), and Clare Higgins (as Irmgard the au pair), bring him food on trolleys to indicate the passage of time, we are transported. The music mixes from masterpiece to masterpiece – a fine job of sound engineering – while the great man chews moodily on a breadstick; splendid! And at the end of the first act the wife, who has sacrificed her singing career to look after the two men in her life, persuades Beethoven to accompany her in one of his songs – he doesn't recognise it. His accompaniment is wayward at first, but thrust forward by Dilys Laye's

Opposite: Peter Ustinov as Beethoven in *Beethoven's Tenth* at the Vaudeville. 1983.

singing he remembers how the notes go, and genius triumphs. The wife has discovered in a few bars 'a reason to have lived'.

Ustinov's performance is stunning. Looking like a Spy cartoon and prowling about the stage with fastidious gestures of the lower arms, he reeks of Vienna, of the coffin, and of Ustinov. Miss Laye is wonderfully tactful, implying the strength and resolution which underlies her mousy exterior, and transformed by music. Clare Higgins copes successfully with a Viennese accent and intelligently with some difficult lines, but lacks variety. Robin Bailey as the critic gets the thankless job of setting the scene (at tedious length) and turns in an adequate but rather twitchy performance. The rest do what they can, but count for little. The old dictum: 'Never act with children, animals or Ustinov' applies.

The jokes are Ustinovian. Anyone might have given us Ludwig's puzzlement over a tape recorder; only Ustinov would have given us his amazement over a tubular steel chair. He also dares to write epigrams, which few modern writers do. Examples: 'When I'm in a good mood I'm a Christian. When I'm in a bad mood I'm a Pagan. This way I avoid blasphemy.' Or 'There is nothing so destructive of faith as knowledge' (familiar?). Or: 'The great drawback about being able to hear is that you're forced to listen.'

What are we left with? A great comic actor in a rich comic creation in an old-fashioned, badly constructed play, which is not much helped by Robert Chetwyn's direction.

Designer-Director

Ultz who designed the Adrian Noble revival of The Comedy of Errors *and both directed and designed* Pericles *at Stratford East talked to Clare Colvin about his work*

There are comparatively few theatre productions designed by Ultz because he finds it difficult to work on more than one project at a time. But if he is not prolific, he makes up for it by the sheer impact of his designs.

Critics are inclined to be divided about the strongly idiosyncratic style. Of his all-white *Twin Rivals* for the RSC, Michael Billington wrote in *The Guardian* that the words 'dressed to kill' could be applied to Ultz's effect on the play. Others found the costumes the only recompense for the evening. *City Limits* commented, 'Ultz's extravagantly showy costumes (like a series of molten wedding cakes) are a treat.' *Event* said: 'If this late Restoration comedy wishes to boast a star, that honour can only fairly go to the costumes and the lighting.' But all the critics, whatever their views, gave the costumes some prominence, rather than just slipping a mention into the final paragraph. Ultz notes the reviews but doesn't let them affect him. 'It's hard enough just having ideas.'

His designs show an awareness of fashion, both street and couture. The cast in Jonathan Gems's *Naked Robots* wore the built-up shoulders and skin-tight lycra, the fleeting fashion of that time. In his designs for *The Comedy of Errors*, which opened at Stratford-upon-Avon in August, he was modifying a jacket, when I saw him, to show more of the Lagerfeld at Chanel influence. Some designs, like those for the pantomines he devised with Martin Duncan, *Aladdin* and *Cinderella*, are influenced mainly by the vivid Ultz imagination.

Dynamic and restless in an interview, Ultz will leap up to demonstrate the effect his style will have on the way an actor moves. Trained as an actor himself, he is acutely aware of what it feels like to be on the inside of the costume. He is 33, with a youthful face, and short fair hair and was dressed in a black Japanese-designed cotton suit when I met him. He reminded me of a dancer in the way he moved, and in his need to demonstrate physically the effect of the costumes.

He had brought with him his costume sketches for *Comedy of Errors* to show the theme that he, together with director Adrian Noble, was trying to suggest – that of a series of comic turns, as in a circus or music hall. He had attended most of the rehearsals and watched Adrian at work. 'It's unusual for a designer, but I only take on one thing at a time, which means I'm poor. Adrian's brilliance is that he lets an actor make the play. There is a feeling that the actor can go in any direction'.

The Comedy of Errors designed by Ultz at Stratford-upon-Avon with Paul Clayton, Peter McEnery, John Dick, Jane Booker and Zoë Wanamaker. 1983.

Ultz follows *Comedy of Errors* with a production of *Pericles* at the Theatre Royal, Stratford East, which he is both directing and designing. It is by no means his first combined role. He recently directed and designed *A Midsummer Night's Dream* at the Canadian National Arts Centre, and also helped to stage the two pantomines of *Cinderella* and *Aladdin*, which were seen at Stratford East and the Lyric, Hammersmith.

'Why *Pericles?* I have always liked the late plays of Shakespeare. I directed *Pericles* at Rose Bruford in workshop and when we did *Aladdin* the first time with its tableau set scenes and spiky movement I knew we had a way into *Pericles*, a way of doing it without apologising for the strange format of dumb show and

255

tableau. Recent productions have seemed almost to apologise for the bizarre requirements of the staging. We are going to use Martin Duncan's music and he will play Gower as well, singing a lot in his high tenor voice. I know there must be a very clear colour grading to be employed in terms of telling a story clearly with a very small cast who are used over and over again. Tyre will have to be a particular colour and Antioch another, so that you can see a man from a red country going to a green country. I am not interested in doing naturalistic work and here you have a romantic old story – a man going through such terrible adversity and bearing it with great patience is comforting to watch. It is a case, as with Gloucester in *King Lear*, ripeness is all.

'I wanted to direct it as well because I have such strong ideas of how to do it. Otherwise I would be trying to direct it through a director. It was the same with *The Dream* which I was asked to design for Sheffield and I said no, I would be doing the whole production, and I felt I would be too rigid to adapt to a director. It is a lovely position to be in when you feel close to a play. So often as a designer you cannot control your destiny.

'I think this is getting to be the age of the director/designer. Look at Philip Prowse, Richard Negri, Voytek, Peter Brook. I don't wish to negate the role of the director, but it may be that the sort of theatre that celebrates the ego of the director should move down. In the experience between seven and ten at night the primary link is between the actors and the audience. So it is actors' theatre really. But everyone needs skilled people controlling the look of what they are presenting and the sound of it. There is no mystery about it – you have a group of people who work well and are talented and you allow them fertile conditions and then monitor it at the end – and that is all, really. It is interesting that designers are now being trained to take part in the whole play. In go-ahead design places like Nottingham, they have to act as well. They are no longer just the people who do the pictures in the background.

'You can be more daring if you do it all yourself. This is not to say that I don't want to work with directors, just that I don't want to work with people who are frightened – frightened of Shakespeare or what people might think of them. Occasionally, of course, you make a terrible mistake and fall flat on your face.'

Ultz has always drawn strongly on the creative, subconscious part of himself, and an idea for a design will often arrive in his dreams. The 16 boxes in *Twin Rivals* were the result of a dream, but the flurry of white costumes were the result of noticing the swashbuckling Restoration revival in the streets of Covent Garden around two years ago. The potbellied bald fairies in his Canadian production of the *Dream* came to him, appropriately, in a dream. Even the name Ultz occurred to him in a dream, and he no longer uses his real name.

'Designers have to use their intuition. John Napier says he can see designs just before he goes to sleep. While you're asleep your subconscious is whirling away and solving the designs. Of course, you have to earn it. In the day you plot and plot and work on sections of the play. Some things you can solve straight off. It just seemed spot on, when I walked round Covent Garden, to use the modern eye interpreting Restoration clothes'.

Ultz came into theatre by a different route from most designers. He trained at the Central School of Speech and Drama from 1967–70 as an actor and drama teacher. He then joined the Sadler's Wells Design School to train as a designer under Percy Harris and Hayden Griffin. He had originally applied to the Central School because he knew he wanted to work in theatre and didn't know of any other way of getting in.

'I went to St Albans Grammar School, and ran a drama club there. My father was a printer and printed school editions of Shakespeare, so from an early age my reading was *The Famous Five* or *Twelfth Night*. I had a model theatre at home and, if you want something really kitsch, there is a photograph of me aged six with some puppets in a Good Housekeeping Manual over the caption "Interest in puppets at this stage can lead to an interest in theatre".'

After a year at Sadler's Wells, he took up an apprenticeship with Hayden Griffin and was assistant designer at the Northcott Theatre, Exeter, which at that time was an outpost of the Royal Court in the West Country, under its director Jane Howell. He worked at the Glasgow Citizens with Philip Prowse, at the Birmingham Rep with John Dove, and at Stratford East as Head of Design around 1978. He designed for Joan Littlewood's last show, *So You Want to Be in Pictures* and he remembers with particular fondness the evenings when the whole theatre was decorated with a theme, and Joan Littlewood would be out scrubbing the steps of the theatre before the critics arrived. He and Philip Hedley devised *Christmas Carol* as a children's party and he loved the generous, heart in the right place feeling of theatre 'for your entertainment'.

Although he acknowledges a great debt to designers such as Griffin and Prowse, he found that learning another style in some ways inhibited his own. 'You cannot help, if you are at all sensitive, acknowledging the house style. Working under the great masters you cannot help working in their way and when you are absorbing other people's work, you are not in touch with your own style. It took years after leaving college for the pictures I used to have in my head to start coming back'.

There is a more contemplative side to Ultz than those who have seen the flamboyant designs might imagine. His multi-media show, *Merrie Prankes*, devised with Martin Duncan in 1980, was to have been his 'swansong' in the theatre, as he had intended to become a monk. He is still involved with the Buddhist Vedanta movement, which preaches unity of faith and non-exploitation of fellow humans and animals.

'It means you don't want to do things on stage that carry on sexist stereotypes. That is why you should be careful about who you work with – if you work with someone who sustains those myths you are going to get upset. I was thinking about my work with Howard Davies last week – you know he will be saying something about people that you approve of. Jane Howell said, "Everything you put on stage is a political statement". Howard has a shining radiance and purity. You know he will always have a committed, left wing, kind and human view of the world. I have had a very close working relationship with John Caird and Adrian Noble, and with Martin the shorthand is incredible. It is good to be able to work with directors you know, because the first show with a new director you are always apologising because you don't know what their reaction will be to your ideas. If you believe certain things, you have to work with people who say things about the human condition that you believe in'.

Virtuoso Actor

Antony Sher – before appearing in David Edgar's new play Maydays *at the Barbican – talked to Peter Roberts about a career that had its beginnings in Cape Town*

I met Antony Sher at the Barbican stage door two and a half hours before he was due to go on stage in the Pit to give his remarkable Rasputin-like interpretation of Tartuffe, where, by the time this appears, he will also have given what promises to be his equally remarkable Molière. Indeed, so physical and so ebullient have been Sher's performances with the RSC since he joined the company last year, to score a notable success as the Fool in Adrian Noble's revival of *King Lear*, that I should not have been in the least surprised if he'd come cartwheeling his way to the interview table perhaps strumming away at a violin or a ukulele as he did as Lear's Fool.

Antony Sher as the Fool in *King Lear* **at the Royal Shakespeare Company. 1983.**

But the man behind all this energy on stage proves to be a relaxed quietly spoken actor, casually but neatly dressed in a denim suit, and who is a very occasional smoker. It's hard at first to relate the interviewee who is still in his early 30s to the performer – that is until he gets under way with the answers showing himself to be both a thoughtful and highly articulate artist not given to taking the easy way out with a glib reply. His experience of the Barbican building's labyrinthine corridors proved invaluable as we picked our way up to Trevor Nunn's office at the top of the building in which we chatted for an hour in the absence of the RSC's boss.

I asked Sher first if he could throw a little light on how he came to choose a stage career in Cape Town, where he was born one of four children of a director of a South African Export Company. 'I was a very shy and introverted boy, not at all the extrovert most people would think would make an actor. Because I'd shown some promise and some talent as a painter everybody assumed that was where my future lay. Actually I was a bit muddled myself and thought perhaps I should try to be a writer – an ambition I've since abandoned. There was not much theatre in Cape Town when I was a boy (though I was lucky enough to see Yvonne Bryceland in the original production of Fugard's *Hello and Good-bye*), so what led me on was not so much the live performances I saw around me, as some of the films that came in and some books in the tiny drama section of the school library. I remember one in particular of Alec Guinness which showed Guinness's famous facelessness (which he now uses as it stands for a part like Smiley) transformed by elaborate make-up, and I found that magical. All those Methuen Playscripts and indeed *Plays & Players* coming out to us in the 1960s whetted my appetite to come to London. So it was very exciting when I'd made it to London and on my first evening went to see Paul Scofield in Osborne's *The Hotel in Amsterdam* – what an evening – to see not only Scofield live, who I had admired from afar, but also to see him in a new play by Osborne at the Royal Court itself!

'I went to talk to my actor-writer cousin Ronald Harwood about my uncertainty whether to try to be an actor or a writer: he advised me to attempt to get into a drama school since the experience of going through an acting academy could always be useful should I in the end become a writer. RADA turned me down (they sent word to say not only had I failed the audition but that they recommended I think of some other calling) but I eventually got into the Webber Douglas.'

I first noticed the name Antony Sher when *Goose Pimples*, Mike Leigh's improvised play, transferred to the Garrick from Hampstead in 1981, but on leafing through some old programmes at that time I spotted the same name in Willy Russell's first West End musical, *John, Paul, George, Ringo . . . and Bert*, in which Sher had played Ringo on its transfer from the Liverpool Every-man to the West End in the early 1970s . . . How had that come about? 'Well, when I'd finished my course at the Webber Douglas I realised I could not go back to South Africa but there were problems in getting Home Office permission to stay and work here. So I was lucky to get on to a post-graduate drama course run in conjunction with Manchester University, Manchester Poly-technic School of Theatre and Granada TV who ran the Stables Theatre in Manchester. And I was even luckier to move on from there to the Liverpool Everyman at a very exciting time in its history when it was being run by Alan Dossor and attracting a number of up-and-coming people like Jonathan Pryce, Trevor Eve and Alison Steadman as well as Willy Russell. I think I was very lucky to be at a place like the Liverpool Everyman under Dossor (and later at the Nottingham Playhouse under Richard Eyre) because they allowed you – even encouraged you – to be *creative*. And they used to cast quite young companies so that one could play parts like Malvolio or Joxer in *Juno and the Paycock*

that one would never have been allowed to do at other reps. Alan
Dossor was one of a new breed of directors who were very keen
on actors taking responsibility for the plays themselves, responsibility for the political statements in the plays they performed
instead of being regarded just as the theatre fodder. So, very early
on, I learned that acting did not have to be just a totally passive
role involving the carrying out of instructions issued by the
director. And that's something I more and more passionately
believe in. I believe that the best actors can and should 'contribute'. Later I did the title role in *The Government Inspector* which
Bill Gaskill directed in Edinburgh. I learned a great deal from
him – one of the older school of directors I had not experienced
before. I found subsequently that puritans like Gaskill are very
good for actors like me because I can be quite excessive – I can
easily go over the top – so if you have an actor like me with ideas
bubbling away in rehearsal it's a very good combination if that
meets a kind of puritanism in a director. It keeps a check on me.
Bill Alexander who directed *Tartuffe* is rather like that.'

260

It was interesting that Sher's two early West End appearances should have been in what amounted to disguises – as the Beatle Ringo and as the Saudi Arabian business man who only spoke Arabic in *Goose Pimples* and whose appearance in the West End got sucked into the controversy that followed the *Death of a Princess* affair. Taking a leaf out of Alec Guinness's book in earlier years, did Sher revel in making himself up as a completely different character, rather like the photographs of Guinness of the 1950s and 1960s that he'd studied as a boy?

'Yes I think it had something to do with being so very shy – I had to spend hours in the dressing room to get myself on to the stage and before the public. In one show I did in Liverpool I played Enoch Powell and it took me over three hours to get the make-up right. On one occasion the theatre asked me to address a May Day Rally as Enoch Powell. It was a most frightening thing to do for me but I must admit it worked and it did get them into the theatre'.

'Only when I'd got to London and auditioned for David Hare did I find the courage to play a shy young man just like myself – in *Teeth n' Smiles* at the Royal Court and Wyndhams in 1975'.

For many non-theatregoers Antony Sher is Howard Kirk in *The History Man*. I asked him how he had landed such an important role in a series so comparatively early in his career, and what he had learnt about acting for television and acting for the stage. 'Well, first of all, I must say I think stage and television acting are very different. I learned a lot about television acting from Stephen Frears, a wonderful teacher-director, who directed a TV play *Cold Harbour* I was in. He took a lot of time teaching us many things – like for example how *mysterious* you can be on camera, how very often the best moments on camera are when you are not thinking about the lines you have to say at all. In simple terms, the responsibility on stage for telling the story of the play rests with the actor being as clear as possible, but on camera it is the director who has the responsibility of telling the story and the actor can be as remote and mysterious as people are in real life; you can think about other things whilst you are talking which is what people do in everyday life. Very few people – Alan Bates is one of them – are totally successful both on stage and on camera and can be equally effective on both.

'As far as *The History Man* was concerned, I had already established a working relationship with Bob Knight who directed *The History Man* as he directed a play I was in at Nottingham and later a Play for Today which I did. I'm forever grateful that on that basis and against considerable opposition from The Powers That Be that he gambled on an unknown like me for *History Man*. I don't think people realise how important it is for an actor to be backed in that way. Most of my contemporaries who have made it have been championed in their early days by a specific director who believed in their work – Jonathan Pryce with Richard Eyre, Simon Callow with Robert Walker . . .'

A turning point for Sher in the theatre proved to be his *tour de force* of a performance as the Saudi business man, in Mike Leigh's improvised play *Goose Pimples*. How had Sher learned Arabic for that part and what research had he done to end up with such a convincing and moving portrait? 'Well as is generally well known now, when you agree to do a Mike Leigh play you cannot meet the other actors – or rather the other characters – until you have got your own character together and know him inside out. When I took the part on I knew how Mike worked but had no idea I should end up playing a Saudi business man. It was a character we alighted upon little knowing that we were involving ourselves in a near-impossible research task. If, for example, you are playing a Wembley school teacher you can verify all the information you need about such a character but if you are playing a Saudi business man it's not so easy, particularly as the early idea of flying me out to Saudi Arabia proved impracticable. Naïvely, we assumed that a lot of Saudia Arabian people in London would be available and happy to co-operate and advise. But the *Death of a Princess* affair having just happened the Arab community here was very suspicious. So it was very depressing and rather frightening to have so many doors slammed in one's face. At the same time I was trying to learn Arabic with the help of records but three months was just not long enough. Eventually what we did was to devise sections of dialogue in English and then I went to various Arab contacts I had made to have it translated. Of course when the play was in the West End one was very conscious of the controversy it aroused and at the height of it I quite expected to be knifed at the Garrick Stage door each night. I think the controversy was misjudged and most unfortunate because *Goose Pimples* was not in any way anti-Arab.'

Before joining the RSC last year, Sher was at the National to play with Bob Hoskins in Sam Shepard's *True West* directed by John Schlesinger at the Cottesloe. What had it been like to be directed by Schlesinger and to have arrived at the National? 'Well Schlesinger had been a hero of mine since my days in South Africa, so it was a great pleasure to be actually working for him and with Bob Hoskins. But strangely enough I never felt I was at the National at all at the time. You seem to go in and out of the theatre there without anybody taking any notice of you. I was amazed never to have glimpsed Peter Hall in a corridor or anywhere about the place in all the months I was there. When I went on to join the RSC I found a different atmosphere. You felt the RSC directors all took an interest in one another's work and there was much more of a company feel to the place. I suppose the difference is the difference in the names – it's the Royal Shakespeare *Company* and the National *Theatre*. One is a group of people the other is a place'.

Since he joined the Royal Shakespeare Company last year saying that to become a leading actor you have to play leading parts but admitting that he is a 'character' actor and not a 'personality' player, Sher has made a deep impression, in particular as the Fool in Adrian Noble's production of *King Lear* at Stratford last year, and again at the Barbican earlier this year. Because the production was rehearsed in tandem with the revival of the Bond *Lear* seen at the Other Place and The Pit, Noble had an unusually long rehearsal period during which the Sher Fool emerged in the eyes of the critics as something of an amalgam of the great English comics from Grimaldi and Dan Leno to George Formby. I asked Sher to throw some light on the rehearsal procedures behind that creation. 'I had seen Michael Williams play the Fool to Eric Porter's King Lear soon after I came to this country. It was a part that fascinated me but when I came to do it myself I found it frightening. There is not much in the script to tell you what he is. He could be almost anything and if you cast an actor like me in the part he could go in many directions because I'm not going to give a personality performance – I'm going to try to find the character. But it is hard at first to know what direction to go in because there are no clues in the text really. You don't even know how old he is, where he comes from or what he looks like. The only clue is his profession, that of being a Fool. So that's what we started with.'

'On the first day of rehearsal Adrian Noble said he thought that it was the cruellest work he had ever read. With the extra-long rehearsal time we could afford to experiment, and in line with Adrian Noble's views on the play's cruelty it became an appealing idea that the Fool should provoke laughter through some cruel deformity, so I was quite keen to play him as a dwarf, going about on my knees with the help of my hands like a monkey. In fact I spent a lot of time studying the behaviour of monkeys and I was struck by the fact that people responded to them with laughter even though they often seem lost in the deepest melancholy.

'The most exhilarating aspect of the rehearsal was that Adrian was prepared to investigate a crazy idea like that. Bob Crowley was even asked to consider designing a costume that would have enabled me to play the part on my knees. But in fact we found that playing him as a crippled outcast was interesting but was not releasing the text so we set the idea aside. Adrian said "well let's now experiment with the comic side, his function as entertainer. We'll start with a red nose tomorrow". And I must say I found that red nose very liberating so that eventually in experimenting with him as an entertainer and bringing back something of the crippled side to him we found what we had been searching for all the time. When the play opened the critics picked up this idea of his being a succession of English clowns but that was something we had not even discussed. Beckett had come up for discussion at one point but that was all. I never visited any theatre collection to study clowns of the past because I was far too concerned to explore the crippled side of the interpretation. Once we had fastened on the red nose then we investigated various clown routines but they were never based directly on a particular clown or series of clowns. The ukulele, for instance, I think was the idea of the composer Ilona Sekacz who was wonderful in helping me over the fact that I'm tone deaf, can't sing and couldn't really play the violin I'd been given. And as far as the music in the production was concerned Adrian wanted it to hint at the different periods of time and to reflect the sense of disjointed time that is in the text.'

When I went along to see Sher he was re-rehearsing Bulgakov's *Molière* whilst playing in Bill Alexander's production of Molière's *Tartuffe*, newly translated by Christopher Hampton. The Rasputin-like Tartuffe was as unexpectedly fresh as the Fool had been and I asked how it had evolved. 'The earliest ideas I had were to play him against convention, to have him appear in white and be Christ-like – in fact to fulfil Orgon's image of Tartuffe rather than everybody else's image of him. There's an extraordinary build-up for Tartuffe, and having played Molière himself in Bulgakov's play, I appreciated what Molière had had to do to get *Tartuffe* on at all. But my first ideas didn't work and robbed the play of its comedy. I think it is a case of Molière's comic writing being so simple and clear that you cannot interfere with it like that.'

'As well as the idea of the saint we were also looking at hippies and at some of the strange sects of the 1960s which the oddest people followed. But it didn't begin to come together until we found the black image that I play. I followed the Rasputin idea as a result of scratching about to try to find a contemporary or near contemporary figure to relate him to. Quite late on in rehearsal I became interested in the idea of a medieval gargoyle, in the idea of there being a demon in Orgon's house as there are so many lines about the whole house being possessed by a demon. The films of Pasolini and Fellini, both of whom I admire very much, seemed to have the flavour of what I was searching for; I particularly love the way Fellini is so bold in his treatment of grotesque characters in his films.'

During the conversation Sher had made it clear he no longer had ambitions to be a writer* so I asked him whether he still kept up the painting for which he was regarded as something of a child prodigy in South Africa. 'I had stopped painting but it came back later. I do a lot of portraiture now – faces. I see acting as an extension of painting. In my mind acting and painting are very closely linked – acting is painting a different character within one's body. My rehearsal scripts are littered with drawings of the character I'm trying to visualise. I always know when a character is starting to take shape because I know how to draw him.'

Sher's forthcoming appearance with the RSC is as Martin Glass, the public schoolboy in David Edgar's new play, *Maydays*. What was the attraction of this role? 'The joy of it for me is that I'm playing an ordinary human being who is not giving a performance. After doing a lot of energetic and physical parts like the Fool, Molière and Tartuffe, all of which are 'performance' roles, it's nice to play somebody who just has to be himself. He starts off as an idealist young schoolboy heavily influenced by a communist master and ends up in middle age after some extraordinary u-turns in his political thinking back at his middle-class roots.'

'I'm not really a fan of political theatre myself and some of the very good new plays that we did when I was at Liverpool were spoilt for me because at some point a character would get up on a soap box and deliver a message. But David Edgar's *Maydays* is an extraordinary piece of writing. It's a political epic and I suppose you would say that it comes from the same stable as *Destiny*. But I don't think that he could have written it if he had not first done the adaptation of *Nicholas Nickleby* because *Maydays* has all the sweep and scope of a nineteenth century novel covering as it does political life over the last 30 years in Russia, England and America.'

Finally, I asked Sher to explain why he was always most insistent on referring to himself as a character actor. 'I think it must stem from having been quite shy as a boy, of not having the sort of personality that lends itself to going on the stage. The attraction of being an actor lay in getting out of oneself, in being able to turn oneself into different people. When I began in rep in Liverpool I virtually could not go on stage without being encased in three hours of make-up. Later I enjoyed making the changes not only with make-up by doing something else like putting on weight. And when I went on to work with Mike Leigh in *Goose Pimples* he made me realise that character acting should not be the couple of pejorative words that they are usually taken to be. After all some of the greatest feats of acting from people like Olivier and Guinness have been as character actors. But I don't see the term in black and white as Mike Leigh does. For example, one of the greatest performances I have ever seen came from Meryl Streep in the film *Sophie's Choice*. In it she was both a personality actress – Sophie is unmistakably Meryl Streep – and yet there is so much character work, like the mastery of the accent and the detail in the sequences where Sophie is ill. If I could ever give a performance half as good as that one I'd be satisfied.'

*Sher has since published *Year of the King* (Methuen).

1983 Awards

voted for by the London Theatre Critics

Best new play: *Maydays* by David Edgar

Best new musical: *Blood Brothers* by Willy Russell

Best actor: Derek Jacobi in *Cyrano de Bergerac*

Best actress: Judi Dench in *Pack of Lies*

Best director: Yuri Lyubimov for *Crime and Punishment*

Best designer: John Gunter for *The Rivals*

Most promising newcomer: Alexandra Mathie in *Daisy Pulls It Off* and Abigail McKern in *Hay Fever*

Most promising playwright: Jonathan Falla for *Topokana Martyrs' Day* and Sarah Daniels for *Masterpieces*

'Best New Musical' *Blood Brothers* with George Costigan and Andrew C Wadsworth at the Lyric Theatre. 1983.

Left: **'Best Actor'** Derek Jacobi in the Royal Shakespeare Company's *Cyrano de Bergerac*. 1983.

Below left: *Crime and Punishment* produced by **'Best Director'** Yuri Lyubimov with Michael Pennington (front) as Raskolnikov. 1983.

Below: **'Most Promising Playwright'** Jonathan Falla's *Topokana Martyrs' Day* with Gordon Case and Carol Leader. 1983.

PLAYS

Index

PLAYERS